Gordon DeBlaey

**School Policy and Issues
in a Changing Society**

School Policy and Issues in a Changing Society

Patricia Cayo Sexton
New York University

Allyn and Bacon, Inc., Boston

This book is part of the
Allyn and Bacon Sociology Series
Consulting Editor: Amitai Etzioni

Library of Congress Catalog Card Number: 70–135447

Contents

Preface

The central questions explored in this volume in relation to the system of education are:

1. Who will get what education?
2. How can the quality of education be improved to the maximum satisfaction of students, teachers, and citizens?
3. How will we pay for good education?

The first question has the highest priority. It is the question raised by the revolution of rising expectations and by the civil rights, black power, and even the student movements. It gives urgency to the need for change in the quality, amount, and price of what the school system offers.

Rising expectations are generated by increased opportunity in the society. They have been spurred by growth of the urban economy and by the technological revolution in agriculture that drove millions from the land into the cities. It is in the urban metropolitan area that the schools have been most troubled.

The question "Who will get what?" is interwoven with other questions. Hence, this volume begins with a treatment of economics, the cost, of equal opportunity. The issues raised around the question of equity in the system—segregation, intelligence, de-centralization, participation, and so on—place us in the middle of discussions of what and how much.

It is hoped that the book will be of use to those instructors wishing to deal with policy issues in their Social Foundations of Education and Sociology of Education courses.

School Policy and Issues
in a Changing Society

Introduction

STATUS OF THE SYSTEM

It does not require deep analysis to discover that the American system of education is in serious trouble. Signs of distress are everywhere. This volume starts from the premise that the system's trouble stems mainly from its failure to provide equal educational opportunity for all without respect to race or class. Other problems are also present, but most are related to the system's failure in this primary function.

Even the matter of quality education is related to equalization. When we started to educate more than an aristocratic elite in our schools, we found that the new children would not consume the schools' traditional offerings of Greek, Latin, and classical studies. These studies were suitable for educated gentlemen but not for members of an industrial society. Over the years, we have gradually shifted from a classical to a more modern and practical curriculum. We are still on the way to modernization. In general, the most pressing demands for curriculum reform, as well as demands for social reform, come from those who want a greater share of the

1

system's rewards—from the outsiders. Once they get into the system, they tend to change it profoundly.

The central questions explored in this volume in relation to the system of education are:

1. Who will get what in education?
2. How can the quality of education be improved to the maximum satisfaction of students, teachers, citizens?
3. How will we pay for good education?

The first question has the highest priority. It is the question raised by the revolution of rising expectations and by the civil rights, black power, and even the student movements. It gives urgency to the need for change in the quality, amount, and price of what the school system offers.

Rising expectations are generated by increased opportunity in the society. They have been spurred by the growth of the urban economy and by the technological revolution in agriculture that drove millions from the land into the cities. It is in the urban metropolitan area that the schools have been most troubled.

The question "Who will get what?" is interwoven with other questions. Hence this volume begins with a treatment of the economics, the cost, of equal opportunity. The issues raised around the question of equity in the system—segregation, intelligence, decentralization, participation, and so on—places us in the middle of discussions of the *what* of education and the *how much.*

SOCIOLOGY OF EDUCATION

The current status of the sociology of education is one of great expectations. Not long ago the field was virtually deserted. Social scientists pursued more topical or lucrative interests elsewhere—in medical, military, industrial, and other institutions. The new prospects for the field arise from racial conflict in the schools, competition with Soviet education, the growing power of educational institutions, the student revolts, and new federal programs.

Since this arousal originates in the *society* rather than in the human *psyche,* the sociologist is being called upon to define the problems and to help solve them. Psychologists still dominate

FIGURE 1.
The Magnitude of the American Educational Establishment (1969–70)

Institutions		*Administrators and Supervisors*	
Elementary	88,556	Superintendents of	
Secondary	31,203	Schools	13,106
Universities, Colleges		Principals and	
and Junior Colleges	2,483	Supervisors	119,365
Total	122,242	College and University	
		Presidents	2,483
School Districts	20,440	Other College Administrative and Service	
		Staff	82,000
Students		Total	216,954
Pupils in Elementary			
Schools			
Schools (Kindergarten			
through eighth grade)		*Board Members*	
Public Schools	32,600,000	Local School Board	
Nonpublic (Private		Members	106,806
and Parochial)	4,300,000	State Board Members	500
Total	36,900,000	College and University	
Secondary School		Trustees	25,000
Students		Total	132,306
Public High Schools	13,200,000		
Nonpublic	1,400,000		
Total	14,600,000		
College and University			
full- and part-time			
students enrolled			
for credit towards			
degrees		*Cost (in billions)*	
Public Institutions	5,100,000	Current Expenditures and	
Nonpublic	2,000,000	Interest	
Total	7,100,000	Elementary and	
Total Students Enrolled	58,600,000	Secondary	
		Schools	
		Public	$32.7
Teachers		Nonpublic	3.8
Elementary School		Higher	
Teachers		Public	12.0
Public	1,099,000	Nonpublic	7.7
Nonpublic	152,000	Capital Outlay	
Secondary School		Elementary and	
Teachers		Secondary	
Public	904,000	Schools	
Nonpublic	88,000	Public	$4.9
College and University		Nonpublic	0.6
Teachers		Higher	
Public	344,000	Public	2.6
Nonpublic	188,000	Nonpublic	0.4
Total	2,775,000	Total	$64.7

Figures are based on latest available estimates from the U.S. Office of Education and the National Education Association.

teacher training and educational research and development, but the sociologist is making swift incursions into a formerly child-centered domain and is being called upon increasingly to advise in the formulation of educational policy.

Not only is sociology of education now part of the curriculum of many sociology departments, but in the vast network of teacher-training institutions, educational sociology, a subject devoted more narrowly to what goes on within educational institutions, is gaining status relative to other disciplines. Faculties, course offerings, and student interest in the sociology of education have expanded rapidly. What was once associated with social foundation sequences for teachers and with the old masters of teacher training—history, philosophy, theology—has moved closer to experimental science and to education psychology. At the same time, it has entered into an opposite association with another rising star, social work, with which it shares new concerns about social problems, social action, and community development.

There is even an inclination among a few sociologists, including the writer, to draw closer to economics, political science, and a field which might be called the "administration of large organizations." The latter specialty is rather highly developed as a concern of business schools, where a large but limited body of knowledge about the efficient and profitable management of business organizations has been developed. Within schools of education, departments of administration have traditionally presided over the educator's interest in organization, but these key departments have been notably barren in the production of meaningful and relevant research about the unique character and problems of educational organizations.

The advantage the alert sociologist has in his inclination to establish kinships with all the disciplines (history, philosophy, administration, economics, political science, psychology, social work). He can then draw resources from this relationship for the advance of sociological studies.

Educational sociology has tended to add empirical concerns to the rather intense interest in problems prevailing in a field dominated by social philosophers and reformers. The new empiricists tend to share an interest in problems, but their emphasis is sufficiently different to generate considerable conflict with the reformers.

Among sociologists on liberal arts faculties, recognition of the significance of educational institutions has swollen the education section of the American Sociological Association and tempted a growing number of leading sociologists into the study of schools and the youth who populate them.[1]

The content of educational sociology has been limited by the relatively narrow preoccupations of educators and a range of interest that is broader than traditional psychology, but narrower than general sociology. Three topics have dominated texts in the field: (1) the school as a social system, (2) teaching as a profession, and (3) the community milieu of schools. Permeating the field is a concern with social stratification and inequality.

The educational sociologist's concerns about community and stratification trace their genealogy back to the Lynd's Middletown studies and the various University of Chicago studies of school and community. Of these, perhaps Hollingshead's work on Elmtown's youth is the best known.

Teachers-in-training, the chief consumers of educational sociology, are assumed to have a personal interest in teaching as a profession. Inquiries in this field, however, have not yielded much beyond what *organized* teachers already know. Many graduate students in educational sociology are nonteachers—administrators of schools and social agencies, and so on. Administrators have been attracted to the field by its concerns for human relations, intergroup conflict, and organizational issues.

Though these dimensions are broad, they are limited by a traditional myopia. Based on the presumed professional concerns of students, the field has restricted its interests to the school and its immediate community milieu. Little attention has been given to relations between the school system and other major systems in the society, in particular the economic, political, and value systems. Nor has there been much analysis of international systems or comparative education where new clues may be found to interactions among cultures, social systems, schools, and personality. Neither the money

---

[1] About one out of three people in the U.S. population are part of the school system in one capacity or another. As a "large scale organization" the public schools have almost no peer. In 1960, 1,600,000 teachers were employed in the public schools, or more than three times the number of employees in the world's largest manufacturing corporation, General Motors. In 1960, $23 billion was spent on schools, or over 50 percent of state and local payrolls. In 1970, the student population of the nation's colleges will be about seven million.

nor the interest has been sufficient to support such complex inquiries.

One study of 168 instructors in educational sociology courses found that the following subjects are regarded as most appropriate for such courses: social status (85 percent of respondents), social mobility (85 percent), social class structure (84 percent). All these subjects pertain to social stratification. No similar stress was given to power. In fact, 40 percent said that politics should not be a subject of concern, and only 54 percent felt that economics was relevant.[2]

Little is known about power—how it operates in the schools, how it is used to make public policy, or how it relates to power structures in the society. Those who manage schools are often the very people who decide how research funds are to be spent. They are not usually eager to have their own roles and power in these institutions examined. The American Educational Research Association (AERA), an affiliate of the National Education Association (NEA), is the principal professional organization of education researchers. A controlling interest in AERA operations has been held by school administrators and more recently by psychologists, though sociologists increasingly participate. A major AERA product is the 1,564-page *Encyclopedia of Educational Research*. Of the more than 100 topics listed in its index, only a few deal with broad sociological subjects. Ten pages of review are devoted to personality, but the national economy is dealt with in only 4½ pages. The subjects of civil rights, desegregation, and race are absent, as are social stratification and power. The "academic" subjects are almost as neglected as the "social" issues. The interests of developmental psychologists and administrators are, however, clearly visible. What has seriously dampened the spirits of those seeking solutions to educational problems via R and D is the general sterility of the voluminous research reviewed in the *Encyclopedia*. Researchers have dwelt, for example, on evaluating teachers. Usually such evaluations are based on artificial criteria such as appearance, skill in lesson-planning, classroom interaction, ratings by supervisors and students, rather than on student achievement. What is invariably found in this research is that good teachers are almost indistinguishable from poor ones.

---

[2] Richard Gjermund Hoyme, "Educational Sociology" (Ph.D. diss., University of California, January 1961).

Most of this educational research is "applied" yet has no real practical application. As for current research, much of it consists of evaluation of experimental programs. These evaluations are often seriously handicapped by the researcher's inability to control what happens in the experiment. The researcher may find almost no resemblance between the program he agreed to evaluate and the program as it works out.

Reviewing research in the sociology of learning, Sarane Boocock concludes that "one can say very little with certainty about how social factors operate on the student."[3] He feels that the classroom, "the core of the school learning system, presents the most confusing picture."

"While it is clear," he says, "that the teacher and the methods he or she uses are important to the learning process, we cannot yet say just what it is that the effective teacher is or does. Looking at the classroom as a whole, the major finding is also a negative one—i.e., that satisfying group relations, often perceived as the panacea for all education problems, are not related to learning in any direct or consistent way. From what is now known, there is no one type of teacher, teaching, or classroom organization which produces the 'best' results with all students in all areas of academic endeavor."[4]

He concludes that the home environment has an effect on learning (not a new discovery). The nature and extent of this influence is unknown, however. As for peer influence, he concludes, "research on student peer groups, which contains some of the best designed and most conclusive studies, makes it quite clear that many young people will not apply their best efforts to learning tasks unless this is consistent with the norms of their informal cliques and friendship groups. The need is for some imaginative applied research, which will point to ways of channeling these potentially powerful peer group influences to promote intellectual goals."[5]

My own research has led me to conclude that the schools set themselves the almost impossible task of cutting across the grain of "boy culture." Peer-group relationships are of prime importance to boys, but schools generally organize learning so that individual

---

[3] Sarane S. Boocock, "Toward a Sociology of Learning: A Selective Review of Existing Research," *Sociology of Education*, Winter 1966, Vol. 39, No. 1, p. 41.

[4] *Ibid.*, p. 41.

[5] *Ibid.*, p. 41.

competitiveness is emphasized and rewarded. Since they often perceive this as an organized effort to turn them against their peers, many boys resist and are thus lost to the system. This seems to me most especially true of the "disadvantaged" and working-class boys.[6]

However unprofitable most school research has been, the sociology of learning and inquiries into the internal structure and functions of educational institutions offer some fresh prospects. What happens in the classroom and school, however, is often controlled from outside. These control centers are found in the society itself and in various institutions. They are found especially in such places as government and private economy where public policy is formulated and key decisions made. Examination of these control centers may yield more practical advantage than the usual classroom studies.

The greatest challenge for the sociologist of education, and for sociologists in other problem areas, is public policy. The adoption of massive federal school-aid programs reveals the urgent need for, and appalling dearth of programmatic advice based on sound research. The ominous and unanswered question is: Can social research rise to this unique opportunity and provide policy makers with sound guidelines for the promised reform of the nation's schools?

The establishment of about a dozen regional research centers in the country with federal funds has given a leading role to R and D as an approach to educational problem-solving. This approach of course, is an old and serviceable concept in industrial and military organizations. It performed its first "miracles" in the modernization of agriculture. Land-grant colleges, set up in each state by federal land grants during the Civil War, reached out to individual farmers, studied their needs, brought problems back to the laboratories, produced solutions, and employed agricultural agents to communicate the new knowledge to the farmer. Concurrently R and D in agricultural mechanization increased production and reduced costs. Eventually it drove the farmer from the land to the cities where the new social problems of the migrant were unattended by similar urban efforts at problem solving.

During the ten-year period ending in 1963, about $100 billion

---

[6] Patricia Cayo Sexton, *The Feminized Male: Classrooms, White Collars, and the Decline of Manliness* (New York: Random House, 1969).

was spent in the United States by public and private sources on R and D activities, mainly in defense.[7] As in agriculture, industrial research has mainly helped in product development, but it is also used to examine markets and organization functions.

Defense spending has left little in the federal budget for research in health, education, and welfare. The political breakthrough into federal aid, however, has stimulated federal support of large R and D centers, regional laboratories, and policy centers. The function of these centers is to discover and disseminate new knowledge about education.

The product of educational research cannot be evaluated yet, but the establishment of these centers is recognition of (1) the role of the federal involvement in educational problems, (2) the need for a massive approach to the definition and resolution of such problems, and (3) the need to bring schools out of isolation and into the mainstream of society.

R and D spending on education in 1958 was about 1 percent of that allocated to it in the Public Health Service and less than that spent in such agencies as the Forest Service, Commercial Fisheries, and the Bureau of Sport Fisheries and Wildlife. Since 1958, spending on educational research has more than quintupled and is expected to climb steeply when defense spending is reduced. In chemical and other industries, as much as 20 percent of all spending goes for R and D. In education, the equivalent spending has been about one-tenth of 1 percent of total expenditures.

We cannot predict whether educational research will be as productive as it has been in agriculture, medicine, industry, and the military. The "product" of education is very different from other products and far less tangible or measurable. Perhaps this kind of research will be as unproductive as the scattered, inconsequential, yet massive volumes of educational research to which we are already accustomed. We will not know until we try it out.

The research approach used in the past has not been geared to the pressing problems of the schools. Locally financed schools and state departments of education have had neither the interest nor resources to finance major reforms in education.

---

[7] In the early forties, annual federal expenditures on Research and Development were about $74 million, about half in agricultural research. By 1956, spending had risen to $15.2 billion. Most of this (about three-fourths) went to defense, atomic energy, and space research. About 98 percent went to the natural sciences and 2 percent to everything else.

Until the advent of federal programs, most national school research was conducted by the NEA, a private organization. In the past, the U.S. Office of Education and most school research operations have come within the NEA orbit of influence. Because of the detachment of the federal government, educational research has been spotty and local.

Recently federal funds have supported several major surveys of the nation's schools. The University of Pittsburgh's Project Talent surveyed talent and its development in the nation's secondary schools. Another million-dollar study, terminating in the Coleman Report, surveyed elementary and secondary schools as well as students in the nation with a view to discovering the extent of inequalities, particularly in relation to black achievement.

Both these giant surveys suffer, as well as benefit, from the enormous quantity of data generated. Both contain treasures of previously untapped information. The data, in fact, seem almost too vast to manage. The surveys point up what has perhaps always been the most troublesome problem in social research—the problem of analysis. What do the data mean? How should they be interpreted? Unfortunately, analytic skill has not yet equalled the technical skill of data collectors and recorders.

A third national survey is under consideration which promises to be the precursor of many others. It will be conducted by the Educational Testing Service, a private organization that is part of the "new educational establishment," the Conant-liberal arts-Carnegie Foundation cluster. Its purpose is to assess the achievement of students and schools in the nation. In one interpretation, it is an effort to identify schools that are not fulfilling their promise and to make all schools publicly accountable for their performance. The effort has not been warmly received by school administrators.

The private foundations have also participated in educational R and D. They have been principally interested in higher education, however.

THE SYSTEM

As a sociologist I tend to think of wholes rather than parts, of systems rather than specialized units. So I think of the school *system* rather than some specific unit such as Parker School. The generalist in medicine and the sociologist are alike in this respect. When a man has a mysterious breakdown of function, the wise physician looks beyond superficial symptoms. He tries to understand the man's total physical and emotional makeup. He probes for the bodily or psychic origins of distress. After a general examination, he may then refer the patient to a specialist who knows more about the particular part (subsystem) that is in distress.

Social systems are similar in some ways to the human body. The special problem with social systems is their vastness. They are so scattered, so complex that even the most informed observers do not comprehend them in their full dimension.

The school system is very sensitive to scrutiny. It is not alone in this respect. There was a time when religious men held the human body to be sacred and forbade its dissection and investigation. So too with the heavenly bodies which were regarded as a supernatural domain. Social systems are sensitive in similar ways. They fall within the domain of man's powers, and too close a look may threaten those who control the system and wish to maintain it as it is. This is not to suggest malice or conspiracy, yet it is obvious that most men guard their turf jealously. Some will even kill to repel invasion. Thus, as in the National Assessment, we find school administrators (the executives of the system) opposed to examination of their schools. They are not unique in this resistance to interrogation. None of us like it.

The system's size and sensitivity often blunt our powers of analysis. The system is both too large and too concealed to be easily understood. Because we do not understand it, we rush about trying to offer first aid. We may stick a bandage (Head Start, Upward Bound, new styles in reading) on the newest wound, but the sickness remains. The remedy that is regarded by most educators as a cure for all ailments is *money*. Usually when the patient complains, we go to his side and pour money, but only in small amounts, on the wound. Sometimes it helps, sometimes not. Its effect may be only to pacify without reaching the true ailment.

That we should respond in this way to complaints is perhaps inevitable. The school system is political. It responds to power, pressure, votes, and citizen action. It is publicly financed, and it should be as accountable and vulnerable to expressed public will as any other public institution. Politics involves competition for favors and resources among various interest groups, and the payoff is usually large enough to keep things quiet for a time.

However, unless effective programs are given sufficient financial support, their effect will be minimal. It is my own view that the two cannot be offered together until we come to terms with—examine and comprehend—the nature of the *system* which we confront.

I hope herein to move toward such an understanding, but one volume cannot be definitive. It can only identify some basic structures, functions, and pathologies of the system.

Participants in the schools usually cannot see beyond the local school or their own particular problem. So the teachers—who are usually as impotent as the enlisted soldier in war—draw fire that might be better aimed elsewhere. And the disadvantaged family is regarded by many as the cause of, rather than the victim of, the system's malfunction.

I wish I could say that sociological models of social systems can give students a significant insight into the nature of the real system. These catalogs of concepts are often unilluminating codes for what is already obvious. They may tell us the patient has one head, two feet, and can walk and run. True, but not much help.

The most striking thing about the system is its size and growth. We are now at a point indeed where the size of the learning force exceeds the work force. If one considers only the *number* of people enrolled, without regard to the *period* of their enrollment, the learning force of 100 million is now larger than the labor force. About two million elementary and secondary teachers and about a half million college teachers instruct this learning force.[8] If we took school as seriously as we take work, we might be persuaded by the size of the learning force to pay more attention to schools than to institutions that employ people.

Increases in the learning force have been paralleled by a rise in the costs of learning. About fifty billion dollars a year is now spent on formal education, the public share being about thirty-four billion.[9]

---

[8] Recently, the highest rate of increase in school enrollments has been in higher education. In 1950, enrollments were about 2½ million; by 1965, they were 6 million; and by 1974, they may be 10½ million.

In 1970, 63 million enrolled in formal education—5.3 million in preschool, 34.2 million in elementary school, 15.1 in secondary school, and 8.4 million in higher education.

Enrollment rates have also climbed rapidly in vocational, technical, and professional training outside the public school system, from about 15½ million in 1950 to 25 million in 1965 and an expected 48.7 million by 1974.

[9] In addition to formal schooling, an estimated $195 billion is spent each year on mass media, educational technology, and R and D activities.

The rising costs of education have seriously strained an antiquated tax system. Some school systems, when refused needed tax increases by voters, have been forced to close down for varying periods of time. The property tax, the source of most local school revenues, is unable to carry the burden of increased costs. In the rural past, wealth was concentrated in land, and the property tax was the best way to tap national resources, but wealth now is concentrated in fewer hands and in other kinds of assets. State sales and income taxes have helped relieve the load on property taxes, but state governments are notoriously loath to invest money in the city, where fiscal overburdens from various urban needs leave too little money for schools. In recent years, the budget troubles of Catholic parochial schools have threatened to add new burdens to public finance. Massive federal aid to public schools now seems indispensable, and limited federal funds are at last being provided.

The federal presence is felt also in programs aimed at equalization, assessment of school efficiency, court orders to desegregate schools, and federal efforts to provide education through media other than the public schools. In the last few decades the federal government has generally been far more responsive than state government to the urban popular will. Federal intervention has tended, therefore, to have a liberalizing effect on public education.

Net investment in public schools has risen substantially in recent years. As a percent of GNP, investment rose from 5.11 in 1959 to 6.65 in 1967. Spending for formal education is rising by about 10 percent a year, faster than the increase in GNP.

A strong current in education, generated by both conservatives and radicals, questions the value of money as a requisite of quality education. Even some of the extreme inferences drawn from the Coleman Report suggest that money does not matter—in fact, that *schools* do not matter so far as student achievement is concerned.

Obviously money doesn't count for what it *should* in the schools. We should be able to buy far better education with the money spent. Hopefully we will find more efficient ways of doing things. But, as matters stand, the only thing that *does* seem to count is money. It buys better teachers, better supervision, more books and materials, small class size, individual attention, good health and psychiatric care, pleasant buildings and good playgrounds, excursions to the outside world, and so on. It might, of course, be preferable to give the money directly to disadvantaged parents and families rather than to school programs that produce poor results. These families could use it to buy better housing and neighborhoods, better food and clothing, better health and recreation. But we are unlikely to siphon off money from needy schools in order to subsidize needy families. Ideally we would give adequate funds to both.

Some skeptics take the view that only when the system cracks up will something new and better be born. If necessity is the mother of invention, they say, then the deprivation of funds to run traditional schools might produce an invention that would be superior to what we have now. Maybe. In a sense the Philadelphia experiment with Schools Without Walls is such an adaptation. The wall-less school was generated out of the shortage of school buildings and is an invention to be reckoned with. The "revolutionary defeatist" view may not be without some logic and historical precedence, but it seems to appeal only to those who have little to lose if the system breaks down. Parents, children, teachers will resist such a course if alternate and safer routes are open. In the end, however, they too may come to it if other roads lead only to dead ends.

I regret that I find too little material on three major subjects that lie close to the inner workings of the system: politics, financing, technology.

In the eyes of many educators, politics are too dirty to associate with the schools. In fact, the association is an old one. Schools have always been in the thick of politics. Such involvement has often been modestly clothed in nonpartisan dress, but it can be as real and dirty as the partisan variety. Teachers have usually been told to keep out of politics, and until recently, they have dutifully obeyed. Citizens have been expected to soft-pedal demands (which are political) for more and better education and to leave important decisions to professional educators. Until recently, they have done so. Such detachment seems to be ending as the pretenses of nonpartisanship are understood.

More good research and analysis are needed to trace decision-making in the schools and to determine *who* makes decisions and how the politics of education really operate. We know there is a large body of state law and regulation that seriously circumscribes what schools may do. In general, state departments of education are far more political and influential than the dissatisfied urban parent knows. State school authorities allocate funds, set standards, certify teachers, and in some cases even appoint local school boards.

At the federal level, the NEA has been more influential than the U.S. Office of Education. NEA policy has been influenced by school administrators. These school executives have also generally dominated the nation's schools (with the consent of small merchants, lawyers, and others who sit on local school boards), as well as public departments of education and teacher-training institutions.

School administrators and officials have sought to prevent federal control of the schools by opposing categorical aid. They want the federal government to give general aid to schools, funds that are not earmarked for specific purposes. The local and state authorities would then decide how the general aid is to be spent. The citizen must decide, then, whether state or local control is to be preferred to federal control. Critics of the schools contend that state and local controls have failed to produce good schools. They see categorical aid as a lever for change and improvement. School systems, they say, would then be required to create new programs or improve old ones in order to qualify for federal funds.

Since Americans are increasingly a single people in a shrinking nation, a *nationwide* perspective on the schools seems a necessity. Although decentralization of power, especially down to the smaller community level, seems desirable, the federal government may be better able than other levels of government to provide the new funds, ideas, and programs we need in our schools.

As for the third omission, we know that modern life is closely linked to technology. Man creates this technology, but the technology in turn dramatically affects man's behavior, culture, and society. It provides the material base on which social organization is built. A change in that base permits swift and profound changes in the whole human condition. Today's way of life little resembles our grandparents' (and perhaps will even less our grandchildren's)— not only in what we *own* but in what we think, believe, and do—because of the technological leaps of recent generations. Technology has produced autos, jet planes, telephones, TV, refrigerators, washers, and the like. Our grandparents did not have them and that is what, principally, makes us different from them.

Usually our response to social problems takes the form of technological innovation. Transportation and communication, the bloodlines of war and commerce, have been most transformed by technical invention. The classroom and school system are, however, technically primeval. The book, the blackboard, the ball-point pen are the chief technical adoptions in recent centuries. At the same time, amazing transformations have occurred in learning *outside* the classroom. Films, radio, records, and TV have become more influential than teachers in informing, instructing, and socializing the young. The powers of these media, however poor their programming, may be responsible for much of youth's discontent with the traditional classroom. Yet they have invaded the classroom of only the more advanced and wealthier school systems.

Even with Marshall McLuhan as inspiration, the full impact of TV on our society has not yet begun to be measured. For the young, music and the recording industry have produced a new way of life—a youth culture—and a language, message, and system of values that are largely outside established channels of communication. As for the printed word, publishers have seriously altered our reading habits by offering highly readable material in small packages at low cost. Their product—the paperback—has perhaps done more than school teachers to encourage reading and literacy in the general population. Yet so slow are schools to adapt to change that even pocketbook editions of the classics are sometimes scorned by traditional teachers. What is popular or pleasurable, in this view, cannot be educational. For this reason, few teachers make as much use as the corner drugstore of the pocketbook's natural appeal to readers.

Then there is the computer. As we are told repeatedly, its powers are staggering. Yet we can only guess at its educational uses. The heavy investments of big industry may ensure its instructional future, but there are problems. As a teacher, the computer is mechanical rather than human, and relative to other instructional media, very costly. To purchase its time, school systems will have to make large investments in capital equipment. Such equipment will undoubtedly displace many teachers. It will also greatly alter the system of learning, including the design and size of schools and classrooms, the relations among teachers and students. Purchase of expensive equipment—computers, teaching machines, and other devices—will require a careful calculation of costs and benefits. What we get may not be worth the cost.

Business investments in educational hardware already run over a billion dollars a year. Big industry is required by these investments to move also into the production of the software that is the content of instruction. A videotape, for example, must be *about* something. That something is curriculum, subject matter, software.

The machine needs something to process. This need tends to transfer control over many basic educational decisions from professional educators to big business. Already industry employs as software experts many of the top curriculum people who once worked for school boards.

The political influence and the general impact on the school system of technology and the technology makers have not been calculated or carefully predicted. The technology *makers* may have an even greater impact than the technology itself. The most powerful interest group in our society—big industry—is for the first time moving directly into the schools. In the past, only publishing and construction have been much involved with schools. As a result, educational dollars have been spent building schools and stocking them with textbooks. Recently, a variety of industries have come on the scene. Their interest is in selling their new products. To accomplish this, they may support increased financing of schools and a decision-making process that can expedite the purchase of new products. Some industries have actively supported decentralizing budget and purchase functions in urban schools because of their difficulties in breaking through central bureaucracies.

In regard to the overall system, this volume does not dwell on some of the primary relations between school and society. Certainly the problem of equal opportunity cannot be settled in the schools alone. Those who are most unhappy with the schools are mainly unhappy about their general lot in life. They want good jobs, a decent income, a fair share of life's rewards. They see better schools as a means of qualifying them for a better, all-around break. Schools can indeed help to qualify them, or *some* of them, for better jobs or whatever they are seeking, but when the schools fail to qualify them, there is another way around. We can change the *qualifications*. We can change what it requires to qualify for rewards in the society and/or in the schools.

For example, suppose once a year our society held a footrace and divided the wealth of the society among the winners. Entrants would qualify for the race by successfully completing twelve years of schooling under professional trainers. Handicaps in the race would be based on obedience to trainers and report-card ratings. Handicaps also would be given according to the school's "quality" ratings which vary directly with the amount of money spent on them.

Many of the trainers have never themselves entered the foot-race, and only a few have finished at the top. Most of the trainers are women even though almost all the winners are males. The trainers require that trainees memorize the names, biographies, and finishing speeds of previous winners. They require them to read, write, and answer questions about the history and purpose of the contest. Seldom do trainees get out on the field and run; rarely do they even simulate the motions of the race.

These trainers share a common vocabulary and code of etiquette, and they tend to impose handicaps on students who look, talk, and act differently from themselves. Accusations by the handicapped along this line are so heated that the safety of judges and trainers, and their whole system, is seriously threatened. Responses to the accusations charge the accusers with having (1) inferior genetic endowment, (2) inferior family and cultural background, (3) inferior motivation (ambition, drive).

To pacify complaints, the trainers and judges sometimes work harder to get the heavily handicapped to fit the system—to obey the rules, answer questions correctly, and behave like the trainers.

But now many contestants question the qualifications themselves: What has such training to do with running footraces? Some of them want to change the whole method and content of training. They ask: Why do the judges require this system of training? Why not a different system, better suited to the actual requirements of the contest? Or, why *require* any training at all? Maybe the strongest runners, by their very nature, cannot endure twelve years of even the most related training. Perhaps they cannot endure one year.

Or going further into the heart of the system, they sometimes ask: Why should the society distribute rewards on this basis at all? Why should so much go to so few people? Why should the winners take all, and why should speed be so highly rewarded?

These questions are at the heart of the system and the complaints about it. Contestants are interested in the rewards of society, in the big stakes. Probably few of them would care much about the training system were it not a necessary qualifier for rewards of the society.

In the real, rather than hypothetical, world, we might ask society to give decent rewards to everyone and to equalize these rewards as fully as possible in keeping with the performance needs of the society. We might ask the judges and managers to subsidize only *suitable* training and to exclude no contestants from any contest simply because he lacks *formal* training. We might also ask what contest the system should sponsor. Is the ability to run fast the most valuable attribute of modern man? Just how valuable are the skills of a footrace to the society?

The example is exaggerated, but it may suggest the essence of the system.

For this reason, I have not considered the orthodoxies of academic texts in making selections for this volume. I wish instead to tap some of the most lively minds in the field, whether or not they are sociologists or educators. In some cases I have made selections only because they deal with subjects of interest. Points of view often come clearest in discussion and debate. I have tried therefore to include some selections from the heated dialogue about schools that typifies our era. In several cases, these are reviews of the work of others. In the case of the Coleman Report, it is a critique and response concerning a research document.

The selections are specialized in that almost all concentrate on the *school* system. References to larger systems are usually incidental. I cannot, in one volume, dwell on educational and socializing influences outside the school system. These influences are considerable, but they are almost totally uncharted and are so vast in scope (mass media, family, religion, employment, group membership, ethnicity, and so on) that they cannot be examined here.

ROOTS OF INEQUALITY

In man's experience, resources have usually been scarce, and the struggle for shares of the scarce resources has divided families, tribes, classes, and nations throughout human history.

Religious sects have sometimes tried to persuade men to temper the struggle and sometimes justified systems of uneven distribution which favor their own members. The early Christians, like some of the Jewish sects from which Jesus and the Apostles may have come, were egalitarian in the extreme. "Primitive Christianity," as it is sometimes called, certainly implies a strong bias in favor of equal sharing of resources among all of God's children, and the rich and greedy are explicitly warned about the difficulties of entering the kingdom of heaven.

On the other hand, some Protestant theologies (especially those postulating an elect of God who are predestined to profit from the riches of heaven and earth) have rationalized and stimulated the enrichment of some individuals at the expense of others.

Recently, large and militant sections of Protestantism, in the United States particularly, have turned back to the early Christians and declared war on social inequities. This development has had enormously important implications for the schools, a traditional battlefield in the ancient war between the haves and the have-nots. In many communities, school officials who once accepted and practiced discrimination against the poor and various outside ethnic groups are under fire from an institution that once had given them strong support. Parents with children in segregated or plush suburban schools are now often the subject of impassioned sermons about equality. And all schools have been deeply shaken by court decisions which have applied the moral code of early Christianity to the legal code of the land. All but a few of the Justices who have created the new code are Protestant.

The greatest pressures have come directly from those most closely tied to Primitive Christianity—the blacks, the poor, the outcast—people who have drawn from their faith an inspiration and strength that sees them through danger as they seek justice for their children. In the schools and elsewhere, they have demanded equal treatment and have found support in the Testaments from which some learned to read, often under the guidance of white Protestants.

The schools are in crisis primarily because they have held themselves out as an escape route from poverty and deprivation. The campaign to win back the dropout, for example, claims by inference that success in school leads to success in life. To win public support, schools have publicized data about the relationship between years of school and income earned in later life. The message has come through clearly: education can free everyone from poverty. Naturally the poor and the excluded respond with demands that they be admitted to the Cinderella chambers where chambermaids become princesses.

The schools have not been able to meet their new commitments. The success and riches they offer are still in short supply in the society. The problem is one of distribution. We can produce ample supplies of the necessities (food, clothing, shelter), but we do not have the will to get such supplies to the millions who need them.

In education, we divide scarcity. Because we suffer from what John K. Galbraith has called "public poverty," we have not built enough schoolrooms nor trained enough teachers nor paid teachers enough to keep them in the profession. Expansion of higher learning has not kept pace with demand, and an economy of scarcity has prevailed at this level also. Competition for the prized, but limited, places in college has intensified competition below. Parents, eager for security and status for their children, often fiercely resist sharing with others one of the scarcest and most prized commodities—educational credentials—passkeys to affluence, status, security.

When they can do so, as in the wealthiest suburbs, parents bid up the price of teachers so their own children can jump the test hurdles and qualify for prestigious colleges. In the typical prosperous suburb, the school superintendent will be in trouble if even 10 percent of his graduates fail to be admitted at least to the top state university. The high school principal in the ghetto who sends even 2 or 3 percent of his graduates there will be acclaimed a success.

Most issues of educational policy are rooted in the struggle over this prized and scarce commodity. Few parents will agree, however, that their own children benefit only because others are denied. Their generally proclaimed belief in democratic tenets and the more benign teachings of Christianity force them to seek justification for discrimination.

If we can honestly believe, for example, in the validity of IQ tests as measures of intrinsic ability, it will be easier to believe that schools should favor those with the greatest potential and that the advantages given our own children are deserved and necessary rewards to the fittest.

So the effort to rehabilitate the IQ test as a measure of inherent merit stirs passionate debate on all sides. Dr. Arthur Jensen's claim that the IQ test measures genetically determined intelligence with considerable accuracy has profound implications. It can justify the maintenance of separate and invariably *un*equal schools, tracks, and curriculums where the "superior" of high potential are separated from the "inferior" of low potential. The separation can then be made in the name of justice for the inferior, since only in schools designed to meet their special needs will they at last realize themselves.

In the segregated schools of the South and other sections of the country where poverty is endemic and in Northern urban schools that are pinched for funds, the demand for segregated (neighborhood) schools and special privileges can be justified if we believe in the native inferiority or superiority of particular racial or ethnic groups. Special programs for the gifted, tracking, homogeneous grouping—all rooted in the same soil of scarcity—can be rationalized in the same terms.

Perhaps most school problems could be dealt with more equitably if parents could feel assured that their children would not have to pay for dealing other children in—if they knew we would spend enough to provide adequately for all.

The elimination of tensions caused by the conflict over apparent scarcity may be impossible (except perhaps under a police state), but we can hope that a new society and psychology of abundance would greatly reduce the resistance to change caused by scarcity.

PART I

Equality and Racial Integration

I

Although schools are assumed to be a ladder to success, open and equally accessible to all citizens, one finds that for many they are much more like an obstacle course. Some from the lower ranks of society do, of course, climb the ladder easily. They are usually those who wish to adopt the school culture as their own. Others climb a rung or two. Many others are blocked from movement because of various handicaps imposed on them before they begin their climb.

Inequality of opportunity pervades the school system. It is apparent in what we invest in schools and in the products we turn out of them—the students. Since schools are financed by local and state governments, they depend on what the state and the community are able and willing to spend on education. Some states and local boards can afford to spend a lot, others can afford very little. In education, as in most other things, we tend to get what we pay for. Poor communities are always handicapped in the competition for good teachers, administrators, and counselors. Like other people who work for a living, these professionals are likely to gravitate to

23

communities where salaries are highest and working conditions best. Poor communities cannot afford small class size, expert curriculum advice, good buildings, equipment, and the rest. Nor can the poor state or district offer the same opportunities to students who want to go to college. They are similarly unable to offer the same incentives for students to perform well in lower grades in order to qualify for higher education and good jobs.

The state of Mississippi spent $335 per pupil in its schools in 1966–1967, whereas New York state spent $912 per pupil. The discrepancy cannot be explained by any indifference on the part of Mississippians to education. In fact, Mississippi made a greater effort for its schools and invested more of its per capita income in education than did the Empire State. New York is simply far more able to pay for good schools than most other states of the union, particularly those of the deep South. Because of its inability to pay for education, only about 30 percent of adults in Mississippi are high school graduates, compared with 41 percent in the entire country.

Even within the same state, because of local funding of schools, there are large disparities in school spending. Rich suburban schools spend most and poor rural districts least. The city, with its large low-income ghettoes, are usually somewhere in between. City schools have in the past been in advance of schools elsewhere. They were able to spend more and offer a better general quality of education for the money spent. Since the wealthier and better-educated groups in the population have in recent decades tended to leave the cities for suburban areas, city schools now find it difficult to compete with suburban systems in buying good education.

Beyond these differences, this author's book *Education and Income* describes large inequities that were found to exist even within the *same* local school district (in this case a very large city). It appears that school boards—at least until very recently—have spent less money on schools in lower-income areas. What is perhaps even more important, they have "processed" children from these areas in different ways and tracked them into different destinies.

To an extent that is still largely unknown and uncharted, these local inequities have responded to federal programs to compensate the "disadvantaged," particularly those living in city ghetto areas. The compensatory programs are too new and inadequate, however, to have had much total impact on the schools yet. Some advocates argue forcefully that low-income groups need to be given far more than upper-income groups in order to properly balance the inequities of the past. If these groups have been given less in the past, they should be given more now to make up for their losses. Indications are, however, that total public subsidies to education (especially when higher education is considered) are still awarded in direct proportion to family income levels. That is to say, the higher the income level, the higher the public subsidies tend to be.

Education and Income was perhaps the first book to explore the system of social stratification and the inequalities in a large-city school system. A few anachronisms were left in the excerpt included in this volume to indicate how far the discussion of inequality has come in the past decade. Note was made in the text, for example, of the total absence of articles, studies, and the like dealing with the "culturally deprived" and the proliferation of literature on the "gifted." This of course is no longer the case. The decade of the sixties, in fact, experienced an explosion of attention to the disadvantaged. The impact was felt in the civil rights, poverty, and student movements, and through them, almost every institution in our society. The issue of racial equity has become undeniably the central domestic issue of our time. In 1961, when *Education and Income* was published, it was just breaking forcefully on the horizon.

Later in that same year, 1961, James Bryant Conant's influential book *Slums and Suburbs* was published, calling attention particularly to the vast differences in opportunity found in slum and suburban schools. Dr. Conant warned of the "social dynamite" in the slum and the need to correct the glaring inequities in American education. He pointed out that the transformation of the American high school can be attributed to laws against child labor which removed young children from factories and put them in school. He notes the impact of these new populations on education: "Today 80 percent of the youth ages sixteen and seventeen are in school. What this has meant for the curriculum and organization of the schools raises not one question but many questions. After forty years we are still arguing about the answers."

Though Dr. Conant is preeminently a chemist and a high-ranking administrator, his approach to education has been that of the sociologist. His concern has been with organization, the system of education, and the relation between school and society. "Why we attempt to provide education for *all* American youth," he notes, "is fundamentally a consequence of a basic change in the social and economic pattern of our society." That "pattern" grew out of economic developments which impelled the adoption of child labor laws. The task of educating *all* youths, rather than small elites, has profoundly altered the nature of American public schools, he accurately points out.

Again, looking at schools as a total system, he says, "The place to begin setting standards in American education is at the last rung of the education ladder—the graduate level." More than most of us realize, and particularly advocates of stress on early childhood education, the graduate schools set the standards to which schools, starting even at nursery levels, conform. It is also interesting and perhaps significant to note that the greatest inequities (racial and social class) are found at the graduate level. To correct imbalances in slum schools, Dr. Conant also recommends that we spend more money on these schools, involve parents, decentralize city school administration, and increase employment opportunities for slum youth.

This author's points of disagreement with Dr. Conant are in what seems to be his too ready inclination to equate school achievement with "ability" and his apparent preference for traditional academic curricula and standards of performance.

Educational opportunity, it appears, tends to vary in direct proportion to the income and social class of parents, family, and community. In general, the more you have, the more you get from the schools. The most obviously disadvantaged in the system have been the blacks. Blacks over the age of twenty-five have only an average of nine years of school, while whites have almost twelve. According to almost all indices, blacks suffer the most serious educational disadvantages. They are 12 percent of the entire population but only 3 percent of graduate students. When they go to college, they usually enter poorer schools and lower-paying careers.

These educational inequalities lead to income inequalities. In 1961, the average *lifetime* earnings of males over eighteen who had less than eight years of school was $176,000; for those who had less than four years of high school, it was $235,000; for college graduates, it was $453,000. The college graduate made $277,000 more during his life than the man who didn't finish grade school.

The controversy over these inequalities led, in the mid-sixties, to a national inquiry, sponsored by the U.S. Office of Education, into "inequality of opportunity in the public schools." The results of that inquiry have now become historic documents. Because of the scope of the study and its highly controversial nature, it has been given rather full treatment in this volume. Included here are the Summary statement from the document itself, omitting only the statistical tables and references to the tables, and a critical analysis (Bowles and Levin) of the complete document. The reader should be alerted to the fact that the analysis by Professors Bowles and Levin is a rather technical one and not easy reading. It is fitting that this should be so. The full Coleman Report is a highly statistical one, involving the use of quite sophisticated techniques, such as regression analysis. Since certain clear policy inferences were made by the researchers about the relation between equality and scholastic achievement, the methodology of the study is of critical importance. The reader is urged to give careful attention to this critical analysis and not to be thrown off by some of its technicalities.

Perhaps the reader can formulate some judgments of his own about the Report from the material included here. This author's view of the matter is that, while the research provided invaluable data about the status of our nation's schools, the Report and the policy conclusions were much too hastily drawn from it. Since data analysis inevitably reflects the predispositions and perspectives (biases, if you will) of the researchers, perhaps it would have been advisable to submit the data for analysis to at least several groups with varying perspectives whose views could then have been compared and contrasted.

In brief, the study found significantly *un*equal educational opportunities in the nation's schools. It concluded, however, that only family background has a significant effect on academic performance and that schools make little difference. Social-class integration, it was found, affects the achievement of black students as well as the student's sense of power over his environment. Its policy implications, were its method of analysis accepted as valid, might be devastating. Since schools were found to have no significant effect on scholastic achievement, the policy inference would be to abandon schools and replace them with something that does affect achievement.

Usually the policy inference drawn, however, is that we need not bother to balance existing inequities in schools or spend more on educating the disadvantaged than we now do (at least not on any known practice of the schools), since these measures have little influence on performance anyhow.

The failure of the study to account for about half of the "variance" in achievement has suggested to many (who perhaps already have predispositions to such assumptions) that genetic ability and intelligence is the central factor in achievement. Christopher Jencks, for example, states, "Whether this reflects unmeasured genetic differences in aptitude . . . is a matter for speculation." The new controversy over genetic intelligence and the views of Arthur Jensen are in large part a consequence of the Coleman Report findings, as well as the premature and quite facile assumption that "compensatory education" cannot help the disadvantaged.

Policy conclusions often represent a substantial inferential leap from the data. Looking at the same data, researchers with differing perspectives may draw widely divergent conclusions. Thus, Jencks may say, viewing the Coleman data: "What their children need first and foremost is not academic skill but such 'middle class' virtues as self-discipline and self-respect."* Others might, and have, concluded that what "their children need" is to have the doors of opportunity —in school, college, work—opened wider for them.

Most professional educators maintain that money is the principal ingredient of good education. Though Professor David Cohen (one of the principal authors of *Racial Isolation in the Public Schools*) is skeptical about the validity of this assumption, based on the analysis in the Coleman Report, he shows how financial inequities are generally locked into schools by the wide variations in the financial capacity of local communities. In his article "The Economics of Inequality," he discusses schemes advocated for minimizing these differentials.

II

The issues of school integration and equality are inseparable, as they are in the Coleman Report. In the South, the segregation of races into totally separate school systems has been enforced by law,

* Christopher Jencks, "A Reappraisal of the Most Controversial Educational Document of Our Time," *New York Times Magazine*, August 10,1969.

a system of *de jure* (legal) segregation. In Northern schools, racial segregation has been *de facto,* a product not of law but of the residential ghettoes in which Northern blacks live and of the gerry-mandering of school boundaries.

Many schoolmen claim that racial segregation does not result in inequality. They claim that the separate schools, black and white, are equal in the quality of education offered. The U.S. Supreme Court disagreed with this view in its historic 1954 decision, holding that segregated schools, because of damaging psychological and educational consequences to blacks, are inherently unequal. It called for desegregation with "all deliberate speed." Now, more than a decade and a half later, schools are still almost as racially segregated as they were then.

In more tangible ways, though physical facilities may have been largely equalized in some areas of the South, inequities continue to exist in the total method of processing students in school and in opportunities for higher education.

Probably the most significant statement on the subject of school desegregation, aside from the Supreme Court decision itself, is the U.S. Commission on Civil Rights' report, *Racial Isolation in the Public Schools.* The findings and recommendations from that document are included here. They speak for themselves, simply and to the point. Most of the data for the report come from the same national study that produced the Coleman Report. Attention is given in the analysis to the complicating problems of ghetto housing and the concentration of black ghettoes in the central cities. The report notes the need for better housing patterns and for an attack on racial isolation on a metropolitanwide basis.

The policy implications of the article by Morton Inger and Robert Stout, "School Desegregation and the Superintendent," are clear. The article is not only included here for this reason but also because it offers some basis for hope in solving one of the most resistant and difficult problems of our time, the racial segregation of schools. The authors conclude that superintendents and school boards have considerable authority with the lay public in providing "legitimacy" to school desegregation.

SLUMS AND SUBURBS

by James B. Conant*

The dramatic contrasts between schools in the slums and schools in the suburbs illustrate the impossibility of discussing education without specifying the kinds of homes from which the pupils come. Many of the criticisms of the public schools which we have heard in the last few years have ignored this fact. Furthermore, they have been expressed often in terms too general to be constructive. To speak eloquently about raising standards is of little help unless one specifies what kinds of schools one is considering and defines accurately what is meant by the words "academic standards." The critics of American education, so it seems to me, are under an obligation both to be concrete with their proposals and to be clear as to the premises from which they start their arguments. For example, progressive education has become a synonym for all that is bad about our schools. Yet when my own children were young, some thirty and more years ago, progressive education was the new dispensation we were all supposed to acclaim with joy. Referring to an outstanding progressive private elementary school, time and again my friends would say, "If only I could have attended such a school." Today I hear my children's contemporaries condemning their own progressive education and preparing as parents to do their best to see that "It doesn't happen to my children."

Phrases which were once overprized and oversold have come to stand for whatever one doesn't like about our schools. Yet few, if any, of those who bemoan the evil influence of the progressive educators would send their children into the kind of schoolroom which was common sixty years ago. Looking at the pedagogic revolution impartially and historically, one runs into the following

* From *Slums and Suburbs,* James B. Conant, The New American Library, 1961.

30

stubborn fact. The schools in the forefront of the progressive movement in the first decades of this century were private schools. Close on their heels came the public schools in the high-income suburban areas, where parent-teacher organizations played an effective role in determining what kind of school was kept. Could it be that what the progressive educators thought they had evolved from new philosophic premises was in reality largely a product of a parental revolt against the schools of the nineteenth century? A reforming zeal to provide better schools for one's offspring seems to be the constant factor that unites all the recent generations of American parents. The pendulum swings back and forth with respect to educational slogans.

Professor Cremin of Teachers College, Columbia University, in an excellent book on progressive education, *The Transformation of the School,* has examined American education from 1890 to World War II from the point of view of an historian who understands schools and teachers. He dates the beginning of the progressive movement with the publication of a series of articles in the *Forum* by Joseph M. Rice in 1892, because Rice sought to weave together many separate strands of contemporary protest into a single reform program. Cremin goes on to show how closely the new educational developments of the next three decades were tied to the reform movement in politics and the social concern of such people as Jane Addams. Progressive education on examination he declares "turns out to be nothing less than the educational phase of America's progressivism writ large." Of this phase John Dewey became a major prophet, but he was in no sense the founder, nor were those who were experimenting with new classroom techniques in 1910 all his disciples.

Indeed I think it is illuminating to turn back the pages of history to the 1870s to see what was being done in Quincy, Massachusetts, by a man whom John Dewey once called the father of progressive education. The school board of that New England town, largely under the influence of Charles Francis Adams, the son of the statesman and diplomat of the Civil War period, had engaged one Col. Francis W. Parker as superintendent. This former officer in the Union Army had studied pedagogy in Germany and developed some radical ideas of his own. He and the school board appeared to see eye to eye, and what they accomplished between 1875 and 1879 is told by Mr. Adams in an address which, to me, is of fascinating interest since it presents so vividly the contrast between the old and the new pedagogic approach to the education of young children.

A series of examinations introduced in 1873 had convinced the members of the Quincy school committee that the pupils could "neither speak nor spell their own language very perfectly, nor read and write it with the ease and elegance which is desirable." According to Mr. Adams, the examinations had shown in fact that in far too many cases those examined "could neither read nor write at all!" Then a new system was introduced by Colonel Parker. "The essence of the new system was that there was no system about it; it was marked throughout by intense individuality. . . . Experiments were to be cautiously tried and results from time to time noted." As a school board member Mr. Adams emphasized the cautious approach, also the economical one, but what he actually reports must have sounded radical enough. "The old 'dame school' disappeared at once. In place of it appeared something as different as light from darkness. The alphabet itself was no longer taught . . . little ones were learning to read almost without knowing it . . . a play-table and toys were furnished them . . . the children actually went to school without being dragged there. Yet the reason for this was not far to seek. The simple fact was that they were happier and more amused and better contented at school than at home. The drudgery of the impossible primer no longer made infant life miserable. The alphabet was robbed of its terrors, and stole upon them unawares."

The Quincy reforms were not confined to the first grade, however. The teaching of geography was enlivened by having the children make three-dimensional maps with moistened clay. As an upshot of all the changes, Mr. Adams reports that "the children had ceased to dislike their schoolrooms; and to those who remember as vividly as most persons over thirty do, the whole unattractive, not to say repulsive character both of the old-time school teaching and the old-time school discipline, this change is one for which those who enjoy the advantage of it may well be grateful."

Colonel Parker left Quincy for Boston the year following Mr. Adams' glowing report, and in 1893 moved to Chicago, where he and Dewey came to know each other—which had far-reaching effects on American education. If one reads Colonel Parker's *Talks on Pedagogics* published in 1894 and John Dewey's *School and*

Society published in 1899, the influence of the older school man with a rich teaching experience on the young philosopher is clearly evident. Dewey, and later his followers who were professors of education, added several elements of importance to the new pedagogic approaches of the 1890s and early 1900s. Indeed by 1919, when the Progressive Education Association was founded, the movement had acquired much ideological baggage, some of it related to psychology, some to sociology, and not a little to politics as well. The latter was to prove to be an awkward load to carry and by no means as closely related to the basic principle as was at first maintained. Indeed, since the new pedagogic approach was early accepted in the elementary schools, it would be my contention that the permanent influence of the movement is to be found by examining what actually goes on in the classroom and not what professors of education have had to say about it. In other words, it is important to separate the new techniques of teaching from some of the wider aims of the progressive movement, particularly from those which were manifest in the depression years. To this end, I should like to distinguish sharply between elementary schools and secondary schools.

Confining attention, for the moment then, to the education of young children, I believe any impartial investigator would say that the contrast painted so long ago by Mr. Adams in Quincy would be the contrast between a vast majority of schools in the 1890s and the schools in the 1960s. The major reforms of elementary education which have taken place seem so obvious today that I would challenge anyone to try and set up a school which negated them. Call it a child-centered school, or a humane school, or use Adams' phrase and characterize it as a school "the children had ceased to dislike," the advantages of the new type of school and the new attitude of teachers as compared with the typical school of the late nineteenth century are just not open to argument by anyone familiar with the facts. I am not speaking of particular teaching methods, for example the teaching of reading, but of general methods used by teachers to enlist the interest and enthusiasm of children.

There are many things about our schools today which I join with others in severely criticizing. Some of them can be attributed to those educators who were in the forefront of the progressive movement. Many others are the consequences of parental desires of the 1920s and 1930s which were a reaction against the "too-bookish" schooling of their youth. Some of the critics are fond of comparing the American public high school with either the British Grammar Schools or German Gymnasia today or the American high schools of 1900. To make this comparison is to ignore a second revolution in American education which I have called the transformation of the high school. This transformation was a consequence of the radical change in the laws and customs affecting the employment of youth. A realization of this social change is so basic to an understanding of the problems of secondary education that I shall attempt to summarize a large bit of American history in a few short paragraphs.

Those of us who remember the period between the Spanish-American War and World War I will readily recall both the optimism of those days and the radical discontent. The two went together. Writers and some political figures were highly critical of the American society which they saw around them. The new waves of immigrants which kept arriving in the last decades of the nineteenth century brought people much more difficult to assimilate then those who had arrived in the 1840s and 1850s. In cities and towns where the new settlers clustered, language barriers were overcome with difficulty. In one mining town in northern Minnesota in 1905, I have been told, there were more than a dozen nationalities speaking a dozen different languages.

In the big cities the foreigners were housed in crowded, impoverished, and frightfully unsanitary slums. Cleaning up the slums, Americanizing the immigrants (adults and children) through formal schools and settlement houses, and reforming the corrupt politics of the cities were tasks which seemed urgent to all right-thinking people of the day. The progressive in politics and the conservative agreed on the need for changing many shocking social situations. On certain topics such as trust-busting, the initiative and referendum, women's suffrage, governmental regulation of railroads, and the recall of judicial decisions, there was anything but agreement among the leaders of opinion. Those who considered themselves progressive in politics and who followed Theodore Roosevelt's banner in 1912 would have been in favor of most if not all the reforms I have just listed and would have added conservation of national resources spelled with large and flaming letters. Part and parcel of the progressive movement in politics were efforts to do something about child labor.

When the industrialization of the Eastern states first started, early in the nineteenth century, the laboring force for the mills was recruited from the nearby farms. On farms children as well as youth had always been expected to work long hours. Therefore, to the first few generations of industrialized Americans, it was not strange that in the new mills children as well as adults found employment and worked from dawn to dusk. The same situation had developed still earlier in Great Britain and gradually aroused the social conscience of that nation. The demand for the regulation of the factory work of women and children had been voiced on the other side of the Atlantic long before the nineteenth century was over, as readers of Dickens and his contemporaries well know.

Here in the United States the movement to abolish child labor did not gain momentum until the era of progressivism began. Then regulation of working conditions and the elimination of children from the mills became one of the more important objectives of the reformers. Progress was slow, however, and when in 1916 Congress passed a law prohibiting child labor, the Supreme Court declared the law unconstitutional. But state laws were passed and, more important, the climate of opinion was in process of rapid change. Management and labor altered their attitudes towards the employment of young people. Long before the passage of the New Deal legislation which abolished child labor in factories, public opinion in most parts of the country had demanded that all children be educated before they were sent to work.

Writing in 1902, a professor of education at the University of California said, "Primary education . . . is the education needed for all; which, for the sake of the general good, no citizen can be permitted to do without. Beyond this is the region of difference, of divergence, and it may be added, of very great uncertainty and dispute. Occasionally one hears the prophecy that what we call secondary education will eventually be an education for all." Here was a professional educator at the beginning of the twentieth century wondering if secondary education might some day be education for all, which it certainly was not at that time. Forty years later the Educational Policies Commission of the National Education Association published a book entitled *Education for All American Youth.* While many disagreed with the prescriptions contained in this volume, few if any challenged the title. Four decades had completed the transformation of American secondary schools. Despite the "uncertainty and dispute" that continued to persist, secondary schools became institutions providing full-time schooling for all youth.

Taking the country as a whole, we find in 1910 that some 30 per cent of the youth fourteen and fifteen years of age were employed; twenty years later the figure had dropped to 9 per cent. In the same period, the percentage of youth sixteen and seventeen years old who were employed was cut in half (from 66 to 32 per cent). As the employed figure diminished, the school enrollments increased. The alterations proceeded at a different rate in different communities, but by World War I it was clear that before long the nature of the secondary school population was going to be very different from what it had been when the century began. It is hardly necessary to argue that the change was irreversible. Anyone who doubts this can try to persuade Congress and the state legislatures to repeal the mass of laws that now restrict the opportunities for young people to get jobs. Whether the teacher liked it or not, the high schools were forced to become schools for all. Today 80 per cent of the youth ages sixteen and seventeen are in school. What this fact has meant for the curriculum and organization of the schools raises not one question but many questions. After forty years we are still arguing about the answers.

How we attempt today to provide education is a consequence of the new ideas of those who led progressive education and the subsequent reaction to these ideas. Why we attempt to provide education for *all* American youth is fundamentally a consequence of a basic change in the social and economic pattern of our society. The extreme examples of high schools I have discussed and the perplexing problems facing the teachers in these schools illustrate the wide range of complexities American educators must face. Few in the profession would claim they knew the answers to these complexities. Few would maintain that even with ample resources they were providing a satisfactory education for every one of their students. Therefore they always welcome informed criticism, reserving the right to challenge the critic as to his premises and, particularly, as to the validity of any arguments based on comparisons between schools in different communities, even different communities within a single state. My own premises, I trust, I have made evident. If so, I may then claim the privilege of summing up my conclusions about schools in suburbs and in slums.

SUMMARY

As to the schools in the well-to-do suburbs:

1. The main problem in wealthy suburban schools is to guide the parent whose college ambitions outrun his child's abilities toward a realistic picture of the kind of college his child is suited for.

2. Expert guidance must begin very early in the suburban schools in this process of educating both parent and child in the realities of college admission.

3. The prestige colleges should be seen as institutions for very bright students, the majority of whom will go to graduate school for advanced degrees. Many will enter the professions.

4. The California pattern of higher education, which includes two-year junior colleges, should be examined with care by citizens interested in solving college problems within many states.

5. The place to begin to set standards in American education is at the last rung of the educational ladder—the graduate level. Requirements for admission to law and medical schools and to graduate schools of arts and sciences should include evidence by examination of a wide and solid academic education. The requirements might be as follows: the ability to write a competent essay; a good reading, writing, and speaking knowledge of at least one modern foreign language; a knowledge of mathematics through the calculus; a knowledge of physics, chemistry, and biology at the freshman level of our most rigorous colleges; at the same level of competence, knowledge of American history and political institutions and English and American literature. The implementation of this recommendation might well have a salutary effect upon the education of bright students in both schools and colleges by bringing about what is called for in recommendation 6.

6. All high schools should try to create a climate of opinion that will encourage bright students to elect the kind of wide program that is required of students in the Bronx High School of Science. Such a program means five rather than the traditional four academic subjects a year.

7. Every high school ought to strive for participation in the Advanced Placement Program.

As to the schools in the large city slums:

8. The contrast in the money spent per pupil in wealthy suburban schools and in slum schools of the large cities challenges the concept of equality of opportunity in American public education. More money is needed in slum schools.

9. Social dynamite is building up in our large cities in the form of unemployed out-of-school youth, especially in the Negro slums. We need accurate and frank information neighborhood by neighborhood.

10. The schools should be given the responsibility for educational and vocational guidance of youth after they leave school until age 21. This will require more money.

11. Increased attention ought to be paid in both slums and suburbs to developing meaningful courses for pupils with less than average abilities. To this end consideration should be given by every school and community to the expansion of work-study programs for slow students, and to the provision of at least an auto mechanics shop for boys in every high school in metropolitan areas.

12. Employment opportunities in the large cities must be promptly opened on a non-discriminatory basis. Because of the attitude of management and labor this can be done only through the use of federal funds.

13. The improvement of the education of elementary school children in Negro slums by the expenditure of much more money than at present should have top priority. In terms of the individual attention provided in teaching the basic skills, the instruction in the first few grades of a school in a Negro slum should be *better* than in other schools in the same city.

14. More teachers and perhaps more pay for teachers are necessary for schools in the slums than in either the high income districts of the large cities or the wealthy suburbs. Special training programs for teachers in slum schools are needed.

15. No effort should be spared in slum areas to enlist the support of parents in the education of their children. To this end, adult education programs should be improved and expanded.

16. Big cities need decentralized administration in order to bring the schools closer to the needs of the people in each neighborhood and to make each school fit the local situation.

17. Nonpolitical, honest school boards composed of high-minded citizens who can differentiate between policy-making and

administration are essential. An aroused public opinion is needed to correct the situation in those cities where such school boards do not exist.

I have sought to create a set of anxious thoughts in the minds of the conscientious citizens who may read these pages and who, while living in the suburbs, may work in the city. To improve the work of the slum schools requires an improvement in the lives of the families who inhabit the slums, but without a drastic change in the employment prospects for urban Negro youth, relatively little can be accomplished. Therefore I close by urging that our large city educational problems be analyzed in far more detail than in the past and with a far greater degree of frankness. Neighborhood by neighborhood we need to know the facts, and when these facts indicate a dangerous social situation the American people should be prepared to take prompt action before it is too late.

EDUCATION AND INCOME

by Patricia Cayo Sexton*

I

Much of the debate over education today, no matter how distantly related it may sometimes appear, can be reduced to a simple contest between "mass" and "elite" education. The debate began in this country when the first school was built and has continued unabated to the present moment.

As we look back, it seems clear that, in the past, educational advantages have gone to those who could pay the price—to an elite

* Adapted from *Education and Income: Inequalities of Opportunity in Our Public Schools*, by Patricia Cayo Sexton. Copyright © 1961 by Patricia Cayo Sexton. All rights reserved. Reprinted by permission of The Viking Press, Inc.

of wealth, in other words. Education has not always been free. Advanced education has always been costly. Money has been needed to purchase it. Thus the elite of wealth and the elite of the educated were usually identical.

Today the situation is not so simple. Education through high school in most places is now free—at least for those who can afford the hidden tuition charges and the expense of unemployment.

Higher education is still very costly, yet scholarships are now available for the poor but able.

Our educated elite has expanded and now includes a number of those who came up the hard way, through the ranks.

Many assume from these facts that an elite of ability, rather than an elite of wealth, is receiving most of the educational advantages we now offer. They are pleased by this arrangement, and they are content that our schools are doing a good job of educating an ability elite.

Some, however, question the relationship of "ability" with the old categories of wealth and status. Jacques Barzun in *The House of Intellect* calls attention to the unearned advantage of ancestry and of being born to the elite: "There is no mystery about it: the child who is familiar with books, ideas, conversation—the ways and means of the intellectual life—before he begins school, indeed, before he begins consciously to think, has a marked advantage. He is at home in the House of Intellect just as the stableboy is at home among horses or the child of actors on the stage. Medical schools recognize this truth when they give preference to applicants who are children of physicians."

Yet, strangely, he would not have the elite of wealth and status wait in line with the elite of ability. The old elite must go to the head of the line: "If we remember . . . how frequently talent is born into families with developed intellectual interests, it is at once obvious that the children of such families should be given preference. Their 'need' is of a different order from that of the ordinary good student. Besides, such families are doubtless more prosperous than the average, they have more expensive tastes, and they will want to send not one, but all their children, to college. And it should be one of the best colleges."

Admiral Rickover, on the other hand, argues for a more rigidly administered system of ability grouping. The one we have now, he feels, is too imperfect. Faced with the threat of Soviet educational superiority, we need, he feels, to put all our resources into the education of an ability elite. His complaints about our system are: We are trying to educate a great many students who are not able to learn; some of those who *are* able to learn cannot afford to stay in school; and—most important in his schema—students with "ability" should be segregated from the less able and given special preferred treatment.

Our basic educational error, he feels, was the comprehensive high school, a school which brought together under the same roof, though often in different curriculums, students of diverse abilities and from all levels of society.

Those responsible for this grave error did not know, he claims, that "aptitude for learning above the elementary level was relatively rare." To correct this error, we must segregate the gifted from the masses, much as officers are separated from the men, and we must give them training worthy of an intellectual elite. And the others, the masses? He does not specify what their fate should be, but it is clear he does not think they can contribute much intellectually or that they have any notable amounts of that "rare" aptitude for learning.

The admiral's views are shared by a great many current critics of education. He holds these views despite his verbal recognition that the Soviets, whose educational superiority he fears, seem to excel at "mass" education and that we will have to run to keep up with their educational accomplishments.

He does not recall, apparently, that, though Soviet schools are as authoritarian as military academies, they do not separate the "gifted" from the ranks, their high schools are "comprehensive," they do not give IQ tests, and they *claim* at least that intellect is much more a product of circumstances than of birth. What is more, in admission to college they give some degree of preference to students coming up from the ranks, even though they may seem less able than others.

Keeping up with the Soviets is not the only problem with education designed almost exclusively for an ability elite.

Robert Owen saw some of the other problems. Though Owen paid his respects to those possessing "virtue and talent," he did not go overboard for an ability elite. He saw what many critics of education cannot see: that elite groups, even when selected by the most rigorous tests of "merit and ability" derive their status much more from their "rich carpeted drawing rooms" and from accidents of environment and association than from superior virtue or talent.

Owen made these observations in the highly stratified society of 1830; yet what he saw can be seen just as clearly today, everywhere, in the richest democracy of all time as well as in the settled societies of the Old World.

The system has not changed much; it has simply changed form with a rising standard of living for people at all levels and ranks.

The doors of opportunity have been opened, but not very wide. Those who pass through first are simply newer generations of the same groups who came first in Owen's day. Mostly they are members of the old elites of wealth and status, disguised now as an elite of ability. Others of course pass through before the doors close, but their numbers are small considering the size of the crowd that is left waiting.

In the schools of modern America we still find that children from "comfortless cabins" or, to shift time and locale, from "urban slums" cannot compete with the children of the elite. This is true not necessarily because of any deficiency of talent or ability but because society, being dominated by elites, has given their children a head start and, following the lead as always, the schools have compounded the advantage by providing them with superior educational services of every conceivable variety.

Slum children and Southern Negroes, victims of segregated education and inferior schools, are not the only ones to incur a disadvantage in this arrangement. Everyone in a stratified society incurs a disadvantage, the weight of the handicap decreasing with the approach to the summit.

Negroes of course, both in the South and in the North, bear the heaviest burden of inequities, but they do not suffer alone. Everyone suffers—some much more than others.

Now accumulating evidence shows that even when children from the lower ranks manage somehow to break through despite their handicaps, when they somehow "score" on the tests of "talent and ability" which have been set up to screen them out—even then they often do not make the grade.

So it is that 50 per cent of the "top" 10 per cent of high-school graduates do not go to college. Apparently many of these students know their place, and that place is more likely to be found on an assembly line than in a college. They cannot afford college very often, and they do not feel they "belong" there. Moreover, since they have often been denied, by accident or intention, all information about the mechanics of selecting a college, being admitted, applying for scholarships or financial aid, etc., they would not know how to go even if they were able and willing.

Painful as it may be to face, estimates are that the worker's child in the USSR has *twice* as good a chance of going to college as his US counterpart (*Harvard Educational Review*, Spring 1957)—an ugly fact, but one we must permit to crawl out from under its rock. Only then can we see the size and shape of the adversary.

Of course, in this country an occasional slum child may find his way into a state university, and some will point to this as evidence of equal educational opportunity. Chances are very good, however, that the rare slum child who is admitted to the state university will flunk out in his first semester—without the university's raising a finger to help him with his academic difficulties or noticing his presence or his absence once he is gone. With luck the slum child may manage to hang on in college. When he does, he may finish teachers' college or the school of social work, and with his degree move up into the ranks of the lowest-paid professionals in the field. If this happens, he will be among the relatively few lucky ones in his class.

In a society with an ever-growing demand for high-level skills and a rapidly decreasing demand for unskilled labor, the failure of students who are top-ranking in scores but low-ranking in privileges to go on to college is a grievous loss. But the problem is much bigger than this. Paying respect to riches or status and withholding it from poverty, in either overt or subtle ways, has much more serious consequences in a democratic industrial society than the simple denial of higher education to the less privileged, however great the loss of "talent" may be.

An industrial society, if it is to grow at top speed, as ours must, should call on the full intellectual potential of *all* the people in that society—not just those in Rickover's ability elite. It must, in other words, engage in all-out mass education, with full equality of opportunity extended to all students. This our nation has failed to do.

The "ground swell" for learning has not yet emerged in our country, and under present conditions may never emerge. The knowledge, understanding, and participation required to reach

tests prove that he isn't, so what can you do? The child simply can't learn more."

The truth about IQ scores, however, and about this easy explanation, is that there is no valid way of measuring native, inborn intelligence. In fact there isn't even agreement about what intelligence *is* or what the IQ tests should try to measure—but this is a matter for later discussion.

Another factor responsible for a school system in which lower-income children are neglected and rewards are given in almost direct proportion to family income levels is the belief, held by a surprisingly large number of people in and out of the schools, that preferential treatment *should* be given to upper-income groups and that so-called "gifted" children are worth much more than others. According to this view, the "gifted" (who come almost exclusively from upper-income groups, as this study shows) should be given better teachers, smaller classes, more and better school equipment— the best of everything available. In addition, it is argued, the main focus of the school's attention should be on the problems of these chosen ones.

Concerning the opposite end of the social class totem pole, this author has frequently heard teachers say in private that the "others," usually children from lower-income groups, aren't worth bothering much about and that the best you can do is keep them quiet and busy.

Such an unfortunate attitude seems to go with the general contempt these people often feel for their "social inferiors" and their preference for and desire to associate themselves with the "better" elements in the community. Certainly there is nothing in the situation or in the proven capacities of underprivileged children to indicate that they are "not worth bothering about."

In the final analysis, the neglect of lower-income students and the stratification system of the schools can probably be traced to three principal sources: one, the IQ evasion; two, the before-mentioned contempt, or at least indifference, which is often felt by teachers and others for their social "inferiors," and the irritation caused by their behavior, manners, and appearance; three, the fact that upper-income groups have usually been in control of school. boards and thereby in control of what goes on in the schools and the methods of distributing rewards. In addition there is the fact that very little pressure is applied to the schools by lower-income individuals or groups representing them, while upper-income groups tend to have great influence in the schools and to be active in school affairs.

Resistance to proposals for mass education and the premises on which they are based is great, perhaps because the stakes are so high. As the pioneer sociologist Lester Ward put it, "The proposition that the lower classes of society are the intellectual equals of the upper classes will probably shock most minds. At least it will be almost unanimously rejected as altogether false. . . .

"While the intellectually disinherited always include and are nearly coextensive with the materially disinherited, the former is much the more serious condition. For the intellectual inheritance would bring with it the material inheritance and all the other advantages that are enjoyed by the intelligent class.

"But here we encounter the great sullen, stubborn error, so universal and ingrained as to constitute a world view, that the difference between the upper and lower classes of society is due to a difference in their intellectual capacity, something existing in the nature of things, something preordained and inherently inevitable. Every form of sophistry is employed to uphold this view. . . .

"The difference in the native capacity of individuals is never sufficient to exclude any person from the highest social class. . . . It does not require any great or towering native abilities to enable an individual to maintain his place in the vanguard of society. The minimum natural abilities above the state of pathological imbecility suffice for this."

III

A great deal more money is now being spent by the schools of Big City in upper-income areas. Certainly an argument can be made that in a democratic society the reverse of this should be true, since need is greater in lower-income areas. Present inequalities in school expenditures are:

Drop-Outs: In one low-income high school alone, $192,000 was saved in one year on drop-outs. Education for lower-income students is therefore costing much less than the education of upper-income students, who rarely drop out of school before graduation.

Buildings and Facilities: It is obvious from our data that a great deal more money has been spent for school buildings and facilities in upper-income areas.

Teachers: Considerably more money is being spent on teachers' salaries in upper-income schools, since ESRPs and inexperienced teachers, who are heavily concentrated in low-income areas, are paid less in wages and fringe benefits than regular experienced teachers.

Club Activities: Indications are that most of the advantages of club activities go to upper-income students. These activities take up a great deal of teacher time and are therefore costly.

"Gifted"-Child Programs: These costly programs service upper-income students almost exclusively.

Evening School, Summer School, Parent Groups, Adult Activities: Since these services are provided disproportionately to upper-income groups, whatever costs are involved, in either teacher time or more direct expenditures, are being unequally distributed.

Another Related Cost Item: Each year about $3.6 billion is spent on higher education at the college and university level; this amounts to about one dollar for every four and a half spent on public-school education. Most of this money comes from public subsidies, though seldom from local board-of-education funds. *Most of this $3.6 billion is being spent on upper-income students, who make up the bulk of the college population.*

Possible reverse inequalities are:

Attendance Officers: Because Attendance Department areas did not coincide in any manageable way with our area divisions, the distribution of these services could not be determined. The main function of the Attendance Department, however, is law enforcement, a police rather than a social-service function.

Visiting Teachers: Since the department in charge of the Visiting Teacher program would not release any information, nothing could be determined about the distribution of these services.

Detention School: Detention School and Ungraded classrooms cost more to operate than regular classrooms, and lower-income children receive more "services" from these programs than upper-income children. However, if other educational costs were equitably distributed and counseling, Visiting Teacher, and other services were apportioned according to need, perhaps Detention School services, as well as Attendance Department services, would correspondingly decrease. It could also be expected that, with adequate educational and guidance services for low-income groups, the public costs of crime, prisons, mental institutions, and public-assistance programs would perhaps also tend to diminish.

We suggest, therefore, as a first step in providing equal educational opportunity to all children, that school expenditures be equalized, at the very least, among the various income groups. It may not be possible, or even desirable, to attempt an exact equalization of *facilities,* but it should be possible, as it would be highly desirable, to equalize *expenditures.*

Federal aid to education and other school-finance proposals are not at issue here. High-quality education, however, for whatever income group, costs money, more of it than we do or can raise by present school taxes.

Federal assistance is an obvious and pressing educational need —not so much in Big City as in areas where high-quality schools cannot be supported locally. Yet Big City is directly concerned with schools in other areas, for their products often end up Big City schools.

In these stateside-underdeveloped areas the children most likely to be short-changed are lower-income children, the same ones who seem to pull the short straw everywhere in the country. In this case, however, the deprivation is acute and desperate.

Big City schools too need more money to operate on, much more. Major reforms can hardly be undertaken without money and lots of it. Those concerned about our national destiny should be willing to pay. Nowhere is money more securely invested than in our schools, and nowhere are the returns greater, to upper-, lower-, and middle-income groups alike.

Those concerned about the education of the "gifted" should be aware that switching funds to their education will create shortages elsewhere, and they should be at least prepared to make up the difference with tax increases.

Curriculum

Reading. If it were possible to make only one adjustment in the curriculum offered lower-income children, that adjustment might be made to greatest advantage in the reading program. Reading is *the* basic learning skill. It is the skill from which almost all academic learning flows. It is the skill that puts citizens in touch with the factual basis for making informed decisions. What is even more relevant, it is an almost indispensable requirement for upward movement through the social classes. It opens the door to better, higher-paying, pleasanter jobs and provides greater status and security with rising literacy levels.

As we have seen, lower-income students are particularly troubled by reading deficiencies. Unless the reading levels of these students are improved considerably—and the learning and language skills that derive from them—they will have little chance of competing with more literate students for desirable jobs.

No doubt an improper emphasis is often given to reading and to "book learning" in the schools. Reading is not the source of *all* knowledge. Without experience in the real world, book learning is often worth less than nothing; yet book learning, in large quantities, is an indispensable supplement to the knowledge of the real world. Many educators feel, quite properly, that "bookishness" is too exclusively prized in higher academic circles. This scale of values, they say with much accuracy, frequently produces "drones" who are good at chewing and regurgitating juiceless facts, but who have little imagination, individuality, independence, or real wisdom. All too often, they observe, schools have produced "prize" students with encyclopedic knowledge but without the character or creativity to survive in the world or to produce anything of real value.

What is worse, this lopsided and feverish pursuit of book learning and "intellectuality," to the exclusion of most other skills and virtues, often results in lopsided, warped, and anxiety-ridden personalities, as testified to by the high rates of suicide and mental illness found in very "intellectual" colleges. And sometimes it produces men such as Leopold and Loeb, whose ceiling-high scores on IQ and achievement tests hardly compensated for their moral and psychological deformities.

It is no doubt in reaction to this overemphasis on bookishness at the expense of other intellectual and moral qualities that many educators have tended to devaluate the reading skills and the central place of book learning in the curriculum. But, while this deemphasis is perhaps desirable in some middle- and upper-income areas and with more advanced students, it does not seem at all proper in lower-income areas. It is an *absence* of bookishness rather than an *excess* of it that troubles lower-income students. It is not that they read too much; it is that they often don't read at all. This being true, there is little present danger that they will become too bookish; some few might, but the great majority are a long way from being saturated with book learning. Without highly developed reading skills and some close familiarity with the contents of books and other reading matter, there is small chance that lower-income children will ever be able to compete with upper-income children for the rewards of school and life.

To many lower-income children public libraries are grim, forbidding places, "conspiracies against the poor," in Sean O'Casey's words.

In Big City, libraries in upper-income areas stay open weekends. In lower-income areas, many of them close. The explanation given: children in these areas do not use the libraries. If they do not use the libraries, they must be actively encouraged to do so, and the libraries must remain open in order to permit them to do so. Above all, the library must be a place where they feel welcome and comfortable and where they can find interesting and attractive books to read.

Whatever approaches are used, whatever methods are tried, certainly a situation should not be tolerated in which large numbers of lower-income children spend eight to ten years in school without having acquired high levels of reading and derivative language skills.

Aside from those who have suffered brain damage and those so deeply disturbed as to be beyond reach, no child should be permitted to leave school without having achieved normal facility in reading. The child who does not learn to read in school has been cheated and is almost inevitably doomed to social exclusion and economic denial.

Teaching children to read at age two may be of very questionable value. Teaching them to read even at age six, as many suggest, *may* be premature. But they must be taught at some point, and they should be taught with as little compulsion and as much pleasure as possible.

Judge John T. McWilliams of the Michigan courts claims that prison records show reading retardation to be the "greatest single characteristic common to all inmates," regardless of economic status. Jackson prison records show, he says, that "although most inmates under twenty-five were in the 80 to 89 IQ bracket when admitted, their IQ went up as high as 110 after they were there," improved reading skill being the explanation. Then, perhaps too hopefully, he says: "Wouldn't it be strange and wonderful if the way to prevent drop-outs and delinquency was to teach them to read?"

It would be, but this is too much to expect; reading is not a cure-all; it *is* a cure, however, for at least some of our major educational ailments, and its healing potential should not be neglected.

Other Problems. While reading improvement is of primary importance for lower-income students (and the other language problems that flow mainly out of reading deficiencies), there are many other matters to be dealt with and other curriculum adjustments to be made. Those that occur to us are given here. The list is not complete. Nor do we pretend that it is a blueprint. It is simply what seems reasonable to us under present circumstances.

Some of the suggestions are directly related to the problems of lower-income children. Some are more distantly related and are of more general application.

1. People who understand and sympathize with the problems of lower-income students should be elected to school boards. These people of course should also be imaginative and courageous enough to work out ways of handling such problems, or to hire people who can.

2. Teachers with some zeal for teaching lower-income students should be encouraged to come into the profession.

3. Experimentation with television, teaching machines, and other educational devices should be encouraged in an effort to free teachers for individual and small-group work with students. Properly used, such devices can lift much of the burden of classroom overloading, lesson-planning, and discipline from teachers, while permitting them to do more creative and rewarding work with students.

4. Use of IQ tests should be stopped.

5. More attention should be given to the psychological, medical, and nutritional needs of lower-income students; where community agencies do not provide necessary services, the schools should feel obliged to take on the responsibility.

6. Special attention should be given to the homework problem in lower-income high schools. Where home conditions are not

conducive to study, homework presents a very troublesome problem for students. The citizens' committee in Big City has recommended that homework be increased; if this is indeed advisable, then lower-income students should be given special instruction in study and homework skills, and time should be allowed for students to do homework assignments in school—in study hall, or during a lengthened class period.

7. Wherever it seems advisable, students should be given a voice in planning their own goals and programs of study. It is an educational truism that students learn more, with greater eagerness and less need for control and discipline, when they pursue their own goals rather than others' and when they have some voice in determining what they will do and what they will learn.

Moving away from dull, pointless routines dictated by the teacher, into work on projects of their own choice, solving real problems in real-life situations, will make learning more stimulating and more rewarding for lower-income students. Learning of this kind, then, will be directed toward problem-solving rather than the simple memorization of facts.

8. Free textbooks should be provided, all other student costs reduced or eliminated.

9. There should be more work-study programs. At the same time, purely vocational training should be de-emphasized in the schools, since this training often becomes obsolete before it can be used. Also, special "trade" and "vocational" schools should be discontinued, unless the vocational curriculum is liberal in approach and broad in character. Such schools are often used as dumping grounds for students who are not wanted elsewhere, and often little more than custodial care is provided in them. When more is provided, the skills taught are frequently of too perishable a nature.

10. Techniques for teaching *self*-discipline to students, in a direct rather than an indirect way, should be devised. Students should learn the value of self-discipline (the body, mind, and impulses), and some of the techniques for achieving self-mastery and self-control. This area has not been explored much by educators, or by anyone else for that matter, except in so far as self-discipline is applied indirectly by forces outside the individual.

11. Efforts should be made to encourage more men, of a type boys can readily identify with, to enter teaching. Such efforts are being made to some extent in Big City schools and elsewhere. Prob-

lem schools in low-income areas of Big City now often have a majority of male teachers in them.

12. Children in problem areas should be reached by the schools as quickly as possible. Nursery-school care should be provided as preparation for school and as relief for the working mother.

13. The general "feeling tone" of the schools should be one of love, encouragement, stimulation, equality, rather than high-pressure competition, snobbery, authoritarianism, and cold, impersonal external discipline. Yet it must not be passive, but very active, alert, and aggressive. It should be soft-hearted, in short, but very hard-headed.

Further Research

Much is suspected but little is known about numbers of factors bearing upon social class distinctions in the school, factors which are more intangible than school buildings, facilities, services, etc., in that they depend on the mental attitudes and viewpoints of those associated with the schools, and indeed often on the goals and general nature of the entire society.

Except for sources cited in this study there appears to be a serious shortage of information about teacher, parent, administrator, and student attitudes as they relate to social class.

Rewards. Further research is also needed on the rewards and punishments to which lower-income children will respond. Evidence is, as we have mentioned, that rewards offered in the present incentive system do not excite much response in many lower-income children, the principal rewards being report-card marks and teacher-parent approval. Frequently students do not respond to these rewards because they realize there is little chance of getting them. Often they do not respond because they do not know what the rewards are worth—either now or in later life. They do not respond because they are often so at odds with both teachers and parents that they are more likely to seek their disapproval than their approval.

In order to provide suitable rewards, it would be of great value to the schools to have systematic information about the needs and natural interests of lower-income children, by ethnic and racial subgroups.

College Studies. Studies parallel to this one should be made of inequalities in college and university education. Since curriculum standards in public schools are often laid down by college requirements (initiated at the graduate-school level often: see Earl Mc-Grath, *The Graduate School and the Decline of Liberal Education*), and since college admission practices and opportunities for college success have a profound effect on what happens to students in public schools, the subject would seem to require a large-scale investigation.

EQUALITY OF EDUCATIONAL OPPORTUNITY (THE COLEMAN REPORT)

U.S. Office of Education*

The great majority of American children attend schools that are largely segregated—that is, where almost all of their fellow students are of the same racial background as they are. Among minority groups, Negroes are by far the most segregated. Taking all groups, however, white children are most segregated. Almost 80 percent of all white pupils in 1st grade and 12th grade attend schools that are from 90 percent to 100 percent white. And 97 percent at grade 1, and 99 percent at grade 12, attend schools that are 50 percent or more white.

For Negro pupils, segregation is more nearly complete in the South (as it is for whites also), but it is extensive also in all the other regions where the Negro population is concentrated: the urban North, Midwest, and West.

More than 65 percent of all Negro pupils in the 1st grade

* From the Summary Report of the Survey, *Equality of Educational Opportunity*, U.S. Dept. of Health, Education, and Welfare (Washington, D.C., U.S. Government Printing Office, 1966).

attend schools that are between 90 and 100 percent Negro. And 87 percent at grade 1, and 66 percent at grade 12, attend schools that are 50 percent or more Negro. In the South, most students attend schools that are 100 percent white or Negro.

The same pattern of segregation holds, though not quite so strongly, for the teachers of Negro and white students. For the Nation as a whole the average Negro elementary pupil attends a school in which 65 percent of the teachers are Negro; the average white elementary pupil attends a school in which 97 percent of the teachers are white. White teachers are more predominant at the secondary level, where the corresponding figures are 59 and 97 percent. The racial matching of teachers is most pronounced in the South, where by tradition it has been complete. On a nationwide basis, in cases where the races of pupils and teachers are not matched, the trend is all in one direction: white teachers teach Negro children but Negro teachers seldom teach white children; just as, in the schools, integration consists primarily of a minority of Negro pupils in predominantly white schools but almost never of a few whites in largely Negro schools.

In its desegregation decision of 1954, the Supreme Court held that separate schools for Negro and white children are inherently unequal. This survey finds that, when measured by that yardstick, American public education remains largely unequal in most regions of the country, including all those where Negroes form any significant proportion of the population. Obviously, however, that is not the only yardstick. The next section of the summary describes other characteristics by means of which equality of educational opportunity may be appraised.

THE SCHOOLS AND THEIR CHARACTERISTICS

The school environment of a child consists of many elements, ranging from the desk he sits at to the child who sits next to him, and including the teacher who stands at the front of his class. A statistical survey can give only fragmentary evidence of this environment.

Great collections of numbers such as are found in these pages —totals and averages and percentages—blur and obscure rather than sharpen and illuminate the range of variation they represent. If one reads, for example, that the average annual income per person in the State of Maryland is $3,000, there is a tendency to picture an average person living in moderate circumstances in a middle-class neighborhood holding an ordinary job. But that number represents at the upper end millionaires, and at the lower end the unemployed, the pensioners, the charwomen. Thus the $3,000 average income should somehow bring to mind the tycoon and the tramp, the showcase and the shack, as well as the average man in the average house.

So, too, in reading these statistics on education, one must picture the child whose school has every conceivable facility that is believed to enhance the educational process, whose teachers may be particularly gifted and well educated, and whose home and total neighborhood are themselves powerful contributors to his education and growth. And one must picture the child in a dismal tenement area who may come hungry to an ancient, dirty building that is badly ventilated, poorly lighted, overcrowded, understaffed, and without sufficient textbooks.

Statistics, too, must deal with one thing at a time, and cumulative effects tend to be lost in them. Having a teacher without a college degree indicates an element of disadvantage, but in the concrete situation, a child may be taught by a teacher who is not only without a degree but who has grown up and received his schooling in the local community, who has never been out of the State, who has a 10th grade vocabulary, and who shares the local community's attitudes.

One must also be aware of the relative importance of a certain kind of thing to a certain kind of person. Just as a loaf of bread means more to a starving man than to a sated one, so one very fine textbook or, better, one very able teacher, may mean far more to a deprived child than to one who already has several of both.

Finally, it should be borne in mind that in cases where Negroes in the South receive unequal treatment, the significance in terms of actual numbers of individuals involved is very great, since 54 percent of the Negro population of school-going age, or approximately 3,200,000 children, live in that region.

All of the findings reported in this section of the summary are based on responses to questionnaires filled out by public school teachers, principals, district school superintendents, and pupils. The data were gathered in September and October of 1965 from 4,000 public schools. All teachers, principals, and district superintendents in these schools participated, as did all pupils in the 3d, 6th, 9th, and 12th grades. First grade pupils in half the schools participated. More than 645,000 pupils in all were involved in the survey. About 30 percent of the schools selected for the survey did not participate; an analysis of the nonparticipating schools indicated that their inclusion would not have significantly altered the results of the survey. The participation rates were: in the metropolitan North and West 72 percent, metropolitan South and Southwest 65 percent, nonmetropolitan North and West 82 percent, nonmetropolitan South and Southwest 61 percent.

All the statistics on the physical facilities of the schools and the academic and extracurricular programs are based on information provided by the teachers and administrators. They also provided information about their own education, experience, and philosophy of education, and described as they see them the socioeconomic characteristics of the neighborhoods served by their schools.

The statistics having to do with the pupils' personal socioeconomic background, level of education of their parents, and certain items in their homes (such as encyclopedias, daily newspapers, etc.) are based on pupil responses to questionnaires. The pupils also answered questions about their academic aspirations and their attitudes toward staying in school.

All personal and school data were confidential and for statistical purposes only; the questionnaires were collected without the names or other personal identification of the respondents.

Data for Negro and white children are classified by whether the schools are in metropolitan areas or not. The definition of a metropolitan area is the one commonly used by Government agencies: a city of over 50,000 inhabitants including its suburbs. All other schools in small cities, towns, or rural areas are referred to as nonmetropolitan schools.

Finally, data for Negro and white children are classified by geographical regions. For metropolitan schools there are usually five regions defined as follows:

Northeast—(Using 1960 census data, this region contains about 16 percent of all Negro children in the Nation and 20 percent of all white children age 5 to 19.)

Midwest—(containing 16 percent of Negro and 19 percent of white children age 5 to 19).

South—(containing 27 percent of Negro and 14 percent of white children age 5 to 19).

Southwest—(containing 4 percent of Negro and 3 percent of white children age 5 to 19).

West—(containing 4 percent of Negro and 11 percent of white children age 5 to 19).

The nonmetropolitan schools are usually classified into only three regions:

South—(containing 27 percent of Negro and 14 percent of white children age 5 to 19).

Southwest—(containing 4 percent of Negro and 2 percent of white children age 5 to 19).

North and West—all States not in the South and Southwest (containing 2 percent of Negro and 17 percent of white children age 5 to 19).

Data for minority groups other than Negroes are presented only on a nationwide basis because there were not sufficient cases to warrant a breakdown by regions.

Facilities

For the Nation as a whole white children attend elementary schools with a smaller average number of pupils per room (29) than do any of the minorities (which range from 30 to 33). In some regions the nationwide pattern is reversed: in the nonmetropolitan North and West and Southwest for example, there is a smaller average number of pupils per room for Negroes than for whites.

Secondary school whites have a smaller average number of pupils per room than minorities, except Indians. Looking at the regional breakdown, however, one finds much more striking differences than the national average would suggest: in the metropolitan Midwest, for example, the average Negro has 54 pupils per room—probably reflecting considerable frequency of double sessions—compared with 33 per room for whites. (Nationally, at the high school level the average white has one teacher for every 22 students and the average Negro has one for every 26 students.)

It is thus apparent that the tables must be studied carefully, with special attention paid to the regional breakdowns, which often provide more meaningful information than do the nationwide averages. Such careful study will reveal that there is not a wholly consistent pattern—that is, minorities are not at a disadvantage in every item listed—but that there are nevertheless some definite and systematic directions of differences. Nationally, Negro pupils have fewer of some of the facilities that seem most related to academic achievement: they have less access to physics, chemistry, and language laboratories; there are fewer books per pupil in their libraries; their textbooks are less often in sufficient supply. To the extent that physical facilities are important to learning, such items appear to be more relevant than some others, such as cafeterias, in which minority groups are at an advantage.

Usually greater than the majority-minority differences, however, are the regional differences. For example, 95 percent of Negro and 80 percent of white high school students in the metropolitan Far West attend schools with language laboratories, compared with 48 percent and 72 percent respectively, in the metropolitan South, in spite of the fact that a higher percentage of Southern schools are less than 20 years old.

Finally, it must always be remembered that these statistics reveal only majority-minority average differences and regional average differences; they do not show the extreme differences that would be found by comparing one school with another.

Programs

Just as minority groups tend to have less access to physical facilities that seem to be related to academic achievement, so too they have less access to curricular and extracurricular programs that would seem to have such a relationship.

Secondary school Negro students are less likely to attend schools that are regionally accredited; this is particularly pronounced in the South. Negro and Puerto Rican pupils have less access to college preparatory curriculums and to accelerated curriculums; Puerto Ricans have less access to vocational curriculums as well. Less intelligence testing is done in the schools attended by Negroes and Puerto Ricans. Finally, white students in general have more access to a more fully developed program of extracurricular activities, in particular those which might be related to academic matters (debate teams, for example, and student newspapers).

Again, regional differences are striking. For example, 100 percent of Negro high school students and 97 percent of whites in the metropolitan Far West attend schools having a remedial reading teacher (this does not mean, of course, that every student uses the services of that teacher, but simply that he has access to them) compared with 46 and 65 percent, respectively, in the metropolitan South—and 4 and 9 percent in the nonmetropolitan Southwest.

Principals and Teachers

One percent of white elementary pupils attend a school with a Negro principal, and 56 percent of Negro children attend a school with a Negro principal.

The average white student goes to an elementary school where 40 percent of the teachers spent most of their lives in the same city, town, or county; the average Negro pupil goes to a school where 53 percent of the teachers have lived in the same locality most of their lives.

Other characteristics which offer rough indications of teacher quality include the types of colleges attended, years of teaching experience, salary, educational level of mother, and a score on a 30-word vocabulary test. The average Negro pupil attends a school where a greater percentage of the teachers appears to be somewhat less able, as measured by these indicators, than those in the schools attended by the average white student.

The average white pupil attends a school where 51 percent of the white teachers would not choose to move to another school, whereas the average Negro attends a school where 46 percent would not choose to move.

Student Body Characteristics

The average white high school student attends a school in which 82 percent of his classmates report that there are encyclopedias in their homes. This does not mean that 82 percent of all white pupils have encyclopedias at home, although obviously that would be approximately true. In short, these tables attempt to describe the characteristics of the student bodies with which the "average" white or minority student goes to school.

Clear differences are found on these items. The average Negro has fewer classmates whose mothers graduated from high school; his classmates more frequently are members of large rather than small families, they are less often enrolled in a college preparatory curriculum, they have taken a smaller number of courses in English, mathematics, foreign language, and science.

On most items, the other minority groups fall between Negroes and whites, but closer to whites, in the extent to which each characteristic is typical of their classmates.

Again, there are substantial variations in the magnitude of the differences, with the difference usually being greater in the Southern States.

ACHIEVEMENT IN THE PUBLIC SCHOOLS

The schools bear many responsibilities. Among the most important is the teaching of certain intellectual skills such as reading, writing, calculating, and problem-solving. One way of assessing the educational opportunity offered by the schools is to measure how well they perform this task. Standard achievement tests are available to measure these skills, and several such tests were administered in this survey to pupils at grades 1, 3, 6, 9, and 12.

These tests do not measure intelligence, nor attitudes, nor qualities of character. Furthermore, they are not, nor are they intended to be, "culture-free." Quite the reverse: they are culture-bound. What they measure are the skills which are among the most important in our society for getting a good job and moving up to a better one, and for full participation in an increasingly technical world. Consequently, a pupil's test results at the end of public school provide a good measure of the range of opportunities open to him as he finishes school—a wide range of choice of jobs or colleges if these skills are very high; a very narrow range that includes only the most menial jobs if these skills are very low.

Table 1 gives an overall illustration of the test results for the various groups by tabulating nationwide median scores (the score which divides the group in half) for 1st-grade and 12th-grade pupils on the tests used in those grades. For example, half of the white 12th-grade pupils had scores above 52 on the nonverbal test and half had scores below 52. (Scores on each test at each grade level were standardized so that the average over the national sample

TABLE 1.—*Nationwide median test scores for first- and twelfth-grade pupils*

| Test | Racial or ethnic group | | | | | |
	Puerto Ricans	Indian-Americans	Mexican-Americans	Oriental-Americans	Negro	Majority
First grade:						
Nonverbal	45.8	53.0	50.1	56.6	43.4	54.1
Verbal	44.9	47.8	46.5	51.6	45.4	53.2
Twelfth grade:						
Nonverbal	43.3	47.1	45.0	51.6	40.9	52.0
Verbal	43.1	43.7	43.8	49.6	40.9	52.1
Reading	42.6	44.3	44.2	48.8	42.2	51.9
Mathematics	43.7	45.9	45.5	51.3	41.8	51.8
General information	41.7	44.7	43.3	49.0	40.6	52.2
Average of the 5 tests	43.1	45.1	44.4	50.1	41.1	52.0

equaled 50 and the standard deviation equaled 10. This means that for all pupils in the Nation, about 16 percent would score below 40 and about 16 percent above 60.)

With some exceptions—notably Oriental Americans—the average minority pupil scores distinctly lower on these tests at every level than the average white pupil. The minority pupils' scores are as much as one standard deviation below the majority pupils' scores in the first grade. At the 12th grade, results of tests in the same verbal and nonverbal skills show that, in every case, the minority scores are *farther below* the majority than are the 1st graders. For some groups, the relative decline is negligible; for others, it is large.

Furthermore, a constant difference in standard deviations over the various grades represents an increasing difference in grade level gap. For example, Negroes in the metropolitan Northeast are about 1.1 standard deviations below whites in the same region at grades 6, 9, and 12. But at grade 6 this represents 1.6 years behind, at grade 9, 2.4 years, and at grade 12, 3.3 years. Thus, by this measure, the deficiency in achievement is progressively greater for the minority pupils at progressively higher grade levels.

For most minority groups, then, and most particularly the Negro, schools provide no opportunity at all for them to overcome this initial deficiency; in fact, they fall farther behind the white majority in the development of several skills which are critical to making a living and participating fully in modern society. Whatever may be the combination of nonschool factors—poverty, community attitudes, low educational level of parents—which put minority children at a disadvantage in verbal and nonverbal skills when they enter the first grade, the fact is the schools have not overcome it.

Some points should be borne in mind in reading the table. First, the differences shown should not obscure the fact that some minority children perform better than many white children. A difference of one standard deviation in median scores means that about 84 percent of the children in the lower group are below the median of the majority students—but 50 percent of the white children are themselves below that median as well.

A second point of qualification concerns regional differences. By grade 12, both white and Negro students in the South score below their counterparts—white and Negro—in the North. In addition, Southern Negroes score farther below Southern whites than Northern Negroes score below Northern whites. The consequences of this pattern can be illustrated by the fact that the 12th grade Negro in the nonmetropolitan South is 0.8 standard deviation below—or in terms of years, 1.9 years behind—the Negro in the metropolitan Northeast, though at grade 1 there is no such regional difference.

Finally, the test scores at grade 12 obviously do not take account of those pupils who have left school before reaching the senior year. In the metropolitan North and West, 20 percent of the Negroes of ages 16 and 17 are not enrolled in school, a higher dropout percentage than in either the metropolitan or nonmetropolitan South. If it is the case that some or many of the Northern dropouts performed poorly when they were in school, the Negro achievement in the North may be artificially elevated because some of those who achieved more poorly have left school.

RELATION OF ACHIEVEMENT TO SCHOOL CHARACTERISTICS

If 100 students within a school take a certain test, there is likely to be great variation in their scores. One student may score 97 percent, another 13; several may score 78 percent. This represents variability in achievement *within* the particular school.

It is possible, however, to compute the average of the scores made by the students within that school and to compare it with the average score, or achievement, of pupils within another school, or many other schools. These comparisons then represent variations *between schools.*

When one sees that the average score on a verbal achievement test in School X is 55 and in School Y is 72, the natural question to ask is: What accounts for the difference?

There are many factors that in combination account for the difference. This analysis concentrates on one cluster of those factors. It attempts to describe what relationship the school's characteristics themselves (libraries, for example, and teachers and laboratories and so on) seem to have to the achievement of majority and minority groups (separately for each group on a nationwide basis, and also for Negro and white pupils in the North and South).

The first finding is that the schools are remarkably similar in the effect they have on the achievement of their pupils when the socioeconomic background of the students is taken into account. It is known that socioeconomic factors bear a strong relation to academic achievement. When these factors are statistically controlled, however, it appears that differences between schools account for only a small fraction of differences in pupil achievement.

The schools *do* differ, however, in the degree of impact they have on the various racial and ethnic groups. The average white student's achievement is less affected by the strength or weakness of his school's facilities, curricula, and teachers than is the average minority pupil's. To put it another way, the achievement of minority pupils depends more on the schools they attend than does the achievement of majority pupils. Thus, 20 percent of the achievement of Negroes in the South is associated with the particular schools they go to, whereas only 10 percent of the achievement of whites in the South is. Except for Oriental Americans, this general result is found for all minorities.

The conclusion can then be drawn that improving the school of a minority pupil will increase his achievement more than will improving the school of a white child increase his. Similarly, the average minority pupil's achievement will suffer more in a school of low quality than will the average white pupil's. In short, whites, and to a lesser extent Oriental Americans, are less affected one way or the other by the quality of their schools than are minority pupils. This indicates that it is for the most disadvantaged children that improvements in school quality will make the most difference in achievement.

All of these results suggest the next question: What are the school characteristics that account for most variation in achievement? In other words, what factors in the school are most important in affecting achievement?

It appears that variations in the facilities and curriculums of the schools account for relatively little variation in pupil achievement insofar as this is measured by standard tests. Again, it is for majority whites that the variations make the least difference; for minorities, they make somewhat more difference. Among the facilities that show some relationship to achievement are several for which minority pupils' schools are less well equipped relative to whites. For example, the existence of science laboratories showed a small but consistent relationship to achievement, and minorities, especially Negroes, are in schools with fewer of these laboratories.

The quality of teachers shows a stronger relationship to pupil achievement. Furthermore, it is progressively greater at higher grades, indicating a cumulative impact of the qualities of teachers in a school on the pupils' achievement. Again, teacher quality is more important for minority pupil achievement than for that of the majority.

It should be noted that many characteristics of teachers were not measured in this survey; therefore, the results are not at all conclusive regarding the specific characteristics of teachers that are most important. Among those measured in the survey, however, those that bear the highest relationship to pupil achievement are first, the teacher's score on the verbal skills test, and then his educational background—both his own level of education and that of his parents. On both of these measures, the level of teachers of minority students, especially Negroes, is lower.

Finally, it appears that a pupil's achievement is strongly related to the educational backgrounds and aspirations of the other students in the school. Only crude measures of these variables were used (principally the proportion of pupils with encyclopedias in the home and the proportion planning to go to college). Analysis indicates, however, that children from a given family background, when put in schools of different social composition, will achieve at quite different levels. This effect is again less for white pupils than for any minority group other than Orientals. Thus, if a white pupil from a home that is strongly and effectively supportive of education is put in a school where most pupils do not come from such homes, his achievement will be little different than if he were in a school composed of others like himself. But if a minority pupil from a home without much educational strength is put with schoolmates with strong educational backgrounds, his achievement is likely to increase.

This general result, taken together with the earlier examinations of school differences, has important implications for equality of educational opportunity. For the earlier tables show that the principal way in which the school environments of Negroes and whites differ is in the composition of their student bodies, and it turns out that the composition of the student bodies has a strong relationship to the achievement of Negro and other minority pupils.

❖   ❖   ❖   ❖   ❖   ❖   ❖

This analysis has concentrated on the educational opportunities offered by the schools in terms of their student body composition, facilities, curriculums, and teachers. This emphasis, while entirely appropriate as a response to the legislation calling for the survey, nevertheless neglects important factors in the variability between individual pupils within the same school; this variability is roughly four times as large as the variability between schools. For example, a pupil attitude factor, which appears to have a stronger relationship to achievement than do all the "school" factors together, is the extent to which an individual feels that he has some control over his own destiny. The responses of pupils to questions in the survey show that minority pupils, except for Orientals, have far less conviction than whites that they can affect their own environments and futures. When they do, however, their achievement is higher than that of whites who lack that conviction.

Furthermore, while this characteristic shows little relationship to most school factors, it is related, for Negroes, to the proportion of whites in the schools. Those Negroes in schools with a higher proportion of whites have a greater sense of control. Thus such attitudes, which are largely a consequence of a person's experience in the larger society, are not independent of his experience in school.

OPPORTUNITY IN INSTITUTIONS OF HIGHER EDUCATION

The largely segregated system of higher education in the South has made comparison between colleges attended mainly by Negro students and mainly by majority students easy in that region. Elsewhere it has not been possible in the past to make comparison between educational opportunities because of the general policy in Federal and State agencies of not collecting data on race. In the fall of 1965, however, the Office of Education reversed this policy as a result of the interest of many agencies and organizations in the progress of minority pupils in gaining access to higher education. The racial composition of freshmen of all degree-seeking students was obtained from nearly all of the colleges and universities in the Nation.

These racial compositions have been cross-tabulated against a variety of characteristics of the institutions in the report itself. Over half of all Negro college students attend the largely segregated institutions in the South and Southwest. About 4.6 percent of all college students are Negro.

Whereas the bulk of the institutions (1104) have on the average 20 students per faculty member, those with predominantly Negro enrollment (96) have on the average 16 students per faculty member. Negro students are proportionally in colleges with lower proportions of Ph.D. faculty. This is generally but not always true in the various regions.

Negro students are in colleges with substantially lower faculty salaries. The institutions in the South and Southwest generally pay lower salaries than those in other regions, and the colleges serving primarily the Negro students are at the bottom of this low scale.

Other findings of the study are that—(1) in every region Negro students are more likely to enter the State College system than the State University system, and further they are a smaller proportion of the student body of universities than any other category of public institutions of higher education, (2) Negro students are more frequently found in institutions which have a high dropout rate, (3) they attend mainly institutions with low tuition cost, (4) they tend to major in engineering, agriculture, education, social work, social science, and nursing.

Future Teachers

Since a number of investigations of teacher qualification in the past few years have indicated that teachers of Negro children are less qualified than those who teach primarily majority children, this survey investigated whether there might be some promise that the situation may be changed by college students now preparing to become teachers. To this end, questionnaire and achievement test data were secured from about 17,000 college freshmen and 5,500 college seniors in 32 teacher training colleges in 18 States that in 1960 included over 90 percent of the Nation's Negro population. Some of the findings of this survey are:

1. At both the freshman and senior levels, future teachers are very similar to students in their colleges who are following other career lines. (It should be remembered that these comparisons are limited to students in colleges that have a primary mission in the

training of teachers, and is not, of course, a random sample of all colleges.)

2. Majority students being trained at the college level to enter teaching have a stronger preparation for college than have Negro students; that is, they had more courses in foreign languages, English, and mathematics, made better grades in high school, and more often were in the highest track in English.

3. Data from the senior students suggest that colleges do not narrow the gap in academic training between Negro and majority pupils; indeed, there is some evidence that the college curriculum increases this difference, at least in the South.

4. Substantial test score differences exist between Negro and white future teachers at both freshman and senior levels, with approximately 15 percent of Negroes exceeding the average score of majority students in the same region. (This figure varies considerably depending on the test, but in no case do as many as 25 percent of Negroes exceed the majority average.)

5. The test data indicate that the gap in test results widens in the South between the freshman and senior years. The significance of this finding lies in the fact that most Negro teachers are trained in the Southern States.

6. The preferences of future teachers for certain kinds of schools and certain kinds of pupils raise the question of the match between the expectations of teacher recruits and the characteristics of the employment opportunities.

The preferences of future teachers were also studied. Summarized in terms of market conditions, it seems apparent that far too many future teachers prefer to teach in an academic high school; that there is a far greater proportion of children of blue-collar workers than of teachers being produced who prefer to teach them; that there is a very substantial number of white teachers-in-training, even in the South, who prefer to teach in racially mixed schools; that very few future teachers of either race wish to teach in predominantly minority schools; and finally, that high-ability pupils are much more popular with future teachers than low-ability ones. The preferences of Negro future teachers are more compatible with the distribution of needs in the market than are those of the majority; too few of the latter, relative to the clientele requiring service, prefer blue-collar or low-ability children or prefer to teach in racially heterogeneous schools, or in special curriculum, vocational, or commercial schools. These data indicate that under the present organization of schools, relatively few of the best prepared future teachers will find their way into classrooms where they can offset some of the environmental disadvantage suffered by minority children.

School Enrollment and Dropouts

Another extensive study explored enrollment rates of children of various ages, races, and socioeconomic categories using 1960 census data. The study included also an investigation of school dropouts using the October 1965 Current Population Survey of the Bureau of the Census. This survey uses a carefully selected sample of 35,000 households. It was a large enough sample to justify reliable nationwide estimates for the Negro minority but not for other minorities. In this section the word "white" includes the Mexican American and Puerto Rican minorities.

According to the estimates of the Current Population Survey, approximately 6,960,000 persons of ages 16 and 17 were living in the United States in October 1965. Of this number 300,000 (5 percent) were enrolled in college, and therefore, were not considered by this Census Bureau study. Of the remaining, approximately 10 percent, or 681,000 youth of 16 and 17 had left school prior to completion of high school.

About 17 percent of Negro adolescents (ages 16 and 17) have dropped out of school whereas the corresponding number for white adolescents is 9 percent. Most of this difference comes from differences outside the South; in this South the white and Negro nonenrollment rates are much the same.

The data suggest that the dropout rate is different for different socioeconomic levels, for whereas the nonenrollment rate was 3 percent for those 16- and 17-year-olds from white-collar families, it was more than four times as large (13 percent) in the case of those from other than white-collar families (where the head of household was in a blue-collar or farm occupation, unemployed, or not in the labor force at all). Furthermore, this difference in nonenrollment by parental occupation existed for both male and female, Negro and white adolescents.

The racial differences in the dropout rate are thus sharply reduced when socioeconomic factors are taken into account. Then the difference of 8 percentage points between all Negro and white adolescent dropouts becomes 1 percent for those in white-collar families, and 4 percent for those in other than white-collar families.

The largest differences between Negro and white dropout rates are seen in the urban North and West; in the nonurban North and West there were too few Negro households in the sample to provide a reliable estimate. In the South there is the unexpected result that in the urban areas, white girls drop out at a greater rate than Negro girls, and in the nonurban area white boys drop out at a substantially greater rate than Negro boys.

Effects of Integration on Achievement

An education in integrated schools can be expected to have major effects on attitudes toward members of other racial groups. At its best, it can develop attitudes appropriate to the integrated society these students will live in; at its worst, it can create hostile camps of Negroes and whites in the same school. Thus there is more to "school integration" than merely putting Negroes and whites in the same building, and there may be more important consequences of integration than its effect on achievement.

Yet the analysis of school effects described earlier suggests that in the long run, integration should be expected to have a positive effect on Negro achievement as well. An analysis was carried out to examine the effects on achievement which might appear in the short run. This analysis of the test performance of Negro children in integrated schools indicates positive effects of integration, though rather small ones. Results for grades 6, 9, and 12 for Negro pupils classified by the proportion of their classmates the previous year who were white show that in every case but one the highest average score is recorded for the Negro pupils where more than half of their classmates were white. But the increase is small and often those Negro pupils in classes with only a few whites score lower than those in totally segregated classes.

Those pupils who first entered integrated schools in the early grades record consistently higher scores than the other groups, although the differences are again small.

No account is taken in these tabulations of the fact that the various groups of pupils may have come from different backgrounds.

When such account is taken by simple cross-tabulations on indicators of socioeconomic status, the performance in integrated schools and in schools integrated longer remains higher. Thus although the differences are small, and although the degree of integration within the school is not known, there is evident even in the short run an effect of school integration on the reading and mathematics achievement of Negro pupils.

Tabulations of this kind are, of course, the simplest possible devices for seeking such effects. It is possible that more elaborate analyses looking more carefully at the special characteristics of the Negro pupils, and at different degrees of integration within schools that have similar racial composition, may reveal a more definite effect. Such analyses are among those that will be presented in subsequent reports.

Case Studies of School Integration

As part of the survey, two sets of case studies of school integration were commissioned. These case studies examine the progress of integration in individual cities and towns, and illustrate problems that have arisen not only in these communities but in many others as well. The complete case studies are maintained on file at the Office of Education.

Lack of racial information. In certain communities, the lack of information as to the number of children of minority groups and of minority group teachers, their location and mobility, has made assessment of the equality of educational opportunity difficult. In one city, for example, after a free transfer plan was initiated, no records as to race of students were kept, thereby making any evaluation of the procedure subjective only. Superintendents, principals, and school boards sometimes respond by declaring racial records themselves to be a mark of discrimination.

A narrative of "the racial headcount problem" and the response to the search for a solution is given in the excerpt from the report on San Francisco.

Performance of minority group children. One of the real handicaps to an effective assessment of equality of education for children of minority groups is the fact that few communities have given systematic testing and fewer still have evaluated the academic performance and attitudes of these children toward education. Yet quality of education is to be estimated as much by its consequences as by the records of the age of buildings and data on faculty-student ratio.

Compliance in a small community. Many large metropolitan areas North and South are moving toward resegregation despite attempts by school boards and city administrations to reverse the trend. Racial housing concentration in large cities has reinforced neighborhood school patterns of racial isolation while, at the same time, many white families have moved to the suburbs and other families have taken their children out of the public school system, enrolling them instead in private and parochial schools. Small towns and medium-sized areas, North and South, on the other hand, are to some extent desegregating their schools.

In the Deep South, where there has been total school segregation for generations, there are signs of compliance within a number of school systems. The emphasis on open enrollment and freedom of choice plans, however, has tended to lead to token enrollment of Negroes in previously white schools. In school systems integrated at some grade levels but not at others, the choice of high school grades rather than elementary grades has tended further to cut down on the number of Negroes choosing to transfer because of the reluctance to take extra risks close to graduation.

A voluntary transfer plan for racial balance in elementary schools. The public schools are more rigidly segregated at the elementary level than in the higher grades. In the large cities, elementary schools have customarily made assignments in terms of neighborhood boundaries. Housing segregation has, therefore, tended to build a segregated elementary school system in most cities in the North and, increasingly, in the South as well, where *de facto* segregation is replacing *de jure* segregation.

Various communities have been struggling to find ways to achieve greater racial balance while retaining the neighborhood school. Bussing, pairing, redistricting, consolidation, and many other strategies have been tried. Many have failed; others have achieved at least partial success. In New Haven, Conn., considerable vigor has been applied to the problem: Whereas pairing was tried at the junior high level introducing compulsory integration, a voluntary transfer plan was implemented at the elementary level. Relief of overcrowding was given as the central intent of the transfer plan, but greater racial balance was achieved since it was the Negro schools that were overcrowded. With the provision of new school buildings, however, this indirect stimulus to desegregation will not be present. In New Haven the transfer plan was more effective than in many other communities because of commitment of school leadership, active solicitation of transfers by door-to-door visits, provision of transportation for those transferring, teacher cooperation, heterogeneous grouping in the classrooms, and other factors.

The original plan provided that a student could apply to any one of a cluster of several elementary schools within a designated "cluster district," and the application would be approved on the basis of availability of space, effect on racial balance and certain unspecified educational factors; that students "presently enrolled" at a particular school would be given priority; and that transportation would be provided where necessary.

Desegregation by redistricting at the junior high school level. The junior high schools, customarily grades 7 to 9, have been the focus of considerable effort and tension in desegregation plans in many communities. With most areas clinging to the neighborhood school at the elementary level with resultant patterns of racial concentration, and with high schools already more integrated because of their lesser reliance upon neighborhood boundaries and their prior consolidation to achieve maximum resources, junior high schools have been a natural place to start desegregation plans. Like the elementary schools, they have in the past been assigned students on the basis of geography; but on the other hand, they tend to represent some degree of consolidation in that children from several elementary schools feed one junior high school. Further, parental pressures have been less severe for the maintenance of rigid neighborhood boundaries than at the elementary level.

Pairing of two junior high schools to achieve greater racial balance has been tried in a number of communities. Redistricting or redrawing the boundaries of areas that feed the schools has been tried in other areas. In Berkeley, Calif., after considerable community tension and struggle, a plan was put into effect that desegregated all three junior high schools (one had been desegregated previously). All the ninth graders were sent to a single school, previously Negro, and the seventh- and eighth-graders were assigned to the other two schools. The new ninth grade school was given a new name to signal its new identity in the eyes of the community. The excerpt describes the period following initiation of this plan and the differential success of integration in the different schools.

A plan for racial balance at the high school level. In a number of communities, students are assigned to high schools on the basis of area of residence and hence racial imbalance is continued. In Pasadena, Calif., a plan was initiated to redress this imbalance by opening places in the schools to allow the transfer of Negroes to the predominantly white high school. A measure of success was achieved but only after much resistance. Of interest particularly in this situation was the legal opinion that attempts to achieve racial balance were violations of the Constitution and that race could not be considered as a factor in school districting. Apparently previous racial concentration, aided by districting, had not been so regarded, yet attempts at desegregation were. The school board found its task made more difficult by such legal maneuvering. The excerpt describes the deliberations and controversy in the school board, and the impact of the court decision, which finally upheld the policy of transfers to achieve racial balance.

Segregation at a vocational school. The Washburne Trade School in Chicago seems to be effectively segregated by virtue of the practices and customs of the trade unions, whose apprenticeship programs have been characterized by racial isolation. Washburne has presented the same picture since its founding in 1919 after the passage of the Smith-Hughes Act by Congress. That Act provides for the creation of apprenticeship programs in which skilled workers are trained both in school and on the job. For example, a young man who wishes to be certificated as a plumber may work at his job 4 days a week and attend a formal training program 1 day or more or evenings.

The apprenticeship programs are heavily financed and regulated by the Federal Government through the Department of Labor and the Department of Health, Education, and Welfare. In recent

years the regulations have focused increasingly upon racial segregation within the union structures. One of the causes for this concern
has been the rather discouraging racial pattern in the apprenticeship
schools. Washburne seems to preserve that pattern. In 1960 an informal estimate showed that fewer than 1 percent of the 2,700
Washburne students were Negroes. Half of the apprenticeship
programs conducted at the school had no Negroes whatsoever. This
excerpt describes the state of racial segregation at Washburne and
at Chicago's vocational schools.

Relation of a university to school desegregation. Education is a
continuum—from kindergarten through college—and increasingly
public school desegregation plans are having an impact on colleges
in the same area, particularly those colleges which are city or State
supported. Free tuition, as in the New York City colleges, has no
meaning for members of minority groups who have dropped out of
school in high school and little meaning for those whose level of
achievement is too low to permit work at the college level. A number of colleges, through summer tutorials and selective admittance
of students whose grades would otherwise exclude them, are trying
to redress this indirect form of racial imbalance.

In Newark, Del., the pressures for desegregation in the public
schools have had an effect on the nearby University of Delaware
indicated by the following excerpt:

There are striking parallels in reactions to integration among Newark's
civic agencies, school district, and the University of Delaware. Because
the university plays such a large part in Newark's affairs, this excerpt
examines its problems with school integration.

NOTE ON SURVEY:

*In view of the fundamental significance of educational opportunity
to many important social issues today, Congress requested the
survey of educational opportunity reported in this document. The
survey is, of course, only one small part of extensive and varied
activities which numerous institutions and persons are pursuing in
an effort to understand the critical factors relating to the education
of minority children and hence to build a sound basis for recommendations for improving their education. Probably the main con-*

tribution of the survey to this large and long range effort will be in the fact that for the first time there is made available a comprehensive collection of data gathered on consistent specifications throughout the whole Nation.

Some brief analyses of the data have been made by the Office of Education in the few months available since the data were collected in the latter part of 1965. The results of this effort to determine some of the more immediate implications of the data are included in this report. A small staff in the Office of Education will carry out a continuing program of analysis. More importantly, the data will be made available to research workers everywhere so that they can perform their own analyses and can apply the data to their own special areas of investigation.

The survey was carried out by the National Center for Educational Statistics of the U.S. Office of Education. In addition to its own staff, the Center used the services of outside consultants and contractors. James Coleman of Johns Hopkins University had major responsibility for the design, administration, and analysis of the survey. Ernest Campbell of Vanderbilt University shared this responsibility, and particularly had major responsibility for the college surveys.

The Educational Testing Service of Princeton, N.J., was the contractor for the major public school survey under the direction of Robert J. Solomon and Joseph L. Boyd. It provided existing published tests for use in the survey and carried out the administration of these tests and of special questionnaires developed by the Center staff. Albert E. Beaton of Educational Testing Service conducted the computer analysis in accordance with specifications supplied by the staff of the Center.

Florida State University was the contractor for the nonenrollment study carried out by Charles Nam, Lewis Rhodes, and Robert Herriott. The Bureau of the Census administered this survey as part of its October 1965 Current Population Survey and processed the data.

Raymond W. Mack of Northwestern University directed the team of sociologists who did the case studies of education for minorities in the 10 American cities. The members of this team were Troy Duster, Michael Aiken, N. J. Demerath III, Margaret Long, Ruth Simms Hamilton, Herbert R. Barringer, Rosalind J. Dworkin, John Pease, Bonnie Remsberg, and A. G. Dworkin. G. W. Foster of the University of Wisconsin directed the team of lawyers who did *case studies of the legal and political problems of* de facto *segregation in seven American cities. The members of this team were William G. Buss, Jr., John E. Coons, William Cohen, Ira Michael Heyman, Ralph Reisner, John Kaplan, and Robert H. Marden.*

Other persons outside the Office of Education who contributed to the report were David Armor, Phillips Cutright, James Fennessey, Jeanette Hopkins, Nancy Karweit, Jimmer Leonard. John Tukey of Princeton University provided consulting assistance in the design of the regression analysis.

An advisory committee assisted in the design of the study and in developing procedures for carrying it out. The committee did not participate in the analysis of the data or the preparation of the final report. Its members were:

> *James E. Allen, Jr., New York State Commissioner of Education.*
> *Anne Anastasi, Fordham University.*
> *Vincent J. Browne, Howard University.*
> *Benjamin E. Carmichael, Superintendent of Chattanooga Schools.*
> *John B. Carroll, Harvard University.*
> *Otis Dudley Duncan, University of Michigan.*
> *Warren G. Findley, University of Georgia.*
> *Edmund W. Gordon, Yeshiva University.*
> *David A. Goslin, Russell Sage Foundation.*
> *Carl F. Hansen, Superintendent of D.C. Public Schools.*
> *James A. Hazlett, Superintendent of Kansas City Schools.*
> *Theron A. Johnson, New York State Department of Education.*
> *Sidney P. Marland, Superintendent of Pittsburgh Schools.*
> *James M. Nabrit, President of Howard University.*
> *Thomas F. Pettigrew, Harvard University.*
> *Clinton C. Trillingham, Superintendent of Los Angeles County Schools.*
> *Warren T. White, Superintendent of Dallas Public Schools.*
> *Stephen J. Wright, President of Fisk University.*

A large number of educators were consulted informally in the early stages of the design of the survey; no attempt will be made to list them here. At the same time, representatives of a number of organizations were consulted, particularly, Leroy Clark, John W. Davis, and June Shagaloff of the National Association for the Advancement of Colored People; Carl Rachlin, and Marvin Rich of the Congress of Racial Equality; Max Birnbaum, Lawrence Bloomgarden, and Isaiah Terman of the American Jewish Committee; Otis Finley, and Mahlon Puryear of the National Urban League; Harold Braverman of the Anti-Defamation League; Randolph Blackwell of the Southern Christian Leadership Conference; Rudy Ramos of the American G.I. Forum of the United States, Paul M. Deac of the National Confederation of American Ethnic Groups, and Elizabeth R. Cole of the U.S. Commmission on Civil Rights.

By far the largest contribution to the survey resulted from the cooperative support and hard work of many hundreds of school officials at every level of education and almost 20,000 school teachers who administered the survey questionnaires in their class-rooms throughout the Nation.

The Office of Education will make all the data gathered by this survey available to research workers. It must be done in the form of tabulations or statistics. No information can be revealed about an individual pupil, teacher, local or State school administrator, local or State school system.

ALEXANDER M. MOOD
Assistant Commissioner
for Educational Statistics.

CRITIQUE OF THE COLEMAN REPORT

by Samuel Bowles and Henry M. Levin*

I

In order to determine the extent of racial and ethnic discrimination in the schools, the Civil Rights Act of 1964 requested the Commissioner of Education to conduct a survey which would assess the degree of inequality of educational opportunity across the nation.

The Commissioner of Education responded to this request by

* From *Journal of Human Resources*, Winter, 1968, Samuel Bowles and Henry M. Levin, "The Determinants of Scholastic Achievement—An Appraisal of Some Recent Evidence" (a critique of James S. Coleman et al., *Equality of Educational Opportunity*, Washington: U.S. Office of Education, 1966).

undertaking an extensive survey which sought to determine: the extent of racial and ethnic segregation; the degree of inequality in the provision of school resources among racial and ethnic groups; the performance levels of students of different backgrounds on achievement tests; and the relationships between school and student characteristics on the one hand, and students' achievement on the other.

Complete sets of survey instruments were obtained for about 3,100 schools. These sets of data included information from the district superintendents, principals, teachers, and some 645,000 pupils from the first, third, sixth, ninth, and twelfth grades of these schools.

This huge store of information was analyzed between January and July 1966, and the 737-page report, *Equality of Educational Opportunity*, was published by the U.S. Office of Education in the summer of 1966.[1]

While the Report contains no policy prescriptions, its contents constitute a major challenge to American education. For example, the survey revealed a significant amount of segregation in the North as well as in the South, relatively minor differences in the measured characteristics of schools attended by different racial and ethnic groups, and very great differences in the achievement levels of racial and ethnic groups throughout the country. Since most of the findings have been reviewed previously, we will not discuss them here.[2]

Rather, in this study we shall confine our attention to that section of the Report which examined the relation of school and student characteristics to scholastic achievement. The Report found that:

(1) Per pupil expenditures, books in the library and a number of other facilities and curricular measures show very little relation to achieve-

---

[1] James S. Coleman *et al.*, *Equality of Educational Opportunity* (Washington: U.S. Office of Education, 1966), hereafter referred to as the Report.

[2] For example, see Robert C. Nichols, "Schools and the Disadvantaged," *Science*, Vol. 154 (December 9, 1966), pp. 1312–14; Christopher Jencks, "Education: The Racial Gap," *The New Republic*, Vol. 150 (October 1, 1966), pp. 21–26; James S. Coleman, "Equal Schools or Equal Students?" *The Public Interest*, Vol. 1 (Summer 1966), pp. 70–75; Robert A. Dentler, "Equality of Educational Opportunity: A Special Review," *The Urban Review*, Vol. 1 (December 1966), pp. 27–29.

ment if the social background and attitudes of individual students and their schoolmates are held constant (p. 325); and

(2) The effect of a student's peers on his own achievement level is more important than any other school influence (p. 325).

If correct, these findings suggest a major restructuring of educational policy.

Further, the Report stated that:

(3) There is a small positive effect of school integration on the reading and mathematics achievement of Negro pupils after differences in the socio-economic background of the students are accounted for (pp. 29–30).

It is not surprising, then, that the Report has generated considerable comment by policymakers, educational groups, and the general public. Indeed, the principal author, James Coleman, stated that while the initial intent of Congress may have been simply to identify areas of discrimination, "the intent later became less punitive-oriented and more future-oriented: i.e., to provide a basis for public policy, at the local, state, and national levels. . . ."[3] It is true that although the Commissioner of Education, Harold Howe II, was somewhat diffident about using the Report's findings as a basis for public policy, the findings concerning the determinants of scholastic achievement have quickly found their way into Congressional testimony, other government reports, legal decisions, and policy statements of a wide variety.[4]

The careful reader will see that the authors of the Report took pains to qualify their principal findings, to point to alternative explanations of the data, and to disclaim certainty on many of the

[3] Coleman, "Equal Schools or Equal Students?", p. 70.
[4] See Daniel P. Moynihan, "The Crisis of Confidence," statement presented to the Subcommittee on Executive Reorganization of the U.S. Senate Committee on Government Operations, December 13, 1966; Jim Leeson, "Some Basic Beliefs Challenged," *Southern Education Report* (May 1967), pp. 3–10; Jencks, "Education: The Racial Gap"; U.S. Commission on Civil Rights, *Racial Isolation in the Public Schools*, Vol. I (Washington, 1967); and Floyd McKissick, "Is Integration Necessary?" *The New Republic,* Vol. 155 (December 3, 1966), pp. 33–36. See also the legal briefs filed in behalf of Julius Hobson *et al.*, plaintiffs, and Carl F. Hansen and the Board of Education of the District of Columbia, defendants, Civil Action #82–66, U.S. District Court for the District of Columbia, as well as the opinion on the case that was handed down by Judge J. Skelly Wright, June 19, 1967.

results. Many commentators on the Report have been less cautious and have moved quickly to inferences about the determinants of scholastic achievement which are quite remote from the actual findings in the Report. Others have faithfully reported findings without giving adequate scrutiny to the evidence on which they are based.

In this review we will evaluate some of the principal findings by examining the analyses and the data from which they were derived. Our critique of the findings is directed towards two types of limitation: those pertaining to the survey itself, and the specific limitations that apply to the more widely publicized findings concerning the relation of school and student characteristics to achievement. In the following section, we will describe some inadequacies of the data. In Section III we will show that the finding concerning the ineffectiveness of school inputs must be seriously questioned; in Section IV we will evaluate the apparently significant effect of student peers on achievement; and in Section V we will discuss the findings concerning the effect of integration on achievement.

II. THE DATA

We would like to suggest first that the poor sample response, with its uncertain pattern, and the large numbers and questionable treatment of nonresponses on particular items of the questionnaire provide grounds for suspecting significant errors in the results.

While the sample of schools was carefully selected, the sample response left much to be desired. Complete sets of survey instruments were returned for only 59 percent (689 out of 1,170) of the high schools. Moreover, there is reason to believe that the pattern of sample nonresponses is not random. One characteristic contributing to this bias is the fact that a disproportionately large number of big cities refused to participate in the survey. Thus, in an analysis of metropolitan data one finds an over-representation of suburban relative to city schools.[5] This factor makes the samples on which the

---

[5] In the largest metropolitan areas, schools with over 25 percent nonwhite enrollment had about a one in five chance of being sampled, schools enrolling between 10 and 25 percent nonwhites had about a one in ten chance of being selected. See the Report, p. 552. Since most of the schools with high nonwhite enrollments are found in central cities, the refusal to participate by even one

analyses were based somewhat questionable as replicas of the populations which they supposedly represent.

A second source of error is represented by the large number of nonresponses (no answer, or "don't know") on particular questionnaire items and the survey's treatment of them.

These nonresponses were simply given the arithmetic mean of the responses, an ingenuous treatment which has probably created severe measurement errors in the data. Although the survey made no attempt to analyze the nonresponses,[6] we can still draw a number of inferences about nonresponse biases.

The nonresponse rates for mother's and father's education are particularly important since parents' education represented a prime control for student's social class. Nonresponses on father's education were about 50 percent for first graders, 40 percent for third graders, 41 percent for sixth graders, 21 percent for ninth graders, and 11 percent for twelfth graders.[7] Nonresponse rates for mother's education were as high as those for father's education at grades 1 and 3, and represented 33 percent, 15 percent, and 7 percent at the higher grades. Nonresponse rates for other background variables were also high.

In addition to the fact that nonresponse rates were substantial, there is definite evidence that these missing items were not randomly distributed among the populations under study. Preliminary analyses show the achievement test scores of nonrespondents on these particular items to be significantly below the means of the respondents, with few exceptions. For example, the mean achievement score for twelfth grade nonrespondents on father's education

---

superintendent of schools in a central city could impart a severe bias to the metropolitan data. If a large city did not cooperate in the survey, 20 or more city schools might be eliminated from the sample, whereas if a small district refused to cooperate, only one or two schools were sacrificed. (Because of the confidential nature of the survey information, we are unable to identify the cities that declined to participate.) An attempt to measure the extent of bias due to sample nonresponse was far too limited in scope to make a proper assessment. See the Report, pp. 565–68.

[6] In fact the only effort that was made to check measurement errors was one which compared the responses of 700 students in two school districts in Tennessee with information that was gleaned from school records and from the students' parents. An appraisal was made in order to see if the matched pairs of data for each item were "in agreement." For example, if both sources gave a "don't know" response, the responses were "in agreement."

[7] Nonresponse rates were provided to us by the U.S. Office of Education.

was 43, compared with a mean of 50 for the entire sample and a mean of 45 for those students whose fathers were in the lowest schooling category, "none or some grade school." Likewise, on almost every question that was examined among the nonrespondents, nonwhites were vastly over-represented relative to their numbers in the sample. But despite the high rates and biased pattern of nonresponses on the parents' education and encyclopedia ownership items, these variables were used to control for student background. The significance of these biases will be cited later in an appraisal of a key finding of the study.

III. SCHOOL RESOURCES AND THEIR EFFECT ON ACHIEVEMENT

The Report found that most of the conventional measures of school resources—per-student instructional expenditure, facilities, pupil-teacher ratio, and curriculum—accounted for very little of the variance in achievement scores of students. By combining this finding with the fact that family background accounts for a relatively large portion of the variance, the Report concluded "that schools bring little influence to bear on a child's achievement that is independent of his background and general social context."[8]

When one considers that children possess a wide range of inherited abilities and are products of different preschool environments and other social influences, this finding is not as surprising as it might appear at first glance. But while one would certainly expect student background to be a powerful determinant of pupil achievement, it might also be anticipated that school characteristics have a significant influence on performance levels. Yet the evaluation apparatus that was constructed in the Report was not neutral with regard to which possible influences might account for variations in achievement. It will be shown below that both in the measurement of variables and the statistical procedures used, the research design was overwhelmingly biased in a direction that would dampen the importance of school characteristics. Further, we would like to stress that the evidence in the Report on the effectiveness of school

8 The Report, p. 325.

inputs is far from uniform, and that despite the biases in the design of the analysis, some school inputs appear to have significant effects on achievement.

One can hardly expect to discover the true relationship between school resources and achievement without developing adequate measures of the school resources themselves. Yet the measurement of school resources in the survey was inadequate. Consider first the treatment of instructional expenditure-per-pupil. Theoreticaly, the measure of per-pupil expenditure should reflect differences among students in the amount of instructional resources devoted to their education. Actually, the survey derived no such data, either on an individual student or individual school basis. The measure used in the regression analysis was an average of instructional expenditure per student within an entire school district. School-to-school differences *within* a district (even differences between secondary and elementary schools) were simply ignored.[9]

The averaging of expenditures among all of the schools in a district imparts a severe bias to the data, for the available evidence indicates that the variation in expenditures among schools within a district is likely to follow a systematic pattern.[10] The schools that are attended by disadvantaged children are characterized by substantially lower expenditures than are those attended by advantaged students. Accordingly, the average per-student expenditure for the school district probably overstates the actual expenditures

[9] While the survey amassed complete sets of data for about 3,100 schools, expenditure data were collected for only the 500 or so school *districts* in which these schools were located. (Some of the metropolitan school districts that were included in the survey had 50 or more schools in the sample that was used for the analysis.)

[10] The survey collected expenditure data for the 1964–65 school year. Since that time, some equalization of school resources may have taken place under Title I of the Elementary and Secondary Education Act of 1965. For verification of the inequalities of school resources within school districts, see the following literature: for Atlanta and Chicago high schools, see Jesse Burkhead with Thomas G. Fox and John W. Holland, *Input and Output in Large City High Schools* (Syracuse, New York: Syracuse University Press, 1967). For the elementary schools of Chicago, see Eric C. Thornblad, *The Fiscal Impact of a High Concentration of Low Income Families Upon the Public Schools* (Doctoral dissertation, University of Illinois, Urbana, 1966). For the City of Boston, see Martin Katzman, *Distribution and Production in a Big City Elementary School System* (Doctoral dissertation, Yale University, 1967). For nonfinancial measures of the intradistrict variation in school resources, see Patricia Sexton, *Eduction and Income* (New York: Viking Press, 1961). Also see *Hobson v. Hansen, op. cit.*

for schools attended by students from the lower class and under-states expenditures for schools attended by students from the higher social classes. The limited variation in per-pupil expenditure that is imposed by averaging expenditures over an entire school district reduces the variance in test scores that is potentially accounted for by school expenditures, and thus results in an understatement of the effect of per-pupil expenditure.

In fact, the Report yields evidence that seems to contradict the finding that per-pupil instructional expenditure shows little relation to achievement, for it found that measures of teacher quality, which the survey data show to be highly correlated with the level of teachers' salaries do in fact exert a significant effect on achievement. We suggest that the source of the apparent contradiction is to be found in the fact that, unlike the per-pupil expenditure data which were obtained for school districts only, teachers' characteristics were measured individually and averaged for each school.

The Report states that teacher characteristics accounted for a ". . . higher proportion of variation in student achievement than did all other aspects of the school combined excluding the student body characteristics . . . ," (p. 316) and that they are comparable in importance to the latter (p. 318). We suggest below that the regression approach used in the Report has probably led to a significant understatement of the importance of teacher characteristics and other school resources. But for the present we need only note that according to the survey's own analysis, teacher traits such as verbal facility, educational level, experience, and the educational level of the teacher's mother account for significant variations in achievement.[11]

But the same teacher characteristics that account for significant variations in achievement relate directly to instructional expenditures. In a multiple regression analysis using the survey data, teachers' characteristics explain about three-quarters of the variance in teachers' salaries.[12]

The implication of this evidence is that higher expenditure on teachers' salaries does indeed lead to higher achievement levels among students. Since teachers' salaries dominate the instructional

[11] See Table 3.25.2, the Report, p. 318.
[12] This finding is based upon our analysis of the zero-order correlations found in the *Supplemental Appendix to the Survey on Equality of Educational Opportunity*.

expenditures category,[13] the evidence in the Report strongly suggests that a school-by-school expenditure measure would have shown a stronger statistical association with achievement.[14]

A number of measures of school resources were collected by the survey at the school-by-school level. This procedure avoids the gross aggregation errors imposed by use of the district as the unit of observation, but it is far from perfect, as inequalities in school resources for students of different races or social classes *within* a given school are obscured.[15] In big city schools with racially heterogeneous school populations and tracking, the distortions arising from the exclusion of intraschool variation in school resources are likely to be particularly severe.[16]

A second weakness in the measurement of school facilities is the limited range of facilities measures actually used in the analysis. In a recent review of some policy implications of the Report, the principal author concluded that "Per-pupil expenditure, books in the library, and a host of other facilities . . . show virtually no relation to achievement . . . ," if other aspects of the school are held constant.[17] Yet the host of other facilities measures used in the regression analysis of verbal achievement turns out to have been

[13] Data provided by the U.S. Office of Education suggest that about 90 percent of instructional expenditures are accounted for by teachers' salaries.

[14] If teachers' salaries and the pupil-teacher ratio showed strong positive correlations, the relationship between teacher quality and per-pupil instructional expenditure could be weakened despite the above evidence. Yet in the majority of cases for grades 6, 9, and 12 (those grades for which the expenditures analysis was carried out), the relation was negative, thus strengthening the relationship between teacher quality and per-pupil instructional expenditures. See the correlation tables in the *Supplemental Appendix* to the Report.

[15] Admittedly, collecting resource data on a student-by-student basis poses formidable problems of definition and administration.

[16] In fact, in schools where students are grouped according to ability, the Equal Opportunity data show a statistically significant direct correlation between verbal facility of teachers and the level of ability of students to whom they are assigned. See Henry M. Levin, "Recruiting Teachers for Urban Ghetto Schools" (manuscript in process). Evidence of social class inequalities in the attention and resources devoted to individual children within a given school can be found in A. B. Hollingshead, *Elmtown's Youth* (New York: John Wiley, 1949), pp. 163–204. Less conclusive but highly suggestive further evidence can be found in Max Wolff and Annie Stein, *Six Months Later, a Comparison of Children Who Had Head Start, Summer, 1965, with their Classmates in Kindergarten* (mimeo, 1966), p. 51. Wolff and Stein found that within a given classroom, the more "able" students received much more attention from the teacher. In their sample, non-Puerto Rican whites were more likely to have higher measured "ability" than either Negroes or Puerto Ricans.

[17] Coleman, "Equal Schools or Equal Students?" p. 73.

rather limited. At grades 1, 3, and 6, the *only* facilities measure used was volumes-per-student in the school library. At grades 9 and 12, the library variable was supplemented by one representing the presence of science laboratory facilities. We find it difficult to understand why science laboratories should have an effect on verbal achievement, but in any case, it is unlikely that the effect of the entire physical plant, instructional aids, and other facilities on educational achievement can be assessed properly by considering only science labs and library books.[18]

A particularly glaring example of the incomplete measurement of school characteristics is the absence of a measure of class size in the regression analysis. According to the Report, the pupil-teacher ratio in instruction ". . . showed a consistent lack of relation to achievement among all groups *under all conditions*."[19] This statement is misleading. Since it is the pupil-teacher ratio in the classroom which seems primarily relevant to achievement, the Report's pupil-teacher ratio has been interpreted by some as representing class size.[20] Such an interpretation is in error, for the Report obtained its pupil-teacher ratio by dividing the enrollment of the school by the number of teachers. Yet, schools with the same enrollment-teacher ratios may have significantly different class sizes depending on the average number of hours of teaching required of the instructional staff. The survey's unpublished data suggest that the teaching load per school varies from a low of about four to a high of six hours per day. This range of teaching loads implies a potential difference of as much as 50 percent in class size for schools with the same pupil-teacher ratio. Thus the Report could not possibly answer the question of how class size affects learning, for class size was never used in the analysis, nor was even the cruder measure of enrollment-teacher ratio subjected to scrutiny "under all conditions," as the Report implies.[21]

[18] If science labs and library books were intended to serve as proxies for the whole range of school inputs, the case should have been made explicitly along with evidence to support such a contention.
[19] The Report, p. 312, emphasis supplied.
[20] See Robert Dentler, "Equality of Educational Opportunity . . . ," p. 29.
[21] The Report might have been more circumspect in asserting "a lack of relation (of pupil-teacher ratio in instruction) to achievement under all conditions." Class size is likely to be a significant factor in the teaching of some subjects and an insignificant one in the teaching of others; and while substantial changes in class size may show some effect on achievement levels, very small changes in class size may not show much impact at all. But the Report examined only the relation between the enrollment-teacher ratio for the school

A third shortcoming of the measurement of school resources arises because the survey collected information solely on current school inputs; thus, the analysis necessarily ignores the effects of past influences on present achievement levels. We would expect achievement in the beginning of a school year (when the survey was implemented) to reflect the cumulative impact of past influences rather than simply the school characteristics and attitudes observed at the time of the survey. It cannot be assumed that the characteristics of schools that students were attending at the time of the survey are similar to those of the schools that they have attended in the past. Secondary schools are likely to receive pupils from feeder schools of widely varying quality. To the extent that in a given high school, disadvantaged children attended feeder schools that were less well endowed with educational inputs than those attended by more fortunate youths, the exclusion of past school inputs biases the analysis against finding school resources to be an important determinant of scholastic achievement, because measures of social background will serve to some extent as proxies for the excluded influence of past school inputs.

Although we have no concrete evidence on this point, we suspect that in addition to their direct cumulative effects on achievement, past school characteristics have an effect on student attitudes, and thus they influence indirectly current achievement levels. The teacher attitudes, curriculum, and even one's own perception of personal success or failure in the earlier years of school may have major effects on the development of a child's self-image and sense of personal efficacy.[22] Yet, while recognizing this problem, the authors of the Report chose a research strategy which necessarily ignored the effects of past school experience on current attitudes.

Although the data on school inputs are far from ideal, a careful statistical treatment might have salvaged some major substantive

---

and a single criterion, verbal achievement. Thus it could not possibly tell us about the relation of class size to achievement in physics or remedial reading, and so on.

[22] The authors of the Report did seek to determine the relationship between their measures of current attitudes and current school resources. They report (on p. 323) that the school inputs explain "almost none" of the variation in the measures of "self image" and "control of environment" beyond that explained by social background characteristics of the students. Because of the intercorrelations of social background and availability of school resources, one cannot infer from this finding that current school resources exert "almost no" causal influence on attitudes.

findings. In our opinion, however, the analysis contains a number of conceptual and methodological flaws which, along with the shortcomings of the data, render many of the key findings of questionable validity. Specifically, we will show that:

a. The underlying, highly restrictive model of the relation between school inputs, background, attitudes, and achievement is implausible; and,

b. The criterion that is used to assess the influence of different characteristics on achievement—addition to the proportion of explained variance in achievement scores—is inadequate for the task.

The basic statistical tool that is used to relate achievement to student background and school characteristics is the linear regression model. Current school inputs and the social background and attitude characteristics of the students and their peers (X_1, ..., X_n) are used to predict current school outcomes, as measured by an achievement score (Q).

The authors postulated an extremely simple relationship between achievement on the one hand and current school resources and student characteristics on the other. Their model implies that a student's achievement level is merely the sum of the independent effects of each school resource and background variable, plus a constant, or that

$$Q = a + b_1X_1 + b_2X_2 + \ldots + b_nX_n$$

where a and b_i, ($i = 1, 2, \ldots n$) are constants.

As a description of the process of education, the above formulation leaves much to be desired. The form of the equation implies that the effect on achievement of an incremental unit of a given input does not depend at all on how much of that input is utilized; nor does the effect depend on how much of other inputs are used.

Moreover, in undertaking this analysis, the authors presumably did intend to say something about the unique effects on achievement of school and student characteristics. And despite its conceptual shortcomings, the model chosen by the authors does allow an estimate (b_i) of the unique effect on achievement associated with a unit change in each of the explanatory variables taken separately, the other influences being held constant. Yet while these estimates are an integral part of the regression analysis, they are not disclosed in the Report.

Without the estimates of the regression coefficients (and their standard errors), the educational decision-maker cannot compare the relative effectiveness of different school inputs. Given the fact that schools always operate with limited budgets, the educational decision-maker is presumably interested in the relative effectiveness of those inputs over which he has control. Yet without these regression coefficients, the Report does not yield the relevant information that might assist the decision-maker in choosing the most effective policies. For example, one cannot determine from the analysis which policy is more effective per dollar of expenditure: hiring better teachers or buying more books for the library. Both alternatives are a priori reasonable, but it is likely that one will represent a more efficient device for raising achievement than will the other. The Report yields almost no insights which will aid this type of decision-making.

The most severe deficiency of the regression analysis is produced by the addition to the proportion of variance in achievement scores explained (addition to R^2) by each variable entered in the relationship as a measure of the *unique* importance of that variable. For example, assume that we seek to estimate the relationship between achievement level, Q, and two explanatory variables, X_1 and X_2. The approach adopted in the Report is to first determine the amount of variance in Q that can be statistically explained by one variable, say X_1, and then to determine the amount of variation in Q that can be explained by both X_1 and X_2. The increment in explained variance (i.e., the change in the coefficient of determination, R^2) associated with the addition of X_2 to the explanatory equation is the measure used in the Report for the unique effect of that variable on Q. Thus, if X_1 explained 30 percent of the variance in Q and X_1 and X_2 together explained 40 percent, the difference, or 10 percent, is the measure of the unique effect of X_2.

If X_1 and X_2 are completely independent of each other (orthogonal), the use of addition to the proportion of variance explained as a measure of the unique explanatory value of X_1 and X_2 is not objectionable. X_1 will yield the same increment to explained variance whether it is entered into the relationship first or second, and vice versa. But when the explanatory variables X_1 and X_2 are highly correlated with each other, as are the background characteristics of students and the characteristics of the schools that they attend, the addition to the proportion of variance in achievement that each will explain is dependent on the order in which each is entered into the regression equation. By being related to each other, X_1 and X_2 share a certain amount of explanatory power which is common to both of them. The shared portion of variance in achievement which could be accounted for by either X_1 or X_2 will always be attributed to that variable which is entered into the regression first. Accordingly, the explanatory value of the first variable will be overstated and that of the second variable understated.

The relevance of this problem to the analysis in the Report is readily apparent. The family background characteristics of a set of students determine not only the advantages with which they come to school; they also are associated closely with the amount and quality of resources which are invested in the schools. As a result, higher status children have two distinct advantages over lower status ones: First, the combination of material advantages and strong educational interests provided by their parents stimulate high achievement and education motivation; and second, their parents' relatively high incomes and interest in education leads to stronger financial support for and greater participation in the schools that their children attend. This reinforcing effect of family background on student achievement, both directly through the child and indirectly through the school, leads to a high statistical correlation between family background and school resources.[23]

The two sets of explanatory variables are so highly correlated that after including one set in a regression on achievement, the addition to the fraction of total variance explained (R^2) by the second set will seriously understate the strength of the relationship between the second variables and achievement. Yet the survey made the arbitrary choice of first "controlling" for student background and then introducing school resources into the analysis. Because the student background variables—even though crudely measured—served to some extent as statistical proxies for school resources, the later introduction of the school resource variables themselves had a small explanatory effect.[24] The explanatory power

[23] The authors of the Report were of course aware of this problem and went to some length to warn the reader about the possible resulting biases. Cf. p. 327.

[24] Given the authors' decision to utilize the increase in the proportion of variance explained as the main criterion of signficance for each variable, it would have been desirable to first control for school resources and then include student backgrounds in the analysis in order to see what the latter might add

shared jointly by school resources and social background was thus associated entirely with social background. Accordingly, the importance of background factors in accounting for differences in achievement is systematically inflated and the role of school resources is consistently underestimated.

The same technique was pursued in the analysis of the unique effect of particular school resources and student body characteristics.[25] Similar problems arise in the interpretation of these results, for if any two variables in the analysis are significantly correlated, the unique contribution of *both* of them will be negligible, *whatever the underlying causal relationship*. The appearance of a relatively large unique contribution for a particular school characteristic is a measure of both its effect on achievement and the degree to which it is independent of the other variables included in the analysis. Thus, for example, the fact that the unique contributions of curriculum, teacher quality, and teacher attitudes are zero in all three cases for white twelfth graders may indicate *either* the ineffectiveness of these inputs *or* a significant overlapping of these variables with each other or with other variables in the analysis. The method used in the Report does not readily allow us to distinguish between these two interpretations, although the authors of the Report appear to accept the first.[26]

A further reason why the effect of student background was probably overstated and that of school resources was understated involves the criterion of achievement that was used. All tests of

---

after accounting for the former. Unfortunately the authors "controlled" for background variables first on the basis of the truism: ". . . background differences are prior to school influence, and shape the child before he reaches school . . ." (p. 298). This rationale is misleading since the regression analysis that was used in the Report does not take into account—in any way—the time sequence of the explanatory variables.

[25] The Report, pp. 303–304.

[26] Fortunately we can do better than speculate about the magnitude of the biases introduced by the statistical procedures used, for we were able to examine the computer runs underlying some of the tables in the Report itself. For example, preliminary analysis of both the size and the levels of statistical significance of the regression coefficients underlying Table 3.25.2 of the Report suggest a strong relationship of school resources to achievement, particularly for Negro children. Because of the measurement problems described above and the absence of good estimates of the relative prices of school inputs, it would be inappropriate to make specific policy prescriptions on the basis of the regression coefficients underlying the Report. We are currently pursuing research on the educational production function and the relative prices and effectiveness of the various dimensions of the school input structure.

achievement used in the survey give an advantage to students who are enrolled in academic and college preparatory curricula relative to those enrolled in basic, general, commercial, vocational, and technical curricula.

On the one hand, a high proportion of advantaged students are enrolled in an academic curriculum, a course of studies which concentrates on the development of the very skills which were tested by the survey. On the other hand, a disproportionately large number of disadvantaged children are enrolled in job-oriented curricula,[27] comparatively expensive courses of study that put relatively little emphasis on reasoning, mathematics, reading comprehension, and other verbal skills. For these latter students, job-oriented tests or post-school employment success are more appropriate measures of the effectiveness of their schools. Obviously, one would not want to exclude consideration of the usual achievement scores, but the reader should be made aware of the specific biases involved in using them exclusively to measure performance.

In view of the shortcomings in the measurement of both school resources and achievement and the biases in the statistical techniques and conceptual model of the educational process used, it is surprising that school resources showed any association with achievement at all. Accordingly, we conclude that a much more careful assessment of the importance of different characteristics on achievement is warranted before any policy conclusions can be drawn about the relative effectiveness—or ineffectiveness—of school resources. The findings of the Report are particularly inappropriate for assessing the likely effects of radical changes in the levels and composition of resources devoted to schooling because the range of variation in most school inputs in this sample is much more limited than the range of policy measures currently under discussion.

IV. THE INFLUENCE OF FELLOW STUDENTS ON ACHIEVEMENT

One of the more widely discussed findings in the Report is that ". . . the social composition of the student body is more highly related to achievement, independently of the student's own social

---

[27] For some interesting evidence on this phenomenon, see Sexton, *Education and Income,* p. 177, and also the Report, pp. 95–96.

background, than is any school factor."[28] Accordingly, the Report suggested that ". . . schools appear to have an effect that is dependent upon the average family background in the school—an effect through the student body not through the characteristics of the school itself."[29] We find that an evaluation of the evidence presented in the Report does not support these conclusions, and that the apparent "effects" of the student body on individual achievement can be equally well explained by the deficient statistical controls for social class.

The authors derived their findings on the influence of fellow students from a set of regressions which showed that after controlling for the student's background, his attitudes, and the curriculum, facilities, and staff characteristics of his school, characteristics of his fellow students accounted for a significant increase in the proportion of variance in achievement that was explained. For example, on page 303 it is shown that the unique contribution of student body quality to the proportion of variance in individual achievement that was explained was about 7 percent for Negroes (addition to R^2 of .0677) and about 2 percent for whites (addition to R^2 of .0201) at grade 12.[30]

In general, the individual's social class and achievement are highly correlated with the social characteristics and achievement levels of his classmates. Because of existing residential patterns and the conscious selection of schools by parents, students tend to go to schools with other students of similar backgrounds and achievement levels.

This commonly observed phenomenon is strongly supported by the following table from the Report (p. 296) which shows the percent of total variance in individual verbal achievement that is "accounted for" by the mean score of the school, at grades 1 and 12:

	Grade 1	Grade 12
Negro, South	23.21	22.54
Negro, North	10.63	10.92
White, South	18.64	10.11
White, North	11.07	7.84

[28] The Report, p. 325.
[29] The Report, p. 311.
[30] The measure of student body quality in this particular regression includes verbal and nonverbal mean test scores for the student body, as well as four other items. (See the Report, p. 575.)

In the above tabulation, the school average for verbal achievement is as highly correlated with individual verbal achievement at grade 1 as it is at grade 12. Yet, it is not possible to attribute high correlations at grade 1 to the influence of fellow students since the tests were administered at the beginning of the first school year.[31]

The authors of the Report were aware of the difficult statistical problem of separating the unique impact of school social class from that of individual social class and prudently suggested that any finding showing a strong association between characteristics of fellow students and achievement of an individual:

. . . must be subject to special scrutiny, because it may be confounded by the student's own educational background and aspirations, which will generally be similiar to those of his fellow students. For this reason, throughout the analysis except where indicated, his own background characteristics are controlled to reduce such an effect.[32]

Therefore, the validity of the Report's findings concerning the effects of student peers on achievement balances delicately on the adequacy of the statistical controls for the student's own background. The Report used several measures of student background, but this is clearly a case where the quality of the control variables is more important than sheer numbers of measures. For example, items in the home, the Report's measure of economic status, showed an inconsistent association with achievement, varying from positive to negative among the different grades and racial groups.[33] Of the three most important dimensions of social class—education, income, and occupation—only education of parents was used in this Report.[34] Its sole inclusion—without occupation and income—omits

---

[31] The authors of the Report attempt to show (p. 306) that student body characteristics explain more variation in achievement scores in grades 9 and 12 than in the earlier grades. Their findings for the upper and lower grades are not comparable, however, because the measures that were used as explanatory variables at the upper grades are different from those used at the lower levels.

[32] The Report, p. 303.

[33] The Report, Table 2.221.5, p. 303. The explanatory power of the items in the home measures may have been reduced by the limited variability in response among students. For example, a detailed study of the responses of white sixth graders in the Northeast revealed that of those children who answered all of the relevant questions, over three-fifths claimed to possess *all* of the items.

[34] For an excellent review of the dimensions of social class and their measurement, see Joseph A. Kahl, *American Class Structure* (New York: Rinehart, 1957). Also see Albert Reiss, Jr., *Occupations and Social Status* (New

important dimensions of social class. Parents' level of education tells us little about the income, occupational, and other characteristics of the family, and further, tells us less about a Negro family's social class than about that of a white family.[35] The association between educational level on the one hand, and income and other dimensions of social class on the other, appears to be much less strong for Negroes than for whites.[36]

Thus, the use of parents' education as a primary control for social class background is particularly poor for Negro students. It is no surprise, then, to find that "family background" is a much less powerful predictor of achievement among Negroes than among whites (p. 321). Conversely, given the fact that individual social class, characteristics of fellow students, and the adequacy of school resources are all highly correlated, the particularly defective control for Negro social class may explain why both the characteristics of fellow students and school resources are better predictors of achievement among Negroes than among whites.[37]

If, as we suggest, the controls for the student's own social class are inadequate, the observed association between individual achievement and characteristics of fellow students may denote either an internal influence of student body characteristics on individual performance (as claimed in the Report); or alternatively, it may reflect the fact that, due to the inadequacies of the student background measures, the average achievement test score in a school or the proportion of students who intend to go to college

---

York: Free Press of Glencoe, 1961). Although data on father's occupation were collected in the survey, they were *not used* in the analysis.

[35] Giora Hanoch found that the years of schooling explained less than one-third of the variance in the earnings among males of the same region, race, and age bracket, as reported in the 1/1000 sample of the 1960 Census. See Hanoch, *Personal Earnings and Investment in Schooling* (Doctoral dissertation, University of Chicago, 1965), p. 42.

[36] Walter Fogel found that the correlations between years of education and housing, income, and consumption characteristics in the Los Angeles Census tracts were much stronger for whites than for Negroes. For whites, Pearson correlation coefficients between years of schooling on the one hand, and housing units with all the plumbing, income, and availability of two or more autos on the other were about .62, while for Negroes, the highest coefficient was .264. "The Effects of Low Educational Attainment on Incomes: A Comparative Study of Selected Ethnic Groups," *The Journal of Human Resources,* Vol. 1 (Fall 1966).

[37] The Report, pp. 317, 319, 313, and 303.

conveys a considerable amount of additional information about the social class of a student in that school, even after controlling for variables purporting to measure individual background. That is, measures of the attributes of fellow students serve in the analysis as reasonably good statistical proxies for the attributes of the student himself. If this explanation is valid, much of the variance in achievement scores "explained" by characteristics of fellow students is in fact associated with the traits of the individual student.

Even if the controls for individual social class were adequate, one would still find difficulty in distinguishing the student peer effect from a community effect. This problem exists because the social class and other attributes of one's schoolmates serve as indicators of the type of community in which the student and his family reside, and the statistical procedures used in the Report are incapable of distinguishing between these two effects.[38]

V. THE EFFECT OF INTEGRATION ON NEGRO ACHIEVEMENT

It is unfortunate that one of the most extensively discussed inferences from the Report is one about which the Report is highly ambiguous. In the widely circulated summary of the Report, the authors assert that:

Those (Negro) pupils who first entered integrated schools in the early grades record consistently higher scores than the other groups, although the differences are . . . small.

No account is taken in these tabulations of the fact that the various groups of pupils may have come from different backgrounds. When such account is taken by simple cross-tabulations on indicators of socioeconomic status, the performance (of Negroes) in integrated schools and in schools integrated longer remains higher. Thus, although the differences are small, and although the degree of integration within the school

---

[38] The fact that the fraction of variance in individual achievement scores explained by the average achievement score of fellow students is as high at grade 1 as at grade 12 is consistent with the interpretation that the apparent student peer effects are at least in part community effects operating outside the schools. However, see Alan B. Wilson, "Educational Consequences of Segregation in a California Community," in U.S. Commission on Civil Rights, *Racial Isolation in the Public Schools,* Vol. II Appendices, p. 202.

is not known, there is evident, even in the short run, an effect of school integration on the reading and mathematics achievement of Negro pupils (p. 29).

and in fact they further suggest that:

It is possible that more elaborate analyses looking more carefully at the special characteristics of Negro pupils and at different degrees of integration within schools that have similiar racial compositions may reveal a *more definite effect* (p. 30, emphasis added).

However, later in the Report, the authors heavily qualify this finding:

The effects of the student body environment upon a student's achievement appear to lie in the educational proficiency possessed by that student body, whatever its racial or ethnic composition (p. 307.)

And in fact Coleman has emphatically stressed that the survey revealed no unique effect of racial composition on the achievement levels of nonwhites. Despite the latter qualification, the initial assertion of a specific racial effect has received wide currency. Because of the apparent confusion caused by the difference in emphasis in different parts of the Report, we will attempt to clarify exactly what the Report does show in its analysis of the effect of school racial composition on Negro achievement levels. After controlling for student background and school variables, the inclusion of a variable representing the proportion of students in the school who were white added a small amount to the explained variance in achievement scores. For Negroes in grade 12, the increase in the percent of variance explained was about two-thirds of 1 percent (i.e., addition to $R^2 = .0068$ by including proportion white as an explanatory variable).

This minuscule increase may be attributable to the fact that, as we noted above, the control on student background was particularly poor for Negroes. In general, Negroes who are attending predominantly white schools are representatives of a considerably higher socioeconomic class than are students in all, or largely Negro schools. The higher the proportion white in a school, the more likely the school is to be located in a residential suburban area or white neighborhood of the city; and if a city school, it is more likely to require entrance examinations (e.g., New York City's Bronx High School of Science or Brooklyn Tech, Music and Arts, etc.). Thus the processes of residential and academic selection imply that those Negroes who attend predominantly white schools are drawn from higher social strata and exhibit higher performance levels than those who are found in schools with lower concentrations of whites. On the other hand, the predominantly Negro schools are generally found in the lower class, core areas of the city or in rural areas. They are not generally selective, nor do they have high proportions of students who will go to college. The proportion white in a school thus represents an approximate measure of the social class of Negro students attending the school; the higher the proportion white, the higher—on the average—the social class of any nonwhites in attendance.

Accordingly, the small, residual, statistical correlation between proportion white in the schools and Negro achievement is likely due, at least in part, to the fact that the proportion white in a school is a measure of the otherwise inadequately controlled social background of the Negro student.[39] Thus we find that the conclusion that Negro achievement is positively associated with the proportion of fellow students who are white, once other influences are taken into account, is not supported by the evidence presented in the Report.

We would like to make it clear that the failure of the Report to substantiate this relationship should not lead us to embrace the opposite position, namely, that in terms of achievement, integrated

[39] A specific racial effect is also stressed in the 1967 report of the U.S. Commission on Civil Rights, *Racial Isolation in the Public Schools*, Vol. 1 (Washington, 1967), pp. 113–14. In the Commission's own analysis of the Equality of Educational Opportunity data, the only control for social class was the education of parents, which was termed low (less than high school graduation), medium (high school graduation), or high (more than high school graduation). Accordingly, the analysis of the Civil Rights Commission is also plagued with inadequate control for students' social class. See also the separate appendices to the Commission's report, Vol. II. Wilson, in his study done for the U.S. Commission on Civil Rights, found that after controlling for other factors, the racial composition of the school had no significant direct association with Negro achievement. The apparent "effect" of integration had arisen because "the Negro students who attended integrated schools had higher mental maturity test scores in their primary grades, and come from homes better provided with educative materials." See Wilson, "Educational Consequences of Segregation . . . ," p. 185.

schools are worse (or no better) for Negroes than segregated ones. The Report simply does not provide conclusive evidence one way or the other.

VI. CONCLUSION

In this appraisal we have attempted to show that some of the Report's most widely publicized findings concerning the determinants of scholastic achievement, namely, those relating to the ineffectiveness of school resources, the influence of student peers, and the effects of integration, are not substantiated by the evidence. We have attempted to show that both the measurement of the school resources and the control of social background of the student were inadequate, and that the statistical techniques used were inappropriate. By no means do we wish to suggest that the actual relations are the opposite of what the Report concludes or that further research will not substantiate some of the Report's findings; but until better evidence is found, we will have to remain agnostic about which relationships prevail.

Equality of Educational Opportunity addressed itself to some of the most difficult questions that our society faces: what are the determinants of different educational outcomes, and what is the relative importance of each of the relevant influences? Unfortunately, the survey that led to the Report was handicapped by a severe time constraint. It was also hampered by a more serious impediment, for the learning processes by which different influences alter achievement are largely unknown, and no set of data and statistical analyses can easily compensate for a missing theoretical framework.

The Report has a distinct contribution to make, but not directly in the arena of educational or social policy. Rather, its strength lies in the fact that it has stimulated a great deal of thought and new research efforts to uncover the largely unknown and complex relationships among family, school, and community influences on one hand, and educational outcome on the other. Further, it has provided some of the necessary data to test the new hypotheses that it has stimulated. In short, while the Report did not provide the answers, it has brought us closer to being able to use large scale research efforts as a basis for making intelligent policy decisions for our schools.

THE ECONOMICS OF INEQUALITY

by David K. Cohen*

It is hardly news that some schools are rich and others poor; nor is it a surprise that the rich ones are likely to be found in well-to-do communities, and the poor ones in less affluent places. The news is that efforts are now underway to eliminate such differences in school expenditures.

During the past three or four decades, many states have sought to reduce financial disparities among school districts through "foundation" or "equalization" programs that provided aid to local districts. But large inequalities persisted. In recent months, however, lawsuits have been filed in six states that seek to compel the states to assume responsibility for eliminating differences in per pupil expenditures among rich and poor districts. These court actions raise a number of fundamental issues, both economic and educational.

The disparities around which all this activity centers are considerable. In Arkansas (the state with the lowest average expenditure for public schooling), the highest-spending 10 per cent of the districts in 1961 devoted $160 or more per pupil to the education of their charges, and the lowest 10 per cent spent $99 or less per pupil; in New York (the state with the highest average outlay for schooling), the top 10 per cent of the districts spent $465 or more, and the

* From *Saturday Review.* April 19, 1969, Vol. III, No. 16. Copyright 1969 Saturday Review, Inc.

lowest 10 per cent spent $333 or less on each student. Studies in individual states since then show that such disparities persist.

Local tax revenues, which cause part of the problem, are unequal for two main reasons. First, the central cities usually experience more than average competition for tax dollars; they have more problems which local taxation is supposed to alleviate (poverty, aging, ill health), and they provide services for people who work there, but live elsewhere (fire and police protection, sanitation). Thus, a smaller proportion of the average property tax dollar is available for spending on schools in central cities than in their neighboring suburbs. One recent study showed that although central cities raised more than $90 per capita in property taxes to their suburbs' average of more than $70, the suburbs spent an average of $60 per capita on schools excluding capital outlays, while the cities spent about $50.

But even if municipal overburden did not exist, the same tax rates would not raise the same amount of money in all communities. Those with more rundown and unproductive land tend to have lower assessed valuations than communities with more well-kept and productive property. Many communities of the first sort are rural (with depleted farmland and underpopulated hamlets), but many others are urban, replete with slums, decaying business districts, and industrial wastelands. The problems of a weakening urban tax base often are compounded by fear of losing the existing jobs and tax revenue entirely.

In any event, when communities with different assessed valuations are taxed at the same rate, the per capita revenue yield varies; communities with the lower valuations raise less even though they make the same tax effort. And when the lower-assessed valuations are found in communities with the greatest poverty and social decay, the result is devastating. For instance, the average affluent homeowner in a well-to-do community is required to sacrifice a smaller proportion of his income to pay his share of an $800 annual per pupil outlay, than would a less well-off homeowner in a central city or depressed rural area. Affluent communities can raise more money for schools at lower tax rates than poor communities can at higher rates. Add to this the heavy burden of municipal services, and the fiscal problems of city schools are compounded.

Programs of state foundation and equalization aid could eliminate these local differences, but generally they do not. The reasons vary from state to state, but a few basic ones are similar. In many states, the aid formulas were designed decades ago to help finance the nonurban districts, which at the time were disadvantaged. Over the years, many of the rural areas became affluent suburbs, and many of the cities grew relatively poor. The state aid formulas, however, have not always been updated. In many metropolitan areas, state school aid programs deliver more dollars per pupil to suburban than to central-city schools. In 1964, for example, Detroit received $189 per pupil from Michigan, while the average suburban receipt per pupil was $240.

But even in those states where efforts have been made to reverse these trends the remedies are only partly effective, because state education departments are reluctant to equalize completely the tax burden among rich and poor districts. It is still easier to raise money for schooling in suburban places like Brookline than it is in Boston. The reluctance to correct this situation, of course, is political. State education departments are answerable to legislatures, which in turn must account to constituents. Parents and schoolmen who are relatively well-off may pay lip service to the idea of equal educational opportunity, but they also will use the political process to protect their advantage and that of their children.

The disparities, then, result both from variations in the wealth of local communities, and from the historic tendency of state education departments to adjust only partly for these local variations. The current burst of activity aimed at eliminating these disparities rests on a few common ideas. One is that levels of support for public schools should not follow such systematic lines of social division as race, wealth, or residence. A second is that the agency best able to remedy differences among districts within states is the state government itself. But it is generally agreed that state government is not likely to resolve fully the issue through the political process, and there is little reason to be any more hopeful about the Congress. Therefore, it is not surprising that the third common idea is that the existing inequalities may violate the Fourteenth Amendment.

The long process of court action has only begun, yet, it appears that if ever there were an idea whose time had come, this would seem to be the idea and ours the time. Since the mid-Fifties, American law and politics have been increasingly occupied with problems of inequality. The concern with intrastate school financing disparities is only the most recent extension of this trend. There is, however, another less apparent reason for its appeal. The last decade of struggle over schools saw efforts at desegregation founder on white resistance and bureaucratic inertia, and programs of compensatory education produce nothing more useful than debates in the liberal press. Lacking any noticeable improvements in either the quality or outcome of slum schools, many of the interested parties (parents, teachers, semi-professional school reformers, and community activists) are abandoning past cooperation in seeking more money or other improvements; instead, they increasingly have fallen to fighting among themselves over who should manage the educational enterprise. This has had a number of disquieting consequences for liberals; they are ideologically fragmented over the question of separatism or integration. Whatever other drawbacks the new lawsuits may have, they are blissfully neutral on the question of who shall control what in the cities.

All of these factors augur well for the proliferation of lawsuits, research, and organizations concerned with intrastate disparities in expenditures for public education. But if the existence of the differences is admitted on all sides, there is no such agreement on whether—or how—they should be eliminated.

The rationales for eliminating the inequities boil down to two. The first is that differences in school expenditures cause differences in the quality of education, and these in turn harm children's achievement, and thus their chances for success. The second is that irrespective of damage to anyone's education, the state has no business making distinctions based on such educationally irrelevant considerations as race, place, or community wealth, as is currently done in nearly all the aid formulas.

The arguments against eliminating the differences follow roughly the same lines. One is that the state aid programs do provide a minimally satisfactory education, and that high-expenditure districts offer not discrimination but leadership. Without beacons of educational excellence, general upgrading of the educational system would be impossible. The other is that neither courts nor legislatures have any business meddling with how much money parents choose to spend on their children's schooling; this is held to reflect an individual's ability and willingness to pay taxes, his concern for education, and his taste in the style of education offered. Any effort to eliminate the differences would infringe individual liberties.

What does the available evidence suggest concerning the merits of these positions?

If one argues—as Arthur Wise seems to, in *Rich Schools, Poor Schools*—that *all* intrastate differences in outlays for schooling must be eliminated, the "beacons of educational excellence" argument becomes a formidable obstacle. The supply of money available for public education is distinctly limited; compelling all districts within a state to spend roughly the same amount would be more likely to level them toward the mean, than to raise all of them up to the top. But the opposition between "beacons of educational excellence" and equalization is not inevitable; it exists only if educational excellence is identified as maintaining the advantages that current school financing arrangements extend to private wealth. One could as well argue that there is nothing intrinsically wrong with spending more on some children than others, as long as the difference results from the free choice of their parents and neighbors. From this view, government is not obliged to make all districts spend the same amount, but only to eliminate any dependence their spending may have upon such things as the personal income of parents, differences in communities' ability to raise taxes, or the formulas under which states aid local school districts.

Remedy, then, would consist of reducing to zero the correlation between measures of community wealth and school expenditures. This would make it as hard for affluent suburbs to spend $800 per pupil per year as it presently is for poor cities or depressed rural towns. Taxation and revenue distribution would have to be a good deal more redistributive than they are, but there is no inherent necessity for sameness. This would doubtless increase fiscal pain in the suburbs and reduce it in the cities, but equal pain in raising money is not the same thing as educational leveling. The second reduces variety; whereas the first only means that it comes no more easily to the wealthy than to the poor.

We can show that irrational disparities can be eliminated without suffocating variety—as is commonly found within American school systems—but it is another matter to prove that this does not infringe liberty. As a matter of fact, it is impossible to prove this point, for the simple reason that equalizing expenditures would indeed infringe liberty. The liberties in question, however, appear to consist of the freedom of those who *have* more to *get* more for less effort, through a system of government taxation and revenue distribution. Thus, the issue is not whether liberties are infringed, but whether they are the sort of liberties that can be allowed to permeate the workings of government.

It is hard to find very poor people who support the liberty of the rich to get more for less effort with the help of government, and it is nearly as difficult to find affluent people who take the view that they should be so taxed as to eliminate the very advantages over less fortunate folk which they either inherited or struggled most of their lives to attain. For this reason, when serious redistribution is sought (whether it be in votes, access to criminal justice, or school finance), it is found mainly through the courts. And the courts have become increasingly skeptical of liberties attained at the expense of others when a) the others are systematically disadvantaged in the economic or political struggle for equality, and b) when the relative disadvantage seems to have obvious and substantial support from agencies of government.

Therefore, it would be no great surprise if the egalitarian revolution were extended to intrastate variations in public school support. But assuming the courts found existing schemes of school support unconstitutional, what would be put in their place?

All the litigation presents dollar disparities as the chief evidence of evil, and there is consequently a profound bias toward conceiving good as the absence of dollar inequalities. Much of the litigation suggests such a remedy. One expression of this view has been proposed by John Coons, which he calls power equalizing. The idea is roughly as follows. A state decides that it wants to divorce variations in expenditures on education from differences in community wealth, and make them depend instead upon community interest in schooling. It decides to use local fiscal effort—the rate at which each community taxes itself for education—as the most convenient indicator of interest in schooling. The state then computes the average assessed valuation (making sure it is assessed uniformly) and determines the state average support for schools. It then arranges the formulas for collecting and distributing aid to education in such a way that districts that tax themselves at or above the state average rate, but fail to raise the state average expenditure per pupil, will receive aid sufficient to make up the difference. Districts that tax at the state average effort (or below) and raise *more* than the average revenue per pupil will turn back some of the excess dollars to the state.

For every bit of effort a district makes above the state average, it could either receive or contribute to state matching funds depending on its wealth. Thus, consider two hypothetical districts—one rich, one poor—both taxed at one mill above average. Let us say the poor one raised $10 per student with its extra effort, and the rich one raised $20. The state would adjust aid so that (in effect) $5 per student was taken from the rich district and assigned to the poor one; equal effort to attain above average schools would be rewarded with equal dollars to spend toward that end.

Of course, this example involves only one possible application of the idea that spending on schools should not be a function of local wealth. The system could as easily be keyed to the highest districts as to the average (which would simply raise all expenditures more), and state reimbursement for above average effort could provide greater or less encouragement of school expenditures by varying the level at which the state matched funds raised by above average local effort.

What is more, dollar equalization would not be irrevocably tied to local tax effort. States could decide to eliminate the local property tax entirely and fund education through state revenues. Or, they could devise some combination of local and state funding, under which individual districts would raise only a statutory minimum, and the state would supply the remainder up to some mandated maximum. In theory, at least, there are many alternative schemes for eliminating the association between community wealth and school expenditures.

There are, however, two substantial objections to any dollar-equalizing scheme. They have both been raised in the cases filed against the Michigan and the California State Departments of Education. The California suit hints that providing equal dollars to districts within a state is no guarantee that equal resources can be purchased, because prices vary from place to place. And both complaints suggest that educational resources should not be allocated on the basis of dollar equality, but educational need. Just as the cost of educational goods and services varies among districts, so does the need for education. Districts where costs are higher, or needs greater, should get more money.

Can variations in the cost of education be adequately measured and priced? Can education be provided on the basis of need? Measuring the cost of anything is no more or less precise than the calculations that lie just behind the dollar signs. It would, for example, be easy to measure interdistrict variations in the cost of teachers, if all we cared about was their height, weight, years of experience, tenure, or certification. But the teacher attributes that produce better student achievement are mysterious. Educational research shows little relationship between their experience, certification, tenure, and salary, and their students' achievement.

There is some evidence that teachers' expectations for their students' performance may influence how well the children do, but this presents other problems. We haven't the faintest idea of whether teachers with more productive expectations cost more; we don't know what a "more productive expectation" actually is; and finally, even if the solutions to these puzzles were as clear as daylight, there is no system of attitude measurement that is both sufficiently precise to single out those teachers whose expectations are the most productive, and sufficiently discreet to avoid the moral and constitutional problems that might attend rating employees of the state on the basis of their attitudes.

Thus, the objective characteristics we can easily measure and price seem of dubious educational value, and the subjective attributes—which may have some causal connection with achievement—provide no handles for effective measurement or pricing.

These conclusions bear directly on the notion of providing state aid on the basis of educational need. The great public concern about poverty has accustomed us to the notion that poor children require more education than the children of the well-to-do. Since more of anything costs more, this notion translated into the idea that effective education for the children of poverty means more money for their schools. On this basis Title I of the Elementary and Secondary Education Act and hundreds of similar state and local programs have been organized and funded, and it is on the same basis that attorneys in Illinois, California, and Michigan have argued that city schools should receive more money than districts with mostly advantaged children.

Because poor children are thought to need more education than other children in order to do as well, the more-than-average education is seen as a condition of producing average achievement. Therefore, the notion of assigning funds on the basis of need is simply a different way of saying that school districts should have some common performance standard.

However, educational research suggests that the present differences in schools' quality produce little difference in their students' achievement. And the recently instituted programs of compensatory education seem only to confirm this finding. Of course, in most cases the variations in school quality are small, and hardly provide a full test of the notion that schools could make a difference. But to a court or a legislature seeking to decide whether (or how) to allocate state funds on the basis of need, these research results might well have a mystifying and disquieting effect. They suggest, simply enough, that schoolmen and researchers haven't much evidence about the educational techniques that might satisfy a need criterion, or how much they might cost. Such news is bound to dampen judicial or legislative enthusiasm for such a criterion of resource allocation.

Finally, all of this assumes that there is something special about school achievement. Although that idea received almost religious attention in the late Fifties, the system of achievement-worship may be breaking down. No one has shown that student achievement is the sole useful criterion of schools' accomplishments. To do so we would have to a) demonstrate that achievement strongly affects adult occupation, income, etc., and b) secure some consensus that these things are more important than such other presumed outcomes of schooling as independence, creativity, or social integration. But the evidence that school achievement adds to the impact of preschool ability upon adult status is slim, and there is a growing agreement that performance on middle-class-oriented achievement tests is not the sole important outcome of schooling.

This leaves educational and political taste as the basis on which to select criteria for measuring school quality. Lacking agreement on the outcomes, we will fight about what's important to measure, and in the absence of measurement systems, we will have no solid basis on which to rest state aid formulas.

Of course, the absence of precise knowledge has never paralyzed state legislatures and school agencies before. They have been organizing and regulating education on the basis of insufficient knowledge for generations. Legislators could decide that it was important to allocate more money to teachers' salaries in rural areas, or to poor schools in cities. The point, however, is that this would be an act of political wisdom or mercy, not educational expertise.

There are other questions, which have little to do with the

technologies of educational or social measurement. There is, for instance, no compelling evidence that state money should go to school districts instead of parents. Such a system might introduce more competition among schools, while increasing the alternatives to families, and in turn, this might result in greater efficiency and differentiation among schools.

A more difficult and complex question that arises is whether the equalization schemes discussed here really would make it as easy for the poor to purchase quality education as it now is for the affluent. There is, after all, more to poverty than the assessed valuation of a person's house; the fact that a given amount of tax effort produces the same dollars for education does not mean that they are equivalent for the poor and the rich. If, for example, the property tax takes a larger proportion of the personal income of the poor than the rich, then the rich still would be less constrained in extending above average effort. And even if aid formulas could take this into account, it would still be easier for the rich to invest around the margins of public education—for books, tutors, etc. It is not clear that the state could compensate for this situation since it would be necessary for the family, not the school district, to be the unit receiving state aid. But none of these points mean that remedy is either unreasonable or unfeasible. They suggest that a dollar-equalization scheme is probably feasible, but that its effect would be limited.

The only question that goes to the heart of the matter is whether dollar equalization would make any difference. An affirmative decision in these cases would set loose profound changes in our system of public finance; the courts would be less likely to take the step if they thought that the only point at issue was discrimination which had no educational impact. Unfortunately, it is not clear whether eliminating existing disparities would produce much change in schools or children. My earlier examples showed that the dollar difference between the lowest- and highest-spending 10 per cent of the school districts in Arkansas was no less than about $60 per pupil per year, and in New York no less than about $130. The evidence from children in programs of compensatory education which cost about that much is that their achievement was no better than that of comparable children who had no more money spent on them. And some programs (such as the More Effective Schools program in New York City) have invested much more—up to $500 per pupil per year; the evidence there is mixed, but even the most enthusiastic reading indicates that it reveals only a small achievement gain.

Of course, these programs often have been done badly, quickly, and many have not been sustained. It is conceivable that the same amount of money applied more steadily, over more years, might have better results. It could be that more money would offer a basis for innovation and experimentation, which might lead to better schools and higher achievement. It is possible that if equalization were keyed to the highest spending district rather than the average, the greater money would produce greater achievement. But if the available evidence does not controvert such statements, neither does it provide much support or encouragement.

Since the evidence is so mixed, and Americans are such devout believers in the efficacy of schooling, litigation to reduce the dependence of school expenditures on district wealth may well meet with success. If it does, many useful results would follow: the existing irrational and discriminatory inequalities in school support would be reduced or eliminated, which would provide a sound basis for federal efforts to reduce wealth-related disparities among states; it also might help build judicial barriers against the use of federal revenue sharing, or bloc grant schemes, to perpetuate or magnify existing intrastate inequalities. Finally, were any or all of these to occur, a more solid and equitable floor upon which to build compensatory efforts would have been constructed.

All these results would be positive. But there is no clear evidence that they would meet the two central problems of public education in our time—its organization along racial lines and its apparent inability to reduce racial and class disparities in school outcomes. In fact, it seems apparent that much of the interest in intrastate fiscal disparities arises precisely from despair over the evident failure of efforts to resolve these central problems. It is more than a little ironic that fourteen years after *Brown,* after years of struggle to improve achievement in slum schools, the newest dimension in efforts to secure equal educational opportunity reminds us as much of the *Plessy* doctrine of separate-but-equal as anything more recent. In a way, of course, that is unfair: these suits do represent a new dimension, undreamed of in the world of *Plessy;* they begin to reach beyond race to the economic determinants of school quality. But in another sense it is not unfair; it reminds us that this new dimension of equal educational opportunity seems to touch the school problems which presently preoccupy us in only an oblique and incomplete fashion.

RACIAL ISOLATION IN THE PUBLIC SCHOOLS

U.S. Commission on Civil Rights*

FINDINGS:
RACIAL ISOLATION: EXTENT AND CONTEXT

Extent

1. Racial isolation in the public schools is intense throughout the United States. In the Nation's metropolitan areas, where two-thirds of both the Negro and white population now live, it is most severe. Seventy-five percent of the Negro elementary students in the Nation's cities are in schools with enrollments that are nearly all-Negro (90 percent or more Negro), while 83 percent of the white students are in nearly all-white schools. Nearly nine of every 10 Negro elementary students in the cities attend majority-Negro schools.

2. This high level of racial separation in city schools exists whether the city is large or small, whether the proportion of Negro enrollment is large or small, and whether the city is located North or South.

Trends

3. Racial isolation in the public schools has been increasing. Over recent years Negro elementary school enrollment in northern

* From the *Conclusions and Findings of a Report of the U.S. Commission on Civil Rights* (Washington, D.C., U.S. Government Printing Office, 1967).

city school systems has increased, as have the number and proportion of Negro elementary students in majority-Negro and nearly all-Negro schools. Most of this increase has been absorbed in schools which are now more than 90 percent Negro, and almost the entire increase in schools which are now majority-Negro. There is evidence to suggest that once a school becomes almost half- or majority-Negro, it tends rapidly to become nearly all-Negro.

4. In Southern and border cities, although the proportion of Negroes in all-Negro schools has decreased since the 1954 Supreme Court decision in *Brown* v. *Board of Education,* a rising Negro enrollment, combined with only slight desegregation, has produced a substantial increase in the number of Negroes attending nearly all-Negro schools.

Population Movements in Metropolitan Areas

5. The Nation's metropolitan area populations are growing and are becoming increasingly separated by race. Between 1940 and 1960, the increase of Negroes in metropolitan areas occurred mainly in the central cities while the white increase occurred mainly in the suburbs. These trends are continuing.

6. The trends are reflected among school-age children.

(*a*) By 1960, four of every five nonwhite school-age children in metropolitan areas lived in central cities while nearly three of every five white children lived in the suburbs.

(*b*) Negro schoolchildren in metropolitan areas increasingly are attending central city schools and white children, suburban schools.

(*c*) A substantial number of major cities have elementary school enrollments that are more than half-Negro.

CAUSES OF RACIAL ISOLATION

Metropolitan Dimensions

1. The Nation's metropolitan area populations also are becoming increasingly separated socially and economically. There are widening disparities in income and educational level between families in the cities and families in the suburbs. People who live in the

suburbs increasingly are more wealthy and better educated than people who live in the cities.

2. The increasing racial, social, and economic separation is reflected in the schools. School districts in metropolitan areas generally do not encompass both central city and suburban residents. Thus, central city and suburban school districts, like the cities and suburbs themselves, enclose separate racial, economic, and social groups.

3. Racial, social, and economic separation between city and suburb is attributable in large part to housing policies and practices of both private industry and government at all levels.

(*a*) The practices of the private housing industry have been discriminatory and the housing produced in the suburbs generally has been at prices only the relatively affluent can afford.

(*b*) Local governments in suburban areas share the responsibility for residential segregation. Residential segregation has been established through such means as racially restrictive zoning ordinances, racially restrictive covenants capable of judicial enforcement, administrative determinations on building permits, inspection standards and location of sewer and water facilities, and use of the power of eminent domain, suburban zoning, and land use requirements to keep Negroes from entering all-white communities.

(*c*) Federal housing policy has contributed to racial segregation in metropolitan areas through past discriminatory practices. Present nondiscrimination policies and laws are insufficient to counteract the effects of past policy.

(*d*) Laws and policies governing low- and moderate-income housing programs, including public housing, the FHA 221 (d) (3) program, and the rent supplement program, serve to confine the poor and the nonwhite to the central city. Under each of these programs, suburban jurisdictions hold a special veto power.

4. Racial and economic isolation between city and suburban school systems is reinforced by disparities of wealth between cities and suburbs and the manner in which schools are financed.

(*a*) Schools are financed by property tax levies which make education dependent on the wealth of the community.

(*b*) Suburbs with increasing industry and increasing numbers of affluent people have a large tax base and are able to finance their schools with less effort.

(*c*) Cities with shrinking industry, a disproportionate share of the poor, and increasing costs for non-educational services to both residents and nonresidents, are less able to provide the required revenue for schools.

(*d*) State educational aid for schools, though designed to equalize, often does not succeed in closing the gap between city and suburban school districts.

(*e*) Federal aid at present levels in most instances is insufficient to close the gap between central city school districts and those of more affluent suburbs.

(*f*) These disparities provide further inducement to many white families to leave the city.

Racial Isolation and the Central City

5. Within cities, as within metropolitan areas, there is a high degree of residential segregation—reflected in the schools—for which responsibility is shared by both the private housing industry and government.

(*a*) The discriminatory practices of city landlords, lending institutions, and real estate brokers have contributed to the residential confinement of Negroes.

(*b*) State and local governments have contributed to the pattern of increasing residential segregation through such past discriminatory practices as racial zoning ordinances and racially restrictive covenants capable of judicial enforcement. Current practices in such matters as the location of low-rent public housing projects, and the displacement of large numbers of low-income nonwhite families through local improvement programs also are intensifying residential segregation.

(*c*) Federal housing programs and policies serve to intensify racial concentrations in cities. Federal policies governing low- and moderate-income housing programs such as low-rent public housing and FHA 221 (d) (3) do not promote the location of housing outside areas of intense racial concentration. Federal urban renewal policy is insufficiently concerned with the impact of relocation on racial concentrations within cities.

6. Individual choice contributes to the maintenance of residential segregation, although the impact of such choice is difficult to assess since the housing market has been restricted.

7. In all central cities, as compared to their suburbs, nonpublic schools absorb a disproportionately large segment of the white school population; nonwhites, however, whether in city or suburbs, attend public schools almost exclusively.

Educational Policies and Practices

8. The policies and practices of city school systems have a marked impact on the racial composition of schools.

(*a*) Geographical zoning, the most commonly used form of student assignment in northern cities, has contributed to the creation and maintenance of racially and socially homogeneous schools.

(*b*) School authorities exercise broad discretion in determining school attendance areas, which in most communities are not prescribed by reference to well-defined neighborhoods or by specific guidelines based on the optimum size of schools.

(*c*) In determining such discretionary matters as the location and size of schools, and the boundaries of attendance areas, the decisions of school officials may serve either to intensify or reduce racial concentrations. Although there have been only a few instances where purposeful segregation has been judicially determined to exist in the North, apparently neutral decisions by school officials in these areas frequently have had the effect of reinforcing racial separation of students.

(*d*) In Southern and border cities, similar decisions of school officials, combined with a high degree of residential racial concentration and remnants of legally compelled segregation, have had the effect of perpetuating racial isolation in the schools.

RACIAL ISOLATION AND THE OUTCOMES OF EDUCATION

1. There are marked disparities in the outcomes of education for Negro and white Americans. Negro students typically do not achieve as well in school as white students. The longer they are in school the further they fall behind. Negroes are enrolled less often in college than whites and are much more likely to attend high schools which send a relatively small proportion of their graduates

to college. Negroes with college education are less likely than similarly educated whites to be employed in white-collar trades. Negroes with college education earn less on the average than high-school educated whites. These disparities result, in part, from factors that influence the achievement, aspirations, and attitudes of school children.

2. There is a strong relationship between the achievement and attitudes of a school child and the economic circumstances and educational background of his family. Relevant factors that contribute to this relationship include the material deprivation and inadequate health care that children from backgrounds of poverty often experience, the fact that disadvantaged children frequently have less facility in verbal and written communication—the chief vehicle by which schools measure student achievement—and the inability of parents in poor neighborhoods to become as involved in school affairs and affect school policy as much as more affluent parents.

3. The social class of a student's schoolmates—as measured by the economic circumstances and educational background of their families—also strongly influences his achievement and attitudes. Regardless of his own family background, an individual student achieves better in schools where most of his fellow students are from advantaged backgrounds than in schools where most of his fellow students are from disadvantaged backgrounds. The relationship between a student's achievement and the social class composition of his school grows stronger as the student progresses through school.

4. Negro students are much more likely than white students to attend schools in which a majority of the students are disadvantaged. The social class composition of the schools is more important to the achievement and attitudes of Negro students than whites.

5. There are noticeable differences in the quality of schools which Negroes attend and those which whites attend. Negro students are less likely than whites to attend schools that have well-stocked libraries. Negro students also are less likely to attend schools which offer advanced courses in subjects such as science and languages and are more likely to be in overcrowded schools than white students. There is some relationship between such disparities and the achievement of Negro students.

6. The quality of teaching has an important influence on the achievement of students, both advantaged and disadvantaged. Negro students are more likely than white students to have teachers with low verbal achievement, to have substitute teachers, and to have teachers who are dissatisfied with their school assignment.

7. The relationship between the quality of teaching and the achievement of Negro students generally is greater in majority-Negro schools than in majority-white schools. Negro students in majority-white schools with poorer teachers generally achieve better than similar Negro students in majority-Negro schools with better teachers.

8. There is also a relationship between the racial composition of schools and the achievement and attitudes of most Negro students, which exists when all other factors are taken into account.

(a) Disadvantaged Negro students in school with a majority of equally disadvantaged white students achieve better than Negro students in school with a majority of equally disadvantaged Negro students.

(b) Differences are even greater when disadvantaged Negro students in school with a majority of disadvantaged Negro students are compared with similarly disadvantaged Negro students in school with a majority of advantaged white students. The difference in achievement for 12th-grade students amounts to more than two entire grade levels.

(c) Negroes in predominantly Negro schools tend to have lower educational aspirations and more frequently express a sense of inability to influence their futures by their own choices than Negro students with similar backgrounds attending majority-white schools. Their fellow students are less likely to offer academic stimulation.

(d) Predominantly Negro schools generally are regarded by the community as inferior institutions. Negro students in such schools are sensitive to such views and often come to share them. Teachers and administrative staff frequently recognize or share the community's view and communicate it to the students. This stigma affects the achievement and attitudes of Negro students.

9. The effects of racial composition of schools are cumulative. The longer Negro students are in desegregated schools, the better is their academic achievement and their attitudes. Conversely, there is a growing deficit for Negroes who remain in racially isolated schools.

10. Racial isolation in school limits job opportunities for Negroes. In general, Negro adults who attended desegregated schools tend to have higher incomes and more often fill white-collar jobs than Negro adults who went to racially isolated schools.

11. Racial isolation is self-perpetuating. School attendance in racial isolation generates attitudes on the part of both Negroes and whites which tend to alienate them from members of the other race. These attitudes are reflected in behavior. Negroes who attended majority-white schools are more likely to reside in interracial neighborhoods, to have children in majority-white schools, and to have white friends. Similarly, white persons who attended school with Negroes are more likely to live in an interracial neighborhood, to have children who attend school with Negroes, and to have Negro friends.

REMEDY:
COMPENSATORY PROGRAMS IN ISOLATED SCHOOLS

1. Evaluations of programs of compensatory education conducted in schools that are isolated by race and social class suggest that these programs have not had lasting effects in improving the achievement of the students. The evidence indicates that Negro children attending desegregated schools that do not have compensatory education programs perform better than Negro children in racially isolated schools with such programs.

2. Compensatory education programs have been of limited effectiveness because they have attempted to solve problems that stem, in large part, from racial and social class isolation in schools which themselves are isolated by race and social class.

3. Large-scale increases in expenditures for remedial techniques, such as those used in preschool projects funded under the Head Start Program, which improve teaching and permit more attention to the individual needs of children, undoubtedly would be helpful to many students, although it is uncertain that they could overcome the problems of racial and social class isolation.

4. Compensatory education programs on the present scale are unlikely to improve significantly the achievement of Negro students isolated by race and social class.

DESEGREGATION

5. Several small cities and suburban communities have desegregated their schools effectively. Although a variety of techniques have been used in these communities, a major part of each plan has been the enlargement of attendance areas. Desegregation generally has been accepted as successful by these communities.

6. Factors contributing to successful school desegregation include the exercise of strong leadership by State and local officials to help implement desegregation, the involvement of all schools in the community, the desegregation of classes within desegregated schools, steps to avoid the possibility of interracial friction, and the provision of remedial assistance to children who need it. The available evidence suggests that the academic achievement of white students in desegregated classrooms generally does not suffer by comparison with the achievement of such students in all-white classrooms. Steps have been taken in communities that have desegregated their schools successfully to maintain or improve educational standards. There is also evidence that non-academic benefits accrue to white students who attend desegregated schools.

7. The techniques employed by large city school systems generally have not produced any substantial school desegregation.

(a) Techniques such as open enrollment which do not involve the alteration of attendance areas have not produced significant school desegregation. The effectiveness of open enrollment is limited significantly by the availability of space in majority-white schools and the requirement in many cases that parents initiate transfer requests and pay transportation costs. Open enrollment also does not result in desegregation of majority-Negro schools.

(b) Other techniques which do involve the alteration of attendance areas, such as school pairing, have not been as successful in producing desegregation in large cities as in smaller cities.

8. The large proportion of Negro children in many central city school systems makes effective desegregation possible only with the cooperation of suburban school systems.

9. Programs involving urban-suburban cooperation in the desegregation of schools, while only beginning and presently very limited, show promise as techniques for desegregating the schools in the Nation's larger metropolitan areas.

10. In large cities, promising proposals have been developed which seek to desegregate schools by broadening attendance areas so that school populations will be more representative of the community as a whole and to improve the quality of education by providing additional resources and innovations in the educational program.

(*a*) Proposals for educational facilities such as supplementary education centers and magnet schools, which contemplate a system of specialized school programs located either in existing schools or in new facilities, and education complexes, which would consist of clusters of existing schools reorganized to provide centralized services for schoolchildren in an enlarged attendance area, would contribute to improving the quality of education and would provide some progress in school desegregation.

(*b*) Proposals for education parks, designed to improve the quality of education and desegregate the schools by providing new centralized school facilities serving a range of grade levels in a single campus, are most promising. Such parks could contribute to improving the quality of education by permitting advances and innovations in educational techniques not possible in smaller schools and could facilitate desegregation by enlarging attendance areas, in some cases to draw students both from the central city and the suburbs. Although legitimate concerns have been raised about the size and complexity of education parks, the new and flexible approaches to teaching and learning they would make possible could provide greater individual attention for each child's needs than is now possible in smaller schools. Additional problems relating to the cost and feasibility of education parks can be met in some measure by the economies which are made possible by the consolidation of resources in larger facilities. Although education parks would require a substantial new investment, it is within the range of what is feasible if the costs are shared by the Federal, State, and local governments.

RACIAL ISOLATION: THE ROLE OF THE LAW

1. Purposeful school segregation—violative of the Constitution —has occurred in Northern cities.

2. It remains an open question whether school segregation

which is not imposed by purposeful action of school authorities violates the Constitution. The Supreme Court of the United States has not resolved the issue.

3. The courts consistently have upheld State or local action to eliminate or alleviate racial isolation in the public schools against the charge that it is unconstitutional to consider race in formulating school board policies. Only a few States have taken any action to require local school authorities to remedy racial isolation in their schools.

4. Congress has passed legislation aimed at eliminating racial discrimination in the assignment of children to public schools, but this legislation does not appear to dictate the application of sanctions not involving purposeful discrimination.

5. Congress has the power to enact legislation to remedy the inequality of educational opportunity to which Negro students are subjected by being assigned to racially isolated schools.

6. Congress, with its ability to appropriate funds, is the branch of Government best able to assure quality education and equal educational opportunity.

RECOMMENDATIONS

Without attempting to outline needed legislation in great detail, our study of the problem convinces the Commission that new legislation must embody the following essential principles:

1. *Congress should establish a uniform standard providing for the elimination of racial isolation in the schools.* Since large numbers of Negro children suffer harmful effects that are attributable in part to the racial composition of schools they attend, legislation should provide for the elimination of schools in which such harm generally occurs. No standard of general applicability will fit every case precisely; some schools with a large proportion of Negro students may not in fact produce harmful effects while others with a smaller proportion may be schools in which students are disadvantaged because of their race. But the alternative to establishing such a standard is to require a time-consuming and ineffective effort to determine on a case-by-case basis the schools in which harm occurs.

As it has in analogous situations, Congress should deal with this problem by establishing reasonable and practical standards which will correct the injustice without intruding unnecessarily into areas where no corrective action is needed.

In prescribing a reasonable standard, there is much to commend the criterion already adopted by the legislature in Massachusetts and the Commissioner of Education of New York, defining as racially imbalanced, schools in which Negro pupils constitute more than 50 percent of the total enrollment. It was found in this report that when Negro students in schools with more than 50 percent Negro enrollment were compared with similarly situated Negro students in schools with a majority-white enrollment, there were significant differences in attitude and performance. It is the schools that have a majority-Negro enrollment that tend to be regarded and treated by the community as segregated and inferior schools. Although there are many factors involved, the racial composition of schools that are majority-Negro in enrollment tends to be less stable than that of majority-white schools and to be subject to more rapid change.

Similar arguments might be advanced for a standard which would deviate slightly from a 50-percent criterion, but a standard set significantly higher would not be adequate to deal with the problem and probably would not result in lasting solutions.

2. *Congress should vest in each of the 50 States responsibility for meeting the standard it establishes and should allow the States maximum flexibility in devising appropriate remedies. It also should provide financial and technical assistance to the States in planning such remedies.* It would be unwise for the Federal Government to attempt to prescribe any single solution or set of solutions for the entire Nation. There is a broad range of techniques which are capable of achieving education of high quality in integrated public schools. Each State should be free to adopt solutions best suited to the particular needs of its individual communities.

At the same time it is clear that the responsibility should be placed upon the States rather than the individual school districts. The States, and not individual communities alone, have the capacity to develop and implement plans adequate to the objective. The States have assumed the responsibility for providing public education for all of their citizens and for establishing the basic conditions under which it is offered. Responsibility for achieving the goal of high-quality integrated education can and should be placed upon the States under terms which afford broad scope for local initiative. But in many jurisdictions, particularly the major cities, solutions are not possible without the cooperation of neighboring communities. The States possess the authority and the means for securing co-operation, by consolidating or reorganizing school districts or by providing for appropriate joint arrangements between school districts.

To help the States in devising appropriate remedies, the Federal Government should provide technical and financial assistance.

3. *The legislation should include programs of substantial financial assistance to provide for construction of new facilities and improvement in the quality of education in all schools.* In many cases, particularly in the major cities, integrating the public schools will require the construction of new facilities designed both to serve a larger student population and to be accessible to all children in the area to be served. Substantial Federal assistance is needed to supplement the resources of States and localities in building new schools of this kind and providing higher quality education for all children. Federal assistance also can be helpful in encouraging cooperative arrangements between States which provide education services to the same metropolitan area and between separate school districts in a metropolitan area. In addition, Federal financial assistance now available under programs such as aid for mass transportation and community facilities should be utilized in ways which will advance the goal of integration.

Regardless of whether the achievement of integration requires new facilities, Federal financial assistance is needed for programs to improve the quality of education. States and localities should have broad discretion to develop programs best suited to their needs. Programs that are among the most promising involve steps—such as the reduction of pupil-teacher ratios, the establishment of ungraded classes and team teaching, and the introduction of specialized remedial instruction—which enable teachers to give more attention to the individual needs of children. Funds also could be used for purposes such as assisting the training of teachers, developing new educational techniques, and improving curriculum.

4. *Congress should provide for adequate time in which to accomplish the objectives of the legislation.* It is clear that equal opportunity in education cannot be achieved overnight. Particularly in the large cities where problems of providing equal educational opportunity have seemed so intractable, time will be necessary for such matters as educational and physical planning, assembling and acquiring land, and building new facilities. However, since the problem is urgent a prompt start must be made toward finding solutions, progress must be continuous and substantial, and there must be some assurance that the job will be completed as quickly as possible. The time has come to put less emphasis on "deliberate" and more on "speed."

❖   ❖   ❖

The goals of equal educational opportunity and equal housing opportunity are inseparable. Progress toward the achievement of one goal necessarily will facilitate achievement of the other. Failure to make progress toward the achievement of either goal will handicap efforts to achieve the other. *The Commission recommends, therefore, that the President and Congress give consideration to legislation which will:*

5. *Prohibit discrimination in the sale or rental of housing, and*

6. *Expand programs of Federal assistance designed to increase the supply of housing throughout metropolitan areas within the means of low- and moderate-income families.* Additional funds should be provided for programs such as the rent supplement program and FHA 221 (d) (3), and these two programs should be amended to permit private enterprise to participate in them free from the special veto power now held by local governments under present Federal statutes.

In addition, *the Commission recommends that the Department of Housing and Urban Development:*

7. *Require as a condition for approval of applications for low- and moderate-income housing projects that the sites will be selected and the projects planned in a nondiscriminatory manner that will contribute to reducing residential racial concentrations and eliminating racial isolation in the schools.*

8. *Require as a condition for approval of urban renewal projects that relocation will be planned in a nondiscriminatory manner that will contribute to reducing residential racial concentrations and eliminating racial isolation in the schools.*

SCHOOL DESEGREGATION AND THE SUPERINTENDENT

by Morton Inger and Robert T. Stout*

School desegregation is dead—at least temporarily—at least in the opinion of some observers. And white opposition is frequently cited as the reason for its demise. The findings of research conducted by the present authors suggest that this opposition, though unmistakably present, could not have been the cause of the demise. It could not, because it was not even the main cause of the defeat or the delay of desegregation plans.[1] What is more, in the opinion of the authors, the reports of the death of integration are greatly exaggerated.

In view of what were (and are) believed to be the prevailing white attitudes toward Negroes and toward integration, the response of whites in the eight cities studied was surprising. In four of the cities, there was either no conflict or else the opposition took forms—such as legal action—which helped to legitimate the school system's integration plan. In the other four cities, there was active opposition (in varying amounts), but the school system in all four

* From *The Urban Review*, November 1968.
[1] The eight cities studied were Berkeley, California; Coatesville, Pennsylvania; Englewood, New Jersey; Greenburgh School District #8 (Westchester County, New York); Rochester, New York; Syracuse, New York; Teaneck, New Jersey; and White Plains, New York. The cut-off date for the study was October 1966. Except for the case of Rochester, our remarks are confined to events occurring prior to October 1966.

except Englewood was able to retain control of the situation. (Please note that we are talking here about the absence or presence of open conflict, not mere dissatisfaction. In all eight cities there was dissatisfaction.) In seven of the eight cities, even including Englewood, the community ultimately accepted the school system's plan. The exception is Syracuse, but the school administration's plan was withdrawn because of opposition by the city's *Negro* leaders.

During the period studied—the mid 1960s—school integration was perhaps the chief demand of the civil rights movement, and school administrators greatly feared the issue. They thought whites would be so aroused over integration that they would rebel against the school system in general and refuse to support needed bond issues, and, in the case of elected school boards, turn the incumbents out of office. Certainly, this happened in some cities. But our study indicated that this need not happen. It depends to a great extent on how the school leaders handle the issue. If the issue is presented and handled properly, we have evidence that the white community not only can accept the desegregation plan but will subsequently give positive support to the school system and its financial needs.

Boston, Chicago, Cleveland, Oakland, and Buffalo are vivid examples of cities whose school systems were believed by school administrators and others to have been hurt in general by the school desegregation issue. No realistic educator would willingly subject his school system to the strains and wrenches experienced by the school systems in those cities. A public controversy is anathema to the school administrator. Like any administrator, he prefers to 'get on with his work.' But from 1960 through 1966, it was difficult if not impossible for a school system to avoid the issue of school desegregation. Despite the impression one may have received from newspaper accounts, some cities achieved desegregation without experiencing harmful public conflict.

What distinguished the successful school systems from the unsuccessful ones? (Success here being defined as the ability to achieve school desegregation without disrupting the school system.) To begin with, the troubled cities (those that did not achieve desegregation and experienced public disruption of the school system) had school superintendents who took the stand that desegregation was not an essential educational goal. In some of those cities, and in other cities that achieved desegregation only after great delay and cost, the school officials asked the public—through referenda and the submission of the issue to *ad hoc* citizens committees—what *they* thought about the question. This was an indication that the school officials did not believe that integration was a proper educational goal, for few school systems ask the voters to decide educational matters as they arise. In Buffalo, in 1964, when the school system went to the public with the issue of the racial composition of a new school, the result was the adoption of a proposal for a school *more* segregated than even the most ardent neighborhood-school advocates on the board had hoped to achieve.

In the four cities that achieved desegregation with little difficulty, the school officials were convinced that integration was an important goal of the public schools. In two of these four cities, the superintendent went beyond this and proclaimed integration to be a moral necessity. White Plains superintendent Dr. Carroll Johnson could see no reason for submitting the issue to the voters. "Who would ask for a show of hands on a moral issue?" he explained. In an official statement, Rochester superintendent Herman Goldberg announced that segregation was *the* problem with education in Rochester. In addition, he made many public appearances arguing the moral and educational rightness of integration. School integration in Greenburgh School District #8 (Westchester County, New York) began in 1951 as an *educational* necessity for the community. Since that time, the superintendent and school board have become committed to 'heterogeneous' education (i.e., racial and achievement mixtures in the classroom) as a goal in itself. Even in Coatesville, Pennsylvania, where the school board and superintendent exerted little leadership to achieve desegregation and seemed relatively uncommitted to the idea, the school system moved rapidly to desegregate because of the school board's conviction that desegregation was the law of the land. In a fifth city, Berkeley, which differs from the above four in that it achieved desegregation only after a long and bitter public fight, the school board tried as much as possible to leave the issue up to citizens committees. Nevertheless, the Berkeley school staff helped CORE present its statement on de facto segregation (and actually found more segregation than CORE knew about), the school superintendent said that integration was good in itself and needed no further justification, and the desegregation plan was presented to the public as an *education* plan.

Indeed, the differences among the eight cities can be seen as differences in the way the school systems presented their plans to the public. The eight cities range from Englewood (where first the school officials and later the city administration asked the community to vote on how and whether to integrate) to White Plains, where the school administration worked skillfully to keep the issue from ever going to the public. It is relatively easy to rank these eight cities ranging from (top) the ones with the greatest noise level over school integration to the cities (bottom) in which there was virtually no conflict.

If we rank the eight cities on the extent to which the school system opened the issue to the public, we see a striking similarity to the first ranking.

Extent of open conflict and difficulty in obtaining acceptance	Extent to which the schools opened the issue to the public
high	
Englewood	Englewood
Berkeley	Berkeley
Teaneck	Syracuse
Syracuse	Teaneck
Coatesville	Coatesville
Rochester	Rochester
Greenburgh	Greenburgh
White Plains	White Plains
low	*high* ... *low*

Despite many differences between these cities, the school systems that opened the issue to the public the most had the greatest difficulty in obtaining community acceptance. The ones that opened the issue the least had the least difficulty in obtaining acceptance.

To explain our ranking of the cities on their opening the issue to the public:

Englewood is at the top because of the repeated polling of the public.

Berkeley is ranked second because of the school board's constant referral of the issue to citizens committees.

Syracuse is third because, among other things, the school board's vacillation and indecision drew into the issue many public voices during the policy formation stage.

Teaneck and *Coatesville* clearly belong in the middle, with perhaps Teaneck being placed higher than Coatesville. The Coatesville school board opened up the issue by asking the PTAs to suggest plans for the integration of the schools; no specific plan was suggested by the school board or the superintendent. On the other hand, when the PTA majority urged the board to fight any attempt to integrate, the school board went ahead and integrated anyway. The Teaneck board publicly announced its intention to come up with an integration plan, asked the public for suggestions, and made frequent, heated appearances before public forums on the issue. A clash at one of these forums led one of the neighborhood-school proponents to decide to run for the school board against the 'integrationists.' Yet, unlike the Coatesville board, which never did come up with a plan of its own but adopted the plan suggested by the PTA minority, the Teaneck school board made its own decisions and plans and went against the open hostility of a large and vocal segment of the public and community leaders.

The remaining three cities clearly belong at the 'absence of public referral' end of the table:

In *Rochester*, for the period studied by the authors (that is, prior to 1967), the school board and superintendent made all decisions without referring the question to the public. (As we shall discuss more fully below Rochester's superintendent made an abrupt change in tactics in 1967, putting the issue of whether and how to the public.)

Greenburgh and *White Plains* run a close race for the position of opening up the issue the least, but we believe White Plains stands by itself because of the finesse with which community organizations were co-opted by the school officials and community acceptance was won.

We have considered and rejected the possibility that the *reason* some cities opened up the issue more than others was that they had more opposition. Such a premise is based, in part, on the assumption that the cities with the least open conflict were somehow made up of nicer, more liberal people who would not oppose integration. This notion is not totally supported by the evidence. In all eight cities large numbers of citizens expressed their dissatisfaction with the very notion of integration as well as with the specific plans under consideration.

One lesson of these eight cities is clear. The less the public is asked for its opinion during the period of policy-formation, the greater the likelihood that the public will accept the integration plan. One can pick cities from any point in the scale and find support for this argument. White Plains is especially 'satisfactory' because community acceptance was won from a rebellious community which, one year earlier had twice decided that the schools were already spending too much money.

Coatesville, too, is a good example because, even though the school board went against the opinion of the community organization from which it had solicited suggestions, the community accepted the integration plan without incident. (And this in a city with many Southern rural mores!)

Teaneck is another good example, for despite the vitriolic open conflict *while the board members were making up their minds,* the community quietly accepted the integration plan once it was put into effect. Thirty neighborhood-school advocates tried to get a boycott started, but their own friends dissuaded them.

Even Englewood is a good example. Despite the openness of the conflict, despite the militancy of the civil rights movement, once the school system adopted a plan and put it into effect, the community accepted it without incident.

Because Rochester's superintendent changed tactics in 1967, that city provides a sharp illustration of the point we are making.[2] From 1963 through 1966, the Rochester school system made progress toward integrating its all-white and predominantly white schools. All steps taken were made by the school officials and school board members without referring the question to the public. Except for a few easily handled legal challenges, the Rochester citizenry quietly accepted all the steps taken by the school system. So successful (in their limited way) were these steps and so committed did the superintendent and the school board seem, that the United States Commission on Civil Rights chose Rochester for the location of hearings on school desegregation in the fall of 1966. Yet, in response to his own school board's unanimous directive (May 1966) to have ready by February 1967 a plan for the desegregation of all of Rochester's elementary schools, the superintendent did *not*

[2] As we have indicated, our study ended as of October 1966. Our information on Rochester since that date was obtained by Morton Inger while working in the Center for Urban Education's Rochester project, directed by Dr. Gladys E. Lang. See *Resistance and Support for School Desegregation Proposals: A Study of Parental Reactions in Rochester,* by Gladys E. Lang, Morton Inger, and Roy Mallett (Center for Urban Education, 1967). The interpretation of the Rochester events expressed herein is that of the authors of the present article and should not be ascribed to the Center or to Dr. Lang.

adopt a plan. Instead, he broadcast four plans to the public without indicating any moral or educational necessity for adopting any particular plan. Thus having been asked *whether* as well as how to integrate, Rochester's white citizens—some of them, anyhow—expressed their strong opposition to the idea of cross-busing. Six weeks after the superintendent threw the plans out to the public, the school board, which had ordered a plan, rejected all four desegregation plans.

Although an argument could be made that the public opposition arose because the rejected plans were more far-reaching than the earlier steps which had been accepted, we believe the earlier steps would have been rejected as well, had they been placed before the voters without the educators having argued strongly for their acceptance. The experience of the other cities indicates that it is not the size of the step taken but the way it is presented that elicits widespread, active opposition. When Berkeley's small step—to desegregate just one junior high—was opened to the public, intense opposition forced the board into a bitter recall election. When Teaneck opened up its decision, there was great trouble, but when the board closed it down—*not reducing the plan,* but taking responsibility for the decision—the trouble ended.

Contrary to the fears of schoolmen that a school system could not escape being hurt if the integration issue came up, in all eight cities the public—as of our cut-off date of October 1966—had not only accepted the system's integration steps but had supported bond issues and reelected the school board members who had taken these steps.[3] When school board elections occurred *before* implementation of a plan, incumbent school board members did not fare well. But when the elections occurred *after* implementation, the incumbents were re-elected. The other side of the coin can be seen in Rochester. So long as Rochester's school board was strongly urging desegregation and implementing desegregation plans without consulting with the public, the school board members were easily re-elected. But after the board *retreated* from its stand, a neighborhood school advocate was elected to the board for the first time.

The hallmark of these success stories is that the school officials

[3] Though Syracuse's integration *plan* had to be withdrawn, all the *steps* it had taken were accepted by the public.

presented desegregation as a proper goal of the educational system and, in some cities, as an educationally beneficial change. In the cities where acceptance was won with the least conflict, an additional key element is that the public was not asked for its prior approval. The important consequence of this form of presentation is that the issue did not become a battle between Negroes and whites.

In Chicago, Cleveland, Boston, Buffalo, and some Southern cities, the school issue stirred up a battle between the civil rights organizations and the whites who are opposed to integration. In our eight cities, by contrast, the school system adopted integration as its own goal, thereby giving legitimation to the idea. If a battle arose in these cities, it was between an accepted governmental body and a group of dissident citizens.[4] It is important to note, in this connection, that even the relatively uncommitted Coatesville school board told the community that segregation was in violation of the law of the land and indicated its intention to desegregate *before* it even had a plan. It was only after the Coatesville board made its intentions clear that it went to the community for suggestions. Thus, the people of Coatesville were asked for suggestions in the context of governmental (the school board) approval of integration. The people of Coatesville, then, were not asked for a show of hands on integration. This would explain why the Coatesville School Board was not deterred by the PTA vote against integration; the school board had already made its decision.

In Teaneck, the school board was uncommitted to any specific integration plan. Indeed, the Teaneck board did not agree on a plan until two nights before the meeting at which they formally adopted it. This uncertainty, which was known to the public, did have the effect, as we have noted, of opening up the issue and making it a public controversy. An election campaign for the school board was fought out over the issue; and when work leaked out that the board had agreed on a plan, three councilmen crashed an executive session of the board to protest their decision. At the public meeting the next night, 1,400 people (estimated to be 3 to 1 against the plan) crowded into the meeting room, shouting and shaking their fists. Overwhelmed by the commotion, the board members called a five

---

[4] Syracuse and Englewood witnessed a battle between white and Negro groups; but in these two cities the battle was over specific integration plans, not over whether to integrate or not.

minute recess to collect themselves; they then came back and adopted the plan by a vote of 7 to 2.

From that point on, any community response had to be to a governmental decision. Governmental decisions are legitimate; for many people, this is enough to settle the issue. For the committed opponents, the road of opposition is difficult. This was clearly the case in Teaneck, for the outburst at the school board meeting was the last open attack on the Teaneck school board. The opponents filed law suits (and lost) and conducted a vigorous election campaign a year later. The legitimating effect of the governmental decision can be seen by comparing that election with the school board election which was held while the board was still making up its mind. In February 1964, while the board was still uncertain, two proponents of the neighborhood school 'concept' were elected to the board, while one incumbent who was known to be favoring the superintendent's integration plans squeaked past a third pro-neighborhood school candidate by only 21 votes. To indicate the virulence of the feelings in Teaneck at that time, one of the pro-neighborhood school candidates told the superintendent during the campaign, "I know you're not a Communist, but you talk like one, you act like one, and you propose policies the Communists favor." That candidate was elected. But in the election *following* the adoption of the integration plan, all three candidates favoring the board's integration plan defeated the three neighborhood-school candidates by a 7 to 5 margin.

The importance of governmental action as a legitimating force can be seen further in the matter of attitudes toward integration. In three of our cities—Syracuse, Englewood, and Coatesville—the school board members were unanimous in their negative feelings toward civil rights demonstrations, yet they approved of integration. It is generally believed that the public as a whole *dislikes* civil rights marches and school boycotts and integration, but our study indicates that when the issue is presented in a certain way, the public *accepts* integration. Apparently, the community tends to accept the idea if it comes from a legitimate governmental body such as the school board. The significant task for government, then, would be to prevent race relations from becoming simply a conflict between 'those Negroes' and 'us whites.'

When the government opposes integration, as superintendent Benjamin Willis did in Chicago, or abstains from the issue and defers to the public, as the city government did in New Orleans from 1956 to 1961 and as the school board and superintendent did in Buffalo at one point, integration is robbed of legitimacy, and the issue becomes a matter of competing demonstrations. When the school systems in Syracuse and Englewood referred the issue to the public at critical points, the void left by the abstention of the government was filled by competing white and Negro groups. The conflict that emerges from such confrontations frightens most people away, and many whites say no to the whole disturbance, including the idea of integration which 'caused' it.

By contrast, the *actions* of the board in Rochester, White Plains, Greenburgh, and Coatesville were accepted by the public. Integration in these cities was achieved not by demonstrations and boycotts but by legitimate school officials who promoted it in the name of educational and moral values. Consequently, the actions taken by these school boards, though not exactly what the public would have demanded if they had been asked what to do, were accepted by the public.

Does this analysis speak against democracy? We think not. We are not advocating secrecy in government or deals made behind closed doors. Although we feel that public leaders should not ask the people what to do, we do believe they should say what they did and why. More specifically, asking the public what to do on issues as they arise is a particularly dangerous thing for a *school official* to do.

School administrators and—in most cities—school board members are not politicians. Hence, they can make no demands upon the parties or their leaders. Yet, being in the public sphere, they are subject to demands from all sectors of the community. The consequence is that school governing bodies are unprotected from mass grievances. Furthermore, not being politicians, school officials are not skilled at 'reading' the grievances. That is, they can not discriminate among the many voices they hear. Is the man or the group who shouts the loudest the one you should listen to? What is the significance of a petition bearing 6,000 signatures opposing desegregation? A political leader with a ward organization can answer these questions, but a school administrator or board member has only hunches—and these are the hunches of amateurs.

There *is* a way for schoolmen to go to the public: to act and later stand for re-election. Schoolmen who ask the public what decisions they should make—especially on such a hot issue as desegregation—risk the incapacitation of the school system. Furthermore, this violates the trust of the public, for these men were elected (or appointed by elected officials) to govern the schools.

Why did the eight communities we studied accept the plans and re-elect the officials responsible for them? The citizens in these cities are certainly no more liberal on race relations than the citizens in most other cities. The answer must be that the people in these cities were satisfied with the men and the desegregation policies. Democracy does not mean that all the people make all the decisions. The fundamental requirements of democracy are met if the people have ample opportunity to influence or unseat the decision makers, if those who govern can be held accountable by the people. Actual day-to-day decisions are left to representatives of the people, who expect these representatives to 'get on with it' without referring all the decisions to them. In fact, democracy is served when the representative accepts responsibility for the decisions. The people of Englewood and Syracuse wanted the same things the people in the other cities wanted: peace, progress, and prosperity. By dodging responsibility and asking the people how and whether to integrate, the officials of Syracuse and Englewood failed to give their citizens what they wanted. The officials in the other cities desegregated the schools (in varying degrees), kept the peace, and were able to get on with other fundamental educational problems.

By way of a summary, we offer the following advice to school officials. If you will treat integration as a routine educational matter and proceed to implement your integration plan without asking for a show of hands, the community will accept the steps you take. Furthermore, integration is not dead. So long as America remains a plural nation, integration shall remain a continuing *internal* need, one that is not dependent upon the demands of individuals and groups. Certain *groups* may no longer speak as though they want integration, but the *nation* needs integration as much as it ever did.

PART II

Intelligence and Testing: Labels and Expectations

The issue of genetic intelligence continues to raise its head in discussions of equal educational opportunity. For a long time the issue was laid to rest, at least in the North, by the Supreme Court decision on segregated schools and by the growing public awareness that segregation and deprivation, rather than lack of native intelligence, was responsible for the failure of many students in school. In the South and other places, the issue has always been an active one.

Through Arthur R. Jensen, educational psychologist at the University of California, the issue has been revived and given national attention. In particular, the American Educational Research Association (NEA) and the *Harvard Educational Review* have given his views a wide general audience. These views were especially noted by many people who assumed that efforts at compensatory education had failed and, moreover, could not possibly succeed. The failure, they seem ready to assume, must lie in the disadvantaged child's inferior genetic intelligence and in his consequent inability to learn as others do. In this view, it is inequality in the native ability of children, rather than the inequality of schools or society, that determines the success or failure of students.

Since the *Harvard Educational Review* would not grant permission to reprint any part of the article appearing in that journal, that article is of necessity omitted here. In any event, it would fill much of this volume in its original form. Instead, this volume contains an article by Phillip Whitten and Jerome Kagan, and Dr. Jensen's response in *Psychology Today* to comments on that article. Comments from three other sources are also included to give the reader some idea of the nature of the controversy. These are: Grace Rubin-Rabson, "Behavioral Science Versus Intelligence" (*The Wall Street Journal*); the present author's comments on a volume by David A. Goslin (*American Sociological Review*); and psychologist J. P. Guilford, "Intelligence Has Three Facets" (*Science*).

Among the issues raised are the validity of IQ tests as measures of native, genetic ability, the extraordinary complexity of human intelligence, the significant improvement in IQ scores among all racial groups over the years, the serious social, psychological, and environmental handicaps of low-income groups and racial minorities, the dangers of generalizing about racial characteristics, and the successes of compensatory education programs. The reader should be warned that some of the technical issues raised by J. P. Guilford will require close and patient attention.

Tests of ability are used by the schools to sort out students, label them, and make certain predictions about their prospects for academic success. This author's comments in "Measures of Worth" deal with some of the uses to which tests of various kinds are put in the schools. Joseph Lederer describes the "sorting out process" and the scope of tracking and of ability and homogeneous grouping in the nation's schools. Mainly he is concerned with the "possible effect on teacher expectation of a whole gamut of institutionalized practices," including grouping, testing, and permanent records of students.

Dr. Robert Coles carries the issue a step further in his review of the work on teacher expectations of Robert Rosenthal and Lenore Jacobson. Dr. Coles, undoubtedly one of the great men of our times, takes a favorable view of this research and of the power of teacher expectation and the child's own concept of his ability to learn. To be sure, research of this kind on expectations is pioneering and, therefore, also rather tentative. It does suggest, however, that the sorting out process and teacher expectations can also provide formidable barriers to student achievement.

The sorting out process is not an incidental matter for students. It affects the child's image of himself. Put in low-ability groups, he is likely to see himself as stupid—or conversely smart, if put into top-ability groups. In the low groups, he is likely to be slighted academically and prepared for a relatively low occupational position in later life. In brief, this sorting very much influences what a student learns, what he thinks of himself, and what he will be in later life.

In the Washington, D.C., schools, Federal Appeals Judge J. Skelly Wright held that the practice of tracking students into totally separate groups based on tested ability violated their constitutional rights. His opinion was upset but not before it had deeply shaken the confidence of many parents and educators in these accepted grouping practices.

JENSEN'S DANGEROUS HALF-TRUTH

by Phillip Whitten and Jerome Kagan*

"Compensatory education has been tried and it apparently has failed." With these dramatic words, Arthur R. Jensen, Professor of Educational Psychology at the University of California at Berkeley, began an article in the *Harvard Educational Review* [Winter 1969], that revived the old argument about the relative effects of heredity and environment in the determination of intelligence. Jensen went on to argue that the finding that black people score, on the average, 15 points below whites on I.Q. tests is evidence that "genetic factors are strongly implicated in the average Negro-white intelligence difference." Though only 10 of its 123 pages are devoted to race and

* From *Psychology Today*, August, 1969. Copyright © Communications/Research/Machines, Inc.

intelligence, the article, as *U.S. News and World Report* reported before it actually appeared, has indeed sent "shock waves . . . rolling through the U.S. educational community." For within a matter of days the article had made headlines, particularly in Southern newspapers, and had been used extensively by the defense in a Virginia suit fighting the integration of Greensville and Caroline County schools.

What is shocking, though, is not the use and distortion of Dr. Jensen's hypothesis by white supremacists, for this was to be expected, but rather the way in which Jensen, himself, may have misinterpreted the data.

The article is a long and eloquent statement of his thesis, highly sophisticated in terms of both psychometric and population genetics. The data he brings to bear on the subject, it appears, may have serious flaws, but the real danger lies, as it does in all the social sciences, in the interpretation of the data, and that is where Jensen may have gone truly astray. Indeed, Jensen's very first statement, as we shall shortly demonstrate, is a dangerous half-truth placed out of context.

Jensen writes that the hypothesis that genetic factors may be responsible for the lower I.Q. of black children is "anathema to many social scientists," and though many have denounced it, "it has been neither contradicted nor discredited by evidence." He goes on to state that to reject "any reasonable hypothesis on purely ideological grounds is to argue that static ignorance is preferable to increasing our knowledge of reality." On this point we are in full agreement with Jensen; that is why we have chosen to criticize his hypothesis solely on scientific, and not ideological, grounds.

But in order to consider Jensen's assertions it is first imperative that we review carefully *exactly what it is that Jensen did and did not say.*

Two concepts derived from genetics are essential in understanding Jensen's argument: genotype and phenotype. Genotype refers to the gene structure of an individual, his fixed genetic make-up. Phenotype refers to the actual physical, anatomical, physiological and psychological characteristics of a person and always reflects a combination of genetic and environmental influences.

Jensen attempts to determine the relative proportion of genetic structure and environmental influences that determine the phenotypic trait we call intelligence. He estimates that environment accounts for approximately 25 per cent of the variability in I.Q., and genetic factors account for the remaining 75 per cent. He buttresses his argument with an impressive array of statistics derived from studies of identical twins reared apart and unrelated children reared together. But, as even Jensen concedes, inheritance is a statistical concept stating a probability, but void of meaning when applied to an individual.

For example, one can argue that genetic factors account for 80 per cent of the variance of the heights of all white males in the U.S. It is *erroneous* however to conclude that gene structure accounts for four of the five inches Bill is taller than Bob.

Jensen concedes that I.Q. tests measure a narrow and a select sample of all the various forms of human accomplishment.

"Had the first I.Q. tests been devised in a hunting culture," Jensen writes, "general intelligence might well have turned out to involve visual acuity and running speed rather than vocabulary and symbol manipulation."

Jensen accepts the I.Q. test as an index of intelligence and shows that I.Q. scores are more similar among closely related people than among unrelated people. He proceeds to discuss racial differences in intelligence and the genetic aspects of racial differences, again being careful to forewarn that "the important distinction between the *individual* and the *population* must always be kept clearly in mind in any discussion of racial differences in mental abilities or any other behavioral characteristics."

Jensen surveys the now-vast literature on Negro intelligence and reports correctly the well-known fact that, on the average, Negroes score about 10 to 15 I.Q. points lower than the average of the white population. This finding is relatively uniform across many different tests of intellectual ability.

Jensen then attacks the environmental explanations for the observed racial differences in intelligence. The major implication for the compensatory education programs, he suggests, is that they may not work for black populations.

There are, therefore, two parts to the Jensen argument. The first states that the lower I.Q. scores of black children are due in part to genetic factors. The second argues that compensatory education, being based on environmental assumptions, may be of little help to them. Let us deal with the logic of these two arguments in that order. Although Jensen is correct in stating that I.Q. scores are more similar for people with similar genetic constitutions and blacks usually obtain lower I.Q. scores than whites, it does not necessarily follow that the lower I.Q. scores of black children are due to genetic factors.

In a reply to Jensen in the *Harvard Educational Review* [Spring 1969], James F. Crow, a population geneticist at the University of Wisconsin, states:

"It is clear, I think, that a high heritability of intelligence in the white population would not, even if there were similar evidence in the black population, tell us that the differences between the groups are genetic. No matter how high the heritability (unless it is 1[100 per cent]), there is no assurance that a sufficiently great environmental difference does not account for the difference in the two means, especially when one considers that the environmental factors may differ qualitatively in the two groups . . . It can be argued that being white or being black in our society changes one or more aspects of the environment so importantly as to account for the difference."

The error in Professor Jensen's logic can be illustrated easily, using stature as an example. There are genetic determinants to a person's height; the more closely related two people are, the more similar their stature. It is also true that children living in the rural areas of most Central or South American countries are markedly shorter than children who live in the urban areas of those countries. If we were to follow Jensen's logic we would conclude that the shorter stature of the rural children must be due to a different genetic constitution. However, existing information indicates that this is not a reasonable conclusion. The shorter stature of the rural children is not due to heredity, but to disease and environmental malnutrition. As a matter of fact, the heights of children in most areas of the world, including the United States, have increased considerably during the past 20 years because of better nutrition and mass immunization against disease during the first five years of life. The increase in stature is a result of change in environment, not of changes in genetic structure. However, these environmentally determined changes in stature do not disprove the fact that height is inherited. The essential error in Jensen's argument can be stated succinctly. Jensen assumes that if a trait is inherited, then any differences between two populations on that trait must be due to genetic factors.

This argument is fallacious for there are many ways to obtain differences among populations on traits that are partially inherited. Some of our most eminent behavioral geneticists take a similar point of view. Professor I. I. Gottesman of the University of Minnesota, for example, notes that, "even when gene pools are known to be matched, appreciable differences in mean I.Q. can be observed that could only have been associated with environmental differences." Moreover, in one study of 38 pairs of identical twins—that is, twins with exactly the same genetic structure—it was found that when they were reared in different environments the average difference in their I.Q. scores was 14 points. Further, at least one quarter of this group of identical twins reared in different environments had differences in I.Q. scores that were larger than 16 points. This 16-point difference is larger than the average difference between black and white populations. Gottesman concludes, "Differences observed so far between whites and Negroes can hardly be accepted as sufficient evidence that with respect to intelligence the Negro American is genetically less endowed."

Other evidence casts doubt on the validity of Jensen's conclusions. For example, a longitudinal study of infants being conducted in our laboratory at Harvard suggests that middle-class white children perform better than lower-class children on tests closely related to intelligence tests. These differences between middle- and lower-class populations occur as early as the first and second years of age in white populations of similar ethnicity and, therefore, similar genetic structure.

Detailed observations of the mother's interaction with the child in the home indicate that the lower-class infant does not experience the quality of parent-child interaction that one sees in middle-class homes. Specifically, lower-class mothers spend less time talking and smiling with their infants and they do not reward the child's maturational progress. The lower-class mother does not play a lot with her child and is less consistent in her treatment of him.

Our theories of mental development suggest that these specific deficits in the experience of the lower-class child should retard mental growth and lead to lower intelligence-test scores. The most likely determinants of the black child's lower I.Q. score are absence of a quality of parent-child interaction in the home during the opening years of life, and nutritional deficiencies in the pre- and postnatal environment.

A serious problem in interpreting the lower I.Q. scores of black children is the fact that many black children are afraid of the examiner or do not realize they are being tested. As a result they obtain lower scores than they would if time were taken to establish a good relationship with them. This conclusion is supported by the work of Dr. Francis Palmer of the City University of New York. Dr. Palmer gave mental tests to middle- and lower-class black children from Harlem. However, each examiner was instructed to delay any testing with any child until she felt that the child was completely relaxed and understood what was required of him. Many children had five, six and even seven hours of friendly play with the examiner before any testing began. Dr. Palmer found very few significant differences in mental performance between the lower- and middle-class populations. This is one of the few times such a finding has been reported and it seems due, in part, to the great care taken to insure that the child comprehended the nature of the test questions and felt at ease with the examiner.

Another serious issue is the belief that the I.Q. score is a measure of some pure entity—a trait that is similar to eye color. This is highly unlikely. An I.Q. score is the result of a host of factors including the amount of knowledge the child has, the extent to which he is attending to the examiner, and his motivation to do well. For example, on most I.Q. tests the child is asked to define words such as "orange" or "penny" and he is asked to draw a design from memory. He is also often asked questions that he may not understand. For example, one question on the Stanford-Binet Intelligence tests asks: "Someone discovered the skull of Christopher Columbus when he was 12 years old. Why is that silly?" If a child had never heard of Christopher Columbus or did not know the meaning of the word "skull" or was upset by the fact that a skeleton was being discussed, he would fail.

It does not take much reflection to realize that the I.Q. test is a cultural invention, not a biological characteristic, and it is not very likely that genes would influence an I.Q. score in any simple manner. Moreover, 15 to 20 per cent of our population of children change their I.Q. scores by at least 15 points and some children change as much as 60 points between six and 10 years of age. The backgrounds and family experiences of these children suggest that the increase was due to the child's motivation.

However, the most important point is that genetic constitution does not produce a specific I.Q. score, such as 85 or 115. Rather, *genetic constitution sets a range of mental ability* (or of height) for a population, not a specific I.Q. score (or a specific height).

The genetic structure of Caucasians seems to dictate an adult stature that ranges between four and seven feet, but it is misleading to think of an adult height of five and a half feet as 50 per cent genetic in origin.

Knowledge of genetic structure is most useful in understanding the limit beyond which a child probably cannot improve. Thus genetic determinants are most likely to influence mental talents that are extremely difficult to obtain, such as creative genius in mathematics or music. Genetic factors are *not* likely to be important in the acquisition of those skills that most children are capable of obtaining. It is the opinion of the authors that learning to read, to write and to add are relatively easy skills, well within the competence of all children who do not have serious brain damage. It is not reasonable to suggest that genetic differences between black and white populations could be responsible for the black child's difficulty in mastering school-related tasks. It is likely that 90 out of every 100 children—black, yellow or white—are capable of adequate mastery of the intellectual requirements of our schools. We should concentrate our efforts on determining the conditions that will allow this latent competence to be actualized with maximal ease.

The second assertion of Jensen's essay, namely that compensatory education is not likely to help black children, is also vulnerable to criticism. In the first place, the value of Head Start or similar programs has not been adequately assessed, and in the second, qualitatively different kinds of compensatory programs such as those described by Bruno Bettelheim in his recently published *The Children of the Dream* have not even been attempted in this country, though they have been spectacularly successful in Israel.

It is not fair to suggest that special tutoring or compensatory work has failed merely because eight or 40 weeks of a Head Start Program organized on a crash basis failed to produce table increases in I.Q. score.

It would be unreasonable to assume that feeding protein to a seriously malnourished child for three days would lead to a permanent increase in his weight and height if, after 72 hours of steak and eggs, he were sent back to his malnourished environment. Research indicates that children who have good tutorial contact *do* increase their I.Q. scores while they are being tutored; but when they are released they regress to their original scores. Jensen, himself, cites similar findings in a footnote to his article, but then, amazingly, concludes that this constitutes evidence for his assertion that compensatory education has failed. Dr. Earl Schaefer of the National Institute of Mental Health argues that we must maintain contact with the child. We cannot invest one year in compensatory work and assume that our job is done. It *may be* that compensatory education is of little value in helping children, but this concept has not been tested in any adequate sense.

Although Jensen inserted several caveats in his article, it seems likely that there will be those who will impulsively scan his essay or its vulgarizations in the popular press and conclude that the black child's poor school performance is a result of genetic taint. This conclusion is logically erroneous, empirically unproven, and socially dangerous.

RESPONSE, ARTHUR JENSEN REPLIES

by Arthur R. Jensen*

The article "Jensen's Dangerous Half-Truth" by Phillip Whitten and Jerome Kagan [August] actually attacks Whitten's and Kagan's half-truths. This is the easiest form of criticism: don't deal with the real issues presented by the author; simply distort them ridiculously and attack the distortions. Such was the response of Whitten and Kagan to my article. I can . . . best disabuse *Psychology Today* readers by summarizing succinctly what my article is actually about.

More than one year ago the Board of Editors of the *Harvard Educational Review* solicited from me an article for their Winter 1969 issue on the general topic "How Much Can We Boost I.Q. and Scholastic Achievement?" Their letter of solicitation outlined the main points to be discussed in the article, with particular reference to the contribution of heredity and environment to intelligence and

* From *Psychology Today,* October, 1969. Copyright © Communications/ Research/Machines, Inc.

scholastic performance, an evaluation of efforts to raise I.Q. and scholastic performance of disadvantaged children, my position on social class and racial differences in intelligence, and my own research on the triple interaction among the variables intelligence, associative learning ability, and socioeconomic status. The resulting article of 123 pages—the longest ever published by the *Harvard Educational Review*—discussed each of these topics in considerable detail. Here, very briefly, is the gist of what I said on each topic.

COMPENSATORY EDUCATION

First, I reviewed the conclusions of a nationwide survey and evaluation of the large Federally funded compensatory education programs, an evaluation by the United States Commission on Civil Rights, which concluded that these special programs had produced no significant improvement in the measured intelligence or scholastic performance of the disadvantaged children whose educational achievements these programs were specially intended to raise. The evidence presented by the U.S. Commission on Civil Rights suggests to me that merely applying more of the same approach to compensatory education on a larger scale is not likely to lead to the desired results, namely increasing the benefits of public education to the disadvantaged. The well-documented fruitlessness of these well-intentioned large-scale compensatory programs indicates the importance of now questioning the assumptions, theories and practices on which they were based. I point out, also, that some small-scale experimental intervention programs have shown more promise of beneficial results. I do *not* advocate abandoning efforts to improve the education of the disadvantaged. I urge increased emphasis on these efforts, in the spirit of experimentation, expanding the diversity of approaches and improving the rigor of evaluation in order to boost our chances of discovering the methods that will work best.

THE NATURE OF INTELLIGENCE

I point out that I.Q. tests evolved to predict scholastic performance in largely European and North American middle-class populations around the turn of the century. They evolved to measure those particular abilities most relevant to a particular curriculum and type of instruction, which in turn were shaped by the particular pattern of abilities of the children the schools were then intended to serve. I.Q. or abstract-reasoning ability is thus a selection of just one portion of the total spectrum of human mental abilities. This aspect of mental abilities measured by I.Q. tests is very important in our society, but is not the only set of educationally or occupationally relevant abilities. Other mental abilities have not yet been adequately measured; their distributions in various segments of the population have not been adequately determined; and their educational relevance has not been fully explored. I believe that a much broader assessment of the spectrum of abilities and potentials, and the investigation of their utilization for educational achievement, will be an essential aspect of improving the education of children called disadvantaged.

INHERITANCE OF INTELLIGENCE

Much of my paper is a review of the methods and evidence that lead me to the conclusion that individual differences in intelligence—that is, I.Q.—are predominantly attributable to genetic differences, with environmental factors contributing a minor portion of the variance among individuals in I.Q. The heritability of the I.Q.—that is, the percentage of individual differences variance attributable to genetic factors—comes out to about 80%, which is the average value obtained in all the relevant studies now reported in the literature, with values extending over a range from about 60% to 90%. These estimates of heritability are based on tests administered to European and North American populations and cannot properly be generalized to other populations. I believe we need similar heritability studies in minority populations if we are to increase our understanding of what our tests measure in these populations and how these abilities can be most effectively used in the educational process.

SOCIAL-CLASS DIFFERENCES

Although the full range of I.Q. and other abilities is found among children in every socioeconomic stratum in our population, it is well established that the I.Q. differs on the average among children from different social-class backgrounds. The evidence, some of which I refer to in my article, indicates to me that some of this I.Q. difference is attributable to environmental differences and some of it is attributable to genetic differences between social classes—largely as a result of differential selection of the parent generations for different patterns of ability. I have not yet met or read a modern geneticist who disputes this interpretation of the evidence. The geneticist C. O. Carter remarked, "Sociologists who doubt this show more ingenuity than judgment." I have also read at least three prominent sociologists who are students of this problem—Pitirim Sorokin, Bruce Eckland, and Otis Dudley Duncan—and all agree that selective factors in social mobility and assortative mating have resulted in a genetic component in social-class intelligence differences. As Eckland points out, this conclusion holds *within* socially defined racial groups but cannot properly be generalized *between* racial groups since barriers to upward social mobility have undoubtedly been quite different for various racial groups.

RACE DIFFERENCES

I have always advocated dealing with persons as individuals, each in terms of his own merits and characteristics. I am opposed to according any treatment to persons solely on the basis of their race, color, national origin, or social-class background. But I am also opposed to ignoring or refusing to investigate the causes of the well-established differences among racial groups in the distribution of educationally relevant traits, particularly I.Q.

I believe that the cause of the observed differences in I.Q. and scholastic performance among different ethnic groups is scientifically still an open question, an important question, and a researchable question. I believe that official statements, apparently accepted without question by some social scientists, such as "It is a demonstrable fact that the talent pool in any one ethnic group is substantially the same as in any other ethnic group" (U.S. Office of Education, 1966) and "Intelligence potential is distributed among Negro infants in the same proportion and pattern as among Icelanders or Chinese, or any other group" (Dept. of Labor, 1965) are without scientific merit. They lack any factual basis and must be regarded only as hypotheses. It would require a full article just to describe the ugly personal and professional consequences of challenging this prevailing hypothesis of genetic equality by suggesting alternative hypotheses that invoke genetic as well as environmental factors as being among the causes of the observed differences in patterns of mental ability between racial groups. The fact that different racial groups in this country have widely separated geographic origins and have had quite different histories which have subjected them to different selective social and economic pressures make it highly likely that their gene pools differ for some genetically conditioned behavioral characteristics, including intelligence or abstract-reasoning ability. Nearly every anatomical, physiological and biochemical system investigated shows racial differences. Why should the brain be an exception? The reasonableness of the hypothesis that there are racial differences in genetically conditioned behavioral characteristics, including mental abilities, is not confined to the poorly informed, but has been expressed in writings and public statements by such eminent geneticists as Kenneth Mather, C. D. Darlington, R. A. Fisher, and Francis Crick, to name but a few.

I indicated several lines of evidence that support my assertion that a genetic hypothesis is not unwarranted. The fact that we still have only inconclusive conclusions with respect to this hypothesis does not mean that the opposite of the hypothesis is true. Yet some social scientists speak as if this were the case and have even publicly censured me for suggesting an alternative to purely environmental hypotheses of intelligence differences. Scientific investigation proceeds most effectively by means of what Platt has called "strong inference," which means pitting against one another alternative hypotheses that lead to different predictions, and then putting these predictions to an empirical test.

DYSGENIC TRENDS

More important than the issue of racial differences *per se* is the probability, explicated in my article, of dysgenic trends in our urban slums, as suggested by census data showing markedly higher birth rates among the poorest segments of the Negro population than among successful, middle-class Negroes. This social-class differential in birthrate appears to be much greater in the Negro than in the white population. That is, the least able among Negroes have a higher reproductive rate than their white counterparts in ability, and the educationally and occupationally most able segment of the Negro population has a lower reproductive rate than their white counterparts. If social-class intelligence differences within the Negro population have a genetic component, as in the white population, the condition I have described could create and widen the genetic intelligence difference between Negroes and whites. The social and educational implications of this trend, if it exists and persists, are enormous. The problem obviously deserves thorough investigation by social scientists and geneticists. The problem should not be ignored or superficially dismissed out of motives of well-meaning wishful thinking. The possible consequences of our failure seriously to study these questions may well be viewed by future generations as our society's greatest injustice to Negro Americans.

LEARNING ABILITY AND I.Q.

The last part of my paper deals with my theory of two broad categories of mental abilities which I call intelligence (or abstract-reasoning ability) and associative-learning ability. These types of ability appear to be distributed differently in various social classes and racial groups. While large racial and social-class differences are found for intelligence, there are practically negligible differences among these groups in associative-learning abilities, such as memory span and serial and paired-associate rote learning. Research should be directed at delineating still other types of abilities and at discovering how the particular strengths in each individual's *pattern* of abilities can be most effectively brought to bear on school learning and on the attainment of occupational skills. By pursuing this path, I believe that we can discover the means by which the reality of individual differences need not mean educational rewards for some children and utter frustration and defeat for others.

My article in the *Harvard Educational Review* has widely provoked serious thought and discussion among leaders in genetics, psychology, sociology and education who are concerned with these important fundamental issues and their implications for public education. I expect that my work will stimulate further relevant research as well as efforts to apply the knowledge gained thereby to educationally and socially beneficial purposes. The whole society will benefit most if scientists and educators treat these problems in the spirit of scientific inquiry rather than as a battlefield upon which one or another preordained ideology may seemingly triumph.

BEHAVIORAL SCIENCE VERSUS INTELLIGENCE

by Grace Rubin-Rabson*

The physical scientist can with certainty predict the conditions under which water will boil, but a man's boiling point is not so readily determined. So complex is the behavior of a living thing, so intertwined the reaction of subject and investigator that one wonders whether the behavioral scientist can ever achieve the precision, the validity (the agreement between a score or measure and the thing it reputedly measures), or the replication (re-examination under identical conditions) available to the physical sciences.

Still, he must persist. When his work with people affects public policy, the behavioral scientist bears enormous responsibility. In these circumstances, since publication in a professional journal does not in itself guarantee merit nor the validity of conclusions, an objective review of the work's premises, its design, the raw data, the manner and accuracy of procedure and computations and the statistical techniques employed is in order.

Each human being is unique; there is no other in the world like him. Approach one for study and, like the chameleon under changing light, he reflects the confrontation and is no longer the same. Approach more than one, sum up the results in neat statistical arrays and the averages describe no particular individual in the group. Design tests to analyze his abilities, his interests and aptitudes, and he is subjected to a mass-standardized procedure that,

* *The Wall Street Journal,* Tuesday, July 1, 1969.

like mass-designed furniture, fits everyone to a degree and no one exactly. Devise skillful experimental techniques to test some aspects of his behavior under social pressure—and it must be some small aspect that can be cleanly isolated—and a hopefully valid conclusion can be drawn about this small aspect. But these are again group findings, not necessarily true of every individual in the group.

DESPAIR?

Nor is human behavior a composite of bits pieced together in a simplified and artificial laboratory staging, but the response to a complex situation of a whole being prompted and defined at any moment by his entire intellectual and emotional experience.

Faced with this obstacle, the experimentalist might well throw up his hands in despair. Contrasted with him, his colleague practicing psychotherapy does not despair, but goes blithely on his loving and persuasive way, unconcerned about the validity of his constructs, content that, for whatever reason, his patient improves. Truly it has been said: The psychotherapist uses important concepts that he cannot validate while the experimental psychologist validates unimportant concepts that he cannot use.

The behavioral scientist is himself a complicating factor, for he is human too, expressing his own needs in his choice of profession and specialized area, the problems he selects to investigate, the methods and materials he organizes for the investigation. Despite his careful conscious objectivity, it follows from his choice of problem that he may be unconsciously biased toward a particular outcome and, by subtle cues—perhaps heightened enthusiasm in his voice and gestures—convey the desired responses to his subjects or his co-workers. There is no fraud here, only a fairly obvious example to suggest the hazards inherent in keeping the experiment free of the experimenter.

In the early, quieter years of this century, American psychologists became interested in the area of intelligence testing. Little was known then about intelligence, little is known now, though the study of its theoretical and biopsychological structures has begun. A British psychologist, Liam Hudson, says of this somewhat over-extolled attribute, recognized by everyone but acceptably defined by no one: "The field is still in its pre-Copernican state: The classical experiments have yet to be done, and the while, our research grows in on itself, and becomes encapsulated. What good ideas there are, are stumbled on in true somnambulistic fashion; and only occasionally recognized as good."

So routine is intelligence testing now that the "I.Q. test" has become an accepted part of the school and clinical scene; so entrenched its use, the testers have ceased to question its validity, if ever they did.

The test result is a composite, dependent on natural endowment, in a measure on school skills, on the confidence engendered by success in school and extra-school skills. School skills, in turn, depend on natural endowment plus adequate learning. From a poor start of faulty learning and cumulative confusion, the inevitable lack of skills and self-confidence pervades the test itself. The added handicaps then further obscure the natural endowment factor in the test result.

THE "ALL-IMPORTANT" IQ

The "intelligence-quotient" is a source of joy and obligation when high, of a dragging sense of mediocrity when centered around the average, of bitter and permanent pain when low, affecting an entire life. Instances of all three have appeared in the press within this year.

The first reports a "girl genius" with an I.Q. of 154-201, depending on the test. Even for an imprecise measure of an elusive concept, this is a range to give one pause. Is this genius an equal among college professors, or is she a genius destined for history? Which score goes down on her record? Does it make any difference? If these wide-ranging scores show a consistent upward trend, either the successive tests were easier, or this mathematics wizard, with sufficient practice, finally broke the code. Intelligence tests have a basic similarity, and test scores tend to increase with exposure to testing. On a second use of the same test, some test-item responses, failed the first time, will be available, not through increased intelligence, simply through investigation.

Another instance, one hard to believe, is the hurtful misuse of testing in evaluating small Mexican-American children in two California school districts. As reported in the press, on the basis of a

Binet test administered in English, with a cut-off point of 70, certain of these children qualified for the Educable Mentally Retarded group. But when, some time later, the test was administered in Spanish, scores increased as much as 28 points, an average of 13.

To the horror of the humiliation of these children and their families, and the demoralizing effects of remaining in a slow group, add the lingering barbarism of a cut-off point on a test standardized on middle-class, English-speaking American children, and for this reason, unsuitable to these children, to Puerto Ricans newly arrived, to Negroes of the deep South, to Indians isolated on reservations, though all of them, presumably, are attending some kind of American school.

A well-designed "culture-free" test may avoid the problem of cultural unsuitability, though it shares with the "culture-associated" test the fundamental drawback, as Hudson says, that classical experiments have yet to be done. Moreover, the tests predominantly used in schools and clinics are culture-associated.

Intelligence is not measurable at a point; should the tests be far more reliable than they currently are, the individual intelligence could be located only in a broad zone, a zone five to ten points on either side of the resulting I.Q. Depending on the quality of the test itself, on the examiner, on rapport, on physiological state, on anxiety, on test practice, on errors in administration and scoring, among an assortment of influences, a considerable variation can be taken for granted. How then, at any specific moment, whether for these or any other children, can one decide that the I.Q. of 69 goes to the retarded class and that the I.Q. of 70 remains with the normal class? Uneasy lies the head of the examiner who must make these decisions.

More uneasy still lie the heads of the expert witnesses at the Sirhan trial. The concepts now available to the psychology professions clearly proved inadequate for a decision in a life and death situation, however helpful such concepts may be in the clinic. Confused and contradictory as they were, a "third ear" might have heard an alert defense's briefing, gleaned from the text-books, on persuasively aberrant responses and courtroom capers. The psychology professions are still young, and though precocious, perhaps not yet ready for the role of expert witness.

Sirhan, an example of the mid-range I.Q., seems to have been tested twice, with an earlier score of 89 and a later 109. Does he, then, barely belong to the average group and at the same time to the group superior to 75% of the population? If the two tests were different, then this is one more instance of large discrepancies in measures of the same thing; if the same test was used twice, then some of the possible reasons mentioned earlier apply. Were the tests suitable for an Arab boy brought up in another milieu even though attending an American school?

Teachers, being human too, are influenced by I.Q.s, and for this reason alone such designations might be dropped. Teacher expectations depend on scores, and these expectations are reflected in pupil response. In the experiment of Rosenthal and Jacobson a group of randomly selected children, assigned to a teacher initially led to believe the group superior, showed large increases in the intelligence quotient, one more example of the self-fulfilling prophecy. Long ago, without the extensive labors involved in such a study, the poet Goethe observed: "If one treats a person as if he were what he ought to be and could be, he will become what he ought to be and could be."

Will not the reverse hold equally true? If an individual is stigmatized as "low I.Q." or "mentally retarded," will not his unhappy family, his teachers and everyone around him consistently treat him as such, thus condemning him for life and confirming once more the self-fulfilling prophecy?

By coincidence, two reports involving the genetic factor in intelligence came to public attention at the same time. One implies a superior, the other an inferior, gene for intelligence in two ethnic groups. Lord Snow, the English writer, gracious to the people honoring him, flatteringly but unscientifically ascribed high Jewish achievement to superior intellectual genes. To this the Jews replied, realistically, "Poppycock." Traditional among Jews, they said, is the love of learning; with Maimonides, they believe the goal of life to be the accumulation of knowledge and the perfection of the human mind. These are social, not genetic, influences; motivation and striving in terms of this tradition account adequately for achievement in a permissive environment. When the young know that achievement is possible, they are motivated to achieve. In any case, Jews, like all people who have moved about the earth's surface, are not genetically pure, but mixed.

The other, somewhat over-publicized report of Dr. Arthur Jensen, while making several important points, concludes that lower average intelligence and scholastic performances of Negroes may involve genetic as well as social factors. His proposal that education be revised for children of lower intelligence, regardless of race, is strongly to be seconded. When the encrusted barnacles on American education are at length scraped off, may the mass procedures now employed for all children, irrespective of individual talent, finally give way to approaching the individual child in terms of his unique gifts and perceptions.

In addition, Jensen warns, with a higher birthrate among lower class Negroes (he does not mention the accompanying higher death rate) than among the comparable white group, the intellectual gap will widen, making an increasing proportion of Negroes unemployable except at unskilled labor. His proposal that Negro leaders advocate control of the birth rate can also be warmly seconded—for all people, world-wide.

MIXED GENES

The American Negroes, too, are a mixed people. Few of them are now pure blacks. Under many black skins lie white genes; and under nearly a quarter of white skins (as of 1960) lies an African element in the inherited biological background. In these circumstances, and until more is known about it, the attribution to any group of superior or inferior genes for intelligence seems untenable. Such attribution is, in any case, socially unproductive.

Certainly the genetic factor is basic in intelligence and determines the upper limits of its growth. However, as in every other biological aspect, intellectual growth depends on other factors for its development: Adequate physical nourishment, especially in pregnant women and young children, and a stimulating environment. The stimulating environment must include not only the contributions of home and formal education, but a psychological ambiance assuring equality, full acceptance and a realistic expectation of achievement. When, after some decades, these conditions truly exist for the Negro, one can consider comparing him with other groups. By then, no one will.

Philip Vernon, a British psychologist, in his recent book, "Intelligence and Cultural Environment," stresses social influences in the development of intelligence: "Clearly, the major barrier to the fuller realization of human potential lies in the realm of adult values and child-rearing practices." And, to quote Dr. Hudson once more: "The intelligence of young children grows, it seems, into the spaces that parents and teachers allot it. What we expect of them, children tend to become."

In an atmosphere of protest, an old world dies, a new one lies aborning: New insights, new curricula, new teaching methods, particularly for handicapped learners, wherever they come from, whatever the reasons for the handicap. Each contributes his talents; each must be served according to his needs. What difference do a few points in a questionable test-score make? Invidious comparisons, in the world community, as in the family community, only arouse ill-will.

Let us move into more constructive areas.

INTELLIGENCE HAS THREE FACETS

by J. P. Guilford*

Many a layman who has taken a psychologist's intelligence test, especially if he did not do as well as he thought he should, has the conviction that a score, such as an IQ, does not tell the whole story regarding intelligence. In thinking so, he is absolutely right; traditional intelligence tests fall far short of indicating fully an individual's intellectual status. Just how far short and in what respects have not been well realized until very recent years during which the whole scope of human intelligence has been intensively investigated.

This is not to say that IQ tests are not useful, for they definitely are, as years of experience have demonstrated. Intelligence-quotient tests were originated more than 60 years ago for the purpose of

* From *Science*, Vol. 160, May 10, 1968, pp. 615–620, copyright 1968 by the American Association for the Advancement of Science.

determining which children could not learn at normal rates. This meant that the content of IQ tests weights heavily those intellectual abilities that are pertinent to school learning in the key subjects of reading and arithmetic, and other subjects that depend directly upon them or are of similar nature psychologically. IQ tests (and also academic-aptitude tests, which are essentially similar) predict less well at educational levels higher than the elementary grades, for at higher levels subject matter becomes more varied. Even at the elementary level, predictions of achievement have been poor in connection with the *initial* stages of learning to read, in spelling, and in the arts. The defender of the IQ test might say that intelligence is not involved in such subjects. But he would not only be wrong, he would also be dodging problems.

ONE INTELLIGENCE, OR MANY ABILITIES?

The father of IQ tests, Alfred Binet, believed firmly that intelligence is a very complex affair, comprising a number of different abilities, and he manifested this conviction by introducing tests of many kinds into his composite scale. He did not know what the component abilities are, although he suggested that there are several different kinds of memory, for example. He went along with the idea of using a single, overall score, since the immediate practical goal was to make a single administrative decision regarding each child.

Test-makers following Binet were mostly unconcerned about having a basic psychological theory for intelligence tests, another example of technology running far in advance of theory. There was some concern about theory in England, however, where Charles Spearman developed a procedure of factor analysis by which it became possible to discover component abilities (*1*). Spearman was obsessed with a very restricting conception that there is a universal *g* factor that is common to all tests that have any claim to the label of "intelligence tests," where each test has its own unique kind of items or problems. His research, and that of others in his country, found, however, that correlations between tests could not be fully accounted for on the basis of a single common factor (*2*). They had to admit the existence of a number of "group" factors in addition to *g*. For example, sets of tests having verbal, numerical, or spatial material, respectively, correlated higher within sets than with tests in other sets. The extra correlation among tests within sets was attributed to additional abilities each of limited scope.

Factor analyses in the United States have followed almost exclusively the multiple-factor theory of Thurstone (3), which is more general than Spearman's. In Thurstone's conception, a g factor is not necessary but analysis by his methods would be likely to find it if the intercorrelations warrant such a result. It is not necessary to know the mathematics basic to factor theory in order to follow the remaining content of this article, but for those who wish additional insights the next few paragraphs present the minimum essentials of a mathematical basis. To all readers it may be said that factor analysis is a sensitive procedure, which, when properly used, can answer the taxonomic questions of *what* intellectual abilities or functions exist and what their properties are.

The basic equation in multiple-factor theory, in matrix form, is $Z = FC$, where Z is a matrix of test scores, of order n by N, where N individuals have all taken n different tests. Z indicates that the scores are in standard form, that is, each element $z = (X - \overline{X})/s_x$, where X is a "raw" score on an arbitrary scale, $\overline{X}$ is the mean of the raw scores in the sample of N individuals, and s_x is the standard deviation. In the basic equation, F stands for the "complete factor matrix," which is of order n by $(r + n)$, where r is the number of *common* factors. The addition of n columns indicates that there are n *specific* factors or components, one for each test. In this matrix, f_{ij} is the loading or weight for test 1 in connection with factor J. C is of the order $(r + n)$ by N and represents the scores of N individuals on $(r + n)$ factors. The basic equation means that for each individual his standard score z_{ij} in a particular test is a weighted sum of his $(r + n)$ factor scores, each factor score also in standard form. An assumption for this form of the equation is that the factors are orthogonal (uncorrelated) variables.

The factor-analysis problem is to derive the matrix of common-factor loadings, A, given the score matrix for N individuals in n tests. The interest is in only the r common factors. The analysis ordinarily starts with intercorrelations among the n tests. The reduced (specifics ignored) intercorrelation matrix R is mathematically related to the factor matrix A by the equation $R = AA'$, where A represents only the common-factor components in F, and A' is the transpose of A. R can be computed from empirical data by the equation $R = ZZ'/N$. Starting with the computed correlation matrix R, the problem is to find the common-factor matrix A. Methods for accomplishing this operation are described by Harman (4).

Very rarely, indeed, does anyone using the multiple-factor approach find and report a g factor. The reason is that there are too many zero correlations among tests of intellectual qualities, where one genuine zero correlation would be sufficient to disallow a g factor that is supposed to be universal. My examination of more than 7000 intercorrelations, among tests in the intellectual category, showed at least 17 percent of them to be acceptable as zero correlations (5). The multiple factors usually found are each commonly restricted to only a few tests, where we may ignore factor loadings less than .30 as being insignificant, following common practice.

DISCOVERY OF MULTIPLE ABILITIES

Only a few events in discovering factors by the Thurstone approach will be mentioned. In Thurstone's first major study (6) as many as nine common factors were thought to be sufficiently interpretable psychologically to justify calling them "primary mental abilities." A factor is interpreted intuitively in terms of the apparent human resource needed to do well in the set of tests loaded strongly together on the mathematical factor. A distinction between mathematical factors and psychological factors is important. Surface features of the tests in the set may differ, but examinees have to perform well in some unique way in all of them. For example, Thurstone designated some of the abilities as being visual-perceptual, inductive, deductive, numerical, spatial, and verbal. Two others dealt with rote memory and word fluency. Thurstone and his students followed his 1938 analysis with others that revealed a few additional kinds of abilities.

Another major source of identified intellectual abilities was the research of aviation psychologists in the U.S. Army Air Force during World War II (7). More important than the outcome of adding to the number of intellectual abilities that called for recognition was the fact that where Thurstone had found one spatial ability, there proved to be at least three, one of them being recognized as spatial orientation and another as spatial visualization. Where Thurstone had found an inductive ability, there were three reasoning abilities. Where Thurstone had found one memory ability, there were three, including visual memory. In some of these cases a Thurstone factor turned out to be a confounding of two or more separable abilities, separable when more representative tests for each factor were analyzed together and when allowance was made for a sufficient number of factors. In other cases, new varieties of tests were explored—new memory tests, space tests, and reasoning tests.

The third major event was in the form of a program of analyses conducted in the Aptitudes Research Project at the University of Southern California since 1949, in which attention was first concentrated on tests in the provisional categories of reasoning, creative thinking, planning, evaluation, and problem-solving (8). Nearly 20 years later, the number of separate intellectual abilities has increased to about 80, with at least 50 percent more predicted by a comprehensive, unified theory. The remainder of this article is mainly concerned with that theory.

THE STRUCTURE-OF-INTELLECT MODEL

Two previous attempts to put the known intellectual abilities into logical schema had been made by Burt (9) and Vernon (10), with similar results. In both cases the models were of hierarchical form, reminiscent of the Linnaeus taxonomic model for the animal kingdom. Following the British tradition of emphasis upon g, which was placed at the apex of the system, there were broad subdivisions under g and under each subdivision some sub-subcategories, on down to abilities that are regarded as being very narrow in scope.

My first attempts (11) found that the hierarchical type of model had to be discarded for several reasons. First, there had to be a rejection of g itself, for reasons mentioned earlier. Furthermore, most factors seemed to be of somewhat comparable level of generality, where generality is operationally defined in terms of the number and variety of tests found to represent each ability. There did appear to be categories of abilities, some concerned with discovery or recognition of information, memory for information, productive thinking, and evaluation, with a number of abilities in each category, but there are other ways of organizing categories of abilities. The most decisive observation was that there were a number of parallels between abilities, in terms of their common features.

Some examples of parallels in abilities will help. Two parallel abilities differ in only one respect. There was known to be an ability to see relations between perceived, visual figures, and a parallel ability to see relations between concepts. An example of a test item in the first case would be seeing that one figure is the lower-left half of another. An item in the second case might require seeing that the words "bird" and "fly" are related as object and its mode of locomotion. The ability to do the one kind of item is relatively independent of the ability to do the other, the only difference being that of kind of information—concrete or perceived in the one case and abstract or conceived in the other.

For a pair of abilities differing in another way, the kind of information is the same for both. One of the abilities pertains to *seeing* class ideas. Given the set of words *footstool, lamp, rocker, television,* can the examinee grasp the essence of the nature of the class, as shown by his naming the class, by putting another word or two into it, or by recognizing its name among four alternatives? The ability pertains to discovery or recognition of a class concept. In another kind of test we ask the examinee to *produce* classes by partitioning a list of words into mutually exclusive sets, each with a different class concept. These two abilities are relatively independent. The one involves a process of understanding and the other a process of production. These processes involve two psychologically different kinds of operation.

A third kind of parallel abilities has pairs that are alike in kind of information involved and in kind of operation. Suppose we give the examinee this kind of test item: "Name as many objects as you can that are both edible and white." Here we have given the specifications for a class and the examinee is to produce from his memory store some class members. The ability involved was at first called "ideational fluency." The more of appropriate members the examinee can produce in a limited time, the better his score. In a test for a parallel ability, instead of producing single words the examinee is to produce a list of sentences. To standardize his task for testing purposes and to further control his efforts, we can give him the initial letters of four words that he is to give in each of a variety of sentences, for example: W—— c— s— d—. Without using any word twice, the examinee might say, "Why can't Susan dance?," "Workers could seldom deviate," or "Weary cats sense destruction." The ability was first called "expressional fluency." The kind of information in both these tests is conceptual, and the kind of operation is production.

But the kind of operation in the last test is different from that for the classifying test mentioned before. In the classifying test, the words given to the examinee are so selected that they form a unique set of classes and he is so told. The operation is called "convergent production." In the last two tests under discussion, there are many possible responses and the examinee produces alternatives. The operation is called "divergent production." It involves a broad searching or scanning process. Both operations depend upon retrieval of information from the examinee's memory store.

The difference between the two abilities illustrated by the last two tests is in the nature of the things produced. In the first case they are single words that stand for single objects or concepts. The thing produced, the "product," is a *unit* of information. In the second case, the product is an organized sequence of words, each word standing for a concept or unit. This kind of product is given the name of "system."

In order to take care of all such parallels (and the number increased as time went on and experience grew), a matrix type of model seemed called for in the manner of Mendeleev's table of chemical elements. The differences in the three ways indicated—operation (kind of processing of information), content (kind of information), and product (formal aspect of information)—called for a three-dimensional model. Such a model has been called "morphological" (*12*). The model as finally completed and presented in 1959 (*13*) is illustrated in Fig. 1. It has five categories of operation, four categories of content, and six categories of product.

It is readily seen that the theory calls for $5 \times 4 \times 6$, or 120, cubical cells in the model, each one representing a unique ability, unique by virtue of its peculiar conjunction of operation, content, and product. The reader has already been introduced to three kinds of operation: cognition (discovery, recognition, comprehension), divergent production, and convergent production. The memory operation involves putting information into the memory store and must be distinguished from the memory store itself. The latter underlies all the operations; all the abilities depend upon it. This is the best logical basis for believing that the abilities increase with experience, depending upon the kinds of experience. The evaluation operation deals with assessment of information, cognized or produced, determining its goodness with respect to adopted (logical) criteria, such as identity and consistency.

The distinction between figural and semantic (conceptual)

contents was mentioned earlier. The distinguishing of symbolic information from these two came later. Symbolic information is presented in tests in the form of letters or numbers, ordinarily, but other signs that have only "token" value or meaning can be used.

The category of behavioral information was added on the basis of a hunch; no abilities involving it were known to have been demonstrated when it was included. The basis was E. L. Thorndike's suggestion (14) many years ago that there is a "social intelligence," distinct from what he called "concrete" and "abstract" intelligences. It was decided to distinguish "social intelligence" on the basis of kind of information, the kind that one person derives from observation of the behavior of another. Subsequent experience has demonstrated a full set of six behavioral-cognition abilities as predicted by the model, and a current analytical investigation is designed to test the part of the model that includes six behavioral-divergent-production abilities. In a test for cognition of behavioral systems, three parts of a four-part cartoon are given in each item, with four alternative parts that are potential completions. The examinee has to size up each situation, and the sequence of events, correctly in order to select the appropriate part. As a test for divergent production of behavioral systems, the examinee is given descriptions of three characters, for example, a jubilant man, an angry woman, and a sullen boy, for which he is to construct a number of alternative story plots involving the characters and their moods, all stories being different.

The reader has already encountered four kinds of products: units, classes, relations, and systems, with illustrations. The other two kinds of products are transformations and implications. Transformations include any kind of change: movement in space, rearrangement or regrouping of letters in words or factoring or simplifying an equation, redefining a concept or adapting an object or part of an object to a new use, revising one's interpretation of another person's action, or rearranging events in a story. In these examples the four kinds of content are involved, from figural to behavioral, illustrating the fact that all six kinds of products apply in every content category.

Implied information is suggested by other information. Foresight or prediction depends upon extrapolating from given information to some naturally following future condition or event. If I make this move in chess, my knight will be vulnerable. If I divide by X, I will have a simpler expression. If it rains tonight, my tent will leak. If I whistle at that girl, she will turn her head. The "If . . . then" expression well describes an instance of implication, the implication actually being the thing implied.

SOME CONSEQUENCES OF THE THEORY

The most immediate consequence of the theory and its model has been its heuristic value in suggesting where to look for still undemonstrated abilities. The modus operandi of the Aptitudes Research Project from the beginning has been to hypothesize certain kinds of abilities, to create new types of tests that should emphasize each hypothesized ability, then factor analyze to determine whether the hypothesis is well supported. With hypotheses generated by the model, the rate of demonstration of new abilities has been much accelerated.

At the time this article was written, of 24 hypothesized abilities in the category of cognition, 23 had been demonstrated. Of 24 expected memory abilities, 14 were recognized. In the other operation categories of divergent production, convergent production, and evaluation, 16, 13, and 13 abilities, respectively, were accounted for, and in all these categories 17 other hypotheses are under investigation. These studies should bring the number of demonstrated abilities close to the century mark. It is expected that the total will go beyond the 120 indicated by the model, for some cells in the figural and symbolic columns already have more than one ability each. These proliferations arise from the differences in kind of sensory input. Most known abilities are represented by tests with visual input. A few have been found in tests with auditory input, and possibly one involving kinesthetic information. Each one can also be placed in the model in terms of its three sources of specification—operation, content, and product.

Having developed a comprehensive and systematic theory of intelligence, we have found that not the least of its benefits is an entirely new point of view in psychology generally, a view that has been called "operational-informational." I have elaborated a great deal upon this view elsewhere (15). Information is defined for psychology as that which the organism discriminates. Without discrimination there is no information. This far, there is agreement

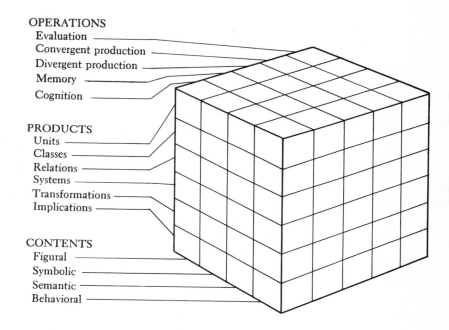

FIG. 1. The structure-of-intellect model.

with the conception of information as viewed by communication engineers, but beyond this point we part company. Psychological discriminations are most broadly and decisively along the lines of kinds of content and kinds of products, from which arise hiatuses between intellectual abilities. Further discriminations occur, of course, within the sphere of a single ability. I have proposed that the 4 × 6 intersections of the informational categories of the SI (structure of intellect) model provide a psychoepistemology, with 24 subcategories of basic information. I have also proposed that the six product categories—units, classes, relations, systems, transformations, and implications—provide the basis for a psycho-logic (16). Although most of these terms are also concepts in modern logic, a more complete representation appears in mathematics.

The operational-informational view regards the organism as a processor of information, for which the modern, high-speed computer is a good analogy. From this point of view, computer-simulation studies make sense. In addition to trying to find out how the human mind works by having computers accomplish the same end results, however, it might be useful, also, to determine how the human mind accomplishes its ends, then to design the computer that performs the same operations. Although a psychology based upon the SI concepts is much more complicated than the stimulus-response model that became traditional, it is still parsimonious. It certainly has the chance of becoming more adequate. The structure of intellect, as such, is a taxonomic model; it provides fruitful concepts. For theory that accounts for behavior, we need operational models, and they can be based on SI concepts. For example, I have produced such a model for problem-solving (*17*).

There is no one problem-solving ability. Many different SI abilities may be drawn upon in solving a problem, depending upon the nature of the problem. Almost always there are cognitive operations (in understanding the nature of the problem), productive operations (in generating steps toward solution), and evaluative operations (in checking upon both understanding and production). Memory operations enter in, to keep a record of information regarding previous steps, and the memory store underlies all.

There is something novel about producing solutions to problems, hence creative thinking is involved. Creative thinking depends most clearly upon divergent-production operations on the one hand, and on transformations on the other. Thus, these two categories have unique roles in creative problem-solving. There is accordingly no one unique ability to account for creative potential. Creative production depends upon the area in which one works, whether it is in pictorial art, music, drama, mathematics, science, writing, or management. In view of the relative independence of the intellectual abilities, unevenness of status in the various abilities within the same person should be the rule rather than the exception. Some individuals can excel in more than one art form, but few excel in all, as witness the practice of having multiple creative contributors to a single motion picture.

The implications of all this for education are numerous. The doctrine that intelligence is a unitary something that is established for each person by heredity and that stays fixed through life should be summarily banished. There is abundant proof that greater intelligence is associated with increased education. One of education's major objectives should be to increase the stature of its recipients in intelligence, which should now mean stature in the various intellectual abilities. Knowing what those abilities are, we not only have more precise goals but also much better conceptions of how to achieve those goals.

TABLE 1

Scatterplot of Expressional Fluency (one aspect of divergent production) scores in relation to CTMM (California Test of Mental Maturity) IQ.

DP score	Intelligence quotient								
	60–69	70–79	80–89	90–99	100–109	110–119	120–129	130–139	140–149
50–59						1	3		1
40–49						2	4	1	
30–39			2	3	4	11	17	6	2
20–29			1	3	10	23	13	7	
10–19	1	5	3	9	11	19	7	3	1
0– 9	1	3	1	4	10	11	2		

For much too long, many educators have assumed, at least implicitly, that if we provide individuals with information they will also be able to use that information productively. Building up the memory store is a necessary condition for productive thinking, but it is not a sufficient condition, for productive abilities are relatively independent of cognitive abilities. There are some revealing findings on this point (18). In a sample of about 200 ninth-grade students, IQ measurements were available and also the scores on a large number of tests of various divergent-production (DP) abilities. Table 1 shows a scatter diagram with plots of DP scores (19) as a function of IQ. The striking feature of this diagram pertains to the large proportion of high-IQ students who had low, even some very low, DP scores. In general, IQ appears to set a kind of upper limit upon DP performance but not a lower limit. The same kind of result was true for most other DP tests.

On the basis of present information, it would be best to regard each intellectual ability of a person as a somewhat generalized skill that has developed through the circumstances of experience, within a certain culture, and that can be further developed by means of the right kind of exercise. There may be limits to abilities set by heredity, but it is probably safe to say that very rarely does an individual really test such limits. There is much experimental evidence, rough though it may be, that exercise devoted to certain skills involved in creative thinking is followed by increased capability (15, p. 336). Although special exercises have their demonstrated value, it is probably better to have such exercises worked into teaching, whatever the subject, where there are opportunities. Informing individuals regarding the nature of their own intellectual resources, and how they enter into mental work, has also been found beneficial.

There is not space to mention many other problems related to intelligence—its growth and its decline, its relation to brain anatomy and brain functions, and its role in learning. All these problems take on new aspects, when viewed in terms of the proposed frame of reference. For too long, many investigators have been handicapped by using a single, highly ambiguous score to represent what is very complex but very comprehensible.

Without the mulivariate approach of factor analysis, it is doubtful whether any comprehensive and detailed theory of the human intellect, such as the model in Fig. 1, could have been achieved. Application of the method uncovers the building blocks, which are well obscured in the ongoing activities of daily life. Although much has already been done by other methods to show the relevance and fruitfulness of the concepts generated by the theory (15), there is still a great amount of developmental work to be done to implement their full exploitation, particularly in education.

SUMMARY

In this limited space I have attempted to convey information regarding progress in discovering the nature of human intelligence. By intensive factor-analytic investigation, mostly within the past 20 years, the multifactor picture of intelligence has grown far beyond the expectations of those who have been most concerned. A comprehensive, systematic theoretical model known as the "structure of intellect" has been developed to put rationality into the picture.

The model is a cubical affair, its three dimensions representing ways in which the abilities differ from one another. Represented are: five basic kinds of operation, four substantive kinds of information or "contents," and six formal kinds of information or "products," respectively. Each intellectual ability involves a unique conjunction of one kind of operation, one kind of content, and one kind of product, all abilities being relatively independent in a population, but with common joint involvement in intellectual activity.

This taxonomic model has led to the discovery of many abilities not suspected before. Although the number of abilities is large, the 15 category constructs provide much parsimony. They also provide a systematic basis for viewing mental operations in general, thus suggesting new general psychological theory.

The implications for future intelligence testing and for education are numerous. Assessment of intellectual qualities should go much beyond present standard intelligence tests, which seriously neglect important abilities that contribute to problem-solving and creative performance in general. Educational philosophy, curriculum-building, teaching procedures, and examination methods should all be improved by giving attention to the structure of intellect as the basic frame of reference. There is much basis for expecting that various intellectual abilities can be improved in individuals, and the procedures needed for doing this should be clear.

References and Notes

1. C. Spearman, *Am. J. Psychol.* **15**, 201 (1904).
2. For the benefit of the uninitiated, a (positive) correlation between any two tests means that if certain individuals make high (low) scores in one of them they are likely also to make high (low) scores in the other.
3. L. L. Thurstone, *Vectors of Mind* (Univ. of Chicago Press, Chicago, 1935).
4. H. H. Harman, *Modern Factor Analysis* (Univ. of Chicago Press, Chicago, 1967).
5. J. P. Guilford, *Psychol. Bull.* **61**, 401 (1964).
6. L. L. Thurstone, "Primary Mental Abilities," *Psychometric Monographs No. 1* (1938).
7. J. P. Guilford and J. I. Lacey, Eds., *Printed Classification Tests* (Government Printing Office, Washington, D.C., 1947).
8. We are indebted to the Office of Naval Research, Personnel and Training Branch, for continued support, and for additional support at various times from the U.S. Office of Education and the National Science Foundation, Biological and Medical Sciences Division.
9. C. Burt, *Brit. J. Educ. Psychol.* **19**, 100, 176 (1949).
10. P. E. Vernon, *The Structure of Human Abilities* (Wiley, New York, 1950).

11. J. P. Guilford, *Psychol. Bull.* **53**, 267 (1956).
12. F. Zwicky, *Morphological Analysis* (Springer, Berlin, 1957).
13. J. P. Guilford, *Am. Psychologist* **14**, 469 (1959).
14. E. L. Thorndike, *Harper's Magazine* **140**, 227 (1920).
15. J. P. Guilford, *The Nature of Human Intelligence* (McGraw-Hill, New York, 1967).
16. ———, *ibid.*, chap. 10.
17. ———, *ibid.*, chap. 14.
18. ——— and R. Hoepfner, *Indian J. Psychol.* **14**, 7 (1966).
19. Expressional Fluency is the sentence-construction test illustrated earlier.

MEASURES OF WORTH

by Patricia Cayo Sexton*

Teachers and Testing is in many ways an admirable book—scholarly, significant, and refreshingly lucid. My quarrel is with the inferences drawn from some of its rich data—shocking and damaging inferences.

The research on which the book is based (part of a larger study of the effects of testing on students, tests users, and society) inquires into the uses of standardized tests in schools, and into the roles, responses, and experiences of teachers with respect to them. The data are mainly from a Project Talent questionnaire survey of 1,140 teachers in 75 public secondary schools (a stratified sample of the nation's 21,000 secondary schools) and from a mail survey of over 800 public elementary schools in three Eastern states. They show that standardized tests are widely used in schools to make most vital decisions about students.

An average of three tests are given each year to some 50 million children. Group intelligence tests account for 25 percent of tests

* From *American Sociological Review*, December, 1968, Comment on *Teachers and Testing*, by David A. Goslin, N.Y.: Russell Sage Foundation, 1967.

given through the sixth grade. Two-thirds of secondary schools use group intelligence tests, 85 percent use achievement tests, 88 percent use college admission tests, 52 percent use multi-aptitude tests, two-thirds use interest inventories, and 32 percent use personality inventories. The *extent* of testing is positively related to per pupil expenditures, but their *use* is negatively related. That is, fewer tests are given in low-income schools, but there the tests are more often used to judge students.

Thirty-seven percent of secondary school principals say tests are used "very often" to "assess the potential learning ability of pupils," and 45 percent say they are used "very often" to inform pupils about their abilities. Teachers think much weight should be given to tests in putting pupils in special classes, recommending them for college, advising them about vocations, and making other important decisions about them.

Though most teachers think tests should be used to judge students, they definitely do *not* think they should be used to judge themselves or the school. (A child's failure on tests, then, is his own failure, not the teacher's or the school's, and the test becomes a useful rationale for resisting institutional change). Despite the teachers' recognition of the importance of many tests, they seem quite disinclined to prepare students in the specifics of test-passing or to alter their class behavior as a prelude to testing ordeals. Some college-bound students have the advantage over others of advance preparation by teachers. But, in general, tests have little effect on teaching methods or course content.

Most teachers have great confidence in the accuracy of tests, and an astonishing proportion believe that intelligence tests are largely a measure of innate intellectual ability. Even more astonishing, counselors, the child's closest school advisers, are more convinced than teachers that tests penetrate deep genetic truths. Moreover, the greater the "psychometric sophistication" of teachers and counselors (that is, the more courses in testing they've taken) the greater is their reliance on these frail devices as certain signs of a child's innate intelligence. Only 4 percent of secondary teachers think intelligence tests measure "only learned knowledge"—and only .7 percent of secondary counselors, 8 percent of elementary parents, 12 percent of secondary students, and 14 percent of American adults. Through the use of various divining rods, standardized or otherwise, 68 percent of secondary and 72 percent of elementary teachers feel "fairly sure I know how intelligent most of my pupils are."

The data indicate that most teachers know very little about tests. Elementary and private school teachers are especially untrained and uninformed. Yet almost three-fourths of elementary teachers say they administer tests each year, and in 80 percent of elementary schools, teachers are routinely given the intelligence and achievement scores of students, to do with what they may.

Teachers, then, are given test scores, know very little about what they mean, but tend to assume they largely measure genetic endowments. The author cites a study by Rosenthal and Jacobson in which randomly selected children showed an average gain over controls of 25 IQ points in one year after teachers were told, falsely, that remarkable IQ gains could be expected from these children. This is "genetic IQ"?

If a man insisted on pointing a loaded gun at you with the safety off, after repeated requests to desist and warnings that the gun is dangerous, you would be well advised to quickly disarm the man. Together, he and the gun, are a menace. Teachers armed with tests of "ability" (which they and the testers assume to be genetic ability, even "partly"), are a similar menace. Yet the author wishes only to change the gunman, to educate him. He feels "explicit consideration needs to be given to the problem of teacher training in the field of measurement." "Aside from possible modifications in the curriculum of teacher training institutions to include more formal training in testing, increased sophistication on the part of elementary teachers might be achieved through the publication of a short booklet designed explicitly to deal with the problems faced by elementary teachers in their role as testers. Such a booklet might be prepared under the sponsorship of the American Psychological Association and distributed *en masse* to elementary teachers through the American Council on Education, the National Education Association, or some similar organization. Furthermore, school systems and testing specialists within them might be encouraged to initiate informal training programs or clinics for teachers."

Such suggestions are like proposing that the National Rifle Association and the Mafia be charged with cleaning up crime and gun abuse, for it is precisely the educators, the testers, and the psychologists (protests of some to the contrary) who have *mis*educated teachers and counselors about the meaning of tests of "ability."

The author acknowledges that there are likely to be certain advantages to pupils if teachers do not accept test scores as genetic measures. "How one reconciles this proposition with the facts in the situation, namely, that intelligence tests do measure innate abilities to some degree, however, is less clear. It is probably unrealistic to consider seriously attempting systematically to dupe teachers into thinking that tests do not measure innate abilities . . ." He offers no supporting evidence for these claims, even though the heavy burden of proof is clearly on those who extravagantly claim that testing products reveal innate qualities of the mind, wholly or partially.

After looking at the startling data in this volume, I would offer some counter inferences as follows:

1. Schools should abandon the use of all tests that purport to measure anything remotely labelled intelligence, apititude, or ability. While genetic differences in intelligence are probably as large as genetic physical differences, I have seen not one shred of real evidence, in this book or elsewhere, that these fragile exercises have any power to discern such in-born mental aptitudes. It has been shown repeatedly that belief in the validity of these tests leads to self-fulfilling prophecies about student behavior, and that scores vary wildly according to student motivation, teacher expectations, and the extent to which teachers prepare students for test success. Worse, the tests have been and are used to limit the performance of Negroes and other lower socioeconomic groups, to legitimate that malfunction, and to excuse the school's failure to educate. They are used to justify doctrines of racial and ethnic superiority. Given the persistent and growing misuse of these tests, perhaps they ought to be forbidden by law, as they are in Norway.

2. Instead of preparing booklets on testing, we should impress on teachers and others that whatever our genetic endowment, very few of us make anything like full use of the potential we have, that the human mind is exceedingly "stretchable" and trainable, whatever its genetic component, and that human intelligence seems to involve such a complex network of responses (including performance, behavior, judgment, etc.) that we cannot hope to adequately define it, let alone pin it down to mere paper and pencil exercises.

3. Given the growing power of tests as measures of a person's worth, all the major tests of achievement (including college boards, graduate record exams, etc.) should come at last into the public domain. They are far too important to be left so exclusively in

private hands. Taking them out of these hands would provide no panacea, but it would help to make clear that these tests are the "geopolitical center" of education, that they can determine what shall be taught, and that they do now determine who shall get what in the schools. As such, they deserve continuing public scrutiny. After informed and responsible public decisions are made about the content and uses of tests, their powers can then more legitimately grow. After defining the knowledge and skills we wish students to have, we may then train them massively and intensively to acquire this knowledge and pass the tests. In doing so, we may by-pass many schools where so much time is now wasted. However, the interests vested in testing are enormous (far in excess of 150 million tests sold each year) and far more respectable than, say, the National Rifle Association. These interests will not be easily dislodged.

SORTING OUT STUDENTS

by Joseph Lederer*

Ability grouping is the classifying of pupils with reference to intelligence or achievement, or both, for the purpose of instruction.[1] In the United States it was applied only sporadically until 1920. Earlier, grade-level grouping had been the rule, determined solely by the child's chronological age.

Then ability grouping began to burgeon, along with the testing movement. The two go pretty much hand in hand, as testing is the main way our schools measure ability. A prominent example dating from the 1920s was the Detroit XYZ Plan. As determined by intelligence and achievement tests, the X group comprised the system's 20

* From "The Scope of the Practice," *The Urban Review*, a publication of the Center for Urban Education, Vol. 3, No. 1, September, 1968.

percent highest students, Z the 20 percent lowest, and Y the 60 percent in between. In 1926, 36 cities out of 40 with populations of 100,000 or more had elementary school pupils in some or all grades classified into ability groups.[2]

The wave continued to crest into the 1930s before subsiding. The spirit of the New Deal was egalitarian, and grouping by ability was considered undemocratic. In addition, the practice was thought to have been discredited by educational research. Underlying many objections was the conviction that the goals of education are much broader than academic achievement alone and can be reached more adequately when pupils are not grouped on the basis of academic ability. Even so, in 1948, one of the lean years for ability grouping, 53 percent of 1,598 city school systems used it in one or more schools.[3]

The latest great upsurge, which is still in progress, began in the late 1950s. The Soviet Union's first sputnik (1957) and the Conant Report (1959) focused sharply on the special needs—slighted for some 20 years—of academically gifted children and stimulated a new, intensified demand for ability grouping, especially at the secondary level. Suburban schools, which had formerly been among the most reluctant to adopt 'special' school situations, began leading the way in honors classes and programs.[4] In these programs for the gifted (usually students with IQs of 130 or more) first-year college courses are sometimes offered to pupils still in high school. It should be added that the past decade has also seen an appreciable increase in special classes for the handicapped and retarded.

The NEA Research Division[5] found that in 1958–59, 77.6 percent of the school districts 2,500 and over in population were making some use of ability grouping in elementary grades, and that 90.5 percent were making some use of it in secondary grades. Of all the districts reporting, 51.7 percent said they were adding or expanding ability groupings in elementary grades, and 67.3 percent said they were adding or expanding it in secondary grades. Less than 1 percent reported curtailing ability grouping at either level.

According to the U.S. Office of Education,[6] special provisions for the gifted are more common in secondary than in elementary schools and have been increasing in recent years. About one-third of the gifted children in special education were elementary school pupils.

A survey of elementary school administration and organization made in 1958 and 1959[7] showed that 72.1 percent of the public schools reporting grouped pupils in grades one through six heterogeneously and 16.9 percent grouped homogeneously. In grades seven and eight, 60 percent grouped heterogeneously and 34.4 percent homogeneously. The question of trends was also raised. Some 46 percent of the responses predicted an increase in homogeneous grouping, 47.1 percent predicted no change, and 3 percent gave no answer. Both those who were using heterogeneous grouping and those who were using homogeneous grouping were in general agreement on predictions. Only 8 percent of the respondents who grouped homogeneously suggested a change toward heterogeneous grouping.

In a study such as the one cited above, the terms 'homogeneous' and 'heterogeneous' may be somewhat deceptive. The fact is, elementary school classes are often termed 'heterogeneous' despite a certain amount of ability grouping: the kind, for example, where pupils are divided into several groups for reading, and into entirely different groups for instruction in arithmetic, while in other areas (e.g. physical education) the class may work as a unit.

As for principals' responses on various educational trends,[8] 52 percent of the principals in large elementary school districts reported an increase in the extent to which pupils were grouped by ability or achievement levels between 1957 and 1961; only 7 percent noticed a decrease in such grouping. For all sizes of school districts, 46 percent of the principals claimed a shift toward greater use of ability grouping. An increase at the secondary level was reported by nearly two-thirds of all the secondary school principals. Eighty-one percent of the large schools recorded an increase of such grouping in the same period.

"It seems fairly clear," summarizes an NEA research memo dated September 1962, "that ability grouping is becoming more and more prevalent and is likely to continue to do so."

A nationwide sample of elementary school teachers was asked whether they approved of ability grouping into separate classes in elementary schools on the basis of IQ or achievement test scores.[9] Some 58 percent approved; 33 percent disapproved; and about 9 percent said they did not know. Of those who had not taught under ability grouping, 46 percent approved; of those who had taught under ability grouping, 79 percent approved; and of those who had taught under both plans, 63 percent approved.

Secondary school teachers, in the same survey, were asked whether they favored ability grouping in academic subjects such as mathematics, English, and foreign languages. Eighty-seven percent were in favor; 8.6 percent were opposed; and 4.1 percent had no opinion. Eighty-two percent of those who had not taught under such grouping were in favor; 87 percent of those who had taught under ability grouping approved it; and some 91 percent of those who had taught under both plans gave their approval.

According to this poll, a substantial percentage of even those teachers who had no experience of ability grouping—particularly secondary school teachers—approved it.

In small schools, special classes may become uneconomically small and the cost of homogeneous grouping programs prohibitive. The larger the school, the easier it is to introduce such programs. Thus, one of the elements that make ability grouping more practicable today than ever before is the exploding school population. In 1959 the median enrollment for all public high schools (grades 7–12) in the United States was 278 and every fifth high school in the nation had an enrollment between 100 and 199.[10] Since then enrollments have shot up and there has been an enormous consolidation of small schools. The tiny rural district, for example, may soon be a thing of the past.

When ability grouping is applied to all grades and used in all schools in a system, it is called *tracking*.[11] As yet there exists no comprehensive statistical study of tracking on a nationwide basis. We do know that partial or complete tracking is a common practice in American secondary schools. Students are often assigned to clearly defined tracks labelled 'college preparatory,' 'vocational,' 'commercial,' 'general,' or 'engineering.' For example, math in ninth grade can be algebra or business math or basic math.

An expected result of the track system is a curriculum planned for differences by adapting the total curricular program to ability levels. The hope is that the track system will increase teachability by limiting ability range.

Variations of the track system permit pupils to choose their electives from any track, no matter what their specialization. A few schools permit no deviation from the track. Even where tracks prevail, some courses remain heterogeneously grouped, but the track itself is a form of ability grouping.[12]

Illustrative of a system designed to meet the needs of big-city education is the multitrack plan adopted by Washington, D.C. in 1956, offering four areas of study: honors, college preparatory, general, and basic.[13] In June 1967 Judge J. Skelly Wright ruled that Washington's tracking plan condemned Negro and poor children, on the basis of inappropriate aptitude tests, to a 'blue collar' education in lower tracks distinctly unequal to that provided white children in upper tracks. Many Negro schools had no honors track, and few white schools had the 'basic' or lowest track. Judge Wright ordered an end to tracking in Washington.

Although ability grouping along the lines we have been discussing is the most commonly practiced homogeneous grouping pattern in our public schools, it is not the only one. An NEA research memo, dated July 1966, enumerates 25 grouping practices and proposals, including split-grade plan, multigrading, dual progress plan, intraclass grouping, Dalton plan, and Trump plan, and comments that the list is "by no means comprehensive." Also, as already mentioned, schools may combine several kinds of grouping: e.g. homogeneous in 'skill' courses like reading and math, and heterogeneous in 'idea' courses, such as social studies.

The central concern of this paper is not grouping *per se,* but rather the possible effect on teacher expectation of a whole gamut of institutionalized practices, of which tracking is but one example. A rule of thumb might be stated (or, more accurately, overstated) as follows: whenever a teacher inherits someone else's evaluation of a pupil, that teacher also inherits an expectation. This can come by way of grades, IQ tests, numerous achievement tests, and recorded comments by teachers and counselors on the pupils' personality and maturity.

Dr. Miriam Goldberg estimates that at least 80 percent of the nation's school districts have 'cumulative record cards' for their pupils.[14] The teachers have easy access to these record cards on which, sooner or later, are probably entered the child's IQ score, his percentile ranks on various achievement tests (reading, math, science, social studies) in a representative sample of American school children, the observations of teachers and counselors, and, in some cases, percentile ranks on interest areas: mechanical, computational, scientific, artistic, musical, clerical, etc. Some systems have two permanent record cards: elementary (kindergarten through sixth grade) and secondary (seventh through 12th grade).

There are no nationwide statistics as to the availability of IQ scores to classroom teachers; but, as a rule, if a child has taken an IQ test, the score is available to his teacher. As far as teacher expectation is concerned, the IQ score is only one of many factors. These things go in waves. Today reading tests seem to be more in vogue than the once dominant IQ tests for purposes of homogeneous ability grouping. One reason for this is indicated by a study in which children with IQs above 120 and below 90 were removed from a fifth grade class;[15] nevertheless, the range of reading ability in terms of grade norms among the remaining pupils spread from 2.7 to 11.2. Not very homogeneous.

In any discussion of teacher expectation—even when limited to institutionalized practices—there are bound to be a good many intangibles. Much depends on the proclivities of the individual teacher along with the demands on her time. She may make frequent, or occasional, trips to the files in order to pore over pupils' permanent records or she may barely glance at, or even ignore, the profile sheet furnished her.

Three different attitudes to the question under discussion can be expressed roughly as follows:

1. The function of a teacher is not to have expectations but to teach!

2. Don't even attempt to minimize teacher expectation. The realistic course is to hone it into a sounder, more precise instrument.

3. There are significant new findings to suggest that academic results would be far better if every teacher had high expectations of every pupil.

Without weighing the evidence in support of these positions, our organizational preferences, whatever they might be, are, in a sense, vacuous. After all, there are many ways of organizing classes, schools, systems—from the 'lock-step' type of instruction (where everyone in the same classroom is expected to do the same things at the same time and at the same rate) to experiments in 'enhancing,' 'modifying,' 'maximizing,' and 'enrichment.' Organizational reforms do not necessarily provide the answers. For example, it is not enough to say: let us abandon homogeneous grouping altogether and return to some modern equivalent of the little red heterogeneous schoolhouse; for even within one classroom the teacher may divide the class into subgroups, individualize instruction, differentiate homework assignments and hold higher expectations for 'more able' students. Nor are nongraded classes a panacea, since, in fact, very careful grouping is a preliminary to this type of organization.

Many questions remain to be asked of *any* organizational plan. How much leeway is allowed for spurts and plateaus in intellectual achievement and for the fact that a child can have more talent in one area than another? How flexible is the program in use, how much opportunity to break out of the mold? Are teachers encouraged to make reevaluations as a matter of course or is the tendency to perpetuate inherited groupings?

The trend, as we have seen, is toward increased testing, grouping, evaluating and record keeping, all of which play a part in shaping teacher expectation, as well as pupil self-expectation. If it can be demonstrated that academic achievement is, in any significant degree, *determined* by expectation, then the time has come to scrutinize these practices as never before.

Footnotes

1. Many schools try to disguise the ranking of classes with 'neutral' labels such as X, Y and Z or Robins, Bluebirds and Orioles. Nevertheless, by eighth grade, if not earlier, children generally have a pretty good idea of their relative placement.
2. Henry J. Otto. *Elementary School Organization and Administration.* New York: Appleton-Century-Crofts, Third edition, 1954.
3. Otto, *op. cit.*
4. I am grateful to Dr. Miriam Goldberg of Teachers College, Columbia University, for calling attention to this fact in conversation.
5. National Education Association, Research Division. *Administrative Practices in Urban School Districts, 1958–59.* Research Report 1961–R10. Washington, D.C.: the Association, May 1961.
6. Romaine P. Mackie and Patricia Peace Robbins. *Exceptional Children and Youth: Special Education Enrollments in Public Day Schools.* Washington, D.C.: U.S. Department of Health, Education, and Welfare, Office of Education, 1961.
7. Stuart E. Dean. *Elementary School Administration and Organization.* Washington, D.C.: U.S. Department of Health, Education, and Welfare, Office of Education, Bulletin 1960, n 11, Chapter 10, 1960, pp. 67–73.
8. National Education Association, Project on Instruction. *The Principals Look at the Schools.* Washington, D.C.: the Association, April 1962.

9. National Education Association, Research Division. "Teacher Opinion Poll." *NEA Journal* 50: 62; April 1961.
10. "Public Secondary Day Schools." *Statistics of Education in the United States*. Washington, D.C.: U.S. Department of Health, Education, and Welfare, Office of Education. 1958–59 Series n 1, 1961.
11. John I. Goodlad. *Planning and Organizing for Teaching*. Washington, D.C.: National Education Association, Project on Instruction, 1963.
12. Carl F. Hansen, *et al.* "For the Able Student—What?" *NEA Journal* 47: 13–15; October 1958.
13. Carl F. Hansen. *The Four-Track Curriculum in Today's High Schools*. Englewood Cliffs, N.J.: Prentice-Hall, 1964.
14. John I. Goodlad. "Classroom Organization." *Encyclopedia of Educational Research*. New York: Macmillan, Third Edition, 1960.
15. See, for example, a description of the research conducted by Robert Rosenthal and Lenore Jacobson.

WHAT CAN YOU EXPECT?

by Robert Coles*

The moment a child is born, it joins a particular kind of world. A doctor has done the delivery in a hospital, or a midwife has done it in a rural cabin, or the baby has emerged unassisted. That baby learns how to sit up, walk, talk, play, dress, and eat. Genes have a lot to do with the child's appearance and appetites and growth, but what *happens* to anyone, infant or grownup, is almost inevitably ordained by the laws of nature. A boy might have it in him to become a tall, strong, energetic man, and a girl might have it in her to become an unusual beauty, but without proper food they will not survive infancy, let alone reach adulthood in anything like the condition they might have attained, had life been more generous.

All this is common sense, but a common sense that is often

* *The New Yorker,* April 19, 1969. Reprinted by permission; © 1969 The New Yorker Magazine, Inc.

missing in arguments over the rights and powers of those two antagonists "nature" and "nurture," each of which has its strenuous partisans. Nor is the struggle only abstract, ideological, or philosophical. When a subject such as what goes to make up "intelligence" is debated, very concrete and practical issues are involved. If intelligence is to be considered something fixed and precise, a biological "given," then teachers are right to separate the quick-witted child from the slow one, and to look upon themselves as agents for each kind of child: the child comes to school with a good, fast mind, an average one, or a slow one, and the school's job is to find out and act accordingly. This teacher works well with fast learners, that one with the dull child; So-and-So has a knack for those in the middle, who respond to her and go as far as they can as a result of her attentive ear, her light, gentle touch. On the other hand, "intelligence" can be considered a complicated and variable activity by which the mind, under certain circumstances—and what is favorable for one person can be the opposite for another—meets up with facts and situations and comes to understand them, act upon them, gain some control over them. This view places great stress on complexity and variability. Idiots can have astonishing powers of recall; geniuses can be dumb about so very much; writers can barely know how to count; any number of brilliant social scientists can't write a straight sentence. More to the point of our present national problems, children can be stubbornly, impossibly backward in school but shrewd, imaginative, and resourceful at home—or, more likely, on the streets and in the alleys.

At this point, the anthropologist and the psychiatrist (and perhaps the merely intelligent teacher or parent) may remind us that some children grow up in a family, a neighborhood, a town where schools mean a lot and the children's achievement in them means everything to their parents. Such children learn that it makes a difference if they pay attention to the teacher and do what she says; others literally learn not to learn. One boy's parents are well-to-do and ambitious, but he is afraid to learn and so has what child psychiatrists call a "learning block." His brain seems normal but his mind won't, for any number of reasons, take in the facts and put them together. A blurred, indistinct world seems safer—an attitude obviously the result of certain experiences. Many children have no such psychological problem but still don't do well at school—because they come there, as it is now put, "disadvantaged" and "deprived." A number of physicians and nutritionists and neurophysi-ologists argue that a diet low in critically important vitamins, minerals, and proteins causes serious damage to an infant's brain, so he comes to school retarded not by disease or injury but by the repercussions of a nation's social and economic problem, which becomes an intense personal problem for millions of families. Yet even if poor parents can provide their children with decent meals and medical care and clothes—which is not usual—there is a larger issue. Do parents give their children confidence, or do they feel discouraged about life most of the time? It takes a lot of persuasion, subtle suggestion, charm, or even force to make an infant the kind of child teachers like: well scrubbed, eager, obedient, responsive. Mothers who live in broken-down tenements, who never know when the next few dollars will come, have little energy left for their children. Life is grim and hard, and the child has to learn that. He learns it and learns it and learns it—how to survive all sorts of threats and dangers, why his parents have given up on school, why they have fallen on their faces. He learns about racial hatred, the state of the economy, technological change; he learns whether he is an insider or an outsider, whether storekeepers and property owners and policemen treat his family with kindness and respect or with suspicion and even out-and-out contempt. By the time a child of the ghetto comes to school, his knowledge might well be what has been awkwardly called "the intelligence of the so-called unintelligent as it appears in sly, devious, and haunting ways."

The teacher may know all that but have little time to ponder the social and psychological forces that make children so very different from one another before they have had a single day of school. To the teacher, the differences are a beginning, not an end. Six-year-old children are what they are, and they are quickly found out by their teachers and school psychologists and by "objective criteria"—by all those intelligence tests, each with its own twist, its own special, prideful, reasonable (or extravagant) claims. These tests are employed to separate children by "tracks": fast, medium, slow. The theory is valid; the able and gifted ones will not intimi-date the fearful and slow ones, nor will the slow ones cost the fast ones their right to learn at a speed they find congenial. Yet those who score well in the tests take an interest in schoolwork and become known as first-rate students; those to whom teachers and the work they assign are a big bore or a big fright become the "problem child," the "disruptive child," the slow-witted or stupid one—no matter how bright they may be "underneath."

Well, what can the poor overworked, underpaid teacher do about all that? Can he be responsible for our nation's injustices, for its history of racial strife, for the regional circumstances that doom white Appalachian children and Indian children and Mexican-American children as well as black children? Can schools make up for lacks and shortages and cruelties at home? Can a few hours in a classroom, even one run by the most capable and best-intentioned of teachers, really change a sullen, troubled child's destiny? Can it be that teachers in dozens of ways, for dozens of reasons, determine which children will eagerly absorb their lessons and which ones will say maybe or positively no? Can the child's performance in school be considered the result as much of what his teachers' attitudes are toward him as of his native intelligence or his attitude as a pupil?

A book with the dramatic and suggestive title of "Pygmalion in the Classroom" (Holt, Rinehart & Winston) has a lot to say about the whole issue. The authors are Robert Rosenthal, a Harvard social psychologist, and Lenore Jacobson, a San Francisco school principal, and their study has to do, in the pedantic words of their subtitle, with "teacher expectation and pupils' intellectual development." They began their work in 1964, when they gave the "Harvard Test of Inflected Acquisition" to most of the children of what they have called the Oak School, an elementary establishment on the West Coast. (The only ones not tested were to leave the school before the next round of tests.) The test had prophetic powers, the school's teachers were told: "As a part of our study we are further validating a test which predicts the likelihood that a child will show an inflection point or 'spurt' within the near future. This test which will be administered in your school will allow us to predict which youngsters are most likely to show an academic spurt. The top twenty per cent (approximately) of the scorers on this test will probably be found at various levels of academic functioning. The development of the test for predicting inflections or 'spurts' is not yet such that *every* one of the top twenty per cent of the children *will* show a more significant inflection or spurt in their learning within the next year or less than will the remaining eighty per cent of the children."

There is no "Harvard Test of Inflected Acquisition." Dr. Rosenthal and Mrs. Jacobson had a mission to fulfill, and they knew that such a name would impress schoolteachers of the second half of the twentieth century; when someone out of Harvard comes around to estimate "inflected acquisition," a woman who struggles to teach boys and girls their letters and numbers can only be grateful for the assistance afforded by Progress and Science. The children were really given the useful Flanagan's Tests of General Ability, or TOGA. TOGA is one of a hundred tests most teachers don't know about. They do know, however, that social scientists are smart. So the Oak School teachers had reason to believe they were aiding research by lending their children to an experiment that would help establish the value of yet another manmade "instrument"—the name given all those questionnaires and tests by the psychologists and sociologists who make them up. Naturally, the teachers also believed that they would become privy to interesting and important information. The Oak School divides each grade into fast, medium, and slow tracks, and TOGA supposedly supplied lists of pupils for all three tracks of each grade. TOGA apparently could spot the "spurters," or "bloomers," and the teachers were let in on the discoveries, though they were cautioned not to tell what they knew to any children or parents. But what really happened was that Dr. Rosenthal and Mrs. Jacobson had arbitrarily selected the names; the TOGA scores had nothing to do with it. A third-grade class made up of fast learners might supply only one or two children to the honor roll of the "Harvard Test of Inflected Acquisition," and a first-grade class that seemed extremely slow might present eight or nine children headed for better things indeed. If any of the children on the lists turned out to be "special," it was because their teachers were told they were or were going to be.

Teachers have a lot to do besides reading and rereading the names of a few children who just might be headed for a kind nod from fate, and the Oak School went about its regular business for a year, interrupted only by two more bouts with TOGA. Then our two authors returned to Cambridge with the "data." Teachers are always grading their pupils—how they are getting along in each subject, how they behave, what their "attitude" is. All that, too, went East to the computers. The teachers were asked for more information: How successful might the children be; were their achievements in class the result of native ability or, say, a capacity for pure drudgery; was this child "appealing, well adjusted, affectionate" and that one "hostile and motivated by a need for approval"? What did the authors and their research assistants discover? Their report—"Pygmalion in the Classroom"—is full of charts and graphs and statistics and percentages and carefully weighed statements, but there are conclusions that have great significance for this nation, preoccupied as it is with severe educational problems of many kinds. Among the children of the first and second grades, those tagged "bloomers" made astonishing gains in the later tests: "About every fifth control-group child gained twenty IQ points or more, but of the special children, nearly every second child gained that much."

The lesson in the book is clear: All sorts of young children did very much better in school than others like them, presumably because their teachers *expected* them to become "bloomers," and TOGA's putative prophecy was fulfilled so conclusively that even hardline social scientists were startled. They were also taken aback by other results. The greatest gains were among the Mexican-American children, a "minority group" with "cultural disadvantage" and "cultural deprivation." Despite these condescending labels, the Mexican children became much better students in their teachers' eyes, too. What is more, the children who looked classically Mexican did better than those who looked a little "Anglo," which prompts the authors to speculate, dryly, that "the teachers' pre-experimental expectancies of the more Mexican-looking boys' intellectual performance was probably lowest of all. These children may have had the most to gain by the introduction of a more favorable expectation into the minds of their teachers." But the teachers were not won over by the remarkable improvement; the Mexican children still were rated low in "adjustment" and intellectual curiosity. Harvard people might know something, the teachers appeared to agree, but these miraculous improvements had come about because of something that had nothing to do with the teachers and their attitudes as educators, as men and women who believe in some children and view others, right from the start, as hopeless. Yet maybe a teacher can silently let a child know that good things are, incredibly, around the corner because the experts say so. A teacher's faith is apparently not required—only her loyalty to experts, the secular gods of the twentieth century. Dr. Rosenthal and Mrs. Jacobson are quite aware of the effect a pair of scientists armed with tons of paper can have on opinions. What obviously surprised *them* was the substantial and persisting nature of that effect, obtained in spite of the long-standing prejudices of teachers. "One wonders whether among these minority-group children who over-represent the slow track and the disadvantaged of Oak School their gains in intellectual competence may not be easier for teachers to bring about than to believe."

The prejudices of teachers—and the effects the prejudices have on learning—come across on almost every page of this book. Bright children who were labelled "bloomers" were found more pleasant and attractive by their teachers; slow children labelled "bloomers" were grudgingly viewed as "more autonomous but less affectionate." When children in the lowest track inexplicably improved, the teachers became confused and angry: "The more such a child gained in IQ, the more unfavorably he was evaluated by his teacher in almost every respect." The authors remark, ironically, that "if a child is to show intellectual gains, it may be better for his intellectual vitality and for his mental health as seen by his teacher, if his teacher has been expecting him to gain intellectually. It appears that there may be psychological hazards to unexpected intellectual growth."

What actually happened in the Oak School? The authors of "Pygmalion in the Classroom" admit that they don't know. Before they tell about their project, they offer a more general discussion of what I suppose is best called the "self-fulfilling prophecy" as it takes place in everyday life, in the practice of medicine and psychiatry, and in the education not only of children but even of animals. Banks have failed simply because frightened people *believed* them to be in trouble. Certain groups of people have always been considered to be by nature inferior and uneducable, and because they have been treated so, they have appeared so, behaved so, and confirmed the beliefs of their oppressors. And patients feel better, get better, because they are persuaded that a given pill will do its job. There is evidence that even something as tangible as surgery draws upon psychological overtones for its success. In 1961, Henry K. Beecher, professor of anesthesiology at the Harvard Medical School, published in the *Journal of the American Medical Association* an article called "Surgery as Placebo." He described a new operation to relieve angina pectoris, and reported that the benefits of it were the result "of what happened in the minds of the patients and the surgeons involved." Experiments revealed that surgeons who believed enthusiastically in the new method brought relief to patients four times as often as the skeptical surgeons did. It even turned out that a feigned operation, done under anesthesia and believed by the patient to be a complicated surgery, was equally effective. Psychiatry has not even begun to settle the issue of which treatment works for what reason. Entire mental hospitals have been suddenly transformed by the arrival of a new drug or "technique," and just as quickly the old despair and gloom have reappeared. Psychiatric theorists argue fiercely, attack one another in dense, muddled language—often enough to conceal from themselves, let alone others, the ever-present hunch that the mind is healed not only by rational explanations, however intricate and compelling, but by experiences (in the doctor's office, outside his office) that have to do with faith, reassurance, suggestion, persuasion, all of which a doctor can first inspire or offer out of his heart, and later nervously dress up in elaborate language that is respectably scientific.

"To summarize now what has been learned from research employing animal subjects generally," the authors say, "it seems that those that are expected to perform competently tend to do so, while animals expected to perform incompetently tend also to perform as prophesied." In describing an experiment, Dr. Rosenthal relates animals to children in a way every teacher might think about: "At the beginning of that study experimenters assigned allegedly dull animals were of course told that they would find retarded learning on the part of their rats. They were, however, reassured that 'it has been found that even the dullest rats can, in time, learn the required responses.' Animals alleged to be dull, then, were described as educable but slow. It was interesting in the light of this to learn that of the experimenters who had been assigned 'dull' animals, forty-seven per cent believed their subjects to be uneducable. Only five per cent of the experimenters assigned 'bright' rats were equally pessimistic about their animal's future. From this result one wonders about the beliefs created in schoolteachers when they are told a child is educable but slow, deserving but disadvantaged."

In the Oak School, "disadvantaged" children suddenly came to life and made astonishing gains. Yet they were given no crash programs, no special tutoring, no trips to museums; their teachers were simply told that those particular children bore watching. Another research project is needed if we are to discover how teachers go about letting children know they have a special destiny. No doubt dozens of signals are made: gestures, postures, facial expressions, a manner of approach, a choice of words and the way they are spoken, a look in the eyes, a touch of the hand. Soon the child gets the message—perhaps in the best way, unself-consciously. He begins to feel the teacher's feelings, the pleasure of approval, and begins to learn more. There comes a time when the issue is not only emotional but intellectual, when a teacher's expectations become a child's sense of prideful achievement, which in turn enables *him* to expect more—of himself.

"Pygmalion in the Classroom" is not meant to be a popular book, though as books written by social scientists go it possesses an exceptionally accessible narrative style. The writers are not afraid of a readable and lively sentence, and they mix blunt social comment with the most complicated statistical equations and tabulations. Without attempting eloquence, they have achieved the matter-of-fact eloquence that goes with an original, imaginative study of people and their doings with one another. The authors constantly remind us of the ethical dimensions of scientific work. After all, they might have persuaded the teachers of Oak School to think less of certain children and to feel right about expecting nothing—right because scientists have said that it is useless to expect much but *decline* in certain children.

I like the way Dr. Rosenthal and Mrs. Jacobson question themselves, their moral purposes, and state their loyalties—ultimately to man as more than the sum of all labels and categories, and to man as full of hidden as well as apparent possibilities, for the good and for the bad. And I also like the title of this book. At the end, Eliza Doolittle is quoted: "The difference between a lady and a flower girl is not how she behaves, but how she's treated." In Shaw's "Pygmalion" a professor helps make a slattern into a lady, but in the Greek legend the issue is more momentous, a matter of life and death—which is what the alternatives are for our schoolchildren.

PART III

Community Control and Decentralization

Failing to achieve school desegregation in Northern schools because of resistance on the part of whites as well as the growing minority populations in the cities, the citizens in some communities began to raise questions about who should control the ghetto school. If the present managers could not improve or desegregate the schools, should not the local residents themselves see what they could do? The demand for community control seemed to fit the general premise on which American schools are organized: that the small school district, the local community, is the best unit for administering the school. It also seemed to fit the initiatives of the U.S. Office of Economic Opportunity (the poverty program) and its community-action efforts to elicit "maximum feasible participation" in communities. Certainly community districts in the city are large enough to be semiautonomous. Ghetto communities in the large cities are far larger in school population, in fact, than most local school districts in the nation.

The issue of school decentralization is related to the issue of community control. Even many school administrators feel that big-city school systems are too large to be administered well from on top. Many favor decentralizing some decision making to smaller districts in the city, assuming they could make decisions faster and be more responsive to local needs. Rarely do these administrators want decision making completely transferred to local lay groups. Usually they only want some authority passed down to district administrators. Such partial dispersal of authority to other school managers is hardly what some citizens mean by "community control."

The discussion raises many questions: Who should make what decisions in the school? How much authority should elected lay boards in the community have? How much should administrators retain? What authority will teachers have? How much should students themselves have to say about their own instruction? What is the most efficient pattern of organization, and what pattern will have the best effect on student achievement?

Professor Etzioni asserts that the need is for national movements, not local controls, that national levers of power are more accessible to citizens, and that national efforts are needed to counteract the consolidation of power by elite groups. On the domestic front, he says, "little will be achieved by most forms of decentralization, because the system is already rather decentralized, and the local-ecological units are chiefly controlled by oligarchies which are tighter than the national domestic system."

Community control of schools, says Joseph Featherstone, "spells deep trouble." It will not mean "more money for public education—indeed, one danger is that it could signal further withdrawals of white support from ghetto institutions. It raises risks of confrontations between hysterical whites and black extremists . . . and it always has to be remembered that it does not necessarily mean any change either in teaching or in learning." But, he says, such reservations are beside the point. "The school system is shaking to pieces. There is a crisis of authority, and there has to be a political settlement." Existing institutions are not "representing the interests of ghetto residents," and professionals have served themselves rather than their clients and communities.

Educationally speaking, he notes, the movement for community control "is not a program but simply a response to what are believed to be the failures of integration and compensatory education." In the end, he concludes, the "schools won't be able to pick up the marbles for the rest of the social order."

Albert Shanker's views reflect those of the main body of New York City's United Federation of Teachers of which he has been president. He stresses the need for broad social and economic reforms to end poverty. He agrees that "parents have a legitimate grievance against the rigidities and the remoteness of the central bureaucracy." But, he says, demands for community control evade the need to integrate schools and are not educationally relevant. They are simply offered, he suggests, in lieu of proper funding and quality education as a means of pacifying black militants in the communities who are demanding more black power.

Maurice Berube asserts that community control *is* educationally relevant. The most pertinent educational research, he says, has a common denominator: "the importance of the psychological to the learning process. Whether a pupil feels his efforts can influence and control his future—feelings of identity and self-worth—emerges as a prime learning factor. What a teacher expects of her pupils has great bearing on how much a child learns. And the sense of security of the ghetto community helps students to achieve."

Charles Hamilton, coauthor with Stokely Carmichael of *Black Power,* questions the legitimacy of the whole system of education and insists that we listen to the black community rather than the "experts" in shaping public policy. He describes the issues concerning the system's functioning that are current in the black community and offers an alternate model—a Comprehensive Family-Community-School Plan.

THE FALLACY OF DECENTRALIZATION

by Amitai Etzioni*

In 1947, I was delivering hay from Tel Yoseph, an Israeli kibbutz, to Ein Harod, another kibbutz less than a mile away. The farm manager of Ein Harod signed the delivery papers for twenty-eight bales, and I filed the papers with the office of Tel Yoseph. "How much will Ein Harod be charged?" I asked the clerk. He was astonished by my question. "By Afula prices, of course." Afula is a town not far from both kibbutzim. While the kibbutzim neither use money nor set prices in their internal transactions, they charge each other the prices which prevail in the "free" (i.e., capitalistic) market of Afula. The national kibbutz associations help fledgling kibbutzim, but in general the mechanisms for transfer payments are very weak. No wonder that rather well-off kibbutzim are to be found next to extremely poor ones. And over the years, the rich kibbutzim get richer while the poor ones remain poor.

The kibbutz movement is of considerable interest to those who favor decentralization as a way of providing a genuinely participatory system. But it also illustrates the fact that decentralization often serves ineffectively those values which require a national mechanism that is sufficiently powerful to reallocate sources among local units (a prerequisite for social justice) and the handling of many other "inter-unit," nation-wide issues and values (e.g., the financing of institutions of higher education which would advance the movement).

I am far from being an expert on Yugoslavia, but I understand from those who are that the relatively considerable decision-making power given to small residential and work units generates some similar, symptomatic problems. Thus, for instance, I am told that there is little "income transfer" from the more affluent parts of

* From *The Nation*, August 25, 1969.

198

Yugoslavia to such poverty-stricken, underdeveloped regions as Macedonia, Yugoslavia's equivalent of our South. Efforts to establish inter-local bus lines, especially those which require inter-regional coordination, are said to face difficulties similar to those encountered in attempts to establish rapid transit systems in our cities, when the consent and financial support of a large number of independent local governments are needed.

To generalize, a truly decentralized participatory system will tend to be highly responsive to the needs of the members in each participatory locality, but will tend to neglect inter-local, inter-regional and national needs, both of the allocative (e.g., social justice) type and those which are best served collectively (e.g., a priming of the economy).

Decentralization offers a significant basis for participation. It fosters a citizenry that is informed and in control, tending to make society and its governance more humane. Hence, it is not surprising that many attempts are made to explain, or to explain away, the drawbacks of decentralization. Some anarchists suggest that the values fostered by decentralization are of such high priority that its disadvantages are more than acceptable. Laissez-faire liberals say, as Kenneth Boulding has argued, that once we have a large number of small, competitive political units, the laws of free competition will operate so as to promote various "inter-unit" values without the need for an institutionalized "super-unit" (or national) mechanism.

Another "automatic" solution comes from the New Left; Berndt Rabehl has written, "How will the structure of the city look? It can be divided up into many, individual collectivities of three, four or five thousand men, who center themselves around a factory. Thereby the factory becomes not merely a work center, but a place offering all possibilities for the unfolding of life. Computers will be used to figure what has to be built, how the plans must look, what dangers may appear." This approach ignores moral and political questions, making all of the issues seem to be merely factual. In short, it may be said that what we seek for America is a system that is less centralized than the existing one, but not a system which is completely or even highly decentralized.

This brings up the question of the nature of our national system and what its decentralization would entail. As I see it, the formulation of military, foreign and space policy is centralized, especially those decisions which may involve life or death for millions in nuclear war. If there were a realistic way by which *these* decisions could be decentralized, the welfare of all of us would probably be enhanced. (Even here, however, there would be a hidden assumption: that people are good, at least peace-loving, while governments, ours at any rate, are evil and war-oriented. Possibly the increased participation of citizens in foreign-policy decisions would have the desired effect only when the citizens themselves were liberated from the effects of the centralized society. How we might survive the transition period is a problem almost as intractable as the original one of a decentralized power to declare war.)

For domestic policy, quite a different system seems to prevail in the contemporary United States; hence an approach quite different from decentralization may be required to make the governance of society in this area more participatory and humane. While the foreign-policy state is run chiefly from Washington by generals and bureaucrats in coalition with national power groups, the domestic state is largely fragmented and controlled locally from city halls, state capitals and "private governments" (such as universities and hospitals) in coalition with local power groups and with only spot interference from Washington. Thus, for example, it is empirically incorrect to assume that anyone in Washington has effective control over the educational system; decisions are made by fifty state Departments of Education, thousands of local school boards, and the trustees of 2,000 colleges and universities, with surprisingly little coordination. The same holds for police departments, health and welfare services, etc. Even the funds which come from Washington are spent largely according to local decisions. When national standards exist at all, they are frequently not effectively enforced; the HEW guidelines for desegregation are a case in point.

Domestic policy cannot be *much* more decentralized than it is now. And in considering whether or not to decentralize further, one must take into account that, by and large, the domestic services provided by the federal government—while highly bureaucratic, too-late too-little, slow to reflect innovations, and more slanted toward the middle class than the underclass—are more responsive to human needs, minority groups, etc., than those provided by most local authorities. Some, actually surprisingly few communities, are progressive but the administration of most cities and states (and, I suspect, of the remaining villages) is significantly inferior to that provided by federal agencies on all conceivable criteria. On the local level, power elites can gain their way more readily, nepotism and unvarnished corruption are more rampant, civil service standards are lower, the cost per unit of achievement is higher, and disregard for minorities is greater. It is the pull of national forces—both the organization of people on relief, and HEW—which increases the level of welfare payments, while most states seek to keep it down; the desegregation that has occurred is due largely to nationwide efforts by such forces as the civil rights movement and the Department of Justice, and so forth. It is quite unclear, at least to me, why the sum of the parts of this country is less reactionary (when one reviews domestic programs) than most of the parts taken singly, but I am quite sure that it is so.

Those who favor decentralization, at least if they come from the Left, will say that they have in mind units smaller than states or cities. But even these units—South Boston or East Palo Alto—tend to be monopolized and corrupt in their governance. The reformers may say that they seek still *smaller* units, like the student communes, but these are at best a way of life for a very tiny minority. Moreover, they are too small to attend to most human needs, and the coordination of scores of such units to provide the needed services collectively is nearly impossible.

It is further said that local units can more easily be made participatory. This may be true for a few communities, mainly campus towns and select suburbs, but is not the case for most localities. On the contrary, it seems to me comparatively easier (though still far from easy) to gain participation in decisions made on the national level and to achieve the measure of transformation (e.g., untightening) of which this society is capable by joining into national social movements such as peace, civil rights, and now that of the students. By coordinated effort, scores of Congressmen can be influenced, the outcomes of elections affected, Washington (or the Pentagon) confronted, etc. All this does *not* yield an open, participatory society, but it does fuel more reforms *and* radicalization than most strictly local efforts (as distinct from local projects which are part of a national movement).

Furthermore, I hold, though this cannot be elaborated here, that from a psychological viewpoint, participation will have a restless, Sisyphean quality unless it is tied to causes beyond personal gratification. Without helping to liberate others, without helping to create the *societal* conditions for personal liberation—without *macro*-participation—there cannot be authentic micro-participation. The main opportunities to broaden the participation of all citizens in domestic policies—and, to the degree that the national Establishment does not respond to this pressure, the radicalization of those not yet radicalized—lie in *national* social movements, usually combining a broad critical perspective with mobilization around a specific issue. To anchor this point further, I must digress briefly to indicate my views of the national power structure and of how it may be transformed. The American reality seems to me to stand somewhere between the vulgar conception of the power elite, which sees the control of society as monopolized by one well-coordinated group, and the conception of democratic pluralism, which sees the country taking its direction as the result of interaction among a large variety of autonomous "interest groups." There is, I think, a plurality of national actors, but they are far from being equal in power. In other words, there is a highly *slanted* pluralism, with the country's course being determined to a large extent, but not exclusively, by a not well coordinated group of powerful actors (e.g., the National Association of Manufacturers, the Armed Services), with a significant role being played—especially on the domestic front—by secondary groups (e.g., AFL-CIO) and, occasionally, by the least powerful groups, such as the farm workers.

To view the same structure dynamically, there is an option other than the four now most frequently discussed: disintegration or anarchy, revolutionary change, token ameliorations ("reforms"), or open authoritarianism following a right-wing backlash. The fifth alternative consists of significant *and* accumulative changes that result in a gradual although not necessarily slow transformation to a fundamentally different society.

The extent to which this option is realizable depends directly on whether or not change in the *national* power balance is possible. The more the least powerful groups become politically aware and mobilized for political action on the national level (as is gradually happening with the blacks), and the more they find partners in "secondary" groups which have some power but also have, or can find, an interest in societal transformation (e.g., students, middle-class ethnic minorities), the greater the chance that a fundamental transformation will take place. In short, national movements are an essential propellant for social change. And only *after* such transformation is accomplished can I foresee the conditions under which decentralization would lead not to greater oligarchization but rather to the local transformation of ecological units in the direction of broadened participation.

I deliberately focus here on power, mobilization for political action and national coordination—issues which to some members of the New Left seem rather old-fashioned as compared to "deeper" existential matters. The mere fact that these issues have been raised before does not automatically make them obsolete. And while I can see the appeal of the short cuts offered by the Theatre of the Absurd, the student communes, and even the social islands of the hippies, the integrated and spontaneous way of life cannot, as I see it, be sustained unless the *national* structures are first transformed. Moreover, whatever progress can be made locally, unless it is very microscopic (limited to a few pads or barns), depends on the moral and intellectual sustenance as well as the political protection of a national movement.

There seems to be one exception to this sociological iron law: participation in "private governments" of corporate units as distinct from ecological-residential ones. Universities, churches, hospitals and some places of work can be made more participatory without first transforming the national structures. Again, I am much more confident about the sociological observation than about the reasons. Perhaps this capacity to evolve autonomously in smaller units without first unlocking larger structures is due to the fact that forces of control and sanctioning, that is, the police, are more closely tied to ecological units and elites than to private governments. These governments seem reluctant to resort to such forces because a measure of corporate autonomy serves their interests, and they are afraid—as university faculties so obviously are—that once the government is regularly invited to deal with their rebels, it will stay to deal with them. The result is well illustrated by the relative reluctance of churches, universities and other private governments to call in the police, as compared with the cities of Boston, Detroit, Los Angeles, Oakland and Newark, and by the difficult time Congress has in finding ways to legislate about conduct in the action-space of these private units.

In short, on the domestic front (as distinct from military and foreign policy), little will be achieved by most forms of decentralization, because the system is already rather decentralized, and the local-ecological units are chiefly controlled by oligarchies which are tighter than the national domestic system. The greatest, although far from great, opportunities for mobilizing power toward transformation are on the national level, including unlocking the system for broader local participation. Participation in "private governments" is an exception so far, but it is not clear how long it will remain so; they, too, may become tied into municipal and state sanctioning systems to be controlled like local-ecological units.

A CRISIS OF AUTHORITY

by Joseph Featherstone*

Despite the chaos in New York City, a number of cities are gingerly moving towards some form of decentralization and local control. Worried administrators are trying to read the murky lessons of New York's disaster: it is obvious that any planning for decentralization has to include representatives of all the important political elements in a city. There should be one single plan, instead of half a dozen. Guarantees of teachers' rights have to be spelled out. And if decentralization is preceded by any experimental dry runs, such as the demonstration districts in New York, it will be necessary to delegate powers and lines of authority with a great deal of precision. Such experiments may be necessary on political grounds, but they inevitably work as lightning rods, attracting trouble, offering easy marks for sabotage to those opposing change, and exposing the fundamental issues at stake. The experience of New York with its demonstration districts resounds like a funeral bell with one practical lesson: any experimental districts ought to include some white middle-class areas, and probably should include poor and lower-middle-class whites as well. White parents have to be persuaded

* From "The Problem Is More than Schools," *New Republic,* August 30, 1969.

that they, too, can benefit from lay participation in school reform. The failure to do this in New York—to name, for example, the integrated Joan of Arc district on the upper West Side as one of the model districts—was a major error.

These and other tactical considerations must be weighed, but when all is said, there is no set of techniques for dodging the underlying dilemmas posed by the movement for community control. Lurking like carp below the surface of the school disputes are a number of shadowy issues very nearly without precedent in our history. There are intellectual issues arising out of the new communitarianism of portions of the middle class, and new challenges to the professionalism of the urban bureaucracies. There are the political issues raised by the minority revolutions. And intertwined with these are the educational issues. One of the difficulties in the school crises is that all the questions—each complex and baffling enough in its own right—fuse together, so that protagonists find themselves forced to take sides on a whole range of complex concerns all at once. It seems to me that, under the circumstances, only ideologues and bigots can look at what is happening with undivided minds. Two concerns, both as yet badly-defined, form part of the intellectual background of discussions of decentralization. The first —the widespread sympathy with demands for increased local control—is still only a mood. The second—the attack on professional monopoly of the professions—is as yet reflected in a few weak stirrings of rebellion. Both may become more important as time goes on; ultimately the constituency for community control and reform of the professions may include more than just the oppressed urban minorities.

Race and the collapse of services for the poor fire the movement for community control now, but it also draws on wider currents of feelings. Resentment at the way the cities work has been festering for 20 years. As Nathan Glazer says, the program for community control antedates the black revolution—it was drawn up by middle-class theorists like Paul and Percival Goodman and Jane Jacobs. Nor was it an exclusive concern of a few white intellectuals with a taste for anarchism. In moving out to the suburbs many people were choosing, among other things, to sacrifice certain amenities of city life for a setting in which they had some leverage on government and access to the authorities—or at the very least, choices about such matters as the educational environment in which their children were to grow up. Clearly there were many other reasons for the middle-class exodus, not least of which was the desire to escape the presence of the new black immigrants. And of all places, the suburbs illustrate the extent to which American life is organized in mass national units: their chain stores and their similarities of landscape are reminders that there will always be a limit to how much local control any of us will have in a continental, and even international, economy. But granting all this, I still think Glazer is right: one aspect of the growth of suburbia has been middle-class dissatisfaction with urban services, distrust of the vast city bureaucracies, and aversion to being administered.

This resentment of a distinctly modern condition of powerlessness is shared by portions of the population in all the advanced technological societies. It unites conservatives and radicals—like an SDS girl I spoke to who had worked with some John Birchers against an urban renewal project in South Boston. It is accentuated by the recurring incapacity of majoritarian democracies to come to terms with their ethnic and cultural diversities—an incapacity which has produced waves of separatist (and often reactionary) movements in countries like Britain, Belgium, and Canada. In America, attention has focused on the rise of black nationalism, but a similar mood of resentful communitarianism lies at the roots of the spreading white middle-class revolts against urban renewal plans, superhighways, and ABM missile sites; it is responsible for a measure of the campus unrest, as well. In distinct ways, Eugene McCarthy, George Wallace, and Robert Kennedy were able to tap it in the last Presidential campaign, invoking what Richard Goodwin has called the sources of our public unhappiness. So far it remains simply a mood: it has not been able to crystallize itself into any institutional shape. The main intellectual failure of those who share it has been a reluctance to grapple with the problem that demands for participation and local control have to be squared with the fact that this is a nation of 200,000,000 people, many of whom are organized into hierarchies, bureaucracies, and unions. What is called for is the kind of intellectual enterprise that Paul and Percival Goodman began in *Communitas*, an attempt to spell out real alternatives to our present urban life. What we are getting, instead, is simply a reiteration of the dim aspirations of a troubled middle class for accountability, participation, and a politics of private expressiveness. Nonetheless these dissatisfactions with the urban order, and the call for more participation and local control, are very much in the air: even though their intellectual sources are different from those of the minority revolutions, they have contributed to the declining legitimacy of the urban institutions now under fire.

This mood informs an assault now underway against the bureaucracies and professions. In an explosive new context, the advocates of community control of the schools have revived a traditionally stormy issue in American education: whether laymen or professionals will run the schools. This may signal the slow beginning of an important shift in thinking—not just for blacks, but for the white middle class, too. In the past, radicals and reformers have tended to assume that virtue must dwell with the professionals, whose standards are usually more progressive and universal than those of their clients; local control in the South, everybody knew, spoke in the accents of parochialism and bigotry. This is a classic argument; it remains true today. Its force has been somewhat blunted in recent years, however, as it also becomes plain that large numbers of professionals—in medicine and other fields as well as education—are digging in to protect vested interests from reasonable public scrutiny and accountability. In many cases the professionals are hiding behind obsolete and self-serving credentials and licensing systems. The furor over schools has obscured how general these problems are becoming. In the midst of the Albany legislative sessions on school decentralization, for example, there were a number of skirmishes over hospitals—particularly Harlem Hospital—that raised similar issues. Both hospitals and schools are failing the poor, and lack of money is only part of the problem. In both, the professionals have a natural stake in keeping themselves in charge and the public out—although there are indications that a number of disgusted doctors may end up crossing over to the ranks of a community control movement.

Reform of structures that have simply grown up over the years is clearly long overdue, although this may not be the most opportune moment for a sensible debate. Many children of the affluent are talking as though they wanted to repudiate all professional standards. A few teachers, doctors, lawyers, and others are seriously working to define a new professionalism—one that would serve clients instead of the profession. Up to now, their influence hasn't been great.

Intolerable schools and collapsing health services give the

revolt of the urban minorities more of a focus than middle-class longings for participation; but while it is more specific, it shares many of the same battle cries and poses, with one great exception, similar challenges to the professionals. The exception, of course, is race. A new black community consciousness is stirring; and we are witnessing an ambitious attempt to organize the black ghettoes into a political force around issues like community control of schools.

To take the measure of all these stirrings is far from easy. As with the middle-class left, a good deal of black revolutionary rhetoric barely masks a profound despair; and politics too often becomes a matter of inflammatory gestures, rather than programs. And for all the organizing that is going on, blacks in the cities are still dismayingly weak as a political force. The needles turn in the old, old grooves: people don't vote, leadership in the "community" is divided and greedy, few organizations are capable of surmounting the grinding factionalism. As a political fact, it is wise to remember, black power is still a slogan: real power in the ghetto remains the same as ever, an occasional veto power over the white armies of occupation.

Nevertheless there are signs of a change, particularly in the aftermath of the various community action programs of the war on poverty. In many ways these programs were a bust, provoking long, senseless quarrels among the poor over bones devoid of any meat. In the absence of massive employment and income programs, bitter fights over participation seem rarely to have been worth the candle. But veterans of the poverty programs have been trained to organize; and they emerged from the whole futile process with a conviction that there are plenty of things wrong with the institutions serving ghettoes besides lack of funds. The community action programs didn't produce a revolution, as their hysterical enemies charged; they didn't alter the feelings of the poor about being powerless, as sentimental advocates hoped. They have, perhaps, established an important precedent in the ghetto: successful programs to help the poor probably can no longer be run without the active participation of representatives of the poor. This includes schools.

In the course of a curiously ambivalent assessment of the community action programs, Daniel P. Moynihan pointed out that one of their principal results has been the creation of a new black leadership at a time when minorities are struggling for more power in city politics. Discrimination and the decline of opportunities for unskilled work in the inner-city cores have made blacks more dependent on public institutions than earlier immigrants. At the same time, civil service reform and the professionalization and upgrading of municipal services have denied many entry into the sorts of jobs that were once available through patronage to the old-time ethnic political machines. In a sense, as Moynihan says, the poverty programs have been a substitute for Tammany, a political apprenticeship. Much of the drive for community control of schools in New York has come from people trained to hold meetings, write proposals, operate mimeograph machines, and make trouble for bureaucrats by the various community action programs of the war on poverty. There is no cause to romanticize this process of political development or to exaggerate its progress. Harlem has its full share of the oldest politics of all—jiggery-pokery and corruption. It is too early to say with any confidence that the new leadership emerging will in fact be an improvement on the old. What is clear is that the school crises have joined this new ghetto leadership to another new group, black professionals, ambitious and eager to reform the schools.

There are different priorities in this alliance: for some, schools come second—they are merely a focus for organizing a community. For others—for most of the professionals, and, one suspects, for most thoughtful and active parents—reforming the schools is the main task.

If the new forces in the ghetto succeed they will in the end have to make a settlement with a society that is increasingly meritocratic and committed to more and more "objective" criteria in advancing people to better jobs. Perhaps they will be able to link up with a general reform aimed at loosening up rigid professional structures, making qualifications for jobs rest on performance, rather than credentials. Right now this seems a long way off. The experience of earlier groups with the bureaucracies suggests the need for some perspective: once you break in fully, the walls can help protect you, too, a consideration that will not escape the attention of black professionals as they start defining their roles in community-controlled institutions. The push to organize the ghettoes poses questions that time may answer, but which now look close to insoluble. The rhetoric of the organizers masks a basically conservative aim: many argue that the way to join up with a society that has excluded blacks up to now is to organize as a group. But conservative or not, this tactic exposes the uncomfortable truth that life in America, for all our universalistic pretensions, is organized on the basis of competing racial and ethnic groups. Ethnic identities persist in voting patterns and ways of living: they are vital realities, not a survival from the past. Earlier groups, it must be said, did not usually manage to break in to established institutions, which is what blacks are attempting: the more common pattern was to create their own, on the margins of society—political machines, the crime syndicates, and the Catholic Church being prime examples.

There are no other levers of power within reach: blacks have no money, and in most cities they don't have anything like a majority of votes. They have two perennial weapons of the underdog: the appeal to the universal values—equality, justice—America says it lives by, and the threat of disruption. The first has produced some gains, but is not likely to carry them very much farther, and the second is wearing dangerously thin. So they have to organize, knowing as they do that any effort to organize along racial lines will cut them off from white allies. Many admit the risks involved, that community control will always be something of a sham without massive national jobs, income, and housing programs. An administrator in one of the New York demonstration districts thought about this and conceded: "The reason why we're picking on the schools is that everything else has failed."

Sooner or later discussions of these matters come round to the need for national political coalitions, for which there would seem to be no realistic immediate prospects. The decentralization crisis is in part a reflection of this political failure. Behind the struggle for community control of the ghettoes lies the somber truth about America in 1969: here, as St. Paul says, we have no continuing city, only groups pursuing self-interest to the edge of self-destruction.

Community control of the schools spells deep trouble; many of the criticisms levelled at it strike me as quite sound in theory. There are always going to be sharp limits as to how much one can accomplish simply by staging elections in unorganized communities. Community control will not mean more money for public education—indeed, one danger is that it could signal further withdrawals of white support from ghetto institutions. It raises risks of confrontations between hysterical whites and black extremists; as in New York it can provoke a conservative and racist backlash. And it always has to be remembered that it does not necessarily mean any change either in teaching or in learning.

Finally, however, such reservations are beside the point. The school system is shaking to pieces. There is a crisis of authority, and there has to be a political settlement. The opponents of the movement for community control have said—correctly—that it is a threat to order because if discredits many existing institutions. It does this for the good reason that they aren't representing the interests of ghetto residents. In that sense it is revolutionary, although we should remember that most trade unions, including the UFT, used to operate on the far side of the law, and that peace usually comes about when organized groups know that they have enough strength to come to terms, but not enough to destroy each other.

The opponents of community control have been unwilling to admit how much authority has ebbed away from institutions in the ghettoes. They have been unable to pose any political or educational alternatives. Legitimacy can only be restored by a redistribution of power. The unanswered question in New York City, and elsewhere, is the extent to which any redistribution of power has to be along ethnic and racial lines.

Peace of sorts can come to the schools and other ghetto institutions. How much better they will then be is another matter. Less bureaucracy will be an improvement, as will more parent participation and local accountability, but there is no evidence that any of these reforms will necessarily improve children's learning. The movement for community control is a political phenomenon. It has been the focus of debates on education because there seems no way of moving schools in any direction unless the political dilemmas are first resolved. Educationally speaking, it is not a program, but simply a response to what are believed to be the failures of integration and compensatory education. Actually, integration, like Christianity, has rarely been attempted in any intelligent way. (A notable exception is Berkeley, California.) Its failure in places like New York was political: not enough people wanted it. The same thing is true of compensatory education: no dramatic, expensive attempt has been made anywhere to make schools for black and poor children *better* than schools for the middle class. This, too, has been a political matter: few people are willing to spend that kind of money. (For one thing it might be better spent on jobs and income programs.) While it is true, however, that the final returns are not yet in on integration and compensatory programs, it would be foolish to ignore the depth of our political failures. For some time to come, it will be chimerical to hold out promises of either integration or adequate compensatory programs in most districts of a city like New York.

Throughout the discussions of education, little has been said about parents' involvement, aside from a number of misleading claims on this score from the ranks of those supporting community control. Yet some of the most promising schools in our cities have been on a scale sufficiently small to make participation work. The experience of small privately-financed "community" schools and storefronts has confirmed what some of the better preschool and Head Start programs have discovered: that apart from political considerations, there are sound educational arguments for active parent involvement in schools for younger children—because what parents do and say is more important to the lives of small children than anything a teacher does.

Some thoughtful people in the ghettoes say that these private ventures, at present financed by string and chewing gum, point towards a day when public education as we know it will be dead in our cities, a victim of its inability to resolve its besetting dilemmas. Despairing activists in the community-control movement are saying that they have given up on the public schools, although nobody has any idea of how sources of public money could be tapped to feed private ghetto schools. Over the next few years there may be some experimenting with public tuition grants to groups of parents interested in setting up their own schools. Like decentralization and community control, this will be sold as a sovereign remedy, guaranteed to cure every ill that man or horse is heir to. Again, some skepticism will be in order: the poor have not traditionally fared well at the mercies of the free market. One look at the fraudulent schools supposedly teaching computer programming to ghetto residents should convince anybody of the limits of free enterprise. Still, the crisis may push us that way, and if it does we may have to change some of our historic ideas about education. As David Cohen puts it, the state might come to be seen as the regulator of the schools, rather than the agency that actually operates them. There have been glimmerings of this notion throughout the decentralization controversy in New York: all the different community-control proposals tacitly assumed new responsibilities for state education authorities—regulating such matters as civil liberties and the teaching of bigotry, maintaining standards, and overseeing the distribution of state and federal aid according to equitable formulas.

There is plenty of educational experimenting left to be done, and out of all the present turmoil there may emerge schools that are diverse, and better than those we have. One of the few clear lessons in this whole muddled business, however, is that the schools mirror the society. Its political failures have generated a crisis that schools alone can never solve. At long last, we are learning that the schools won't be able to pick up the marbles for the rest of the social order.

CULT OF LOCALISM

by Albert Shanker*

The schools of America have become the center of a great controversy which reflects the fundamental issues facing our society today. Confronted with the challenge of equality, we are being asked to provide educational excellence for all of our children and economic justice for all of our citizens—both black and white.

How we proceed on these issues is a matter of strategy about which there is presently much disagreement. There are some who wish to take the road of racial separatism, black capitalism and community control of local institutions while others, many of whom are a part of the labor movement, advocate a program of full employment and integration.

Beyond these disagreements, there is the more fundamental matter of the preservation of the democratic ideal for, in effect, we are being asked to do something unprecedented—to establish within the context of a pluralist society the educational and economic conditions for equality without sacrificing the political principle of democracy.

* From "Quality and Equality in Education," *The American Federationist,* March, 1969.

This challenge places the labor movement, and teacher unions in particular, in a crucial position, for no two institutions in America have been more responsible for the realization of equality and democracy than the trade unions and the public school system. The former has given economic dignity and security to millions of immigrants and American Negroes, while the latter has contributed to their cultural enrichment. There has, in fact, been a functional interdependence between the unions and the schools since the latter part of the 19th century, when the labor movement fought for the passage of compulsory education laws. These laws not only re-moved children from sweatshops where they were exploited as cheap labor, but they guaranteed the development of their intellec-tual potential so that as adults they might participate more fully in the political process. I think it is fair to claim that the trade unions and the public schools have been primarily responsible for the efforts to establish a balance between economic equality and politi-cal liberty which must be the foundation for any democracy.

The most significant social movement since the Second World War has been the civil rights revolution in which the unions have played a vital role. In 1951, three years from the Brown v. Topeka decision, the American Federation of Teachers ordered its southern locals to desegregate and throughout the 1960s the American Fed-eration of Teachers and the United Federation of Teachers contrib-uted teachers and funds to the struggle for racial justice. More importantly, as Bayard Rustin has frequently pointed out, not a single civil rights bill could have gotten through Congress without the labor lobby, and this includes the 1965 Elementary and Secon-dary Education Act which represented the first major commitment of the federal government to the education of the urban poor.

While the civil rights movement brought great progress for black Americans, it also revealed the glaring necessity to go beyond legal guarantees prohibiting discrimination. It showed us that the problem of poverty in the rural South and the urban North is tenaciously rooted in our social institutions and that the poor are neither satisfied nor incompetent, as conservatives claim, but are victimized by economic inequity.

There is no better way to illustrate this difficulty than to exam-ine the problems we have had in the field of education. We are faced in New York—and in every urban center in the country—with the massive educational retardation of the poor. Some people have found it convenient to blame individuals for this tragedy. Depending on one's point of view, it is the fault of the teachers, the parents or the children. But I would prefer to look for the root of the problem in a social system that produces poor children and poorly-trained teachers, as well as remarkably uniform educational results in schools where these two groups predominate. Certainly, commonsense should tell us that if a child is brutalized by poverty, if he must come to school without breakfast, attend class with 35 similarly impoverished children, and be taught by an inexperienced and overworked teacher—then surely that child will have difficulty learning to read and write. And beyond commonsense there is educational research, particularly James Coleman's study, "Equality of Educational Opportunity," which indicates that the socioeconomic background of the child and the skill of his teacher are the two major variables that determine educational achievement.

By posing the problem in these terms, we might not only moderate the hostile climate of blame-placing which has obtained in recent years—we might also find a solution to our difficulties.

For I maintain that if poverty is a major factor which contributes to educational retardation, then we must struggle for massive social programs that will eliminate poverty; and no political and economic institution in America is in a better position to lead such a struggle than the trade union movement.

And if a poorly-trained and overworked teaching staff is a second such factor, then we must plan and carry out programs that will improve the quality and performance of that staff; and no group in the field of education is in a better position to accomplish this than organized teachers. Even if poverty persists, I believe we can make our teachers and our schools good enough to enable children to overcome its constricting and debilitating effect. We do not throw up our hands in the face of poverty problems. Schools must still do a job.

In the brief eight-year history of the United Federation of Teachers in New York City, we have taken major steps to make the conditions of teaching conform to its status as a profession.

Through collective bargaining, we have nearly doubled teacher salaries, thereby attracting into the profession many highly-trained individuals who previously could not afford to teach. We have negotiated a transfer policy with the Board of Education which has equalized the distribution of experienced teachers throughout the city so that ghetto schools should no longer be top-heavy with substitutes.

We have pressured the Board of Examiners to liberalize and nationalize its recruitment practices, and it was again under pressure from our union that the Board of Education instituted a six-week summer program during which talented college graduates can earn all the necessary education credits.

We are demanding an internship program that will be a real probationary period for new teachers who would teach only half-time and under complete professional supervision. Not until they are fully trained and judged competent would they be permitted to take total charge of a class. We have also proposed inservice training and supervision for those teachers who consistently perform poorly. And in the area of curriculum, we developed the first Racism in Education Conference out of which grew a campaign, led by the United Federation of Teachers' Afro-American History Committee, to eliminate racist textbooks from the schools.

Most significantly, the United Federation of Teachers has pioneered in what David K. Cohen of the Harvard and MIT Joint Center for Urban Studies has called "the most comprehensive and well-conceived program of educational compensation launched to date in slum elementary schools"—namely, the More Effective Schools program.

Under MES, we have reduced class size in 21 New York City schools to a maximum of 22 pupils and we have provided special services and facilities to meet the needs of these children. The additional operational cost per child in an ME school is almost $500 a year, but this has shown results. A study conducted in 1968 by the Board of Education showed that children in ME schools had made dramatic advances in reading over children in comparable control groups—as much as three-tenths of a school year at the third and fifth grade levels.

The program has been compensatory, but because of its success it has also promoted integration as white parents have wanted their children to benefit from this quality education (more than 200 white families have voluntarily bussed their children to MES 307, which is located in the heart of a Brooklyn ghetto).

Thus there have been major advances because of the efforts of the UFT but, of course, we have not been able to go far enough. We are still faced with a situation in which most of our poor and minority group children perform below standard in reading and arithmetic and, however much we experiment with new methods and techniques, I am afraid this situation will persist until our society is willing to make the investment of resources that will provide genuine quality education for every child. It has been estimated that the expansion of an improved MES program to the approximately 250 other "special service" elementary schools in New York City that need similar help would cost $2 billion over five years and that providing a national program of quality education would require an expenditure of $160 billion over 10 years. When we consider this level of investment, we are no longer talking only about educational reform; we are confronted with the necessity to fundamentally reorient our social and political priorities.

It is not surprising, then, that in the absence of a reorientation, our children continue to fail and their parents grow increasingly frustrated and outraged. Nor should we be amazed that these emotions have given rise to a politically explosive situation which the city fathers of New York and elsewhere are searching for ways to defuse. In New York, this defusion is presently taking the form of school decentralization and I introduce this subject with these skeptical observations because I am convinced that it cannot be understood apart from the volatile political context in which it was conceived and promoted and that it is fundamentally not an educational reform but an attempt to pacify bitter emotions.

Having said this, however, and before offering a more substantial criticism of decentralization, I want to emphasize that I do believe that it has constructive potential, particularly those aspects of it which should enhance both parental concern for the learning of the children and creative community participation in matters of educational policy.

Parents have a legitimate grievance against the rigidities and the remoteness of the central bureaucracy. To the extent that these difficulties have increased the alienation and the apathy of parents, to that extent they must be remedied by bringing the decision-making power closer to where its effects are felt. I favor this because if parents have no interest or influence in their children's education, then the kind of militant parent-teacher alliance that the UFT has always advocated as a means to improve the schools will be impossible to achieve. And, more fundamentally, I favor increased parent and community participation because I know from my experience in the trade union movement that individuals cannot have human dignity until they participate in decisions affecting their lives.

I thus support the broad philosophical and political principles underlying the demands for greater participation. The difficulties in New York City arise not from these demands per se, but from their potential effect on educational and social policy which derives from the political context in which decentralization is proposed. This political context has been shaped by the failure to achieve either the massive resources necessary for quality education or racial integration.

Within this context, decentralization, while not in inherent contradiction to massive funding or integration, is put forth as an alternative to both of them. And once it has been so proposed, it is justified on the grounds that both of the previous policies have proved educationally invalid, an empirical judgment based on the false assumption that massive funding and integration "didn't work," when in fact they had never even been tried. We can, therefore, understand how Dr. Kenneth Clark, a strong and influential proponent of decentralization, can make the following statement rejecting greater public investment in education:

"One of the best things that could happen to public education in the United States in the next two or three years is that it not get any extra money from the federal or state governments and that it be required to raise the quality of performance within its present budget." (*The Center Magazine*, November 1968)

If Dr. Clark's sentiment is widely shared, I am afraid that it will be far more than two or three years before our schools get any extra money because the political pressure for such funds will have been channeled into demands for decentralization.

I think that advocates of decentralization also have turned their backs on integration, some with reluctance, but many with an active enthusiasm for racial separatism. The demand for community control of the schools, we should remember, was first heard during the controversy surrounding the opening of I. S. 201 which took place only months after the emergence of the separatist black power movement. The parents at I. S. 201 had been promised an integrated school by the Board of Education. They were lied to and deceived, they were justifiably outraged and they had the support of the school's thoroughly integrated staff and the UFT. But when, out of their bitterness and frustration, they adopted the view that the previously appointed white principal must be replaced by a black one, they lost their moral authority. Neither the school staff nor the UFT could tolerate an appointment on a racial basis; nor could the vast majority of the citizens of New York.

What occurred after the original dispute at I. S. 201 was a very subtle and effective process of the justification and mystification of racial separatism. The justification process took the form of providing separatism with a cloak of respectability by drafting it into a proposal for school decentralization. The concept of hiring and firing people on the basis of race, which is both morally offensive and politically impractical, was transformed into the demand that each community have the right to control its schools.

Stated in these terms, community control could be interpreted and accepted as part of our progressive democratic tradition. In New York City, I think that the responsibility for dignifying separatism in this way lies primarily with the Mayor's office and the Ford Foundation. Their desire was to accommodate to the demands of black power militants in the hope of preventing an "explosion" (a household word among apprehensive city officials) of racial violence. And they also hoped to satisfy black demands for change without having to invest enormous resources in schools, jobs and housing. Decentralization, in this sense, represents an attempt to give a respectable appearance to what is actually a form of cheap accommodation to militants and a cheap solution to social injustice.

The process of mystification has been a far more unconscious attempt to dignify separatism by endowing it with a certain regenerative capacity. It has occurred in segments of the black community largely as a consequence of the failure by society to meet Negro demands for full equality. For those blacks who have despaired of progress there has been a withdrawal into nationalism, a turning away from social institutions that have proved difficult to change and a concentration on psychological problems which are more immediate and seem to be more manageable. And there has been the inevitable rationalization that this is a progressive shift of emphasis, that one can obviate the need for more and better jobs, homes and schools simply by thinking that "black is beautiful."

A similar process of mystification and withdrawal has taken place in the white community as well. Many liberals who have grown weary of the struggle for social justice are using the rhetoric of black nationalism as a means of justifying their fatigue. They have now convinced themselves that the black poor need "identity" and "pride" rather than economic and political equality and that the primary task of white people is to purge themselves of their racism. I am in agreement with these liberals only to the extent that I do find an undercurrent of racism in their attitudes. Having assumed that the Negro is in need of psychological rehabilitation, they act towards him in a manner that is both condescending and insulting. They romanticize his poverty, pardon all his misdeeds and project him into the role of the revolutionary come to save the white middle class from its boredom and their sins.

These attitudes might be humorous did they not contribute to an atmosphere in which racial separatism has become acceptable public policy. For example, the redistricting proposed by Mayor Lindsay's "liberal" Board of Education in its decentralization plan of December 15, 1968, was a deliberate attempt to impose racial apartheid on the City of New York. What is even more threatening is that as a result of the separatist and nationalist framework within which decentralization has developed, a mood of intellectual oppression and moral absolutism has set in which has made it impossible to discuss social problems with any degree of rationality. The separatists have posed the issue as that of a people struggling to overthrow an oppressor. They have imported concepts of imperialism and colonialism which provide the ideological justification for calling people to arms on the basis of ethnic loyalties. Their cry is, "We destroy you or we perish."

The logical outcome of defining the issue in terms of racial oppression is that demands become absolutistic and non-negotiable. And, because it is impossible to meet these demands within the context of competing centers of influence, a climate of violence and racial hostility must inevitably develop. I think that we must understand the problem of anti-Semitism as a subsection of this larger difficulty. The Jews are a convenient and proximate object of hatred and so they have been singled out, but ultimately they are but one of the many so-called oppressors. The fundamental problem remains the environment of hostility that has been created by those who use primitive oversimplifications, racial myths and irresponsible revolutionary rhetoric to interpret complex social issues.

The mystification which I identified in relation to racial separatism has, like a contagious psychological disease, infected other areas of social thought as well. A mystique has been built up around decentralization and participation that has distorted the genuinely democratic character of these concepts.

Decentralists, I feel, would prefer to dismember rather than democratize social institutions which they despise for being impersonal, technological and centralized. Their protest takes the form of a cult of localism and anti-social individualism and exhibitionism which is most evident today among educated and alienated members of the middle class. This movement is inevitably separatist in its effect since it glorifies and reinforces those characteristics—racial, ethnic, class or otherwise—which differentiate social groups.

And it is also reactionary in that it is fundamentally opposed to political and economic equalization, as well as to those centralized institutions—such as the federal government, the labor movement and the public school system—which have been most responsible for the social advancement of the poor.

Which is all a complicated way of saying that decentralization has no educational relevance except that it might very well increase the problems confronting our schools. The advocates of decentralization claim that it will promote innovation, but small school districts are traditionally conservative and highly dependent on conventionalized commercial products. In fact, the most innovative school systems today are those which are consolidating the resources of localities, thereby broadening the scope and range of their activities.

Nor would decentralization eliminate bureaucracy, inefficiency and unnecessary costs. On the contrary, it would establish inefficient and expensive local bureaucracies which would perform the same dull administrative chores that are presently centralized—only with greater duplication.

And I am afraid that decentralists exaggerate the number of idealists who will flock to impoverished areas once local districts are allowed to compete for staff. Their ranks, which are today quite limited, may be totally decimated by an end to the war in Viet Nam. Moreover, the law of the market dictates that the qualified and experienced personnel will be recruited by the middle class districts where it is easiest to teach, while the ghetto will be forced to make do with those teachers who cannot find employment elsewhere.

I also reject the idea that decentralization will enhance democracy. The cause of democracy is in no way helped by creating power vacuums that extremists and putschists can move in to fill. And once they have moved in, they will not only deny academic freedom and due process to teachers, but they will intimidate the less aggressive members of the community who disagree with their views. More fundamentally, decentralization can be anti-democratic insofar as it caters to local differences and prejudices. Liberal teachers will be unwanted in conservative neighborhoods and ethnic and racial affinities with the local population may become prime criteria for selecting staff. In a pluralist society, such practices are discriminatory and intolerable.

A final word must be said about the anti-labor implications of decentralization. John Doar, currently the President of the New York City Board of Education, has succinctly stated the ideology guiding many decentralists:

"Union concepts of security and seniority were formulated in the period of struggle between company and union. Now the struggle is between the Negroes and the unions. . . . It is our position that a basic conflict exists between labor union concepts and civil rights concepts. Something has to give." (*Fortune* magazine, January 1968)

Doar's statement is an invitation to total disaster. The loss of security and seniority rights will hurt all workers, but Negroes and other minorities will be most grievously injured because they have been most dependent on these basic guarantees.

Even more dangerous is the kind of conflict which Doar seems to think is inevitable and progressive. It is this very conflict between Negroes and unions upon which both Wallace supporters and corporate executives will thrive, for it sets blacks against whites and the have-nots against the have-littles, and it enables the rich to get off scot free while the poor struggle with each other over scarce resources. These resources might be increased and this struggle avoided if, for example, corporate profits were more heavily taxed, but instead Doar proposes a school decentralization plan which, however noble his intentions, is equivalent to union-busting.

Despite the many potentially dangerous and regressive features of decentralization, some form of it is in the making. Therefore, I should like to propose several guidelines to help make it a creative reform.

Decentralization must not be permitted to institutionalize racial segregation and, therefore, local districts must be few enough and large enough to contain a heterogeneous population.

Secondly, local boards should have the right to hire and fire the district superintendent, but teachers should be appointed by a central agency. Where there are grievances of parents against teachers or teachers against the local board, there should be recourse to an impartial third party (such as an ombudsman or a civilian review board) whose ruling will be binding. In this regard, no teacher shall be dismissed without due process, which must include the presentation of written charges, hearings and the right of appeal.

And there must be a central focus for all local districts, which should include the establishment of a basic city-wide curriculum, the determination and enforcement of educational standards by a central agency and the evaluation of district performance by that agency.

Finally, we must enlarge the role played by paraprofessionals whose contribution represents the most creative form of community participation to date in the schools. They have freed the teacher to teach by performing many important non-professional tasks and in the process they are receiving the training that will enable them in the future to assume more professional responsibilities. Even more significantly, their employment (there are 20,000 of them working in New York schools) is a pioneering effort in the area of "new careers for the poor" which has tremendous implications at a time when automation is eliminating jobs for the unskilled and the inadequately educated.

Greater community participation in the schools thus can be a progressive reform. It can not only enhance the education process, but it can bring parents and teachers together into a working alliance. But if the regressive aspects of community participation and decentralization predominate, then such an alliance will be destroyed and the children will suffer.

With a conservative Administration in Washington, there may be pressures to cut federal expenditures and accommodate to racial separatism which may not be counter-balanced by sufficient pressure from progressive forces that have been weakened, as we have seen, by the loss of some liberals and Negroes.

Those of us in the labor movement, the civil rights movement and the liberal community who still believe in equality and integration must struggle to prevent the enactment of conservative legislation during the next four years. But we must do more than perform a holding action, for if our schools continue to produce uneducated young people, if poverty, unemployment, and urban decay persist, then the kind of legislation we will need four years hence will have to be that much more radical. We have the forces to take positive action now and, if we do so, many of our former allies can be won back. I believe we can do this because the principles of equality and integration upon which we stand are just and we must do it if our pluralist society is to endure as a unified democracy.

ACHIEVEMENT AND COMMUNITY CONTROL

by Maurice R. Berube*

THE IMPORTANCE OF PUPIL ATTITUDES

There is every reason to believe that community control of city schools will enhance educational quality.[1] *Equality of Educational Opportunity,* the most extensive educational study ever conducted, (commonly referred to as the Coleman Report, after its chief

* Reprinted from the *Institute for Community Studies,* Queens College, New York City, 1968.

[1] It is necessary to make a crucial distinction between the terms school decentralization and community control. Unfortunately, the umbrella word *decentralization* has come to mean all things to all people; it has been adopted by opponents of "meaningful" decentralization, much in the same fashion as the term integration was bandied about five years ago by its enemies. Consequently, the most hostile and active opponent to "meaningful" decentralization, the United Federation of Teachers, claims to support decentralization; just as the Parents and Taxpayers, which successfully defeated integration efforts such as busing, Princeton plan school pairings, and developing educational parks, was nominally in favor of school integration.

This ambiguous word, *decentralization,* no longer has value in clarifying concepts, connoting anything from administrative gerrymander to publicly accountable school systems. On the other hand, the term *community control* is clear: placing educational power with the public, by means of elected school boards with final authority over budgets, personnel and curriculum.

author), emphasized the need for an educational system capable of stimulating a strong sense of self among students. In the U.S. Office of Education's poll of 645,000 pupils throughout the country, Coleman discovered that the secret to learning lay with student attitudes. Attitudes toward self, of power to determine one's future, influence academic achievement far more than factors of class size, teacher qualifications or condition of school plant. "Of all the variables measured in the survey, the attitudes of student interest in school, self-concept, and sense of environmental control show the greatest relation to achievement," Coleman concluded.[2] Furthermore, a pupil's attitude—*"the extent to which an individual feels that he has some control over his destiny"*—was not only the most important of the various elements studied, but it "appears to have a stronger relationship to achievement than do all the 'school' factors *together.*"[3] (Emphasis added.)

Coleman's findings were revolutionary, cutting against the grain of prevalent myths concerning the nature of learning. Until Coleman, most educators did not consider pupil attitudes to be dominant. Rather, they believed that the teacher, her qualifications and background, her working conditions and small class registers, to have the greatest influence on how children learn. Moreover, these educators predicted various strategies to remedy school ills on that premise, so that one simply added more of the same, "compensatory" programs, to help pupils learn.

That approach has failed. Compensatory programs have not justified the claims of their avid proponents. The More Effective Schools Program in New York City, for example, reduces classes and provides saturation services at nearly double the cost of regular programs, only to produce few noteworthy results. After three years of operation, the MES program has not enabled children to read on grade level.

Neither has any other compensatory education program succeeded where MES has so far failed. The U.S. Civil Rights Commission study, *Racial Isolation in the Schools,* found the innumerable compensatory schemes throughout the country to be wanting; none had raised achievement levels. This is not to say, however, that compensatory efforts should be discontinued. In a different atmosphere these programs could possibly flourish.

[2] James Coleman, et al, *Equality of Educational Opportunity,* U.S. Office of Education (Washington: U.S. Government Printing Office, 1966), p. 319.
[3] *Ibid.,* p. 23

Essentially, then, schools will best help children learn when they strengthen pupils' feelings of control over their destinies. That is at the heart of community control of city schools. Big city school systems, unaccountable and isolated, generate feelings of powerlessness and alienation among parents and pupils. Only when these city schools are operated by their various communities can an educational "system" even begin to dispel this powerlessness. And students, developing a greater sense of self-worth, would correspondingly develop a greater motivation to learn.

This entails wholesale reform of the school system, redistributing power to elected school boards. In this sense, a beneficial climate for learning will result as parents have a voice in the running of the schools. The alternative to powerlessness is power.

THE IMPORTANCE OF TEACHER ATTITUDES

What bearing has the "self-fulfilling prophecy" on city schools? One of the unfortunate aspects of urban education is that middle class teachers too often expect too little from the children of the poor. In the case of the black poor, low expectations are often intermingled with racism.[4] The corroborating testimony to this widespread reaction of middle class teachers is overwhelming. For the past two years, the National Council on the Education for the Disadvantaged has singled out the attitudes of middle class teachers toward the poor as damaging to the Head Start programs. Professor Edmund Gordon and Doxey Wilkerson of Yeshiva University, in their evaluation of 76 compensatory programs in the United States, concluded that teacher attitudes were the crucial element in the failure of those programs.[5]

Moreover, there has accumulated a small literature by former teachers on the widespread self-fulfilling prophecies of teachers. These works have gained national prominence, in one instance winning for the author a National Book Award (e.g., Nat Hentoff's *Our Children are Dying;* Mary Frances Greene and Orletta Ryan's *The Schoolchildren;* Herbert Kohl's *36 Children;* Jonathan Kozol's *Death*

---

[4] Robert Rosenthal and Lenore Jacobson, *Pygmalion in the Classroom* (New York: Holt, Rinehart and Winston, 1968), p. 181.

[5] Edmund Gordon and Doxey Wilkerson, *Contemporary Education for the Disadvantaged* (New York: College Entrance Examination Board, 1966), pp. 56–57.

At An Early Age). The following exchange between a new teacher and an "experienced" one, who expects little from pupils, in the *Schoolchildren* typifies a tragic and subtle scene recurrent in city schools:

That same week I'd picked up second-hand copies of NATIONAL GEOGRAPHIC, NATURAL HISTORY, and other magazines for our library shelf. "You're not being fair to them," said Mrs. Abernathy. "You must not make these demands. Stick to the books they can read."

"But I often read to the child from them . . . Last week Carlos almost cried because he couldn't read the caption under a picture of a snowy egret."

"That's what I mean. You're not being fair."

"But then he went to work—he took the magazine home. Thursday he could read, 'This is a snowy egret.' "

"And will that help him in the reader? You're arousing a desire in him for something he can't achieve. We try to treat the child as a decent human being," she concluded—as so often.[6]

Common to these reports is a unifying theme of an "educational system" destroying the minds of its youngsters by breeding into its teachers defeat even before education is begun. As long as this system is left to its own devices, this poisonous climate will prevail in urban schools.

The implication for urban school reform is clear. Middle class teachers, who commute from suburbs to fortress schools in the ghetto, are not likely to develop positive attitudes towards their pupils who are poor, unless some bridge between the two worlds is built. That, too, is an aim of the community-controlled school. No harmony between teacher and parent, teacher and pupil, can begin to exist when both are isolated from each other by a bureaucratic system designed as a barrier. When teachers work together with parents, under accountable school boards, then, their attitudes will be shaped more by the realities of the needs of the school's clients.

A FLEXIBLE STRUCTURE TO ADAPT PROGRAMS

There is more to community control of schools, however, than returning educational power to the public. There must be sufficient

[6] Mary Frances Greene and Orletta Ryan, *The Schoolchildren* (New York: Pantheon, 1966), p. 29.

restructuring of the system to permit this beneficial climate to develop. In short, size is important to the enterprise. In an article in the magazine *Educational Leadership,* Philadelphia Superintendent of Schools Mark Shedd sums up the problem:

The most fundamental crisis in urban education today, as I see it, is a failure to produce organizations capable of adapting the program of a given school to the needs of a given child . . .

The trick, then, is to remake and revitalize through decentralization the quantitatively massive and qualitatively sluggish school systems . . . to create a climate in which beneficial changes can flourish.

The involvement of the community in planning, operating, and evaluating the schools would do much to eliminate the isolation, complacency, and irrelevance of urban education.[7]

Central to reform of the total system is developing units of a size small enough to be "capable of adapting the program of a given school to the needs of a given child." Studies of big city school systems dating back nearly thirty years have recommended such reforms of the system to improve the programmatic possibilities.

Additional studies in the fifties and sixties of the New York City school system reinforced the need to decentralize operations to permit sufficient flexibility in developing programs. The most notable of these, sponsored by the Women's City Club, emphasized local control. A key study that emerged from a Temporary Commission on City Finances, Marilyn Gittell's *Participants and Participation,* observed that the centralized New York City system was incapable of instituting educational change. Gittell described the educational system as inbred and managed by a miniscule number of professionals. She reported that this system was without ability to implement far-reaching policies: "New York City has not witnessed any meaningful change in curriculum, administrative structure, teaching recruitment, appointment and training, or general organization for at least three decades."[8]

The Bundy Report, *Reconnection for Learning,* absorbing the research and recommendations of these forerunners, suggested placing from thirty to sixty autonomous school districts under control of

[7] Mark Shedd, "Decentralization and Urban Schools," *Educational Leadership,* October, 1967, pp. 32–35.

[8] Marilyn Gittell, *Participants and Participation* (New York: Frederick Praeger, 1966), p. 21.

parent dominated school boards. Administratively, Bundy's recommendations blended realistic demographic considerations of ethnic communities in the city with established standards of administrative size.

An ideally flexible and administratively productive school district should account for no more than 20,000 pupils. Using the thirty-three present school districts in New York City, serving 1.1 million students as model autonomous school districts, they would serve approximately 33,000 students—close to the administrative ideal.

It must be emphasized, however, that mere administrative reform is unlikely to result in high academic achievement. Although smaller, flexible school mechanisms can originate and enact educational programs more readily, the essential psychological relation between pupil and school, between teacher and pupil, would still be lacking. Mere administrative decentralization would not create the kinetic atmosphere necessary to improve a pupil's self-esteem and learning motivation, or a teacher's attitude. For that, an intimate involvement of parents and community in the educational structure is required.

WHAT CRITICS SAY

There is one final argument, based on extensive research, that must be made for community control of schools. However, this testimony is best introduced through a back door, through first marshalling the most serious criticism against community controlled schools in the cities. The trouble with local control of the schools, critics maintain, is that such an arrangement closes off the possibility of school integration—what these critics view as the most beneficial educational condition for the black poor—thereby raising the "threatening" spectre of black power separatism.

First, let us consider the case for integration. According to census patterns, most American cities are increasing in racial segregation, and within a generation will have a majority black population. School integration simply is neither feasible nor foreseeable in the near future. The movement of parents for community control was based on this default of the white community. In the fall of 1966, Harlem parents at I.S. 201 demanded that the school be integrated; if integration was not possible, they demanded that those segregated schools be run by the community. In short, recognizing that the integration movement had failed, black school activists sought to make the schools accountable.

Fully aware of this, one critic, Sandra Feldman, a staff member of the United Federation of Teachers, still writes:

"There is a very real danger that decentralization will mean an end to the possibility of school integration in New York City . . ."[9]

"The trouble is that local control is regarded as *an alternative* to integration . . .

Yet integrated schools are not impossible—just very difficult."[10]

Furthermore, this same writer advances the opinion that "integration is essential to their (Negro schoolchildren) achievement."[11] For this statement, the writer refers to the Coleman Report's findings that the self-image of poor, black school children (and consequently their academic achievement), improved in a socioeconomic integrated setting. Coleman also found poor pupils' self-image and academic achievement were raised also in an all-black setting, with middle class Negro pupils. In a later article, Coleman was careful to point out that his findings did not constitute a case for school integration. The significant fact is that a feeling of control over one's destiny influences achievement. This sense of purpose would more readily be encouraged in an educational atmosphere where power was exerted by school parents.

That does not mean that school integration is not a desirable end for other reasons. But it certainly *does not mean* that "integration is essential to achievement." The writer, voicing prevalent views of those hostile to community control of schools, more accurately reflects fears that are at the heart of the local control controversy; fears that "black power," self-determination for black ghettos, threatens the white paternalistic order of the past. Consider the following statements (emphasis added):

"While (local control) has some validity, it is asserted by different groups with differing goals in mind. It is used by *black power militants who regard decentralization as a step toward self-determination for the Negro community;* it is also used by *milder* proponents . . ."[12]

[9] Sandra Feldman, *Decentralization and the City Schools* (New York: League For Industrial Democracy, 1967), p. 3.

[10] *Ibid.*, p. 6.

[11] *Ibid.*, p. 5.

[12] *Ibid.*, p. 2.

"To the extent that an *ascendent separatist point of view prevents groups in the Negro community from coalescing* with white allies to demand increased federal aid to schools, and to the extent that the white community uses *black extremism* as an excuse to turn its back, the children, white and black, will suffer."[13]

To this writer black power, black self-determination, is not only equated with "black extremism," it presents a threat to the old coalition, perhaps, even a threat "of violence." Yet, one can infer from the studies of effects of racial isolation—the Coleman Report, Civil Rights Commission Report, Kenneth Clark's early work—that black school children suffered psychological damage in segregated schools *because the prevalent values in these schools were white.* In such a society, not being in an (white) integrated setting naturally creates a psychology of inferiority. However, the thrust of black power is that there are values in black society as substantial as those in white society—specifically, that "black is beautiful." In this context of a "segregated" school system emphasizing black values, one can conceive of psychological benefit to black children.

That is not to say our society should continue on its present segregated course. It is to say however, that the black ghetto can develop its own values and rationale for success. And it is to say that the black power ideology is "extremist" only to those who are themselves psychologically unable to tolerate black citizens who have the equal opportunity to determine their own fates.

THE SECURITY OF THE GHETTO COMMUNITY

The final argument for local school control, then, rests on the positive values to be found in a ghetto atmosphere. Two sociologists, Andrew M. Greeley and Peter H. Rossi, undertook to evaluate the effect of Catholic parochial education on the life options of its pupils. What they unearthed in their investigations surprised Catholics, educators and themselves. Greeley and Rossi punctured the myth that Catholic schools, financially undernourished, overcrowded and badly staffed, accomplished little for their students. Instead, they learned that Catholics who attended all Catholic schools compared favorably, educationally and in terms of the job market, with the best schools and their graduates in the country. At

[13] *Ibid.*, p. 11.

first, they surmised that these students became successful in later life because Catholic school administrators have the power of admitting only those students they desire. But, even Catholics who were expelled from parochial schools and sent to public schools did well. *By a process of elimination, the sociologists inferred that the ghetto atmosphere of parochial schools generated an ambience of security which helped Catholic students to achieve.* Moreover, Catholics in their ghetto schools were least likely to be intolerant of other ethnic groups since they felt more secure in their ghetto atmosphere than Catholics in public schools.

Greeley and Rossi posed the question:

"Is it possible that the religious community plays the role of a sort of super ethnic group which provides the emotional support a young person needs in order to develop motivation for achievement in his early years?"[14]

They answered their question in the following fashion:

"It ought to be clear that (our findings) . . . call into serious question the assumption that it is necessary, for the health of society, that the religious and religio-ethnic ghettoes be eliminated. Such subcultures do not apparently impede achievement; on the contrary, they may even promote it. In the long run, they may even promote greater tolerance, because they give a person a relatively secure social location and a fairly clear answer to the difficult question 'Who am I.' "

"(There are) . . . two paths to achievement—the way of the ghetto and the way of assimilation—and that . . . the former had clear-cut advantages . . . In the matter of attitudes toward civil liberties, the way of the ghetto seems to have advantages for the larger society as well."[15]

Following the reasoning of Greeley and Rossi, one can conceive of community control of schools in black urban ghettos to promote exactly those qualities of security, identity and purpose. It is just such reasoning that is behind the efforts of black parents to get more black school administrators as identity models for schoolchildren.

SUMMARY

The most recent and pertinent educational research, then, has a common denominator: the importance of the psychological to the

[14] Andrew M. Greeley and Peter H. Rossi, *The Education of Catholic Americans* (Chicago: Aldine Publishing Co., 1966), p. 155.
[15] *Ibid.*, pp. 161–163.

learning process. Whether a pupil feels his efforts can influence and control his future—feelings of identity and self-worth—emerges as the prime learning factor. What a teacher expects of her pupils has great bearing on how much a child learns. And the sense of security of the ghetto community helps students to achieve.

Considered in conjunction with the long list of studies condemning the destructive climate produced by large centralized school systems, these psychological factors constitute a strong case for local control of public schools. Community control is by no means a panacea. There will still be the task of obtaining large amounts of government aid to finance the schools; there still needs to be devised more and better educational programs. But, without the necessary structure to respond to the many particular needs of pupils, more money and more imaginative programs will have little effect.

The first step to better education in city schools is to transfer educational power to a series of autonomous, community controlled local school districts. The rest will follow.

BLACK POWER AND PARTICIPATION

by Charles V. Hamilton*

An article on public policy, race, and education in the United States in the late 1960's cannot overlook the clear existence of tremendous ferment taking place in the various black communities in this country. The nature of that ferment is such that, if we would devise relevant policy for educating vast numbers of black people today, we cannot focus merely, or even primarily, on achievement in verbal

* From "Race and Education: A Search for Legitimacy," *Harvard Educational Review,* 38, Fall 1968, 669–684. Copyright © 1968 by President and Fellows of Harvard College. Also in *Equal Educational Opportunity,* published by Harvard University Press, 1969.

and mathematical skills as criteria for educational improvement. At one time, possibly to the mid-1960 s, it was possible to talk about educational policy largely in terms of "integration" (or at least, desegregation) and assume that plans to implement integration would be dealing with the core of the problem of educational deficiency. This is no longer the case.

Today, one hears wholly different demands being raised in the black community. These demands are better represented by the kinds of resolutions coming out of the workshops of the newly formed (June, 1968) National Association of Afro-American Educators than by the conclusions reached by the report on *Equality of Educational Opportunity* (Coleman Report). These demands are reflected more clearly in the demonstrations of black high school students in many cities for more emphasis on Afro-American history and culture and for better science lab facilities than by the findings of the United States Commission on Civil Rights (*Racial Isolation in the Public Schools*). These demands are more clearly illustrated in the positions taken by the Harlem chapter of the Congress of Racial Equality (CORE), calling for an independent school system for Harlem, and by many of the Concerned Black Parents groups than in policy recommendations found in the statement issued by the Board of Education of Chicago, Illinois in August, 1967 (Redmond Report).

First, I would like to indicate why it is more important at this time, from a socio-political point of view, to put more credence in the wishes of the black community than in the statements and findings of the experts. Second, I would like to give examples of the kinds of things on the minds of some of those black people taking an active interest in new directions for education in the black community. Third, I want to present a sketch of a proposal for dealing with some of the problems in some of the large, urban areas. I am not sanguine that the proposal will be applicable in all places (I assume it will not be), but neither do I believe it possible or necessary to develop one model to fit all occasions. My proposal attempts to combine some of the fervent wishes of a growing number of black people with the clear need to think in wholly new institutional terms. I am fully aware that public policy in this area has been influenced by such dichotomies as "integration vs. segregation" (*de jure* and *de facto*) and "integrated education vs. quality (compensatory) education." My presentation will not use these terms as primary focal points, but it is clear that the main thrust of my proposal will support the involvement of more parents in the school system and the improvement of educational opportunities within the black community. Some critics will view this as an "enrichment" proposal, or as an effort at "compensatory" education, or even as a black power move to maintain any further divisiveness in the society. I simply acknowledge these criticisms at the outset and intend to let my proposal stand on its own merits.

A CRISIS OF EDUCATIONAL LEGITIMACY

It is absolutely crucial to understand that the society cannot continue to write reports accurately describing the failure of the educational institutions *vis-à-vis* black people without ultimately taking into account the impact those truths will have on black Americans. There comes a point when it is no longer possible to recognize institutional failure and then merely propose more stepped-up measures to overcome those failures—especially when the proposals come from the same kinds of people who administered for so long the present unacceptable and dysfunctional policies and systems. Professor Seymour Martin Lipset once wrote:

> Legitimacy involves the capacity of the system to engender and maintain the belief that the existing political institutions are the most appropriate ones for the society. The extent to which contemporary democratic political systems are legitimate depends in large measure upon the ways in which the key issues which have historically divided the society have been resolved.
>
> While effectiveness is primarily instrumental, legitimacy is evaluative. Groups regard a political system as legitimate or illegitimate according to the way in which its values fit with theirs.[1]

And in another place, he has written:

> All claims to a legitimate title to rule in new states must ultimately win acceptance through demonstrating effectiveness. The loyalty of the different groups to the system must be won through developing *in them* the conviction that this system is the best—or at least an excellent—way to accomplish their objectives. And even claims to legitimacy of a super-

[1] Seymour Martin Lipset, *Political Man: The Social Bases of Politics* (New York: Doubleday, 1963), p. 64.

natural sort, such as "the gift of grace," are subjected on the part of the populace to a highly pragmatic test—that is, what is the payoff?[2]
The United States gradually acquired legitimacy as a result of being *effective*.[3]

The important point here is that loyalty, allegiance, is predicated on performance. What decision-makers *say* is not of primary importance, but it is important what black people *believe*. Do they *believe* that the school systems are operating in their behalf? Do they *believe* that the schools are *legitimate* in terms of educating their children and inculcating in them a proper sense of values? With the end product (i.e., their children graduating from high school as functional illiterates) clearly before their eyes at home and with volumes of reports documenting lack of payoff, it is not difficult to conclude that black people have good reason to question the legitimacy of the educational systems.

They begin to question the entire process, because they are aware that the schools, while not educating their children, are at the same time supporting a particularly unacceptable situation. They know that the schools are one of the major institutions for socializing their children into the dominant value structure of the society. Professor V. O. Key, Jr. concluded in his book, *Politics, Parties and Pressure Groups*:

In modern societies the school system, in particular, functions as a formidable instrument of political power in its role as a transmitter of the goals, values, and attitudes of the polity. In the selection of values and attitudes to be inculcated, it chooses those cherished by the dominant elements in the political order. By and large the impact of widely accepted goals, mores, and social values fixes the programs of American schools. When schools diverge from this vaguely defined directive and collide with potent groups in the political system, they feel a pressure to conform.[4]

The relevance of all this is that makers of policy and their advisers must recognize that there is a point beyond which vast numbers of black people *will* become alienated and will no longer

[2] Seymour Martin Lipset, *The First New Nation: The United States in Historical and Comparative Perspective* (New York: Basic Books, 1963), pp. 45–46. (Emphasis added.)
[3] *Ibid.*, p. 59. (Emphasis in original.)
[4] V. O. Key, Jr., *Politics, Parties and Pressure Groups* (New York: Thomas Y. Crowell Company, 1964), pp. 12–13.

view efforts on their behalf, however well-intentioned, as legitimate. When this happens, it behooves decision-makers, if they would search for ways of restoring faith, trust, and confidence, to listen to the demands of the alienated. The "experts" might see integration as socially and educationally sound and desirable, but *their* vision and empirical data might well be, at this juncture, irrelevant. Unless this is understood, I am suggesting that public policy might well find itself in the position of attempting to force its programs on a reluctant black community. And this is hardly a formula for the development of a viable body politic.

A clear example of a paternalistic, objectionable policy is contained in the report of the Chicago Board of Education, *Increasing Desegregation of Faculties, Students, and Vocational Education Programs*, issued August 23, 1967. The Report called for busing black children into all- or predominantly white schools. It contains the very revealing paragraph:

The assignment of students outside their neighborhood may be objected to by Negro parents who prefer that their children attend the segregated neighborhood school. This viewpoint cannot be ignored. Prior to implementation of such a transfer policy the administration must take steps to reassure apprehensive sending area parents that transfer will be beneficial not only in terms of integration but of improved education for their children. The generation of a favorable consensus in the designated sending area is important. *If such a consensus is unobtainable, the transfer program would have to proceed without a popular base.* In the light of the dismal alternatives such a program perhaps should proceed even without consensus, but every effort should be made to attain it.[5]

This is a perpetuation of the pattern of telling the black community what is best for it. My point is that this position will only increase alienation, not alleviate it. At the present time, when the educational systems are perceived as illegitimate, it is highly unlikely that such a policy could lead to success. In order for the program to work, support *must* be obtained from the black community. This means that educational achievement must be conceived more broadly than as the mere acquisition of verbal and mathematical skills. Very many black parents are (for good reason) quite concerned about what happens to the self-image of their black children

---

[5] *Increasing Desegregation of Faculties, Students, and Vocational Education Programs* (Board of Education, City of Chicago, August 23, 1967), p. B-20. (Emphasis added.)

in predominantly white schools—schools which reflect dominant white values and mores. Are these schools prepared to deal with their own white racism? Probably not, and a few summer institutes for white, middle-class teachers cannot prepare them. Are these schools prepared to come to terms with a young black child's search for identity? Will the black child indeed acquire certain skills which show up favorably on standardized tests, but at the same time avoid coming to grips with the fact that he or she should not attempt to be a carbon copy of the culture and ethos of another racial and ethnic group? Virtually all the social scientists, education experts, and public policy-makers who emphasize integration overlook this crucial, intangible, psychological factor. Many concerned black parents and teachers do not overlook it, however. And their viewpoint has nothing to do with black people wanting to perpetuate "separate but unequal" facilities, or with attitudes of "hate whitey." This concern is simply a necessary reaction to the fact that many white (and black) liberal, integration-oriented spokesmen are tuned in to a particular result and overlook other phenomena. They fail to understand that their criteria for "educational achievement" simply might not be relevant anymore.

What I am stating (in as kind a way as possible) is that setting criteria for measuring equal educational opportunity can no longer be the province of the established "experts." The policy-makers must now listen to those for whom they say they are operating; which means of course that they must be willing to share the powers of policy-making. The experts must understand that what is high on the liberal social scientist's agenda does not coincide with the agenda of many black people. The experts are still focusing on the effectiveness of existing educational institutions. Many black people have moved to the evaluation of the legitimacy of these institutions.

American social scientists generally are unable to grasp the meaning of alienation when applied to certain groups in this country. (Most of the recent perceptive literature on alienation and modernization deals with new nations of Africa and Asia.)[6]

---

[6] See: Myron Weiner, ed., *Modernization, The Dynamics of Growth* (New York: Basic Books, 1966);

    David Apter, *The Politics of Modernization* (Chicago: University of Chicago Press, 1965); S. N. Eisenstadt, *Modernization: Protest and Change* (Englewood Cliffs, N.J.: Prentice-Hall, Inc., 1966);

Consequently, Grant McConnell, in an important book, *Private Power and American Democracy,* could write:

In general the use of government has depended on a particular group's capacity to isolate the relevant governmental agency from influences other than its own and to establish itself as the agency's constituency—at once giving an air of validity to its own ends and endowing it with the added disciplinary power of public authority over its own members.[7]

And later:

. . . farm migrant workers, Negroes, and the urban poor have not been included in the system of "pluralist" representation so celebrated in recent years.[8]

Then finally:

It can be readily agreed that if explosive mass movements are a genuine threat to America, a politics of narrow constituencies might be desirable to counter the danger. Small associations probably do provide order and stability for any society. In the United States some associations may serve in this manner to a greater degree than others. The American Civil Liberties Union and the League of Woman Voters have given notable service to American democracy. Trade unions and farm organizations have undoubtedly also been similiarly useful at various times. Nevertheless, it should be clear that a substantial price is paid for any guarantee against mass movements provided by a pattern of small constituencies. That price is paid in freedom and equality. Although the price would be worth paying if the danger were grave, it can hardly be argued that such an extremity is present.[9]

There are voices in the black community (accompanied, as we well know, by acts of expressive violence) saying precisely that the

---

Edward Shils, *Political Development in the New States* (New York: Humanities Press, 1964);

Thomas Hodgkin, *Nationalism in Colonial Africa* (New York: New York University Press, 1957);

K. H. Silvert, *Expectant Peoples: Nationalism and Development* (New York: Random House, 1964);

Lucian W. Pye, *Politics, Personality and Nation Building: Burma's Search for Identity* (New Haven: Yale University Press, 1962).

[7] Grant McConnell, *Private Power and American Democracy* (New York: Random House, 1965), pp. 346–347.

[8] *Ibid.,* p. 349.

[9] *Ibid.,* p. 355–356.

danger *is* grave and that the extremity *is* present. The educational systems are particularly vulnerable, because of their very conspicuous inability to "pay-off."

AN ALTERNATIVE AGENDA

It is instructive, then, to examine some of the major items presented by certain voices in the black community. Clearly, one source of constructive ideas would be black teachers, those persons who not only teach in ghetto schools, but whose children attend those schools (in most instances), who, themselves, grew up in the black community, and who, for the most part, still live in black communities.[10] Approximately 800 such teachers met in Chicago, June 6–9, 1968, in a national conference and formed the National Association of Afro-American Educators. They did not spend the four days discussing the Coleman Report or the report of the U.S. Civil Rights Commission. One could identify four particular areas of concern at that conference, and these areas coincide to a great extent with the issues raised by associations of Concerned Black Parents as well as various Afro-American History clubs in the high schools around the country.

(I) Control

It was generally concluded that the existing educational systems were not responsive to the wishes of the black community. Therefore, those structural arrangements now operating should be changed substantially. The decision-making process in most ghetto school systems was challenged. The workshop on the black school and the black community issued the following statement:

[10] In a column entitled "Quality Teaching in Decentralized Slum Schools," Fred M. Hechinger, education editor of *The New York Times,* wrote: "It seems more realistic and, for the long pull, more constructive to face the fact that part of the answer to the crisis must come through the efforts of Negro teachers. If young Negro college graduates can be channeled into these schools and if their greater identification with the children's and the parents' own background can more easily gain the pupils' confidence and attention, then to sacrifice some of the present licensing requirements may be a small price to pay" (*The New York Times,* April 29, 1968).

—Whereas, the educational systems of this nation have criminally failed the Black youth of this country,

—Whereas, Black parents have not had a voice in determining the educational destiny of their youth,

—Whereas, the Black youth and Black parents are demanding relevant education to meet their needs,

—Therefore, be it resolved that we encourage, support and work to organized local communities to control their own schools through local or neighborhood school boards and further that this organization go on record to immediately implement such plans.

—The goal of the National Association of Afro-American Educators should be Black control of the Black Community schools.[11]

One hears these kinds of statements increasingly among newly politicized people in the black communities. The focus has shifted; emphasis is now on viable ways to gain enough leverage to drastically revise a system. Black people, having moved to the stage of questioning the system's very legitimacy, are seeking ways to create a new system. This is difficult for most Americans to understand precisely because they have assumed the continuing legitimacy of the present educational system.

(2) Parent Involvement and Alliance with Black Teachers

It is becoming clearer and clearer that the major agents of control should be black parents in the community working closely with the teachers in the school. For this reason, if no other, many black spokesmen do not favor various compulsory plans for busing black children out of their communities into white schools, in some instances, miles away from home. Are we to assume that black parents, likewise, will travel miles across town in the evenings to attend PTA meetings—frequently to be surrounded by a sea of white faces, more articulate and with more organized voting strength? The principle of busing overlooks the very important factor of facilitating black parent participation in the child's schooling. If in fact the home has a critical role to play in the educational process, then we would be well advised not to pursue policies which would make that role more difficult.

[11] Excerpt from notes of discussion and reports of workshops of National Association of Afro-American Educators (Chicago, Illinois, 1968). (Mimeographed.)

The participation of black parents in the child's schooling is one of the points high on the agenda of some black people. And it is clearly at odds with one of the stated objectives of the Redmond Report: to bus black children into white schools, but to maintain a quota (no white elementary school would be over 15 percent black; no high school over 25 percent black), in order to guard against the possibility of a white exodus. James Redmond, Superintendent of Schools in Chicago, said: "Chicago will become a predominantly Negro city unless dramatic action is taken soon . . . School authorities (must) quickly achieve and maintain stable racial proportions in changing fringe areas."[12] Trying to placate whites simply is not a matter of top (or high) priority to many black people, especially if it must be done by manipulating black children.

Discussion of parental involvement and control has serious implications for the standards of professionalism we adopt. Black parents might well have different notions about what is methodologically sound, what is substantively valuable. They might well be impatient with some of the theories about teaching reading and writing. And at this stage who is to say that their doubts are not valid? The present approaches have hardly proved efficacious. Therefore, when we get sizeable black parental participation, we are opening up the profession to question and challenge about what constitutes educational legitimacy. No profession welcomes such intrusion from laymen. This is quite understandable; professionals have a vested self-interest. All those years of college courses and practice teaching and certifying exams, all those credentials of legitimacy may be going by the board. But that is precisely what happens in societies which are modernizing, in societies where new groupings—alienated from traditional norms—rise to make new normative demands. It is disturbing, disruptive, painful. It is change. And this is the phenomenon American social science has

---

[12] Quoted in an editorial in *Chicago Sun-Times*, January 12, 1968, p. 27. The editorial, which favored the Redmond Plan, further stated: "That part of the Redmond Plan that has excited opposition calls for fixing immediately a balanced racial enrollment in those all-white schools that are in the way of the Negro expansion. It would be roughly 90 per cent white, 10 per cent Negro. The Negro pupils (who are from middle-class families) would be acceptable to white families and keep them anchored in the neighborhood, whereas they would flee to the suburbs if the Negro proportion became greater than 25 per cent. The plan may not work. If it does it is at best only a holding action until the entire metropolitan area faces up to the demographic realities of our time. But it should be tried."

been unable to come to terms with in the latter half of the twentieth century—especially with reference to the issue of race relations.

(3) Psychological Impact

A third matter of concern to these new black voices is the psychological impact of educational institutions on the black children. Many black people are demanding more black principals in predominantly black schools, if only because they serve as positive role models for the children. Children should be able to see black people in positions of day-to-day power and authority. There is a demand to have the schools recognize *black* heroes with national holidays. There is concern for emphasizing group solidarity and pride, which is crucial for the development of black Americans. And there is very serious question whether a predominantly white, middle-class ethos can perform this function. Again, the Coleman data measure verbal skills and mathematical abilities, but there are other areas of equal importance. One should not assume that symbols of cultural pride are unimportant. Professor Lipset was correct when he described the impact of these symbols, but he was incomplete when he applied them to the United States—when the growing awareness of black Americans is taken into account. He wrote:

A major test of legitimacy is the extent to which given nations have developed a common "secular political culture," mainly national rituals and holidays. The United States has developed a common homogeneous culture in the veneration accorded the Founding Fathers, Abraham Lincoln, Theodore Roosevelt, and their principles.[13]

The schools serve as a major instrument to transmit such a common homogeneous culture. And yet, we are beginning to see black Americans call for the recognition of other heroes: Frederick Douglass, Martin Luther King, Jr., Malcolm X, and so forth. Students are demanding that the traditional Awards Day programs at their schools include such awards as a Malcolm X Manliness Award, a Marcus Garvey Citizenship Award, and Frederick Douglass and Martin Luther King, Jr. Human Rights Awards. We see black writers challenging the idea of a common secular political culture.

[13] Lipset, *Political Man*, p. 68.

John Oliver Killens and Lerone Bennett, Jr. are two prominent examples. Killens captured the mood when he wrote:

We (black Americans) even have a different historical perspective. Most white Americans, even today, look upon the Reconstruction period as a horrible time of "carpetbagging," and "black politicians," and "black corruption," the absolutely lowest ebb in the Great American Story . . . We black folk, however, look upon Reconstruction as the most democratic period in the history of this nation; a time when the dream the founders dreamed was almost within reach and right there for the taking; a time of democratic fervor the like of which was never seen before and never since . . .
For us, Reconstruction was the time when two black men were Senators in the Congress of the United States from the State of Mississippi; when black men served in the legislatures of all the states in Dixie; and when those "corrupt" legislatures gave to the South its first public-school education . . .[14]
Even our white hero symbols are different from yours. You give us moody Abe Lincoln, but many of us prefer John Brown, whom most of you hold in contempt as a fanatic; meaning, of course, that the firm dedication of any white man to the freedom of the black man is *prima-facie* evidence of perversion or insanity.[15]

And Lerone Bennett, Jr. challenged much of American historical scholarship when he challenged the role and image of Abraham Lincoln:

Abraham Lincoln was *not* the Great Emancipator. As we shall see, there is abundant evidence to indicate that the Emancipation Proclamation was not what people think it is and that Lincoln issued it with extreme misgivings and reservations.[16]

A growing number of black Americans are insisting that the schools begin to reflect this new concern, this new tension. We simply cannot assume a common secular political culture. If we continue to operate on such false assumptions, we will continue to misunderstand the very deep feeling of alienation in the black community. And misunderstanding cannot be a viable basis for enlightened public policy. Likewise, it is not only important that Afro-

[14] John Oliver Killens, *Black Man's Burden* (New York: Trident Press, 1965), pp. 14–15.
[15] *Ibid.*, p. 17.
[16] Lerone Bennett, Jr., "Was Abe Lincoln a White Supremacist?" *Ebony*, 23, No. 4 (February, 1968), p. 35.

American history be taught in the black schools, but that it also be incorporated into the curriculum of white schools throughout this country. It is not sufficient that only black children be given an accurate historical picture of the race; all Americans must have this exposure—in the inner city, the suburbs, the rural schools.

Who can predict what the "tests" will show when we begin to expose black children to these kinds of innovations? What sort of impact will this have on the motivation of those "slow learners," those "high risks," those (and here is the misnomer of them all) "culturally deprived?" The legitimacy of the "standardized tests" must be questioned as long as they overlook these very essential components.

(4) Curricula and Instructional Materials

Closely related to the third point is a concern with the kinds and content of materials used, especially in black schools. How are black people portrayed? Do the textbooks reflect the real experience of black Americans in history and in contemporary society? The workshop on instructional materials at the Afro-American Educators Conference concluded:

In each local community black educators must develop a criteria for selection of materials which will be presented to the Board of Education, to local textbook committees, and to the major publishing houses which provide text and supplemental materials to that community. It is incumbent upon us, if we are to serve this society, that instructional material which we select be both educationally sound and incorporate a strong black orientation.

Black classroom teachers must help black students to speak the language of the market place and assist them as they move back and forth between "their own thing and a white American thing." Since all groups usually speak two languages, one at home and within their group and another in the economic world; by nurturing and respecting our own language and effectively manipulating the other we will become a truly bilingual people. This is necessary to achieve a viable economic base . . .

Black teachers must become connected with major textbook publishing firms as authors, editors and consultants to create the materials available on the market. We must pressure major publishers to reflect the needs of black children in schools. We will work for a factual inclusion of the scientific contribution of black scientists to medical and scientific advancement. For example, Dr. Daniel Hale Williams (open heart surgery) and Dr. Charles Drew (developer of blood plasma) must receive their rightful place in elementary and secondary science texts.[17]

These are some of the things on the agenda of many black people as they consider possible solutions of our vast educational problems. It is far too soon to evaluate the results of most of these proposals—in some instances they have not even been implemented. And in most cases they are in the embryonic stage. We are without precedent in these matters, and it would be presumptuous of American social scientists to attempt to prejudge results, or even to suppose that they could. Black people are searching for new forms of educational legitimacy, and in that kind of modernizing atmosphere the traditional criteria for measuring effectiveness might well be irrelevant and anachronistic.

AN ALTERNATIVE MODEL

The rhetoric of race and education, as stated earlier, is prolific with dichotomies of segregation vs. integration, quality education vs. integrated education, compensatory programs vs. busing, and so forth. Too much is assumed by these simplistic terms, and a superficial use of these labels frequently restricts and predetermines discussion at the outset. While this is unfortunate, it is probably unavoidable, given the historical context and the highly emotional atmosphere. Those persons favoring "neighborhood" schools and opposing busing have traditionally been, in the North, white parents and taxpayer groups, usually identified as anti-Negro in their basic racial views. These groups would normally be found opposing open housing laws as well. Therefore their motivations are questioned when they argue that they are essentially concerned about "educational standards" and property values. When it is pointed out to them that white students do not suffer academically and (if panic selling is avoided) property values do not go down, they do not listen. And their intransigence leads their opponents to label them as racial bigots and segregationists.

Proponents of busing and integration see a positive academic

---

[17] Excerpt from notes and discussion and reports of workshops of National Association of Afro-American Educators. (Chicago, Illinois, 1968). (Mimeographed.)

and social value in racially heterogeneous classrooms. Integration to these people is virtually synonymous with quality. And black people who once worked for desegregated schools but who no longer do so are viewed as having given up the fight, as having joined the white racists, and, indeed, as having become black racists and advocates of "Black Power separatism."[18]

I state this simply to acknowledge an awareness of some of the positions taken before I proceed to suggest an alternative educational plan. The fact that my ideas would appear more closely akin to the views of some white segregationists whose ultimate goal is to deny educational opportunity to black people is an *appearance* I cannot avoid. It is important however to point out that a close examination of the ultimate goals of my suggestions will indicate a clear divergence from views held by the segregationists. In other words I am motivated by an attempt to find an educational approach which is relevant to black people, not one that perpetuates racism. The plan I am suggesting is not a universal panacea; it is not applicable in all black ghettos. Where it is feasible—particularly in the large urban communities—I strongly propose it for consideration.

This is a model which views the ghetto school as the focal point of community life. The educational system should be concerned with the entire family, not simply with the children. We should think in terms of a Comprehensive Family-Community-School Plan with black parents attending classes, taking an active, day-to-day part in the operation of the school. Parents could be students, teachers, and legitimate members of the local school governing board. A similar plan is already in operation in Chicago: the Family Education Center. There are two centers, the Westinghouse and Doolittle Centers, which provide basic adult education, prevocational and vocational training, and work experience programs.

Mr. William H. Robinson, Director of the Cook County Department of Public Aid, has stated:

[18] An example of this attitude was contained in the report of the President's civil disorders commission (Kerner Commission). "The Black Power advocates of today consciously feel that they are the most militant group in the Negro protest movement. Yet they have retreated from a direct confrontation with American society on the issue of integration and, by preaching separatism, unconsciously function as an accommodation to white racism" (*Report of the National Advisory Commission on Civil Disorders* [New York: E. P. Dutton & Company, 1968], p. 235).

The Center's most unique feature is the Child Development Program for the students' (parents') pre-school children, who come to school with their mothers and spend the day in a well-equipped, professionally staffed nursery school. Mothers can attend classes with the assurance that their children are receiving proper care and mental stimulation. Thus, the program makes participation in an educational program possible for many recipients who were prevented previously because they could not obtain adequate child care services.[19]

Since the inception of the program two years ago, 1,300 adults and 500 children have been involved in the centers.

This concept should be expanded to include fathers as well, those unemployed and willing to obtain skills. Many of these parents could serve as teachers, along with a professional staff. They could teach courses in a number of areas (child care, auto mechanics, art, music, home economics, sewing, etc.) for which they are obviously now trained. The Comprehensive Plan would extend the school program to grades through high school—for adults and children—and it would eliminate the traditional calendar year of September to June. (There is no reason why the educational system could not be revised to take vacations for one month, say in December of post-Christmas, and another month in August. The community educational program would be a year-round function, day and evening.)

The school would belong to the community. It would be a union of children, parents, teachers (specially trained to teach in such communities), social workers, psychologists, doctors, lawyers, and community planners. Parent and community participation and control would be crucial in the hiring and firing of personnel, the selection of instructional materials, and the determination of curriculum content. Absolutely everything must be done to make the system a functioning, relevant part of the lives of the local people. Given the present situation of existing and growing alienation, such involvement is essential.

If it can be demonstrated that such a comprehensive educational institution can gain the basic trust and participation of the black community, it should become the center of additional vital community functions. Welfare, credit unions, health services, law enforcement, and recreational programs—all working under the

---

[19] Cook County Department of Public Aid, *The Challenge of Change* (Annual report, Chicago, 1967), p. 11.

control of the community—could be built around it. Enlightened private industry would find it a place from which to recruit trained, qualified people and could donate equipment and technical assistance. The several advantages of such a plan are obvious. It deals with the important agencies which are in daily, intimate contact with black people; it reduces a vast, fragmented service bureaucracy which now descends on the black community from many different directions, with cumbersome rules and regulations, uncontrolled by and unaccountable to the community. It provides the black people with a meaningful chance for participation in the very important day-to-day processes affecting their lives; it gives them educational and vocational tools for the future. All these things reflect the yearnings and aspirations of masses of black people today.

The Comprehensive Plan envisions the local school as a central meeting place to discuss and organize around community issues, political and economic. All of the establishments functioning under the plan would provide relevant intermediary groups to which the people could relate. The size of the community involved would vary, with several factors to be considered: geography, number of participating agencies, available funds (from federal, state, and local governmental sources), and manageability. At all times, the primary concern would be about the active involvement of people and about their possession of real power to make decisions affecting the Comprehensive Plan. They would hire consultants and experts whose legitimacy would be determined by their relevance to the community, not by a predetermined set of criteria superimposed from outside.

The proposed Comprehensive Plan attempts to come to grips with the understandable alienation discussed in the first section and with the appropriateness of the agenda items described in the second section of the paper. This plan is better understood when one keeps in mind the premise presented earlier: black people are questioning, evaluating the *legitimacy* of existing educational institutions, not simply searching for ways to make those institutions more *effective*. I am suggesting that we are at a point in the process of modernization and social transformation when we must begin to think and act in wholly new normative and structural terms.

PART IV

The Professionals

The principle of control in American education is that laymen should govern the schools. They do so through elected local school boards, state superintendents, and boards of education. In some states they do so through appointment of these public officials by elected mayors and governors.

In practice, much of the control and authority in the schools passes to the professionals whom these public officials hire. The professionals are on the job full time; they are far more numerous than the laymen; they are paid for the work they do; they are regarded as "trained experts" by the general public. These professionals include administrators, teachers, and other trained people—such as counselors—who work in the schools or manage the school system.

Considering that there are about 107,000 members of local and state boards of education throughout the United States, there are more than 132,000 administrators and about two million teachers, all of whom are on the job full time. In the large city school, there may be a local school board composed of some nine laymen who serve part time without salary and with very little secretarial and research support—while the administrators, the managers of the system, may number four or five hundred. This results in a ratio of about one lay school board member for every forty administrators.

This imbalanced ratio has undoubtedly been one important factor in demands for greater community control (lay control) in the big-city school system. Community people, particularly parents in the ghetto, feel that they lack influence in making important decisions about the schools. They feel underrepresented on the small local school board, and many feel that their opinions have carried little weight with the large "bureaucracy" of administrators and managers who make most of the important operating decisions about the schools.

When the struggle in city schools was over the issue of integration, the conflict was largely between community people (the local parent advocates or opponents of integration) and school administrators who drew school boundaries and were charged with making decisions about busing students for purposes of integration.

For various reasons, as we have seen, very little racial integration was achieved in the typical city system. This being true, the demands of community people shifted in many places to the issue of community control. If ghetto parents could not get their children into integrated schools, they wanted at least to be able to influence decisions and to select administrators in their own community. The shift to this new issue created a new group of adversaries among professionals in opposition to the community. Not only did administrators in many places resist the community's demand to hire and fire their own administrators, teachers also joined the resistance.

In collective-bargaining relationships with newly organized teachers, the relationship between teachers and administrators was originally that of adversaries. Administrators sat on the side of the "bosses" and teachers on the side of the "union" and "workers" in this relationship. Moreover, this relationship grew out of a long history of grievances on the part of teachers who wanted improvement in their salaries, working conditions, and the management of schools but found that administrators consistently stood in the way of change. It was for this reason that many teachers organized themselves into unions. They, too, wanted some of the authority that had long been reserved to administrators.

When the community began asking for authority, however, organized teachers in New York City (and to a lesser extent, in other places) abandoned for the time their traditional adversary relationship with administrators and joined them in opposition to certain forms of community control. The form they seemed to object to most was the community's insistence on its right to transfer, if not hire and fire, teachers. Organized teachers, at any rate, felt that its newly won position of influence in the operation of public schools was threatened by community demands for its own share of influence. Some teachers felt also that their opportunities for promotion to administrative posts would be diminished if community boards were permitted to select their own administrators. At any rate, for the first time on an issue of this kind, the professionals in the system joined forces in opposition to the demands of laymen.

ORGANIZED TEACHERS

Among those responsible for educating the young, teachers are by far the most numerous. Their authority in the school system has in the past not matched their numbers, however. The most important decisions in the schools are made by others, as we have seen—the managers or the laymen or the state legislator or others. Among the key decisions in which teachers have very little say are: design and location of school buildings, financing education, equalization of educational opportunity, size and scheduling of classes, purchase of equipment, supplies and books, uses of school buildings, training of teachers, involvement of parents, the system of grouping students, curriculum, the selection of courses of study. The list is very long. Teachers who are guided by a set course of study and preselected texts have very little to say even about what goes on in their own domain, the classroom. In brief, teachers have had very little effective authority in the *system* of education.

Even in the NEA, the largest and most potent school organization in the country, teachers have historically played a secondary role to the dominant school administrators, even though they greatly outnumbered them in that organization.

The organization of teachers into trade unions, a rapid development in urban schools, starting in New York City, has profoundly changed the general status of teachers in the educational system.

Teachers who have hitherto had almost no collective voice, now engage in formal collective bargaining with dozens of major school systems. Though their demands at the bargaining table have had mainly to do with matters of direct concern to them, especially salaries and working conditions, they have shown interest in a wide range of topics and, in most places, have asserted the right to bargain about anything having to do with schools. They have asked for smaller class sizes and specialized professionals in guidance, reading, health, community relations, and so on. They have often sought to bring parent aides into the school as well as personnel to attend to neglected clerical matters. Although all of these are directly related to teacher welfare, they are possibly just as closely related to child welfare and the general quality of education offered in the schools. Organized teachers resist change of certain kinds but actively promote change of many other kinds. Moreover, they are becoming an effective lobby, in Washington and in state legislatures, for increased aid to schools. They are for the first time a power to be reckoned with in education. The successes and rapid growth of the American Federation of Teachers, AFL-CIO, have provided strong impetus for change in the general approach to education problems even in the NEA. With the increased "militancy" of the NEA, many observers anticipate an eventual organizational merger between it and the AFT.

Traditionally, teachers have been expected to be politically neutral on school issues. Ivor Kraft discusses the influence teachers could have on the schools if they choose to be active, rather than passive, members of the system. He urges that teachers have "a total commitment to academic freedom, and a willingness to undertake political struggles in protecting it." He wishes teachers to provide youth with a "liberating education in the broadest ideological sense. This will probably entail nothing short of a pedagogical revolution in our approach to the social studies." The second political task of teachers, he says, is to align themselves with "conscious, organized, and militant methods of political struggle." Their third task is to "speak up in political forums on matters which go considerably beyond the conventional confines of educational doctrines"—such as housing integration, full employment. Finally, he feels teachers should declare themselves boldly on "at least one overarching ideological position." This relates to the "deep themes of egalitarianism"—"minimal guarantees of economic and social security for all children in all lands." He looks forward to the infusion of youth and new blood into the teaching profession.

Ivar Berg discusses collective bargaining, the special requirements of bargaining for teachers, the lessons to be learned from other groups of organized employees, the threat of technological innovation in the schools, and the need for innovations in the bargaining structure to accommodate the new conditions.

Myron Lieberman and Michael H. Moskow are concerned about the importance of teacher organization at the local level, the rivalry between the NEA and the AFT, the changing attitudes of teachers, and the relation between consolidation of schools and the need for teacher organization.

Teachers, as public employees, have claimed the same rights that organized employees in the private sector have long taken for granted. They claim the right to have some control over the circumstances of their work—wages, hours, working conditions. Most teachers, and almost all citizens, are interested in another question relating to teacher negotiations. They want to know: What impact will teacher demands have on the quality of education?

Lieberman and Moskow, in another section of their text, point out, in response to this question, that it is difficult to measure the effects of *anything*—a new textbook or in-service programs for teachers—on pupil education. Short-run effects are particularly elusive when it comes to measurement. Since teachers have been organized and assertive for only a brief time, it cannot be expected, they argue, that we would know anything yet about the effects of negotiations on education. Certain factors, they claim, tend to bring about better education—competitive salaries, adequate instructional supplies, manageable class size, a good physical plant. We know we want these things, they say, even though we cannot demonstrate with any precision their effect on what children learn. In the long run, they assert, effective employment relations are conducive to better education. To determine how effective employment relations are, we must ask such questions as: Are salaries adequate to attract good teachers? Are the views of teachers heard by the right people? Is communication good? Do teachers have a voice in decision making? We do not yet know how relevant these questions are to quality education. Undoubtedly some more rigorous inquiries will be opened into such subjects in the coming years.

ADMINISTRATORS

As we have seen, the ultimate authority in the schools rests with laymen—on local school boards, state legislatures, state boards of education, the U.S. Office of Education, to name a few. As it turns out, however, these laymen usually turn over much of the actual running of the schools to professional administrators. Often the laymen are too busy, too temporary, or too intimidated by the "experts" and professionals to exercise the authority they legally possess. They hire managers to do the job for them. These managers are the school administrators—superintendents, principals, assistant principals, and their staffs—the managers of state departments of education, schools of education, the U.S. Office of Education, the NEA.

The excerpt from David Rogers' book *110 Livingston Street* (the Brooklyn address of the New York City Board of Education staff) deals with specific aspects of bureaucratic and administrative functioning in relation to the struggle for desegregation of New York City schools.

Organized Teachers

THE POLITICALIZATION OF AMERICA'S EDUCATORS

by Ivor Kraft*

It was the great novelist Thomas Mann who once said that it is not possible to be devoted to culture and at the same time disinterested in politics. For educators in our era this is a particularly appropriate belief.

* From *Kappan,* May 1966.

In the past it made considerable sense to foster the reciprocal slogans: Keep politics out of education, and keep education out of politics. It was a corollary to the state and church maxim. The reasons for this had to do chiefly with matters of expediency in winning the battle for quality public education, not from considerations of principle or educational philosophy. (Our leading educators have always been passionately concerned, and frequently involved, with politics.) When public school teaching was a weak, nonprofessional, female-dominated calling, it could not have survived the crossfires of deliberate political alignments. When the American civilization was in the throes of westward expansion, of absorbing millions of immigrants, of building vast cities and industries demanding disciplined labor, politics was often such a wild and treacherous undertaking in a *laissez-faire* approach to life that public school people were quite wise to shun it like the plague.

The situation is now much different. Teachers are coming into their own, and there are now more than 2,000,000 of them. Education is being spoken of as the nation's leading "growth industry." We spend nearly $40 billion on it annually. Americans have finally been brought to a way of thinking about schooling and learning that makes them routinely willing to undergo considerable sacrifices for the blessings of a "good education."

Also, the nature of political engagement is now submitting to a remarkable evolution in America.

CHANGING FORMS OF POLITICAL STRUGGLE

There is some confusion in coming to terms with the nature of this evolution because we Americans do not always know what we mean when we use the term politics. Is it what Plutarch meant when he called it a way of life—"the life of a domesticated political and social creature who was born with a love for public life, with a desire for honor, with a feeling for his fellows"? Is it what Jefferson had in mind when he said that "politics is such a torment that I would advise everyone I love not to mix with it"? Or is it what that grand old scoundrel of Tammany Hall, George Washington Plunkitt, intended when he declared that a thieving politician is a fool because "with the grand opportunities all around for a man with political pull, there is no excuse for stealing"?

There is probably more of Plunkitt than Plutarch in the traditional American approach to politics. But whatever definition we choose, politics does have to do with administering cities, allocating budgets, and determining what shall or shall not take place in the schools of the nation. Thus, even on the simplest level, many of the chief educational issues of our day are first and foremost political issues and they will yield only to political solutions. This has always been true in the past; it remains true today.

But today, in a rather strange way, the nature of political struggle has become at the same time more abstruse and sophisticated and also more transparent and ingenuous. We all know about the massive impersonal forces, the controlled ballyhoo and the managed press, the coteries of millionaires and power elites that manipulate the things at the very top. But we also know about the immense power that can be concentrated in street demonstrations at the very bottom, hastily scrawled signs held aloft by students with not a cent in their pockets, and the moral force of direct, nonviolent action.

In these still emergent and still somewhat tentative beginnings we are witnessing the birth of a new form of American politics. It is a politics that not only a Jefferson but also a Socrates or a Thoreau would have welcomed and applauded. It is not a politics of ward-heeling, pork-barreling, you-scratch-my-back-and-I'll-scratch-yours. It is a politics of individual participation and commitment, a kind of neo-Greek dialogue in the streets, the early New England spirit carried to a modern level of appropriateness. The civil rights groups, the militant students, the marchers, the signers of ads and the issuers of interdisciplinary mimeographed statements from academia are asking us to relate our own minds, bodies, and ideals to the great issues of the day, to take our fate in our own hands, to break through the immense walls of impersonality and alienation which loom all around us in the landscape of a mass society, to unburden our hearts, and then to roll up our sleeves and set about making the reality of our lives conform to the ideal.

Space does not permit me to discuss in adequate detail the ideological aspects of the educator's role. Perhaps the leading point is the simple one that we need frankly to acknowledge this role, not to shy away from it, and to open up with youth the great and controversial issues of our era. Numerous possibilities—as well as problems—will then emerge and we will need to thrash out a responsible policy as it relates to handling controversial and ideological questions in the public schools.

We need to do this because too many Americans today grow up in a condition of ideological barbarism. Their commitment to the freedom and openness of the American ideology is often lukewarm or even nonexistent. Millions of students depart from the high schools with no grasp of the burning issues that will determine their future as citizens of a shrinking world, with no well-founded beliefs on what it means to live as a free citizen in a democratic, science-dominated culture. Millions of Americans live out their life in ideological ignorance or servitude. This can yield tragic social and political consequences.

IDEOLOGICAL SERVITUDE AND IDEOLOGICAL FREEDOM

An ideological bondsman is a person who identifies with and then accepts the purposes of his bondage as defined by the master. In this regard we have a great deal of ideological servitude in our open society. Not all slaves are deprived of their liberty, and not all prisoners are slaves even though they may be in chains. The inmates of concentration camps who went to their deaths keeping inviolate their own inner purposes as political and social men did not perish in a state ideological slavery but rather as "free" men.

The distinction between those American Negroes who since emancipation have been living in ideological servitude and those who have not is a vital one, and this distinction is well known to all who are deeply concerned about the present struggle for civil rights in America. For one hundred years the official fiction of the South (and parts of the North as well) has been that there are two kinds of American Negroes, a large majority who willingly and freely identify with the superior purposes of white society as defined by the white leaders, and a small minority of criminal and pathological types who must, when occasion requires, be ruthlessly and even brutally suppressed. This sanctimonious but no doubt sincere fiction, which is the kingpin of the southern white supremacy rationale, simply did not take into consideration the possibility that there was a third group of Negroes who saw no way of escaping their bondage while at the same time resolutely refusing to identify with its purposes. This was the group which resisted the ideological slavery of the white supremacy position.

Today one of the great missions of the civil rights movement is not only to rally this third group and free the American Negro from the constraints and terrors of systematic discrimination, but also to free many millions of Negroes who dwell in ideological slavery, for there is regrettable truth in the white supremacy claim that large numbers of Negroes do indeed passively or even willingly identify with the purposes of society as defined by their white masters. A spiritual and ideological emancipation which is profound and irreversible requires more than laws, and more than the formal trappings of an open society. It requires an education which liberates.

Just as the civil rights movement is now providing a liberating education for millions of American Negroes (and whites as well, if they but listen), so America's teachers must learn how to provide all the youth of the land with a liberating education in the broadest ideological sense. This will probably entail nothing short of a pedagogical revolution in our approach to the social studies. This in turn will require of teachers a total commitment to academic freedom, and a willingness to undertake political struggles in protecting it.

MILITANT ADVOCACY IS NEEDED

Our second political task is unflinchingly to align ourselves with conscious, organized, and militant methods of political struggle. As responsible educators we must oppose all forms of violence, the destruction of public and private property, and obstreperous demonstrations for purposes of personal aggrandizement or juvenile sensationalism. This is the Halloween mentality, and ·it has no place in serious social action. But as responsible educators we must not oppose and we must have no fear whatsoever of strikes, boycotts, marches, sit-ins, teach-ins, pray-ins, and all forms of orderly and purposeful demonstration, including nonviolent civil disobedience in redressing deep-seated grievances that have long persisted in defiance of the moral law and the higher orderliness in human relationships.

We must ever be mindful that militant advocacy is squarely in the American tradition, and were it not for those bolder kinds of political struggle we would still be back in the era of the twelve-hour day, of no unemployment compensation, of families condemned to pauperism by industrial accidents that maimed a bread-winner for life and then threw him into the streets with a token $200 payment, of ten-year-old boys working a fifty-hour week in coal mines, of 11-year-old girls working a sixty-hour week in textile mills, of women denied the right to vote, and of American Negroes being beaten and thrown into jail for the mere act of seating themselves at a lunch counter and expecting to drink a cup of coffee side by side with a white man. Social justice was not always handed to us on a silver platter. Men and women had to fight for it, while others sat by idly, clicking their tongues at unseemly ways of protest. Sometimes it takes the passage of twenty-five or fifty years to establish whose ways were seemly and whose were unseemly.

A third thing which educators can and must do is to educate themselves to speak up in political forums on matters which go considerably beyond the conventional confines of educational doctrines. I will cite only one example.

Everyone concedes that one of the keys to achieving integration in our urban centers is a more equitable and enlightened housing policy. We know that residential patterns are often rigidly segregated through shadowy legal, semilegal, and outrightly illegal procedures. We also know that one-fifth of all Americans live in substandard housing. Acting purely as educators, there is nothing we can do about the housing problem, which in actuality is what imposes on us such admittedly makeshift devices as school busing and large educational parks.

But the plot is even more complicated, for housing is also a key to job stimulation and the reduction of unemployment, which would in turn palpably diminish the burden on those teachers who daily struggle with children from impoverished homes. It so happens that a really massive nationwide investment in housing combined with well-planned efforts at urban renewal and city beautification would comprise the single greatest mechanism for expanding employment.

With housing so important a key to all our problems, how can educators afford to remain silent? Ought we not to debate the issue among ourselves and then affirm a nationwide policy?[1]

---

[1] Two million teachers raising their voices for an enlightened housing policy in politically effective forums would certainly help get things moving in the right direction. Moreover, I am persuaded that few things would ultimately raise our prestige higher in the eyes of citizens, legislators, and even students

Finally, the inevitable politicalization of the teaching profession compels educators to declare themselves boldly on at least one over-arching ideological position. This relates to the deep themes of egalitarianism in our history as a nation and within the portentous political disputes which now wrack the globe. The enormous growth of wealth in our society, the great contrast between the American standard of living and that of the rest of the world, and the equally great contrast between the very rich and the very poor in our land invite unavoidable varieties of moral and social catastrophe. Teachers must line up squarely on the side of a reverse movement toward egalitarianism. They must declare in unmistakable language that enough is enough. Teachers must insist that all children be launched in life without arbitrary and extreme handicaps of grinding poverty or bloated, extravagant wealth.[2] In today's world no teacher has the right even to begin to talk with youth unless he can say flatly and honestly that he is on the side of minimal guarantees of economic and social security for all children in all lands. But this alone, if carried beyond the slogan stage, becomes a salient ideological alignment.

CONCERNING NEW BLOOD

Hopefully, we can expect soon to be subject to a benign invasion of our ranks on the part of a new generation of educational militants. These are the young but tried veterans of campaigns that already comprise a glowing page in our democratic history: the freedom rides, the Selmas, the teach-ins. There will be more.

There can be no doubt that many of these young and earnestly committed advocates of a newer, bolder, more "participatory" and

---

than strongly affirmative and informed statements on public policy, such as housing.

[2] Readers will no doubt recognize that this is hardly an original sentiment of mine. It has been repeatedly affirmed by eminent Americans. James Madison put it as follows in the tenth Federalist Paper: "The most common and most durable source of faction has been the various and unequal distribution of property." Justice Louis D. Brandeis said, "We can have democracy in this country or we can have great wealth concentrated in the hands of the few, but we can't have both." And former President Eisenhower warned us about the dangerous powers inherent in the existence of a vast industrial-military complex. At root, these are all variations on the same theme.

activist democratic style as they call it, will see in teaching the most satisfying way of translating their dedication into a career, a way of life to improve the quality of American life. It is well known to us, and we must often confess it sadly, that public school teaching has not attracted the sharpest and most searching minds among the young.

But these activist and militant youth now studying in our colleges and doing good work in our slums happen also to be our brightest and most fearless youth, and they may well bring to public school teaching, if and when they come, a spirit of inquiry and purposefulness that has heretofore been routed more typically into the physics laboratory and the corporation law office.

Let us welcome them with open arms. Let us actively recruit them. We need their faith, their honesty, their brashness, their capacity for welcoming dissent while committed to constructive work among people. This is precisely what American education needs, and they are precisely the ones to help meet this need. Of course they will be boat-rockers, unconventional experimenters, even trouble-makers, perhaps with a tendency to scandalize the local self-appointed guardians of the public morality. In other words, their behavior will be that of typical innovators.

As educators we must defend the new and bold blood. We must not stand by idly while it is shed in vain. The old-timers must join in the new experiments, they must reexamine their old ways and tired excuses. If educators cannot reeducate themselves, then who can? And woe unto us if word gets around that we educators are so set in our ways of teaching the young that we are no longer capable of learning from the young when they have things to teach us.

THE CHOICE IS UP TO TEACHERS THEMSELVES

Will teachers find the strength to grow militant, to affirm real commitments on political and ideological questions? Will they enter into political actions with citizens groups demanding an end to segregated schools forthwith? Will they join in strikes and boycotts if necessary to secure real changes in salary scales, school equipment.

Or will they throw away the undeniable political and moral curriculum innovation?

strengths which they possess, and serve passively in the stormy days ahead as doorkeepers, policemen, and glorified clerks administering an unstable *status quo* in the nation's classrooms?

In large measure the answer to these questions will determine the future of American education.

UNIONIZED EDUCATORS:
SOME COMPARISONS WITH THE
PRIVATE SECTOR

by Ivar Berg*

One can hardly read about collective bargaining developments in public education without wondering whether instructive parallels can be drawn between them and labor relations in the so-called private sector. The parallel (or divergent) developments to which I refer have to do with (1) conditions that foster union membership and help shape the sentiments of the parties in collective bargaining, and (2) the substantive character of the bargaining relationships themselves. Although this article is concerned mainly with the second of these comparative dimensions, let me begin with some brief observations relating to the first.

The American Federation of Teachers and the National Education Association have been helped in their drive to organize teachers by the fact that other public employees (policemen, sanitation workers, etc.) have also organized. At the same time "the consolidation of school districts has been identified as a further cause of the rapid development of negotiation procedures. In 1962 there were only 34,678 school districts in the United States, representing a decline of almost 50 percent in the previous ten year period and nearly 70 percent in the previous 20 year period."[1]

* From *The Urban Review,* June, 1969, Vol. 3, No. 6.

These two trends, 'contagion' and 'bureaucratization,' are among the important parallels between bargaining developments in education and the earlier experience in manufacturing. But while there may be some agreement that relations between teachers and school systems have been deteriorating, there is much less agreement about the best stance from which to move in dealing with the growing interest of teachers in unions and collective bargaining. In the public press several vexing issues tend to crystalize around one question: Are long-familiar patterns of labor relations in the nation's factories and offices appropriate in the dealings professional employees have with public agencies?

The question of whether 'traditional' collective bargaining is an 'appropriate model' in public education is not a particularly helpful one, as there are many, many patterns of relationships in the private sector. While there are *some* elements in some of these relationships that may usefully be compared with those emerging in the public education complex, these are in fact not even nearly precisely analogous cases. This fact immediately raises questions about the utility of popular formulations of the 'problem' of applicability of traditional collective bargaining.

It is worth noting, in this context, that there are also innumerable patterns of relationships within the educational complex.[2] The role of state government, the delegated powers of school boards, the mix of local and non-local financial agencies, the size of school and district units, the types of teacher organizations and the social compositions of geographic regions and sub-regions are among the many variable elements in the equations one might wish to devise in the development of a reasonably useful model for the discussion of the problems and prospects in contemporary public education.

These variabilities lead many to despair over the prospects for collective bargaining in education, and indeed the complexities are numerous. However, the differentiated structure of public educational organizations are not wholly discontinuous with circumstances in the private sector. And too much may be made of the fact that organized teachers, in a given urban school district, are obliged to bargain with school boards that are entirely dependent financially on government—local, state and federal.

The pluralistic economy is not without bargaining structures that are homologous to those prevalent in public education. In the maritime industry, workers and managers have long since dealt with each other sensibly, progressively, even imaginatively; to a substantial degree the terms they reach are fulfilled through federal funds that are allocated to the shipping industry. Another example: after a period of extensive conflict, government contractors at Cape Kennedy have learned how to negotiate effectively with a herd of unions despite the fact that their payrolls are made of nothing more than the winnings that accrue to successful bettors on the space race.

Among the most sophisticated bargaining arrangements are those in the airframes industry. The companies in that industry, including one that receives more money from the federal government than is expended on our entire national war against poverty, bargain not only with the blue collar trades but with professional workers as well. No one need have any doubt that professional social workers (and teachers) have a good deal to learn from Lockheed scientists and engineers on the bargaining strategies that work effectively in dealing with financially dependent employers.

At the same time, newer unions can give teachers useful instructions on tactics regarding public finance. Thus urban hospital employees have managed to use Medicaid grants to states and localities to raise submarginal wages despite the intent that these funds be used in connection with the indigent sick.

These cases would indicate that the financial arrangements operative in public education are not automatically subversive of collective bargaining as we have known it in America for a substantial part of the relatively short time that collective bargaining has enjoyed legal support under the Wagner Act. The companies in the airframes industry have really been federal government 'agencies' (for labor purposes) since the early '40s, while labor's 'Magna Charta' was passed in 1935!

Discussion of the applicability of 'traditional' collective bargaining can also suffer from a too simple view of the directional flow of influences between private and public sector unions. The test of applicability need not be formulated in terms of the old, established styles in the private sector and the new conditions in the public sector as though the former must fit the latter in detail.

Modern technology has already blunted the cutting edge of the strike weapon in many industries and has driven many unions to reexamine their arsenal. In the petroleum industry, the chemical industry, the power industry and the communication industry to name a few, employers have found that, during strikes, they can continue operations for extended periods by using supervisory personnel. However, the teachers of Youngstown, Ohio were able to close down school operations, without a strike, by conspiring with the school board to grant salary increases, without budget increases, that bankrupted (and temporarily closed) the entire educational apparatus during the fall of 1968. The pressures on citizens and on the state's legislators have become much greater than if the Youngstown school board had sought to balance the teachers' demands (regarding salary and educational issues) with the citizens' rejection of budgets requiring tax increases.

Similarly, unionized engineers and scientists in the electronic industries, for example, could learn from Connecticut teachers how to mount successful attacks against professionals who supervise them. These teachers induced the state and national teacher associations (the Connecticut Education Association and the National Education Association) to threaten "a fullscale investigation" of Waterbury's education program and, later, to announce that unless "corrective action" (a $270,000 addition to the budget) was taken, no new teachers who were CEA members could take jobs in Waterbury without violating the CEA's ethical code, thereby losing membership. The teachers also withdrew from *all* extracurricular activities (lunch programs, coaching, clubs, dance chaperoning, etc.). The combination of blacklisting techniques (earlier used so effectively by managers in the private sector!) with what Veblen called strategies of independence, turned out to be highly effective in forcing Waterbury's city fathers to support the school board's efforts to resolve the problem. Professional societies, even those that are subsidized by employers, could utilize these strategies very effectively in a number of American industries.

In a similar case all the teachers in a school district in Connecticut agreed *not* to sign new contracts with a school board, thereby opening their ranks to the active recruiting efforts of other 'employers.' In private industry, technical personnel could withhold signatures from contracts covering trade secrets and patent arrangements. Indeed such cancerous sores may be more painful than the clean incision of a strike.[3] The full enforcement of *all* company regulations would upset the organization in ways that might be permanently disruptive of its productive capacity; the number of rules in most organizations, alone, compels such a conclusion.

Any discussion of the relevance of 'traditional' collective bargaining must take account of the revolutionary implications of changes that are possible through innovations in education. The lag in this area is attributable, on the one hand, to the pitifully small expenditures on research and development in education—"a small fraction of 1 percent of the total investment [$49 billion] in education"[4]—and, on the other hand, to the even more pitiful expenditures (from this sum) on "developmental work which will evaluate and apply the findings of research and demonstrate their practical work."[5] Where industry exends 77 percent of its R and D funds on such developmental work, ". . . . only 10 to 12 percent of the funds expended on educational research and development are devoted to development."[6]

There is, of course, some danger that massive investments in educational technology would simply result in a transformation of a consumer *service* into a technological package that is no more educationally serviceable than the primitive educational approaches currently used. Indeed, there is ample precedent for the conversion of a complex service into a glamorous gimmick, as a number of components of the antipoverty program well illustrate. Even if this is not the case, hardware is certain to transform education in *some* way.

Accordingly, the argument that there is a basic difference between 'professionalism' and the fear of advanced technology shown by blue collar workers may be too glibly drawn. Education may well be touched by innovations already made by psychologists, computer designers, television wizards and others. Meanwhile, the educational apparatus has not been left untouched by an imperfect economy. Education functions to a large degree as a protracted effort to control the size of the labor force by 'cooling-out' millions of young workers who, incidentally, could undoubtedly be educated in much less time than is now spent on the grade school-to-grad school cycle.

An important point here is that taxpayers have been pressed hard in the post-World War II era. And there is mounting evidence that they are beginning to fight further substantial increases at a time when federal and state taxes have been mounting. There have been significant fights in even the most education-conscious suburbs in which the 'financially independent' school districts have found themselves the object of highly politicized battles that attract far more voter concern than do even major election campaigns. Taxpayers who have great difficulty in influencing other tax rates and public expenditures will apparently not squeeze themselves very much further for educational outlays. While most Americans are aware of the income advantages of formal education, and would apparently like to maximize these personal returns, they would like to restrict the size of the investment. It should hardly surprise the citizen or the planner, however, that teachers balk at what they see to be a personal subsidy that helps keep the return on educational investment relatively high for their youthful beneficiaries while the teachers themselves struggle to stay economically abreast of a less educated blue collar population.

Citizens, at the same time, will predictably opt for technological 'reforms' in the educational process itself as a way of economizing on salaries (which dominate annual school district budgets). The consequences will reduce the alleged margin of analytical differences between educators and other workers as Americans begin to talk seriously about the incontestable inefficiencies in the 'knowledge industry.' The public will be no less alert to the benefits of rationalized instructional techniques and the productivities they can purchase from uncomplaining, nonprofessional motors, screens, keys, films, and tubes. It is probable that the cry of 'unlikely prospects' will be voiced by college professors despite the fact that they feel the squeeze even sooner than primary and secondary teachers, as costs in higher education are approaching the ridiculous and the brightest graduates regularly report that academic experiences are far less than sublime.

A considerable part of every formal union agreement is taken up with non-work, non-pay matters. Where in Western Europe the nation state takes up welfare, unemployment, health and similar issues, these are pursued in the United States by unions exclusively, or by unions in tandem with governments. It is therefore hardly surprising that collective bargaining in education already finds itself encumbered with problems outside the classroom and pay envelope complex.

Irresolution of such pervasive problems as segregation pave the way for this and other plaguesome urban issues into the relations among school boards, communities and politicians. Americans have an extraordinary penchant for dealing with problems at one or more removes from the reality of their contexts, and it probably ought not shock us that this is the case in a society with so many misgivings about government.

If teachers bargaining agencies fail to find answers to social problems that reflect themselves in their dealings with school systems, we need not beat them down further when they are already burdened with an unmanageable load of personal, professional and occupational concerns. These concerns are made top heavy by the concerns of parents, politicians, repressed minorities and a new generation of venturesome youths. Meaningful discussion of the role of unions among publicly employed professionals cannot take place if Americans do not either (a) liberate these professionals from some of the obligation to solve problems that are only in part their concern, or (b) accept strife and conflict as the price to be paid for the encumbrances on these professionals that derive from slow reform in the system in which education is embedded.

The Congress, the several state legislatures, the innumerable local governmental units, and courts at all these levels, could clear much of the poisonous air that currently surrounds school boards and teachers. It would be well to start with the redistricting of the states, the enforcement of constitutional rights and the sensible overhaul of foreign policy arrangements including aid programs that senselessly drain off precious funds. Teachers unions simply need not be stuck with the task of shoring up urbanized social systems and of being damned for their members' confusion about their role in the not-so-Great Society. Their confusions are no worse than others' confusions but they suffer directly for them.

Next, it is worth considering that while our political commitment to collective bargaining in the private sector is a positive one, the parallel commitment to collective bargaining in the public sector is a negative one; collective bargaining among civil servants is a necessary evil to most people. Partly this stems from fears of strikes among public servants. But more significantly it stems from the peculiar *legal* status of public employees.

Collective bargaining agreements between public servants and employers are like the hard-to-enforce private agreements in the private economy prior to 1947. These *agreements* did not become *contracts* until Section 301 of the Taft-Hartley Act formally transformed them. This section was included at the behest of employers who were appalled by the rash of strikes in the immediate postwar era and the unenforceability of no-strike clauses in their agreements with unions. The desire to make contracts out of the loose frameworks that were signed in negotiations soon gave way to other employer hopes, however, when *unions* used Section 301 to resist plant relocations as contract breeches! Section 301 does not apply to the agreements of teachers and school systems. As a matter of fact, the problem is the reverse of the one that existed prior to Taft-Hartley, for it is the teachers who cannot secure enforcement of their agreements with employers under the time-honored principle of the sovereignty of government.

The fact that teachers' agreements are unenforceable in courts makes the outcome of negotiations contingent upon the goodwill of the parties. The fears of some politicians, like Mayor John Lindsay of New York City, that union leaders will use the political system, meaning political power, as 'power brokers' are understandable; such relationships were not treated in the Yale Law School books from which this otherwise capable man learned about government. It is apparent, however, that government leaders will *have* to learn about these relationships in the future as all manner of government workers will soon be organized; government officials simply cannot run for office, as Mr. Lindsay did, against collective bargaining.

That there are many unfortunate strikes will not be denied. But it is relevant to note that government workers and government employees must both become practiced in calculating the costs of disagreeing. The lessons are not better learned from non-striking civil servants who use more effective substitutes for strikes! Some officials are discovering that it is not easy to rally public opinion against careful and detailed law enforcement by shrewd policemen or against the subversion of familiar if important fire and building codes by clever firemen. The public may not respond to these efforts in ways that strengthens the 'employer's' hands.

The old-line machine politician headed a number of organizations which he was obligated to *manage* with some expertise. If the modern politician manager doesn't do so, he must fail to accomplish his jurisdiction's legal obligations. This expertise will have to include skills necessary to keep an able work force and to lead that work force. When managers in the private sector have faced this fact they have not infrequently discovered that unions can be a valuable adjunct to the apparatuses over which they have fuller control.

But such a development is inconceivable where the relationship is strained by the politician's misunderstanding of the management enterprise. The 'elected manager' may legitimize his decisions in a court room by legalisms, and in political debate, by consummate political skills. But these decisions *must* also be legitimated with the relevant work force itself in organizational-managerial terms. It need hardly be added that a negative rationale regarding public employees unions can be corrected only by the *stance* of the elected official. Just as the bureaucratic head of a union organization must be an effective operator in an essentially political system so must a political head of public services be an effective operator in an essentially bureaucratic system.

If the general status of 'collective negotiations' in the public sector is a negative one (in contrast to the positive status granted to private bargainers by the Wagner Act) the specific status of the lower-level negotiations that take place within the actual work setting in public bureaucracies is most unclear.[7] Although we know that low-level bargaining over work rules governing day to day operations in a school or a district goes on, as it does in the departments and shops of factories, the precise character of such negotiation is shrouded. Thus, in New York City we know precious little about grass roots bargaining over teacher assignments and transfers. Transfers and assignments, which are among the biggest bones of contention in disputes between community groups and the professionals in school systems, often appear to be worked out in the absence of anything like the monitoring of working rules (hammered out between stewards and first or second line supervisors) in organized industry.

The results of such ungoverned, unmonitored and unnoticed arrangements are no less relevant to an organization and to efficiency in the public sector than in the private. It is interesting that it was the new, liberal members of New York City's lay school board (i.e., *managers*), who pleaded that the right of critics to transfer unpopular teachers was the equivalent of a 'work rule,' and that such *ad hoc* arrangements had existed for years! It is usually the other way around in industry. The transfer procedures in the school cases can be seen for what they indeed were: the outcome of bargains that became the grease to lubricate a bureaucratic machine. However, the machine need not be drowned in such lubricants in an effort to reduce simple frictions.

One of the primary effects of unionism is to highlight such intra-organizational practices. As steel companies discovered in 1959, the year of the great 116-day steel strike, the 'rationalization' of such rules does much to coordinate the segments of an organization that may easily (and only too equitably) solve its unique problems at the expense of other organizational values that need also to be considered. To the extent they are monitored they may be useful to both parties[7] and they are more likely to be sensibly monitored if the lower-level parties to their development do not go off on their own and make accommodations to each others' need at the expense of values that deserve higher priority.

The point is that we may too easily sweep such 'little negotiations' under the rug of 'professionalism' when, in fact, they may serve only the narrowest of interests. What is worse, these convenient deals may be subversive of the commitments of an entire community embarked on progressive reforms that can be stopped cold by employees and their supervisors, or, as in New York City's schools, by school authorities who see benefits in work rules that are negotiated at the margins of the organization.

The fact that school authorities usually do not, particularly in larger districts, control the funds expended for education does make the education manager different from the production manager in some industries, although, as we have pointed out, there is, in this regard, more similarity than difference between the public education industry and those industries that draw most of their incomes from the public purse. The additional fact that, in many systems, the political jurisdiction closest to the relevant educational complex does not typically provide all of the necessary educational funds makes for additional orders of magnitudes of difference between the public and private systems.

Educational responsibilities belong to the several states; the states can delegate some authority to lesser jurisdictions though these lesser jurisdictions have only a *very* limited legal status. And these lesser jurisdictions are typically not self-supporting; the state-city-school district trinity therefore tends to be what sociologists like to call an unstable triad. The resulting combinations of (1) local and state bargaining, (2) local bargaining and state lobbying, (3) local and state 'political power playing' or (4) gradual centralization of policy and funding at state levels, any of which patterns may result from union pressures, are not easily predicted.

One (possibly desirable) outcome of union pressures is that the states will make fewer 'specified-purpose' grants to large communities for educational purposes, and larger amounts of aid in 'block grants,' the expenditures from which may be determined locally and in response, in part, to the necessary outcomes of locally agreed upon policies.[8] States may thus pull back on their impulse to 'police' in advance the funds they grant by allowing the judgments and the wisdoms, applied by their dependent constituents and dependent administrators at the grass roots, to govern specific expenditure arrangements.

In any event the separation of administration from funds, and the dual (state and local) character of responsibility for funding, are somewhat different from the bargaining conditions that prevail when national or international unions negotiate with their opposites in management.

The differences are not so great, however, when the union's relation to an urban school system is compared in gross terms with those between a large local union, say the Kenosha, Wisconsin local of the UAW, and the Kenosha works of American Motors. As in other basic industries, agreements are reached at both levels in that company; it is not at all unlikely that a multilevel bargaining system will replace the community bargaining and state lobbying model that is now widespread in regard to pay and other monetary as well as nonmonetary issues in education. The fact that the certification and employment (hiring) of teachers already has both local and state axes suggests that the model has prospects in a related sphere of concerns that preoccupy teachers and school systems.

Another apparently essential difference between the public and private sector is the pattern of third-party relationships in which employees (and manager-politicians) find themselves enmeshed. Although there is a feeling that public servants are qualitatively different employee types from those on private payrolls, government employees union leaders may gradually disabuse Americans of the intriguing idea that their tax dollars, rather than their consumer dollars, create presumptive moral (and other) imperatives.

It is already clear that privately employed physicians are more immediately linked to the public's welfare than are clerks in the Department of Agriculture's agency for the protection of exotic birds. Needless to say, however, the clerks do not enjoy the same employee rights as doctors regarding the conditions under which they may sell their offerings to their employers. Suburban teachers, meantime, have come to learn first hand that civil service tenure regulations provide almost no protection against attacks by community groups whose sensibilities are offended by textbook references to the United Nations, or by the four-letter words used by pupils in the high school newspapers that teachers serve as faculty advisors.

In the face of these facts, it is not helpful to remind teachers that they owe a special obligation as servants of the public and must remember that they are directly accountable to third parties. These lessons have been learned only too well in many jurisdictions, and public servants, whether in government bureaus or in schoolrooms, may draw very different inferences from those drawn by the casual observer who looks only at the other side of the coin. It is not sensible to see *only* the justifiable interests of third parties whose lives are touched by government employees. These employees' organizational powers may indeed be substantially subversive of 'good' public interests, but they may also be the fragile barrier against 'bad' public pressures.

There may be significant deficiencies in the ways professional services come to be allocated in a school system, as there may be excessive constraints in the procedures unions have imposed on managers in the private sector to assure members that assignments and reallocations of manpower will not have untoward consequences for their promotion possibilities or for their pay envelopes.

In most organized private industries the flow of personnel through the bewildering array of titles, jobs and skill hierarchies is carefully 'structured' in collaboration with union representatives, an arrangement that may be too limiting in the case of professional employees. The discontinuity here may be less associated with the fact that *teachers* are professionals than with the fact that their *superiors* are professionals who seek some degree of freedom in making professional judgments—as do doctors—about how best to pursue a task or objective.

Problems, of course, arise when subordinates feel that the judgments that govern their work efforts are in fact less professional than they are personal, political, or organizational, and none the more appropriate for having been enunciated by a school superintendent, supervisor or department chairman. The assurance that the supervisor's 'door is always open' does not by itself protect the equally profession-conscious employee from arbitrary rule.

There is no analogy between the rights of office workers in an insurance company and the rights and immunities that accrue to civil servants through the delineations and delimitations of civil service codes. Provisions for hearings and other procedural guarantees that protect civil servants are the rule not the exception, a fact which must color the character of civil servants unions' dealings with public officials over such matters as grievances and discipline.

In short, it is not easy to balance the rights of third parties, public employers and managers, and public servants working in the front lines of a public enterprise. Looked at from one point of view, these workers *are* protected by civil service codes and are generally seen to have *obligations* to the public that do not encumber private employees. From a second viewpoint, they are less sensitively caught up in the public's interests than some *private* employees whose work, in the health services for example, is intimately linked with the commonweal. From a third viewpoint, teachers, in particular, are professionals who can perform better under the professional-technical criteria that bear upon the work they do than under the nonprofessional, technically uninformed criteria that may be operative in the thinking of lay critics who move to influence school programs, curricula, or pedagogical practices.

The last point, that professionals should be guided by professional considerations, merges rather easily—too easily, in the judgment of some education critics—with a parallel idea that workers have a considerable investment in their jobs. This investment parallels the more familiar investment in property and involves a development of the conception in America that 'the job belongs the worker'—which is to say that a manager cannot determine working conditions unilaterally or make unilateral decisions that violate a worker's equity, dignity or basic individual rights.[9] The argument could well be made that the professional in large organizations has an even better claim to control the conditions of work than those workers in the private sector whose claims have come to be honored by legislators, courts and arbitrators. It could be further argued that these rights—whether for workers or professionals—are even more significant to employees than narrower economic questions having to do with wages and supplementary benefits. The market, after all, does set a high order of constraint, though by no means total constraint on employers' powers in the economic sphere.

The resolution of this matter entirely in favor of teachers poses some special problems, but this should not obscure the problems of teachers. Teachers do not enjoy the full benefit of market operations because they do not control, in most states, the credentialing process.[10] The result is that 'uncertified teachers' are awarded temporary teaching certificates the effect of which is to depress salary scales.

Similarly, most school jurisdictions (97 percent) utilize single-salary schedules: that is, salary groupings based on academic preparation and service; in 31 states these steps begin with state-mandated minimum salary figures.[11] The effect is to deny *many* teachers (in all fields in which there are shortages) any of the market benefits of their particular scarce skills. In a 1962 study, researchers found that 35 percent of mathematics teachers, 13 percent of physics teachers and 13 percent of language teachers in a sample of school districts were unqualified in the subjects they were teaching; "in some cases, the teachers had not taken college courses in the appropriate subjects."[12] Under these circumstances one can understand the zeal with which 'professionally oriented' teachers might seek through collective efforts to influence their situation; judicious bargaining over job controls could, indeed, prove advantageous to both professionalism and economic well being.

But there is another side that suggests that whatever the benefits such a formulation implies, it leads to monopolistic controls and, potentially, to abuses. One of the reasons for seniority claims, for example, is to increase the senior employee's choices in the employment setting. The result may be that the younger, less experienced and more easily intimidated teachers get the more taxing assignments. There is thus likely, in the thinking of many, to be a conflict between 'the job to be done' and the managers' flexibility in doing it. The problem is not unlike the public's investment in the training, for example, of psychiatrists (through loans, G.I. bills, etc.) who foresake the larger community in favor of lucrative Park Avenue practices.

The problem is not an insoluble one. 'Traditional' collective bargaining has not destroyed 'management rights'—or even limited them in any significant fashion. What has happened is that as employers face new conditions requiring adaptations in the assignments and rules governing work, they have simply had to pay to gain these rights; simultaneously they have changed the work process by capital investments. Both answers are open to the boards and legislators, as well as the supervisory professionals who deal with teachers. Monopoly does not automatically mean inflexibility, as we long ago discovered in the field of public utilities. That it *can* mean rigidity and maladaptation is shown by the case of railroads in which managers have been even *less* inventive than a generally unimaginative group of union leaders.

Since public services, unlike steel or glass, cannot be stockpiled, and 'managers' in the public services cannot relocate their operations, the labor market situations facing private and public managers are, once again, different. Even the 'lockout' does not serve well as an organizational counterpoise to the bargaining powers of organized public servants. Indeed these servants can create far greater difficulties than those facing private employers because they can disrupt service by tactics that go well beyond those familiar in production.

Even wider social problems, like unemployment or 'racism,' do not press in upon managers in the private sector to anywhere near the degree that such urban problems press in upon school systems. While it would be desirable to unburden teachers from major responsibilities for solving these problems, it is more than just desirable that public servants do not add to the complexities born of racial, social and political conflicts. Government and school officials are, by definition, not exempted from dealing with public problems while private employers may isolate their bargains with employees from their political gestures regarding minority groups, urban blight and other societal issues.

It is important that we cease our preoccupation with strikes by public servants. Taking a longer view, it must be recognized that all groups of workers in America need and deserve rights to participate in shaping their work and the conditions of the work. In the short run there will be strikes and it is reasonable to suggest that as the parties discover the cost of this type of radical disagreement, they will learn, themselves, the limitations of the strike as a weapon. Since strikes loosen other forces over which the parties have no control, they will be avoided more and more.

Needed are innovations in the traditional bargaining *structure* to accommodate the facts outlined in this article—also structural innovations in the public arena to encourage the development of new styles of bargaining. Budgeting arrangements are among the most crucial of these issues. The trick is to avoid breakdowns that pave the way for strikes and to deal with strikes in legal terms only if the penalties are related to the facts and to the complications discussed in this article.

There has been much discussion of late about the introduction into school systems of paraprofessionals whose understanding of a community might facilitate the translation of educational practices to fit local conditions. On the face of it such a development might make a good deal of sense. The use of paraprofessionals might also 'break' the monopoly of professional teachers in a given school system. The prospects are at least as great, however, that these paraprofessionals would be enrolled as members by teachers organizations. Meanwhile, an organized professional labor group would be attentive to the possibility that such a move would be inspired by the need for jobs for community members rather than by educational philosophy; such a group would also be concerned about the use of competitive cheap labor.

A sensible approach to this problem can be developed within the bargaining process with appropriate guarantees and trade-offs. Employers need merely recognize the organizational problems facing teachers. The economic implications of educational jobs are obviously serious; not only are teaching positions involved but, because of the normal mobility process of teachers-to-administrators, there are contract awards at stake as well.

One final need: an ombudsman for pupils and teachers so that the bargaining process between teachers and school systems are not unduly encumbered by citizens' complaints which are not easily processed in two-party collective bargaining.

References

1. Michael H. Moskow, *Teachers and Unions*. Philadelphia: University of Pennsylvania, Wharton School of Finance and Commerce Industrial Research Unit, 1966, p. 4.
2. *Op. cit.*, Chapters I, II, III, and IV.
3. For a discussion of teachers' inventiveness in this area, see Moskow, *op. cit.*, p. 193 ff.
4. *Innovation in Education: New Directions for the American School*, A Statement on National Policy by the Research and Policy Committee, Committee for Economic Development, July 1968, p. 29.
5. *Ibid.*, p. 30.
6. *Ibid.*, p. 30. The figure is between $49 and $59 million. To get some idea of the amount of money expended one may note that it is about equivalent to the *difference* between the $920 million and $870 million (for R and D) costs estimated by the two aerospace companies who bid on the now-famous TFX airplane. These estimates were undoubtedly too low, and represented only a very small part of the

two total program costs. See Robert J. Art, *The TFX Decision: McNamara and the Military.* Boston: Little, Brown and Co., p. 133–136.

7. See Ivar Berg and James Kuhn, "Bargaining and Work Rules Disputes," *Labor Law Journal,* 1962.
8. The agreements between school systems and unions are not, as indicated earlier, legal, enforceable contracts. The parties agree and the substance of all points is embodied in a policy statement *by the school system's* leaders; good will is supposed to pick up the slack so that the agreement will come to govern practice 'as if' a contract had been signed.
9. See Eli Ginzberg and Ivar Berg, *Democratic Values and the Rights of Management.* New York: Columbia University Press, 1963, especially Chapters 10–12.
10. In most states teachers are not even represented on licensing boards. In contrast, "Physicians, attorneys, and dentists constitute the entire membership of such boards in all states, while even barbers and beauticians constitute majority groups in 44 and 38 states, respectively." Professional educators are specifically excluded for licensing bureaus in ten states. See Moskow, *op. cit.,* p. 76.
11. *Op. cit.,* p. 69.
12. *Op. cit.,* p. 75.

COLLECTIVE NEGOTIATIONS FOR TEACHERS

by Myron Lieberman and Michael H. Moskow*

Just as it is virtually impossible to show that better education results from a specific raise in teacher salaries or the adoption of a specific textbook or the introduction of an in-service program, so it is usually impossible to show that better education results in the short run from collective negotiations. This impossibility is not a valid objection to collective negotiations, just as the impossibility of demonstrating specific educational improvements from specific salary increases is not a valid objection to such increases.

* From Rand McNally, 1966, pp. 12–17.

Certain factors tend to bring about better education. Among them we might include competitive salaries, adequate instructional supplies, manageable class size, and a well-ordered physical plant. None of these things guarantees better education. It is possible to have all of them and still lack good education. But just because it is impossible to demonstrate the specific educational benefits, if any, resulting from specific changes in these factors, we are hardly justified in concluding that there is no need to make the changes.

The same holds true for effective employment relations. In and of themselves, such relations do not guarantee better education, but they certainly do tend to bring about better education over the long run.

By way of analogy, we know that children should eat some fresh fruits and vegetables. But, because one cannot demonstrate a health improvement resulting from a week's consumption of fresh fruits and vegetables, it would be silly to argue against their consumption on a long-range basis. In the case of collective negotiations, a more complex set of relationships is involved, but the underlying rationale is the same. In the long run, effective employment relations are conducive to better education.

Nevertheless, if collective negotiations do help to bring about more effective employment relations, it can be assumed that they also help to bring about better education.

What is meant by "effective employment relations?"

Are salaries adequate to attract and keep qualified teachers? Do teachers feel that their views, criticisms, suggestions, and grievances get heard in the right places by the right people? Is there clear and rapid communication where it is needed? Is there sufficient administrative discretion but not administrative license? Granted, some of these criteria could be elaborated in more detail, but there is surely a broad area of agreement as to the meaning of "effective employment relations."

Collective negotiations can be regarded as a tool. Like any tool, it can be misused. When it is, criticism should be directed against its misuse. Thus it is no argument against collective negotiations that it has been unsuccessful in isolated situations. At the same time, a tool that never is used properly is probably worthless. Hence, although a realistic evaluation of collective negotiations must be concerned with its use in specific situations, the outcome in many cases over a period of time must be considered. Otherwise, there is a real danger of identifying collective negotiations with a specific result which is not typical or inherent in its use.

Collective negotiations must help get the educational job done. Unless its alleged advantages are ultimately reflected at the classroom and the school levels, they are not worth the effort to achieve them. It is too early to assert that collective negotiations are proving successful in many school districts, but there is reason to believe that they could be successful with a better understanding of the problems involved.

The need for effective teacher representation at the local level. One of the most important factors underlying the emergence of collective negotiations has been the absence of strong teacher organizations at the local level. Let us elaborate on this point briefly.

Taking 1960 as the point of departure, there were 7,135 local associations affiliated with the NEA, which enrolled about 49 per cent of the nation's public school instructional staff. The state associations affiliated with the NEA enrolled about 93 per cent. Although exact figures on membership in local associations are not available, the overwhelming majority of teachers were undoubtedly members of local associations affiliated with the NEA.

The important factor to bear in mind is the wide gap between organizational effectiveness at the state and local levels. Historically, teachers have relied mainly upon state organizations and state legislation to advance their interests and views. Although a state approach is essential, its one-sided emphasis is evident from data on local associations. A study of these associations conducted by the NEA's Research Division in 1958–59 showed that:

1. Approximately 64 per cent of the local associations had annual dues of less than $4.00.

2. In 34.9 per cent of the associations, not a single committee presented a written report during the entire year; in 54.4 per cent of them, there were two or fewer written committee reports during the entire year.

3. Less than 13 per cent of the association presidents had any free time for association work.

4. Although about two-thirds of the local associations had building representatives, the functions of the latter were predominantly membership promotion and distribution of literature.

5. Only 6.7 per cent of the local associations employed either full- or part-time paid staff, and only an additional 3.6 per cent were considering such action. Typically, paid staff consisted of an office secretary.

6. About 77.3 per cent of the associations reported expenditures of less than $1,000 for the year.

7. Only 26.4 per cent of the associations sent a representative to all meetings of the board of education.

8. In 1957–58, 83.9 per cent of the associations sent two or fewer communications in writing to the school authorities during the entire year, and 93.5 of the associations received two or fewer communications in writing from school authorities.[1]

Although these data refer only to local associations affiliated with the NEA, comparable data on AFT locals would probably reveal a similar situation. As a result of the organizational inadequacies at the local level, school boards almost always set the salaries and working conditions of teachers unilaterally. At times, local teacher organizations recommended improvements in working conditions prior to final determination by boards of education, but such recommendations could be rejected without explanation if the boards so desired. The only recourse for dissatisfied teachers was to change their jobs, a costly recourse indeed for established personnel. Furthermore, most teachers had to change to systems in which the procedures for determining conditions of employment were no better than those in the system they would be leaving.

Broadly speaking, therefore, the collective negotiations movement grew, and is growing, out of the appalling lack of teacher effectiveness in dealing with local school administrators and school boards. The pace of the collective negotiations movement and its nuances in particular school systems are influenced by many factors, but it would be unrealistic to overlook the fact that collective negotiations are a response to basic occupational needs of teachers.

Many educators believe that collective negotiations are chiefly a reaction to ineffective school administration. This view is an oversimplification. Although an ineffective school administration can stimulate the development of collective negotiations, an effective administrator cannot always avoid them. Events clearly beyond the

---

[1] National Education Association, Research Division, *Local Associations-Organization, Practices, and Programs, 1958–1959* (Washington, D.C.: National Education Association, 1960).

control of the school administration may bring about collective negotiations. Therefore, it is a mistake to regard collective negotiations as merely a crisis-inspired reaction, or to assume that there must be something wrong with administrators who must negotiate with teacher organizations. On the other hand, organization leaders often feel that a poor administrator is the best organizer, and there is no doubt that such an administrator is often conducive to teacher organization and militant action.

Changes in teacher attitudes. Inadequate representation of teacher interests at the local level has been a pervasive characteristic of American education for many years with only intermittent and sporadic protests by teachers. For various reasons, teachers accepted such inadequacy in the past, but they are becoming less tolerant of it.

In a 1952 study conducted by the NEA's Research Division, superintendents were asked: "If no group has been recognized for collective bargaining, what are the primary reasons why this procedure has not developed?" Ninety-four per cent of the superintendents replied that the procedure was not deemed necessary, presumably by the teachers and the administration. Clearly, no such result would be forthcoming today.

Organizational rivalry. The organizational rivalry between the NEA and the AFT is perhaps the most important single factor underlying the rapid spread of collective negotiations. Ordinarily, the state associations affiliated with the NEA have more influence in the state legislatures than the state federations affiliated with the AFT. Strategically, the associations find it to their advantage to set the framework for negotiations at the local level through state legislation. Such legislation is more likely to be drafted in accordance with association than federation policy. Its indirect result, however, is to speed up resort to collective negotiations at the local level.

In the early 1960's, state and local education associations tended to permit AFT locals to choose the time and place of elections to determine which organizations would represent teachers at the local level. More recently, however, the associations have begun to realize that this is extremely short-sighted strategy. Thus, instead of waiting for AFT locals to take the initiative in the relatively few communities where such locals have a good chance to win, more associations are taking the initiative to secure representation rights.

Both the NEA and AFT are under increasing pressure to demonstrate that each can do more for teachers than its rival. Gains by state or local affiliates are immediately used as propaganda elsewhere; losses and failures are no longer matters of merely local concern. Also each organization gives widespread publicity to its most advantageous agreements. The result is that teachers elsewhere tend to have higher expectations and demands. By the same token, national and state organizations must help their local affiliates avoid setbacks in negotiations, not merely for the sake of the members in the locals concerned but because of the wider organizational ramifications of such setbacks. Just as both the NEA and AFT publicize their successes, so they publicize situations wherein affiliates of the rival organization have supposedly bungled the task of representing teachers effectively.

Larger school districts. The decrease in the number of school districts, and consequent increase in the size of the remaining ones, is also contributing to the need for collective negotiations. The decrease in the number of school districts is rather impressive: 104,000 districts in 1947, 59,000 in 1956, and 26,000 (operating districts) in 1964. While much of this decrease has taken place in rural areas which have not participated in collective negotiations, its effects generally are conducive to collective negotiations in several ways.

First, the larger the school system, the more important it is to develop collective procedures for dealing with staff problems. In a small school system, matters can be resolved on a personal basis. There are too few teachers to support an organization anyway. Psychological elements are extremely important also; the larger an employee group becomes, the more likely it is that a few of its members will be willing to take aggressive action on behalf of the group. Also, the sense of personal participation in policy-making is easily lost in a large school system. This loss creates the need for mechanisms by which large numbers of teachers can influence policy or express their views effectively.

It should not be overlooked that collective negotiations have certain advantages for school administrators in large school systems. The larger the system, the more the administrator needs collective procedures to ascertain staff views and desires. In a small system, the administration has no problem ascertaining staff views; in a large system, a systematic approach is essential. Thus as size of school system increases, collective negotiations appears more advantageous, at least in some respects, to the school administration as well as to the teachers.

Size of system plays an important role in organizational dynamics. The larger the system, the easier it is for teachers to support a local organization which can represent their interests. In addition, large districts are prime targets for organizing activities. A given amount of organizational resources will usually reach more teachers in large school systems than in small ones.

Finally, it is probably no accident that collective negotiations have emerged first in large city systems characterized by slum areas, heavy teacher mobility, hierarchical administration, and other phenomena which tend to make teachers more receptive to collective mechanisms for solving their problems. The teacher sees big corporations, big unions, big government, and other powerful forces all around him; small wonder that he feels the need for a collective approach in the big city environment.

The "snowball" effect. Every time a teacher organization and a school board negotiate collectively, they make it more difficult for other teacher organizations and school boards to justify their refusal to do so. A sort of herd instinct operates here. A school board which is reluctant to be the first or only board in its state to negotiate collectively may find it easy to be the tenth board to do so. Each state law that places some obligation on school boards to negotiate makes it easier to convince other legislatures that they ought to enact such laws. Similarly, the leaders of teacher organizations may find it embarrassing to be left behind in what appears to be the wave of the future to their constituents.

Developments outside of education. Teacher attitudes toward collective negotiations have changed, but the problem of explaining the reasons for this change remains. One important reason appears to be developments in fields other than education itself. In some states, negotiation rights for teachers have come about as the result of legislation providing such rights for other kinds of state and local public employees. This fact suggests that teacher attitudes toward collective negotiations in public education have been influenced by developments in other areas of employment, especially public and professional employment.

It is apparent that some of the basic ideas now being espoused by the NEA as well as the AFT originated in private employment. Exclusive representation by the majority organization of teachers is a case in point. Exclusive representation has been national policy in private employment since the Wagner Act, but its acceptance in local, state, and federal public employment has been a slower process. As its acceptance in public employment increases, arguments against it in public education, on the grounds that the latter is a *public* enterprise, are correspondingly weakened.

The fact that public employees constitute an increasing proportion of the total labor force is also important. When there were relatively few public employees, procedures for determining their conditions of employment were not such a significant problem of public policy. As public employment increased from 8 per cent of the total nonagricultural labor force in 1947 to 14 per cent in 1965, the need to develop effective procedures for determining conditions of public employment grew more acute.[2] The fact that public employees are becoming a more significant group at the polls also increases legislative interest in this problem.

Teachers have been reluctant to identify with industrial workers, but they frequently have highly visible common interests with other public employees. For instance, all state and local public employees, including teachers, may be required to belong to a single state retirement system. The upshot of such arrangements is that teachers tend to be interested in developments in other areas of public employment, and, in some states, to be directly affected by them. Although the interrelationships between teachers and other groups of public employees vary from state to state, there is no doubt that teacher attitudes toward collective negotiations have been influenced by developments in other areas of public employment in some states.

It is also apparent that employment relations in the federal service are having a considerable influence upon negotiation procedures in public education. The prestige of the federal government and its willingness to engage in collective negotiations with federal employees are providing strong encouragement and leverage for advocates of collective negotiations in public education. "If the

---

[2] U.S. Department of Labor, *Manpower Report of the President, 1963* (Washington, D.C.: Government Printing Office, March, 1963), p. 17; *Monthly Labor Review*, LXXXVIII (October, 1965), 1254.

federal government can negotiate collectively with its employees, including teachers, lawyers, and other professional workers, so can local school boards." This is an attractive argument even though it may not always be a valid one.

Administrators

THE BUREAUCRATS

by David Rogers*

The civil service mentality, reinforced by the examination system, has hampered the schools at every turn. Many [New York City] headquarters staff often hesitated to formulate advanced desegregation plans, for example, for fear of offending some of the administrators and supervisors and losing what little influence they had to effect even minor reforms. After a while, they too, and this includes staff personnel in those headquarters units most directly involved in desegregation planning, would feel obliged to retreat behind one or another legalism that supposedly prevented them from recommending more far-reaching desegregation proposals. Sometimes, the tendency to invoke particular rules or by-laws as a justification for inaction was not so much a matter of being against a desegregation plan as it was an attempt at personal and organizational survival. And the more tradition-bound officials were, the more attached they were to rules.†

* From *110 Livingston Street,* by David Rogers. Copyright © 1968 by David Rogers. Reprinted by permission of Random House, Inc.
† Social scientists have coined the term "'bureaucratic personality" to characterize such forms of behavior, and suggest that they are prevalent in large civil service organizations. A preoccupation with rules, procedures, and traditional ways of solving problems is generally seen as the hallmark of this personality type. The New York City schools have more than their share of such people; the board recognizes this fact, but civil service laws preclude doing much about it.

One top-level commissioner in the Mayor's Commission on Human Rights, who had dealt with the Board of Education on the desegregation issue for many years, described some of the professionals he encountered: "When Gross came in we told them what they need is leadership. There is no flow in that kind of bureaucracy. The Board of Education is like an old man with arteriosclerosis. They make a good statement and it sits there like a heart pumping, but there are no veins or the veins aren't working. They are hardened. The bureaucracy is so paralyzed. They are slaves of their own past frame of mind. In other words, they set up ideas and lose sight of the fact that if they set the ideas up they could change them too. They became enslaved by the structure that they themselves had been responsible for setting up."

It was on the desegregation issue, perhaps more than on any others, that this bureaucratic outlook prevailed. The neighborhood school was an axiom, basic and unshakeable; many of the rules that were cited to justify the status quo followed logically from this axiom. Questioned about school construction and zoning, the educators recited the old rules. Even after the board had made numerous policy statements on construction to the effect that schools would be built in fringe areas where possible or where practicable, headquarters professionals continued to quote the old policy to justify building them as neighborhood schools.

On zoning, though the board had added integration and utilization in 1957 as criteria for zoning decisions, particular plans were sometimes evaluated on the basis of other, more traditional criteria. For example, some plans were rejected because they violated the rule that there be no skip zoning—that is, that pupils not transfer across a contiguous school district.

One leader of a white civic group reported her conversations with Central Zoning Unit staff over feeder patterns they had developed for junior high schools in several boroughs. They told her with some pride how they had rearranged zoning patterns without violating traditional Board policy. "They kept trying to show me how they could break with the old without breaking with the old," she recalled. "It was a little bit like verbal gymnastics, because there wasn't much desegregation coming out of their plans. Many of them wanted to desegregate and it wasn't their fault, because they were bound by old zoning rules. It was sad to see them try to do something they couldn't do within the framework they followed and try to make themselves feel good about it. If it were up to them alone, at least some of them would have discarded old zoning rules."

FRAGMENTATION, FIELD REBELLION, AND PROTECTIONIST POLITICS

Two other key features of the system are its lateral and vertical divisions. The fragmentation of headquarters into various power blocs and cliques, and the rebellion and non-compliance of field officials with headquarters directives, contribute substantially to the school system's failures.

Despite the formal and legal centralization, the school system is in fact informally decentralized and quite anarchic. Invariably, when authority is centralized in large, bureaucratic organizations and dispersed across numerous headquarters units, the ranks become alienated and rebel. This has happened in the New York City schools.

Flooded with so many directives from so many bureaus, angry at how little headquarters knows about local conditions, and frustrated by the red tape, many field personnel of the New York City schools concluded that headquarters could usually be disregarded. This was not just a minority view held by a few rebellious field officials, but was part of their shared outlook, and one was a deviant if he did not follow it.

One field superintendent who had formerly been a high-ranking headquarters official said: "At the field superintendents' association meetings you'd see this distinct division between the district men and the headquarters men. The latter were regarded as in an ivory tower by the men in the field. Anything coming out of headquarters from someone of peer rank they regarded with a jaundiced eye. Now I'm out in the field, I'm one of the boys, and I'm also somewhat infected with their attitudes. I often find myself grumbling: 'Why don't they consult with us?'"

Field superintendents and principals often reinterpret directives to mean that they should do what they can to implement them in the light of their own superior knowledge of local conditions. Such reinterpretations could be anything from "passive sabotage" (as in Open Enrollment, when Negro and Puerto Rican parents were not informed of transfer opportunities) to more active efforts (such as telling parents at the end of the school year of the many costs and hardships involved in bussing their children out of the district or local school). If the directive was on a relatively noncontroversial matter, it might simply be filed away and disregarded.

The fragmentation comes about as a result of the elaborate vertical and horizontal differentiation of the system, dividing it up into a series of separate power centers.

Divisions

In both desegregation and decentralization, the significant power blocs have been the elementary, junior high, and academic and vocational high school divisions. Innovation threatens the position or even the survival of these units.

By 1965, when the board formulated its first decentralization proposals, the divisional offices had become solidified within the system with much authority and informal power. They added to their staff at headquarters and took over decisions on staffing, curriculum, budgeting, and basic pedagogical and administrative matters for their units. At the least, they had strong veto power over decisions made by higher level officials.

Each divisional office was generally supported by its principals' association in the field. Occasionally, the associations were even informally encouraged in their opposition to reforms by headquarters officials.

The divisions were a focus of strong loyalties. At headquarters especially, one was known as a high school or a junior high school man and often identified as a protégé or ally of a strong personality within a division. Appointment to the superintendency, as well as to other top administrative and field posts, involved the influence of particular cliques formed within the divisions. Superintendent Donovan, for example, was known as a "high school man," partial to other high school men in his selection of people to serve on key committees. The late Dr. Joseph Loretan was a "junior high school man." There were constant clashes between these divisions and personalities.

These loyalties, cliques, and internal power struggles were an essential element in headquarters politics, with respect to routine matters as well as innovation. Administrative studies of the system indicate that the divisions were often insulated from one another and tended to approach routine staffing, curriculum, and budgetary questions from the perspective of their own specialist logics. They functioned as separate baronies that just happened to be part of a larger structure. Predictably, the divisions competed in trying to secure larger shares of the scarce resources of the system. "What will this do to our unit?" was the usual question when reforms were discussed.

The high school division was generally regarded as the most powerful unit. "There's an old saying around the board," explained a headquarters person, "that there is the New York City school system, and then there is the high school division." Some academic high schools had achieved a national reputation over the past several decades for their programs; many of their award-winning students went on to top colleges, where they won more honors. Some of the vocational high school programs had a similar reputation, though some were justly criticized for their outdated curricula, and for ethnic and class segregation.

The junior high school division perhaps had the most problems, the result of its ambiguous position. It was the most recently established of the four divisions, and it had trouble getting accepted as a bona fide unit. The New York City school system used to be organized in an 8–4 arrangement and there was resistance to the 6–3–3 organization introduced in the late 1920s. Some elementary and high school officials held out to the bitter end.

This division's officials have felt for many years that they have never been given the status, power, and salary scale that they merited. Junior high school staff, and especially principals, have been lobbying for a long time to get salaries equivalent to those of high school principals, on grounds that they have equal responsibilities and training. They say that they deal with pupils at an especially difficult period in their growth and development, and they resent the "stand-offishness" of high school officials and the unwillingness of the latter to see this.

The junior high school division was often viewed as the stepchild of the system. And its curriculum and programs were often poorly coordinated with those of elementary and high schools. Furthermore, the concept of the four-year comprehensive high school, discussed publicly since the early 1950s, and the middle school, threatened its future. *

Elementary school principals were allowed, sometimes encour-

* See my discussion below on these concepts in the context of desegregation controversies.

aged, to move up to junior high school posts, but the same opportunity had not generally been granted the junior high school principals to move up to the high schools. Junior high school spokesmen demanded equal salaries, perhaps partially to compensate for their lower status, and were denied that as well. They were constantly told in these symbolic ways that their division was the weakest in the entire system.

Personal factors contributed to the division's problems, too. The junior high school division needed a strong and able administrator, given its anomalous position within the system. Instead, it suffered from weak leadership in its early years. Later, in the 1950s and 1960s, its leaders began to struggle among themselves and alienated many other headquarters officials. They were in a difficult position and compounded their difficulties by their inability to maintain amicable working relations with administrators outside the division.†

Salary scales preoccupied officials in all divisions. Elementary school principals received the least, followed by the junior high and high school staffs. The difference in salary between the junior high school and elementary school staff was only about $600, which led to much resentment among junior high school officials. The status hierarchy and tensions that existed generally affected the response of people in the divisions to headquarters pressures for desegregation and decentralization.

The commitment to their divisions often took on a remarkable intensity. "If you just said the word 'junior high school,'" a headquarters official said, "some of these people would literally have a religious experience. This is an interesting question of semantics, the

† Students of administration note that the status of "middle" groups in organizations is often a source of much strain, both within the range of middle status occupations themselves and in their relations with lower and higher ranking groups. Dr. Leonard Sayles suggests that this problem is endemic in both blue collar and professional hierarchies. Middle groups often face an ambiguity of status that leads to attempts at monetary, political, and status improvement. They feel that their training and skills are virtually the equivalent of those of top-level people, and resent the fact that this goes unrewarded. A vicious cycle often gets established: failure to secure more rewards and status reinforces doubts about the importance of the job, leading to more efforts to gain recognition, new evidence that the job is not appreciated, and renewed efforts to raise one's status through pressure tactics and grievances. Among unionized blue collar workers, wildcat strikes are quite common from within this group. Professionals often respond by rebellion and behind-the-scenes struggles for status and power. This characterization fits the situation and behavior of many junior high school officials in the New York City schools. See his *Behavior of Industrial Work Groups,* New York. Wiley, 1958, pp. 49–56.

way a particular word or concept would evoke such feelings. People would tell you the wondrous things their division had done in New York City. Their division was their whole way of life. They meant it in a professional as well as political sense."

The other major blocs, in addition to the Board of Examiners and divisions, were the Board of Superintendents,* the Council of Supervisory Associations, particular bureaus, the district superintendents, and the principals' associations.

The Council of Supervisory Associations is a major symbol of traditional bureaucratic politics. Formed in 1963 to represent all the field supervisors—principals, department chairmen, district superintendents, administrative assistants, and various staff personnel—it has opposed virtually every suggested innovation on desegregation or administrative reform. The Council upholds the neighborhood school, and it defends it against all demands for desegregation, even to the point of having led open rebellions against Calvin Gross and the lay board during the controversy over pairings and implementation of the Allen Report recommendations for junior high and high school desegregation. When Alfred Giardino presented his proposed reforms in February, 1967, concerning examination procedures, the CSA went to Albany to prevent the necessary legislative changes, even though the Board of Examiners itself came to accept, however reluctantly, Giardino's proposals.

Field supervisors, especially district superintendents and principals, who are the backbone of CSA, resent the unilateral way in which the lay board and top headquarters officials usually propose innovations. The field supervisors felt threatened as civil rights and other integrationist groups began to influence top decision makers at headquarters, and when headquarters formulated actual desegregation plans without consulting them, the field supervisors revolted.

District superintendents obstructed desegregation, both in

---

* The Board of Superintendents included divisional and bureau heads, all of whom had associate superintendent rank, plus the superintendent. This group was abolished in 1961, when the Board of Education underwent some organizational changes in top positions, though it continued to function informally for a few years after that. It made major policy decisions on pedagogical and administrative matters and reportedly hemmed in the board and superintendent with precedents and traditions whenever there was any discussion of possible innovations. It was a symbol of much of the status quo politics that had existed before Calvin Gross arrived in 1963.

policy-making and implementation. They strongly resisted most of the original pairing plans, not only because they were attached to the neighborhood school idea, but because many of them resented the fact that headquarters had taken over much of the authority that they used to exercise informally. The district superintendents made most zoning and site location decisions, even though these decisions were supposed to be made at headquarters. When Gross was superintendent, he rarely communicated with them and didn't take them into his confidence, nor, apparently, did the lay board. Many district superintendents as well as principals have made the same complaint, however, about Superintendent Donovan as well, whom they condemn for "not touching base with us, but making the big decisions on impulse," as one of them put it.

At a private meeting of the lay board in 1964 attended by representatives of local school boards, parent associations and district superintendents, for purposes of discussing the proposed pairings, the revolt took place in dramatic fashion. "A district superintendent got up," recalled an informant who was present, "and shouted at Gross in anger, saying that he didn't care what happened to him for making the speech, but that he would absolutely refuse ever to be a party to such a bunch of trumped-up and politically inspired and expedient plans that were so educationally unsound. He accused Gross of becoming a tool of civil rights leaders and suggested that this could hurt the schools. This meeting included all the district superintendents, and after he finished, they gave him resounding applause. I was surprised to see this insubordination before a group of outside citizens."

PART V

The Student Movement and Higher Education

Students are the "consumers" of education. Except for some college students, most do not pay for education out of their own pockets. Unlike the customer in the store, they have very little choice about what they consume. Indeed for most of their school lives, not only schooling but also a rather set curriculum of education are compulsory for all youth and enforced by law. Gross failure to comply (truancy) is punishable by imprisonment (detention), but even less dramatic forms of noncompliance carry heavy penalties. If a student fails to learn (consume) the educational product offered, he may suffer loss of status, income, or opportunity for the rest of his life.

It is ironic that the rising period of compulsory education should be one of our society's proudest achievements. No other society requires so much schooling of its citizens. The requirement grows not only out of our ability as a nation to pay for education but also out of our impulse to equalize educational opportunity. When education is not compulsory, the dropouts are usually those who are already disadvantaged. When attendance is required, we assume some education is likely to rub off even on resistant students and—like it or not—these students will be better prepared to face their futures.

This extensive compulsory and semicompulsory quality of education is one of the major sources of the new discontent of youth. People who love freedom, as perhaps all people do, are likely to become restless when subjected to such extensive compulsion. The situation can be difficult enough when we feel we enjoy or profit from what we are forced to do, but when we feel there is neither much pleasure nor profit in our efforts, we may be ready for rebellion. The restlessness is felt by those both inside and outside the system, the successful and the unsuccessful. Those outside resent the system's failure to incorporate them, and those inside resent their not altogether willing confinement.

The discontent of youth stretches out across a long continuum. A relatively small minority of youth are seriously discontented with our society and its educational institutions. The majority are relatively accepting of both. But perhaps almost all young people, like most adults, are somewhat discontented about *some* issues. Few of us have no gripes or grievances at all. The most serious discontent has perhaps always been found among the "delinquent," the violators of law as well as social norms—but this has usually been a voiceless and inarticulate discontent, often finding its expression only in acts of violence. A powerful new source of articulate discontent has been found in recent years among the most privileged groups in the society—among middle- and upper-class honor students attending some of the most prestigious universities in the country. Much of this dissatisfaction, of course, has been triggered by the rising discontent of the disadvantaged—by the civil rights, poverty, and black power movements—but having reached these higher stratified levels, it has assumed an identity and a shape of its own.

It is argued by some that the student movement is ephemeral, that students have no lasting stake, status, or power in the educational system and will never form an important part of its "power structure." They argue, moreover, that the moods of youth shift very swiftly, that the militance of today will become the passivity of tomorrow, that the leaders of the movement will graduate from college and move on into the establishment, never to be heard from again except as defenders of law and order. The professionals, they say—particularly teachers and college faculty—have gained most from the various student- and parent-generated crises in education and that, in fact, this gain for faculties results in a further loss in status and options for students.

It is too early to draw any conclusions about the longevity of the student movement or its impact on schools. Certainly the rebellion has rattled the colleges, but how profoundly it will change them is another matter.

As for the public schools, while the revolt of black students has probably had some impact, the general student rebellion has not struck with any force. The discontent present has led to a proliferation of high school organizations and chapters of Students for a Democratic Society and to the creation of hundreds of "underground" high school newspapers, but it has had no apparent permanent effect on the structure of education.

In regard to the student movement, several types of articles are included in this section. The article by Stephen Spender presents a global perspective on the revolt of youth, describing the "religious" nature of student discontent in France and elsewhere in contrast to the more political discontent of Czech students.

A rather lengthy selection from an important document, the Cox Commission report on the crisis at Columbia University, is included as a review of the specific causes of the events taking place there as well as some of the general characteristics of the student rebellion.

Finally, Carl Cohen's article on democracy and the curriculum puts the case for faculty "responsibility" in the governance of universities. He advocates democratic decision-making, believes that most faculty and students honestly want what is best for the university, but he feels that only faculty have the authority and competence to make curricular decisions, though students must have a role in the ongoing debate.

THE YOUNG REBELS

by Stephen Spender*

What do the students want? Statements have been made by students, reports by committees, books have been written by journalists, to answer this question. When one has read a few of these one begins to wonder—which is the student movement about, the society or the university? For it soon becomes clear that the students have two sets of complaints, two sets of demands, one about the university, one about the "society." Sometimes the two are merged and the university is seen as "a microcosm of the society."

Since the war, we are reminded, there has been an immense expansion of university education all over the world. The consequent increase in the university population, with corresponding increases in courses, tests and examinations, and in practical arrangements about dormitories, housing, etc., has been so great that personal relations between teachers and taught have largely broken down. The university has become a faceless education factory. Lectures are given through TV to overflow audiences, tests are made by mechanical systems, professors are unapproachable, the student thinks of himself (or thinks that he is thought of or likes people to think that he thinks that he is thought of) as a number on a computer card.

In addition to the depersonalization of the student-teacher relationship, the teachers themselves have begun to think that they are in a similar, depersonalized relationship with the university: with the regents, chancellors, vice-chancellors, presidents, alumni and the immensely overgrown administration. Indeed, younger members of the faculty often identify with the students in thinking

* From *The New York Times Magazine,* March 30, 1969. © 1969 by The New York Times Company. Reprinted by permission.

that both are dealing with an impersonal machinery of administration and knowledge distribution.

All this is a bit exaggerated, but one can see it being built up into the great historical explanation of why the university went wrong (like those accounts of the burial grounds full of bones of nameless illegitimate babies next to convents, which explain the decadence of the monasteries). There are, of course, good professors who are friendly to their students and there are small seminars, just as there were monks who didn't cohabit with nuns.

There are similar complaints, partly true and partly exaggerated, in France and West Germany. There is the absurd centralization of French education, all directed from the ministry, so that the minister can sit in his office knowing exactly what every student in a certain class studying a certain subject is reading at any hour of that day (exaggeration, of course). In most West German universities, professors remain the unapproachable old princelings, hedged round by their assistants, they always have been. An attempt was made with the founding of the new Freie Universität in West Berlin after the war to alter this and form a new democratic university, "a community of teachers and taught," but it largely collapsed through a combination of overcrowding, political complications and internecine disputes. In Italy, matters are still worse. Professors are so badly paid that most of them, to be able to afford to teach, have to take other jobs. I have no space here to discuss universities in Asia, but they are slums for students who know that without a university degree they won't get jobs and that with it the chances are enormous that they won't do so either. Perpetual revolt here reflects perpetual despair.

In America the stated demands of the students are that they should have voices in deciding who teaches them, what they study, how they are governed. They demand, on the university level, participation—that is to say, sitting with faculty members on committees where decisions are made, and having a student senate or parliament that can debate university policies.

Another complaint of the student militants is against the relations of the university with the power structures of the surrounding society and the representation, in American universities, of governmental, military and industrial interests: Dow Chemical, the Institute for Defense Analyses, the C.I.A. and the R.O.T.C.—which are bound up with militant policies the militant students detest. Today these are symbolized by Vietnam. The presence of these organizations is resented not only because of what they are and what they stand for, but also because, the students feel, they cast ideological shadows across the university and "prove" that its ultimate purpose is to instill in them the attitudes of the military and industry.

In France the militants also suspect the state of infusing capitalist ideology into the university. Daniel Cohn-Bendit in his book, "Obsolete Communism: the Left-Wing Alternative," writes about his fellow students of sociology at Nanterre forming the opinion that the American industrial psychology they were taught was a weapon for helping the world *bourgeoisie*. In being trained as sociologists the students were being enlisted to support the system. (Apart from this there was the worry as to whether they would get any employment anyway.) Alain Touraine, one of the teachers at Nanterre sympathetic to the students, remarked in an interview: "If the study of sociology didn't make one sensitive to social problems, it would be a bit surprising." So the Nanterre students of sociology and political science formed groups (*groupuscules*), which approached their subjects with the idea of interpreting them as two-edged instruments that they were being taught to use in defense of the society but that could also be turned against it and used for the defense of "*la révolution.*"

There is a problem special to American universities that has greatly preoccupied the students, and that is racialism. This is a problem that certainly cannot be dissolved in "participation" or, as might happen in cases of recruiting for industry or military purposes, simply be removed from the campus. The blacks are there on the campus, and even if they segregate themselves from the whites, their absence is felt. It is a problem that involves the students more than the administration, for ultimately its solution lies in the relations between black and white students. The importance of racialism as a new element in the life of the campus was evident during the Columbia uprising, when the question of building or not building the proposed gymnasium on Morningside Heights—which involved the racial problem—became a central issue. As every reader will know, the university had arranged that the blacks of neighboring Harlem would be able to use the gymnasium; but at the same time the students disputed the conditions under which they were to do so, and they charged that the administration had been highhanded in its relations with the neighborhood.

I am not concerned here with the rights or wrongs of this. What far outweighs them is the importance of the black-white confrontation that they symbolize. The white students at Columbia, in opposing the building of the gymnasium, had shown their eagerness to join with the black students in a situation that made black and white one community.

As most readers will recall, the white students were rebuffed, their advances rejected by the black students. There is a parallel here to the relation of the Sorbonne students with the young workers. At the time of the general strike in France following on the student revolt, the students marched to the Renault factories on the outskirts of Paris and asked the young workers to join them. Like the white students at Hamilton Hall who, after joining the blacks were then asked to leave, the Sorbonne students were coldly received by the workers and then asked to go home.

Yet, rebuffed as they were, I think that the attempt to form a community of the young who shared their ideals was what American and French students most deeply wanted. Their "demands" and "confrontations" were real, but they were improvised, and shifting, and always had the look of symbolic causes that referred to issues beyond themselves. One could not move among the students who had "liberated" buildings at Columbia and at the Sorbonne without realizing that what most closely answered their "demands" was the communal life they had temporarily achieved. When they called the "liberated" buildings "ours," they indicated what they meant by the revolution: the commune.

The authors of the Cox Commission Report, "Crisis at Columbia," quoted from an eyewitness of the events during the occupation of Low Library:

". . . . Always meetings and more meetings lasting long into the night. Participatory democracy. There was a real community spirit; everything belonged to everybody; the building was 'liberated'. . . . Here was a single commune in which adult hypocrisies did not apply any longer, where people shared and shared alike, where democracy decided everything . . ."

With their Gallic intensity, the students occupying the Sorbonne, with their discussions in the Grand Amphithéâtre and many classrooms spilling over into the "liberated" Odéon Theatre, diffused a similar excitement. A professor at Paris who had little sympathy with the "movement" told me that he had never seen his students so beautiful, so inspired. Students who were stupid and silent in class suddenly became eloquent and comprehending.

In his famous interview with Jean-Paul Sartre, Daniel Cohn-Bendit was surprisingly modest about the political achievements of the students, declaring, at the headiest moment of their success, that they could not possibly achieve any revolution, and might at most be instrumental in tipping over the Gaullist regime. In fact, at one moment it looked as if they would do this. He said that all they had done was to "launch an experiment that completely breaks" with the surrounding society, "an experiment which will not last but which allows a glimpse of a possibility; something which is revealed for a moment and then vanishes. But that is enough to prove that something could exist."

This strikes to the truth of the "movement of March 22nd" (as the Nanterre students called themselves), and is perhaps more revealing of their aims than were their stated demands. What they wanted was to perpetuate the revelation of that moment, which was the revolution. Their dilemma was that they could not perpetuate it without real political revolution, but that real revolution would probably destroy it.

Norman Mailer and Diana Trilling have commented on the "existential" character of the marchers on the White House in the spring of 1967, and the students of the Columbia uprising. What both the American and the French students wanted was to realize a state of being within a political form of such a kind that it would not blight or destroy that state of being. They were not ignorant of the fact that most revolutions of the present century have first frozen and then killed the original revolutionary impulse. Hence, their desperate invocations of Castro, Che Guevara and Mao as upholders of the revolution that remains in a state of liquefaction, "*la révolution permanente.*" Hence, also, the insistence-on "spontaneity"; the refusal of the outstanding figures in the movement to accept the idea that they were "leaders"; the repudiation of any suggestion that they should put forward a "program"; their distrust of all existing political movements (apart from Castro's) of the left as well as the right; their insistence on youth, because the young are physically and mentally alive to the possibilities of combining the greatest release of their subjectivity with the greatest degree of objective action. They have not yet become enclosed in either public or private worlds, and can fervently echo the paradoxical sentiment conveyed in a delightful slogan on the walls of the Sorbonne: "The more I make revolution the more I make love, the more I make love the more I make revolution."

It might be misleading to say that the true aims of the student movement are religious rather than political. Nevertheless, one finds oneself constantly forced back onto religious example to describe them. For it is in religion rather than politics that the revolution precedes the goal, and that the aim of the revolutionaries is—when they have gained power and have overthrown the conflicting systems —to retain the original vision, the *élan* of the first demonstrations and manifestoes which were, in the existence of the revolutionaries, the already accomplished revolution. The "glimpse of a possibility; something which is revealed for a moment and then vanishes" describes not so much the Marxist revolution as the Christian vision of the "kingdom of heaven which is within."

I do not mean by this that the students who burned automobiles on the barricades and those who "liberated" the private papers of a university president and then published them are saints. What I do mean is that their protest is ultimately that of their idea of "life," upheld against a society which to them spells death. Their slogans ("Imagination seizes power," etc.), their insistence on the values of a total self-awareness merged into political consciousness and the epithets that they use to describe the powers that be— sclerotic, paternalistic, bureaucratic, etc.—all dramatize a conflict between the living forces and the social death. If the students of the spring of 1968 had to choose between political necessity and personal self-realization they would have chosen self-realization. Everything they did, I think, showed that.

The revolt of the students at Nanterre, began with demonstrations in favor of the rights of boys and girls to enter one another's dormitories. In this the students were not just asserting their sexual needs. They could easily have got round any rules frustrating them. They were demonstrating the identity of personal values with public rights. Sex meant "life" in their political-existential revolution. More dubiously than with sex, "pot" is revolutionary to students because it stimulates awareness of the sensation of being alive.

The grievances and demands of the students, the issues and confrontations—reasonable or unreasonable as they may in themselves be, excusable or deplorable—express their total rejection of the depersonalizing forces of modern society. The feeling of the young is that the aims, the powers, the "production" of this world are opposed to the spirit, flesh, imagination, instincts and spontaneous self-realization that are life.

To avoid the embarrassing connotations of that word "life," I would have preferred to substitute some such phrase as "individual self-awareness." But in fact the students are not great upholders of individualism. They are communalists—rather than communists—believing essentially in the shared consciousness of the group that accepts their life values and rejects the death ones. The individualist, with his self-cultivation and his development of his intellectual or aesthetic sensibility, seems to them to seek after a superiority that cuts him off from the group. Here again the student movement is closer to a religious than to an aesthetic or intellectualist outlook.

In all this, however, the students are far less original than they look. Their protest is only the most recent manifestation of the idea of a struggle of those who have chosen to reject the riches of the world (which the students call the advertised products of the consumer society), in favor of a psychically and spiritually richer community of the chosen, which is recurrent through history. One need not regard their movement as a throwback to chiliastic revolts. Ever since the industrial revolution at the end of the 18th century, there has been an underground struggle between the "life forces" and the immensely powerful inhuman and impersonal ones of the scientifically equipped modern state. Ever since the Romantic movement, literature has been schizoid with this struggle. It continues in an unbroken line from William Blake, to Nietzsche, Carlyle and Ruskin, to D. H. Lawrence and Henry Miller, to the beatniks—to mention only a few names. It is significant, too, that critics of the students, when not attacking them for being communistic or anarchistic, attack them for being fascist. For the most revolutionary and the most reactionary movements do have this in common: their starting point is usually condemnation of materialistic, modern, bourgeois civilization.

So far I have only described what the students want in terms of what they are against, which they call "the consumer society." Since they refuse to put forward a program, or to have leaders, or to support a party, it is difficult to say what they are *for*. But some students at the Sorbonne could be quite forthcoming when I asked them about this. In fact, one of them, over coffee, took out pen and paper and made me a diagram of the society of the future. It consisted of little boxes that were autonomous groups of people running their own lives, by democratic discussion, in industries, factories, villages, universities, etc., and sending representatives to a center where those responsible, instead of giving orders to the autonomous groups, received information from them as to their plans, and related it to the plans of other similar groups.

When I went to Israel a few weeks later and asked at the *kibbutzim* how the community of a *kibbutz*—where there was an industry or an agricultural settlement—coordinated its plans with other *kibbutzim* and with the state, the picture I was given of the members of the group discussing their plans and then coordinating them with the plans of other settlements, through a center, seemed to me close to the kind of society of which the French students would approve (though Israel is too exceptional in its structures and economy to be taken as a model).

The students had this vision of their goal but little idea how they get there. However, they were confident that just because they were a different generation they would avoid the mistakes of young people in the thirties who fell into the traps of Fascism or of Communism. I am not so sure.

I was in Czechoslovakia in July, 1968, and I found the attitudes of the Czech students very different from those of their French, West German and American colleagues.

The Czech students do not care for the revolutionary talk of their Western colleagues. As some of them explained to me, they have lived through the euphoria, the horror, and finally the boredom, of revolution. What they want is to have, within the context of a socialism that they have no wish to overthrow, some individual freedom. They feel, rather bitterly, that American, French and West German students have been glutted with too much democracy, so that they are fed up with it. One of them remarked to me drily that the Czech students, during the past 10 years, would have been grateful for only a few of the freedoms that the Western students complain so much about. Recently, in Ramparts, a Czech student leader, Jan Kavan, declared: "For us, the classic liberties are of the utmost importance. . . . I have often been told by my friends in Western Europe that we are only fighting for bourgeois-democratic freedom. But somehow I cannot seem to distinguish between capitalist freedoms and socialist freedoms. What I recognize are basic human freedoms."

The Czech students also criticize the French students for their burning of automobiles on barricades, their destructiveness, their professed contempt for the consumer goods with which—as with freedom—the Czech students feel that the Westerners are glutted, so that they cannot draw a line between having too much and having too little. As one of them said: "The French students want to remodel the whole society according to patterns of the inner life, but in doing this they neglect the material means which are needed in order that one may enjoy an inner life."

All this is anathema to the Western students, and meetings between them and their Czech colleagues have ended without much mutual understanding. This is a pity, for under the rhetoric there is a great deal that they might learn from one another. The real cause of the misunderstanding is that the Westerners are Haves, the Czechs are Have-nots. The Westerners have the freedoms and the material goods, which the Czechs are extremely short of. But even on the crude level of having or not having, here, with goodwill and a genuine desire to understand, there is much to discuss. For instance, to what extent are the Western freedoms real, and to what extent are they illusory? Those who have no freedoms are certainly in a position to explain to those who have them, and treat them so lightly, their reasons for thinking that students in Eastern Europe could benefit from Western freedoms, which do not seem illusory to them. On the other hand, there are certainly reasons why Western students feel their freedoms to be illusory. The same goes for a discussion about consumer goods. Those who have almost none are in a position to explain why, up to a certain point, labor-saving devices can be accessories to a better life. Perhaps what is wrong in the West is not that freedom is illusory and consumer goods destructive of values of living, but that people do not know how to use either in order to extend the values of living.

A Czech student, commenting on the methods used by the Western students, said to me: "They occupy their liberated buildings on the campus—so what? When they are in them what can they do except play table tennis?" Under the rather sneering tone, a real question is being posed here. Supposing—to press the question further—the student extremists succeeded in wrecking the universities, which they consider microcosms of the society. What then do they do? The students in Paris left the university and tried to join the workers, but the workers, some of whom—the young ones— were interested when they were invited into the university, were not interested when the students who had traded their mess of pottage for a pottage of mess asked to join them. Students who give up being students to become revolutionaries immediately put themselves into competition with professional politicians, trade unionists, etc., who have their own plans for a better society.

Obviously, the student revolution, after the phase of occupying buildings—which might be called the phase of demonstration—has now reached a turning point. It is likely that it will become split between those students who accept participation from the university as the answer to their demands, and those students who remain "revolutionary." There will be student senates and parliaments where topics of general university policy will be debated, as they have been at the *Konvent,* the student parliament at the Freie Universität of West Berlin. There will be student-faculty committees to arrange courses, and perhaps even to appoint teachers.

Having gone far to meet the student demands, the university will take steps to protect itself from extremists who regard it as a microcosm of the society, and who think it reasonable to begin their revolution by attacking the society at its weakest point, the university itself, without reflecting that in doing so they are also destroying their own base.

The combination of participation, self-protection by the university and wrecking tactics by the extremists, seems likely to lead to increasing concentration of the university on itself and its own problems. A type of student who likes attending committees and managing the affairs of whatever institution or family he belongs to, is likely to emerge. He is just as likely to be a Republican as a revolutionary.

If this happens it will be because the students could not answer the question put by the Czech student: So what happens after you take the buildings? At Columbia, when this question was asked, the answer, if not "Play table tennis," was "Take another building."

Although the problems of the Czech students are different from those of the Westerners, I think that what happened in Czechoslovakia still might provide a model for students elsewhere to reflect on. The Czech students did not seek to overthrow the society. They did, though, stand for values—in their case, human freedom—

which the government did not grant. Proof of their seriousness about these objective demands was that they did not insist on the making of them as a monopoly of their youth. They supported whoever made them—for example, senior members of the university faculties and intellectuals of the Writers' Union. They had a clear program of aims within the university, and other aims within the society, which they pressed. In fact, they defined themselves quite consciously as a pressure group. Beyond this, they regarded the university as an institution that was inside the society—in the sense of not attempting to disrupt it—but outside it, in the sense of being independent and of maintaining standards critical of the society.

Put like this, it seems to me that there might be a parallel development of universities in the West. To try to convert the university into an instrument for wrecking the society is totally self-destructive. But there are plenty of things in the society of which the university might be critical and on which it might exercise influence as a pressure group. There are even causes that seem peculiarly the concern of youth, in which the students might really make their pressure felt (for example, the mass media and the commercialization of means of communication). The young, considered as a social group, have every right to claim that they are the section of society most open to corruption by the mass media and advertising. In the same way the young, being the inheritors of the earth, have a particular interest in exercising pressure to oppose the destruction and pollution of the earth. It seems to me curious that, during the weeks when miles of the California coast near Santa Barbara were being polluted by oil from undersea wells, the students, busy making life impossible on their campuses, made no protest against the desecration of the most beautiful coast in the world, their world.

Beyond issues such as the corruption of the mind, the destruction of the landscape and the pollution of the atmosphere—which are more the concern of the young than of the old—there lies the world. There are reasons quite other than those of understanding one another's tactics that the students of America, Eastern Europe, Asia and Latin America should try to understand one another. The attitude of the students toward problems of freedom and productivity should be discussed internationally because they are really world problems. The students should surely ask to send representatives as observers to meetings of United Nations organizations, which have bearing on the fact that while the standard of life is going up in one half of the world, it is going down in the other half. Problems of population, feeding, youth, education and illiteracy vitally and immediately concern the young. One could wish that rebellious students showed more interest in them.

The universities are extremely vulnerable, if either governments that pay for them or students who belong to them choose to destroy them. If they are not destroyed, they are extremely strong—so much so that it sometimes seems to me that, in America, one begins to see on the campuses, which resemble city states, the emergence of an alternative civilization. It is nonsense to be misguided by the "presence" on the campus of vested and governmental interests into thinking that the university is simply a reflection of the society. The university is the students, the young, and in some way their life is much in advance of the society from which they come. The students lead a life, not just as a result of their own efforts but as an effect of the institution, that is more egalitarian, more open to "direct democracy," more communal and certainly more civilized than that of the surrounding society. The universities are probably the institutions in our society in which freedom is most truly felt. It is just for this reason that some students realize that the freedoms in the democracy outside the university are so largely deceptive.

The power of the universities lies, then, essentially in their position as centers of a life more disinterested, more democratic, more critical than that of the society. The problem for the present generation of students is to exercise this power—the power of criticism—within the limits of what is possible, without destroying the university. It is an immense responsibility; for on the one hand they have more power than they realize, on the other hand they may well throw it away, not just for themselves but for future generations.

CRISIS AT COLUMBIA*

by the Cox Commission*

I. STUDENT ATTITUDES AND CONCERNS

A. General Characteristics

1. The present generation of young people in our universities is the best informed, the most intelligent, and the most idealistic this country has ever known. This is the experience of teachers everywhere.

It is also the most sensitive to public issues and the most sophisticated in political tactics. Perhaps because they enjoy the affluence to support their ideals, today's undergraduate and graduate students exhibit, as a group, a higher level of social conscience than preceding generations.

The ability, social consciousness and conscience, political sensitivity, and honest realism of today's students are a prime cause of student disturbances. As one student observed during our investigation, today's students take seriously the ideals taught in schools and churches, and often at home, and then they see a system that denies its ideals in its actual life. Racial injustice and the war in Vietnam† stand out as prime illustrations of our society's deviation from its professed ideals and of the slowness with which the system reforms itself. That they seemingly can do so little to correct the wrongs through conventional political discourse tends to produce in the most idealistic and energetic students a strong sense of frustration.

Many of these idealists have developed with considerable sophistication the thesis that these flaws are endemic in the workings of American democracy. They argue that their form of pres-

† See pp. 317–319.

sure—direct action, confrontations, sit-ins, and (in some cases) physical violence—applied at points of institutional weakness, is a legitimate political tool comparable to the other forms of pressure— large political contributions, covert lobbying, favoritism, and the like—effectively applied by those who would lead society astray.†

For some of these students their universities have become surrogates for society. The university administration is close at hand. One can bedevil and strike out at it. If the frustrated activist cannot beat the system, he can at least insist that his own university should not lend itself to evil. There are a smaller number who see the university as a place of shelter untouched by the evils of society. They suffer profound shock when they find that the university, and therefore they as parts of it, are not so far removed. In their view this makes them guilty of complicity in profound social and moral evil.

2. Six thousand years ago an Egyptian priest carved on a stone the lament: "Our earth is degenerate . . . children no longer obey their parents." Impatience and antipathy for authority have always been hallmarks of youth, yet today one encounters the irony that this most promising of all student generations appears unusually antagonistic to all forms of restraint and peculiarly violent in social or political protest.

May not the fault lie with the older generation? Unless we are prepared to concede that ours is a sick society too corrupt to be saved, we must acknowledge that we have failed to transmit to many of the ablest young men and women either a sense of the values of reason, order, and civility or an appreciation of the fact that freedom depends upon voluntary restraint. We have managed

† The argument of these students, stated in a little more detail, is as follows: Our governmental system, which in theory depends upon popular will, imperfectly expresses that will, because of the development of institutional failings of several sorts: for example, the political party system, the workings of influence and economic power, lobbying, and deficiencies in public education. As a result, when government and society are moving in tragically wrong-headed directions, these institutional weaknesses prevent recalling it to the true path by means within the tradition of political democracy. Direct action, confrontations, sit-ins, and (in some cases) physical violence applied at points of institutional weakness are political tools fairly comparable to the large political contributions, covert lobbying, favoritism, cocktail parties, and other *sub-rosa* power techniques used by the "Establishment." Such countervailing pressures either must be counted an acceptable part of the democratic process, or, if not, then American democracy is so far dead that its principles cannot be invoked as a restraint upon direct forms of action.

to convey the idea that, because some of the values we upheld are outdated and others were always wrong, the remainder must also lack merit.

The sources of this shortcoming are not easily identified. One source may be our actual or seeming slowness and resistance to change where change is plainly required. Others may be inherent in our current civilization. The insight of the social sciences and the honesty of the arts have taught us to look at ourselves stripped of our pretense, and what we see is unlovely. We have the honesty and courage to see ourselves as we are, but perhaps, as Archibald Mac-Leish suggests, we lack the greater Hellenic courage to see man stumble and fall, yet avow his nobler capacity. It became unfashionable among forward-looking intellectuals 30 or 40 years ago to speak of progress, virtue, and wisdom, or to examine the supports on which they rest.

Size and complexity, as elsewhere in modern life, enormously increase the difficulties of communication and response. The growing demands of each teacher's own field of knowledge and the opportunities for applying it in government and industry divert him from close personal intercourse with his students. (Paradoxically, it is usually the teacher actively engaged in applying his knowledge to society who is most interesting to the largest number of students.)

It is sometimes said the schools and colleges exert too much pressure upon students. In the case of many seemingly irrelevant scholastic requirements there may be something to the charge. Certainly the intense busy-ness that afflicts both faculty and students discourages easy discourse and diminishes the quality of personal relations. Yet the problem is not so much one of pressure as of pressure for the wrong things. Many students are not being given responsibilities which sufficiently challenge their capabilities. The formal structure of most universities is authoritarian and paternalistic in relation to students, and it often excludes even the faculty from important aspects of university policy. Columbia inherited more than its share of this style. Bringing students closer into a community of all the parts of a university, including the process of decision-making, would promote that intimate exchange of ideas and experiences which is vital to maturity. It would also aid them in learning how to control rapidly changing technological, social, and cultural conditions.

The last point is best illustrated by the unfortunate alienation of the older graduate students and youngest faculty members— those who have only recently finished their own formal training or who are still in that intermediate stage of being half-student, half-faculty member. They are in a peculiarly advantageous position to help bridge the gap between generations. When they feel aggrieved, misunderstood, or exploited, they understandably ally themselves with any other elements within the institution that are unhappy and desirous of change. When communication between them and their more influential (and usually older) colleagues in the faculty and administration becomes attenuated and when they are denied effective participation in decisions that are vital to them, political tactics based upon muscle may become an appealing substitute for reasonable discussion. This factor was plainly evident during the April disturbances at Columbia where many of the junior faculty took parts encouraging to students in the buildings.

When decisions are made largely on the basis of who has the most power, especially when power is concentrated in a formal authoritarian structure, more and more people within the institution will be dissatisfied. When the decisions are made after full and frank discussion of the various issues involved, and with all opinions being taken into consideration, cohesion develops and effective teaching about the ways in which a democracy should operate is possible—in fact, an actual demonstration takes place. The radical demonstrations for "student power" illustrate what can occur when thoughtful groups trained to criticize and dissent are forced into the tactics of manipulation instead of the rational correction of defects in education and research.

3. During the years in which the present university students were in secondary school the gap between the generations was widened by marked changes in speech, conduct, dress, and manners. Although older people generally disapproved the changes, the more exaggerated the new styles became the more they were promoted by entertainers and influential mass media. The cycle became self-sustaining. Inflated rhetoric and violence began to spread through contemporary society—again largely because the mass media give them the greatest attention. Among the young, inflated rhetoric and bizarre personal appearance have become symbolic behavior indicating disapproval of the "Establishment" and the older generation. As the number of late adolescents and young adults increased in relation to older people, the young

became increasingly aware of their power if only they were willing to reject conventional restraints.

The conflicts of style and removal of customary restraints breed antagonisms and even distrust; thus, they increase the tendency to resolve problems by strongly emotional and often intolerant lines of action. And, to a degree, even violent obstruction (as in April) becomes a form of generational self-expression.

4. The size and complexity of the large universities in an urban society increase the alienation of students and, as we shall see, there is too little at Columbia to offset the feeling. One form of response, which must be mentioned among the causes of violent demonstrations, is the romantic reaction against complexity, rationality, and restraint, which has become a small but pervasive thread in student life.

In philosophy, it is illustrated by the popularity of Anarchism.

In politics, the appeal of rigid doctrine with simple explanations becomes irresistible. A simplistic demonology purportedly describing the "Establishment" that controls "the system" comes to explain all the hardships and injustices resulting from the complex cross-currents of a technological society and the selfishness and blundering awkwardness of man. Che Guevara and Frantz Fanon have become folk-heroes for some radicals. Others wait for the day when the students will be joined by proletarian workers in a Marxist (or Maoist) revolution.

At Columbia more than a few students saw the barricading of the buildings in April as the moment when they began meaningful lives. They lived gloriously like revolutionary citizens of Paris. They liberated buildings and flew the Red flag. Men and women shared alike without restraint. The marriage ceremony performed in a liberated building by a chaplain attached to the University symbolized the glorious moments of truth. Later, a graduate student, asked to explain to us why he had joined in the seizure, replied that, although he had participated in civil rights activities and every possible peace demonstration, all had come to nothing, but in April, in the buildings, he and others knew that at last they were taking effective action for things worthwhile. The mixture of political and social romanticism varied widely from individual to individual. Many took part without political motivation.

Obviously, romanticism is only one form—probably a minor form—of response to the gap between social and political ideals and social and political performance. Many students who join in civil disobedience, direct action, and other forms of obstructive protest see their tactics as necessary catalysts of social reform in an age when conventional political methods have proved inadequate. The sit-down strikes of 1937–38 and the sit-in demonstrations of the civil rights movement are cited as proof that, whatever the legality or illegality of obstructive tactics, "they work."*

These general characteristics of student attitudes are intensified at Columbia by the urban environment and the conditions of student life. We discuss these problems later. Here it is enough to point out that Columbia's student body, while less radical than others in its activities, is probably among the most politically sophisticated and liberal. This is the result partly of tradition, partly of environment, and partly of the processes of selection (including self-selection among high school students).

At Columbia, as at other universities, students' opinions cover the entire spectrum of political life. But two issues command unusually broad agreement among the young and engage their deepest emotions: the peace movement and racial justice. Both were causes of the April disturbances.

B. The War in Vietnam

During Dr. Truman's testimony he observed:

Some of us have felt for a very long time that if it were inescapable that the current war in Vietnam had to continue on, it was debatable whether university communities could survive, because the tension is not only among students but in faculties, and the whole fabric of the institution is strained.

In a sense, I think there have been two battlefields in the war. One in Vietnam, and the other on our university campuses. And they are not good places for battlefields.

The Vietnam war is the overriding concern of nearly all students. For them it is a matter of life or death—to kill or be killed. For many, it is an immoral war and all who support it are immoral; it should be stopped at once—how stopped is a detail irrelevant to

---

* For further discussion of this aspect of the background of the upheaval, see pp. 25–29.

men of commitment. The consensus among students and most of the vocal intellectual community appears to validate their criticism, hence differing opinions are condemned with earnest righteousness.

The uncertainties of the draft, moreover, and the overbrooding threat of nuclear warfare have intensified every grievance and frustration.

Student opposition to the war has many forms. Student activists have taken part in nearly all the peace and anti-draft demonstrations. Just as some learned the tactics of obstructive protest in the civil rights movement others gained experience in rallies at draft boards and recruiting stations.[*]

The university became the focus of both criticism and frustration wherever it could be linked with the defense establishment; in furnishing class rankings to draft boards, in making facilities available for ROTC programs, in permitting recruitment for the Armed Forces or war-related industries, and in government research. Militant young men and women, frustrated by their inability to shape a vastly complex society upon an issue that seems both moral and simple, turn to make their weight felt on nearer and more vulnerable institutions. On the war, therefore, even more than on other issues, the university becomes a surrogate for society and the New Left has evolved political theories asserting that the university is a microcosm of society in order to rationalize the transference. Many large universities—Wisconsin, Michigan, and Harvard among others—have experienced seriously obstructive demonstrations against their alleged complicity in the war in Vietnam.

Students at Columbia appear typical of the students at other large universities in these respects. The opposition to the war is more vocal, perhaps, than in the south and parts of the midwest, but it is not discernibly different from other universities in the northeast or on the west coast.

Militant groups have lashed out at Columbia, as elsewhere. Although the demonstrations were neither as large nor as disruptive as others, Columbia experienced at least her numerical share of incidents as the fighting in Vietnam intensified. In May 1965, violence broke out, which the City police were called to suppress,

---

[*] We do not suggest that obstructive protest has been in any sense characteristic of either the civil rights or peace movements. Such tactics were exceptional and, at least in the civil rights movement, even those exceptions were usually associated with the unconstitutional suppression of other forms of expression.

when protesters formed a human chain to block the Naval Reserve Officers Training Corps from entering Low Library† in order to hold final review ceremonies. On November 15, 1966, 200 students, organized by SDS, marched into Dodge Hall in order to "ask a few questions" of a recruiter for the Central Intelligence Agency (CIA) who was interviewing prospective applicants for employment. One day later, on November 16, 150 students marched to President Kirk's office in Low Library with a letter demanding an official statement of non-cooperation with the CIA. In February 1967, 18 students engaged in a sit-in demonstration, blocking access to the rooms in Dodge Hall where CIA interviews were to be conducted. On April 20, 1967, 300 SDS members and sympathizers filled the lobby of John Jay Hall where recruiters for the U.S. Marine Corps had set up tables. The next day 800 anti-recruiting demonstrators milled about Van Am Quadrangle, together with 500 counter-demonstrators sympathetic to campus recruiting. On February 28, 1968, a 200-man picket line, sponsored by SDS, marched toward Low Library in protest of the presence of recruiters for Dow Chemical Company; 80 Barnard and Columbia students left the march to stage a sit-in demonstration in Dodge Hall. On March 27, 1968, SDS led more than 100 students in a march through Low Library in a demonstration against the Institute for Defense Analyses.

We list these incidents here simply to show that issues connected with the Vietnam war had repeatedly stirred large demonstrations prior to last April's disturbances. By then, attention had focused upon Columbia's connection with the Institute for Defense Analyses. The connection was emphasized beyond its intrinsic importance, but it became a symbol of Columbia's participation in the war for many critics of the national policy in Vietnam. As such, it was manifestly an explosive issue.

C. Civil Rights and Community Relations

The cause of racial justice, more than any other issue, brought students out of the political lethargy of the 1950's and, like the Vietnam war, engrossed their deepest emotions. Today the "racism"

† Low Library is the central administration building at Columbia. It is no longer used as a library.

they condemn encompasses not only active racial discrimination but continued acquiescence in the poverty, the denial of opportunity, and the human suffering that segregation in ghettos make integral parts of the Negro and Puerto Rican experience. Racial issues and the war on poverty also engage the active support of a larger segment of the student body than any other issue, with the possible exception of the war in Vietnam. At Columbia the presence of racial issues, symbolized by the projected gymnasium in Morningside Park, undoubtedly had much to do with the breadth of the faculty and student support for those who sparked the April uprising.

Columbia's location epitomizes the conflicts and intensifies the emotional commitments and frustrations of the movement to relieve racism and poverty. Situated on Morningside Heights, the University looks down on the flats of Harlem, one of the most depressed of all urban ghettos. Millions of black people must have looked up at the institutional buildings as symbols of the affluence of a white society; remote, unattainable, and indifferent. Hundreds of Columbia students who came to the University and then went down into Harlem with high ideals of social justice, but little prior experience with the realities of urban poverty, have been shocked by immersion in the ghetto. Not only the strongest criticism of the projected gymnasium but also important support for the seizure of the buildings came from the College Citizenship Council whose members were actively in touch with Columbia's poorest neighbors.† A University official suggested that the response of these students was a case of well-intentioned but naive overreaction. Many of us have also come to acquiesce in "the realities," with more or less discomfort, but one wonders whether the sensitive students' perception is not closer to the truth.

D. Grievances and Problems of Black Students

One of the outstanding features of the most recent wave of university demonstrations has been the central role of self-conscious black students. Especially within the past year, Negro students on campuses, large and small, throughout the country have made unprecedented efforts to bring about changes in campus life increasing their

† The Citizenship Council is engaged in important social service programs and other forms of community assistance in the Morningside and Harlem areas. Many students contribute time and energy to these activities and thus are drawn into continuous contact with the local areas.

participation and enhancing respect for their identity. Their goals included changes in curriculum, personnel, admissions, and living conditions. Sometimes they worked alone as more or less organized black students, sometimes in loose, temporary coalition with predominantly white organizations. Always they were moved by an intensely self-conscious design to act as black students and to make "black" a proud symbol. Indeed, a recent accomplishment, mainly attributable to Negro college youth, is the unprecedented semantic reversal of the negative racial connotations formerly associated with the words "Negro" and especially "black."

Similarly, there is reason to think that the role of the black students at Columbia was uniquely important, for it may well have been their decision to request the white demonstrators to leave Hamilton Hall that converted a somewhat unfocused, noisy, disorderly, all-night demonstration into an unprecedented uprising involving the occupation of five campus buildings.

In analyzing the particular grievances and problems of black students as related to the April disturbances, one must first note the importance of their perceptions and experiences of their contemporary environment, some long-standing and some recent, some general and some unique to Columbia. Thus, black students have been profoundly influenced by, and react sharply to, shifts in the civil rights movement, just as they are extraordinarily sensitive to the political and cultural meanings and uses of race in contemporary society. The much publicized generation gap may well have even more effect upon black youths than others, for they are keenly aware that the movement for changes in the status of the Negro has been spearheaded by the young, especially by the initiative and energy of self-conscious, and increasingly race-conscious, Negroes in college. Public issues, such as the Vietnam war, the youth movement, and the worsening crisis of the ghettos, concern them no less than socially conscious white students, and probably not very differently except where their concern is racially self-conscious or influenced by a rather sophisticated awareness of the identity yet separateness of the demands being made by and for Negroes, the poor, and the young.

Thus, as students at Columbia, the black students are affected like all other students by their perceptions of the quality of student life and the apparent attitudes toward students of both faculty and Administration. Yet, even while they share this important degree of common experience with others, black students are uniquely influenced by their perception of the manner in which Columbia has dealt with small but successive generations of Negro students.

Historically, the enrollment of Negro students at Columbia has been very small, and those few have been isolated in different schools. Recently, Columbia, like a number of other Ivy League colleges where competition for admission is keen, has made serious and successful efforts to increase the enrollment of black students. Some of them come with a markedly different preparation from the rest of the student body. Their social, economic, and educational backgrounds create very real practical problems of adjustment. Yet nothing effective is offered to ease the transition. Until this is changed, the more that is done to enable promising young men from rural areas or urban ghettos to obtain a university education, the deeper the dilemma grows.

We do not imply that the black student body of Columbia is homogeneous in terms of class, income, or educational achievement. As among the white students, grievances, protest, and political consciousness (and black consciousness in the case of the Negro) bear no necessary relationship to cultural, economic, or educational advantages. In the recent past and now, middle-class black students have been among the leaders of protest.

One experience common to all backgrounds, however, has been the impression that Columbia is a discriminating, indifferent, frequently hostile world, just because it is dominated and peopled by whites. Even the instruction and curriculum emphasize that black students are moving into another man's world. Black students are a small minority. There are very few, if any, black deans, black professors, or black instructors with whom to identify. The courses ignore the history and culture of black people. The curriculum often strikes them, like other students, as irrelevant, perhaps more because its relevance is not made clear than because it is actually irrelevant. The shortness with which these basic facts can be stated must not be allowed to obscure either their reality or substantive importance.

Often the situations that bother students grow out of the very efforts to remedy past injustices. A Columbia undergraduate wryly gave this insight into one kind of situation that affects self-image. In substance, he said: "We know that we are admitted to Ivy League colleges, although we would not make it under normal standards of admissions policy, because black people engaged in demonstrations, rioted, and otherwise pressured the white establishment. This tells us we are not up to the competition—at least by those standards. At the same time, the knowledge lessens our incentive for academic achievement. This seems to say that the same pressures will get us into law schools and other graduate study regardless of our achievement." The student who made this statement had too good judgment to mean it without many qualifications. The ability of black students is high, and most would be accepted under a suitable standard. The point, needless to say, is not whether the statement is absolutely true, rather that the creeping doubt or kernel of truth probably created in him or his fellows both some insecurity and some frustration.

There are still evidences of apparent prejudice. Some fraternities appear still to discriminate against black students. Occasional incidents have arisen involving restrictions imposed by the national, parent organization. Sometimes, uncomfortable feeling arises at mixers. At Columbia, the security guards were long allowed to follow the unforgivable practice of inspecting black students' identification cards when they entered college buildings although the white students were passed without notice. (Later Vice-President David B. Truman halted the practice.)

The black student is also currently under another set of psychological pressures that comes from both the resurgence of social consciousness in youth and from the Black Power movement. He feels a conscious obligation to help the less fortunate and subconscious pressure to prove his militancy. His reaction may be increased by a sense that he is enjoying education and opportunities denied to many less fortunate Negroes.

At Columbia, the Negro students had not shown signs of collective militancy until rather recently. One incident of record was the seizure of 1,500 copies of an issue of the *Jester*—the student-humor magazine—in the spring of 1967, upon the ground that it contained an article offensive to the Negro race. Columbia's black students took little visible part in the increasing number of protest demonstrations against the projected gymnasium in Morningside Park through 1966, 1967, and the first three months of 1968. Some of them must have been troubled by the contrast between their own seeming indifference and the active efforts of white students who joined civil rights and other organizations in Harlem in demonstrations seeking to block the construction.

The complex responses of black students in the April events were suggested in added dimension by a close observer who was discussing the black students' seizure and barricading of Hamilton Hall. Among other things, he stressed the aim of Negro students to be taken seriously as people:

What was the cause? Whether they would accept it or not, I believe their basic course was to dramatize the unresponsiveness of the University, primarily to them. But that's not easily sold or easily acceptable to [one's own] consciousness.

The more acceptable way of selling that [to oneself] would be [to speak of] the unresponsiveness of the University to the community and to its very real needs; and in doing that, they get an extra dividend. They demonstrate their identification—the student's identification—with the community to which the University is unresponsive. Whatever guilt they may [feel] about having advantages which the average kid of their age in Harlem doesn't have, is somewhat ameliorated by this action which is—to take their phrase—"for the black brothers in the ghetto." And they get publicity while they do it.

Q. Earlier, when you were asked about the motivation for the demonstration in Hamilton Hall, you replied in much better chosen words than I have, that the aim was to be taken seriously as people, to be responded to as people, to be recognized and to have the University respond in a meaningful way. I was wondering if one raised the same question about the students in the other buildings, whether the answer would be just the same.

A. It would be identical, but fundamentally similar . . . The difference would be probably in the complexities. In the case of the Negro students in Hamilton Hall, another ingredient would be that, by this act, they were demonstrating they were part of the movement, and "movement" is very important. Such action helps to deal with guilt, too, not being the privileged Negroes, pets of the white establishment but as militant as Malcolm, Stokely, and Rap.

The black students who occupied Hamilton Hall were not unmindful of the complexities of the gymnasium controversy, although they also saw the symbolic racial issue. But they were most consciously concerned with the demonstration of their power, for the very practical reasons already noted.

II. UNCERTAINTY CONCERNING THE ROLE OF THE UNIVERSITY

In examining the conditions of student life which make for unrest at American universities it is important not to overlook the fact that the universities themselves are in a state of transition where they, consciously or unconsciously, face exceedingly complex yet fundamental issues concerning their functions and curriculum. The lack of accepted answers to such basic questions not only impairs institutional cohesion within the university as a whole, it also promotes student dissatisfaction and unrest.

Although we lack any special insight into the nature of these problems—indeed, most of us would disclaim the qualifications for dealing with them—still it seems important to say enough to illustrate the connection between the disturbances and the uncertainties concerning the universities' role in current society.

A. The Role of the University in Relation to Society

The increasing complexity and sophistication of all aspects of the industrial and social order have enormously increased the demands upon universities to join in applying to practical uses the knowledge, skills, and equipment they assemble. State and federal governments, industry, foundations, and community organizations are constantly calling upon individual professors for active participation in action programs as well as for expert opinion; and both the professors and their institutions value the opportunity. Universities, as others have said, have become knowledge factories with much wider and possibly more powerful constituencies than the students whom they educate. At least some branches of the university, moreover, are attracting to their faculties a new type of academician— the man of action as well as intellect whose interest is not the pursuit of truth for its own sake but to shape society from a vantage point combining academic security, intellectual weapons, and political action.

The trend raises questions of extraordinary difficulty, of which we mention only two.

1. What is the proper role of the university in the immediate practical application of knowledge to military, industrial, social, and economic problems? During the hearings before this Commission it was suggested that Columbia's relations with her neighbors would be immeasurably improved if, instead of buying up SRO buildings and driving the tenants from the vicinity, the University would

bring the expertise of her doctors and social scientists to the aid of those unfortunate occupants who resorted to crime, prostitution, and drugs. Witnesses also argued that West Harlem affords endless opportunities for the School of Social Work to do work of immeasurable aid to the community.

Perhaps the answer is that the universities must expand in these directions, but the expansion will not be without costs. Since the time, energy, and money diverted from pure research at universities will not be replaced anywhere else in society, the diversion of academic resources would limit the seeds of progress. Furthermore, without radical revision of curriculum and methods of instruction, the professors so engaged would have still less time than today for work and informal association with students.

2. If universities are to be actively engaged in social endeavor, how and by whom are decisions to be made concerning when, how, where, and to what uses their knowledge shall be applied? Choices have to be made: there are not enough hours and resources to go around and often the alternatives conflict with one another. Moreover, the more the application of knowledge brings the university into involvement with society, the more apparent it becomes that the choices depend on judgments of social and political policy. When students see work being done at a university on the application of science to spreading death and destruction in Vietnam, but little evidence of similar work on eliminating poverty and racial injustice, they are naturally concerned about the decision-making process. Are the choices left to individual professors? If so, are the choices really left to them? What if their political decisions seem badly mistaken?

Making decisions on the application of its knowledge to society must, to some degree, politicize the university. One is thus forced to inquire how politicization of the centers of knowledge affects pursuit of the ideal of detached, objective search for truth. And this leads back to the initial question concerning the university's role in the application of knowledge.

B. The Curriculum

Students are widely dissatisfied with the formal educational curriculum of American universities. That dissatisfaction, although not assigned by students as a ground for the April disturbances, un-doubtedly helped to make them sufficiently restless for other motives to stir them into joining the uprising. Thus, many of the students who occupied Fayerweather Hall had long been critical of the educational offerings of their respective departments and some had earnestly sought discussion and change. Immediately after the police action and in subsequent weeks, most schools and depart-ments quickly established joint faculty-student panels whose efforts were to be devoted, in part, to a review of curricular questions. Large numbers of students and faculty realized that if the curricu-lum (which is the students' chief contact with the university) seems "irrelevant" or worse, the student is bound to ask why he should worry about maintaining the university against hostile assault.

The central educational assignment of American colleges and universities has long been to prepare functionally effective people for rather definite roles in industry, finance, government, and the established professions. The young man whose motivation parallels accepted categories of career, status, and prestige has little reason to question the universities' curricular offerings or performance; they do this preparatory job exceedingly well, and often give the indi-vidual lasting scholarly or cultural interests.

But the simple fact is that a constantly growing proportion of the best students does not look forward to careers molded along the established lines of professional or business success. The point can be proved statistically, but it is enough to illustrate it by reference to the tremendous interest in social service work and the Peace Corps and, conversely, to the difficulties established business firms and their professional advisers now face in recruiting.* Although most professors will rush to deny that their offerings are in any sense vocational, one suspects that a good many of the vocal com-plaints of the irrelevance of the curriculum are attributable to the fact that the kind of education offered by our colleges and univer-sities has not changed as sharply as the interests of the most vocal

* We have been referred to a most provocative paper dealing with Colum-bia College students, written by Mr. Stanley Raffel, now a graduate student in the Department of Sociology. In the paper he notes the disturbing fact that, although almost half the freshman class entering in selected years intended to enter the *academic* profession, by graduation the number had dropped to a little more than one-sixth. Mr. Raffel apparently concludes that the Columbia College environment actually turns academically motivated college students toward professional careers as a second or third choice.

and energetic students. One cannot help being impressed by the enormous enthusiasm that goes into "liberation schools" and extra-curricular as well as "anti-curricular" offerings.

One also wonders whether the charge of "irrelevance" that both undergraduate and graduate students level at the curriculum is not a way of challenging a mode or style of academic life that has remained unchanged at the core since the nineteenth century, or—some will say—since the earliest European universities. The revolutionary changes in technological and social conditions, the vastly different composition of student bodies, and the enormously increased opportunities for human attainment may well require equally radical changes in the university scholar.

One other source of student disappointment in the university should be noted. Perhaps because of less certainty about their status, career goals, and broader aspirations, perhaps for much more complex reasons, more sensitive and intelligent students than formerly are looking to the university to help them discover what life is about. Yet most of these are disappointed. Too little of the whole elaborate paraphernalia of academic activities appears to be concerned with the conduct of a man's life. J. D. Salinger's Franny gives this insight:

I don't think it would have all got me quite so down if just once in a while—just *once* in a while—there was at least some polite little *perfunctory* implication that knowledge *should* lead to *wisdom,* and that if it *doesn't,* it's just a disgusting waste of time! But there never is! You never even hear any *hints* dropped on a campus that wisdom is *supposed* to be the goal of knowledge. You hardly ever even hear the word "wisdom" mentioned! Do you want to hear something really funny? In almost four years of college—and this is the absolute truth—in almost four years of college, the only time I can remember ever even hearing the expression "wise man" being used was in my freshman year, in Political Science! And you know how it was used? It was used in reference to some nice old poopy elder statesman who'd made a fortune in the stock market and then gone to Washington to be an adviser to President Roosevelt. I'm not saying that happens to everybody, but I just get so upset when I think about it I could die.*

We do not mean to imply that the proportion of students who are worried about wisdom and therefore share Franny's disappointment is high. We know many teachers who help their students

---

* J. D. Salinger, *Franny and Zooey* (Bantam Books), pp. 146–147.

toward the understanding of life's unanswerable questions, not so much by precept as by example. One witness suggested to us, perhaps with more than a touch of irony, that no one should be so foolish as to look to a university to help him discover what life is about. But, despite the doubts and qualifications, it seems to us that the university should not be allowed to remain that "irrelevant" to the questing student, if only because there is presently no other institution that claims all knowledge as its province. Until such students are more convincingly shown that universities are addressing themselves to such questions, their disappointment will remain at least a latent source of disaffection.

III. SOCIAL ATTITUDES TOWARD DISRUPTIVE DEMONSTRATIONS

The forms in which student protests find expression are normally affected, in marked degree, by the social and moral judgments of a wider community. For even if those judgments were wholly rejected by most students—and they are not—still they would be operative facts with which the student leaders must deal as a matter of tactics. Thus, one of the conditions contributing to the April disturbances at Columbia was the prevalent moral uncertainty over the acceptability of the seizure of buildings as a means of influencing reform.

The past decade has seen a marked change in attitudes toward the acceptability of disobedience, harassment, and physical obstruction as methods of influencing social and political action. Tactics that would have been so widely condemned 10 or 15 years ago as to be self-defeating are now accepted and approved in many quarters as moral endeavors to achieve worthy ends. This is especially true among political liberals and youth. The spreading use of such tactics and the much, much wider spirit of tolerance toward their use not only increased the likelihood of resort to physical seizure and occupation of buildings but enabled the rebels to escape unanimous condemnation and gain widespread support among students and faculty once the seizure occurred.

We need scarcely recall the national events in the civil rights movement that spread tolerance for passive disobedience of unjust laws, then for deliberate confrontation with officials enforcing arguably unconstitutional restrictions upon freedom of expression, and finally for the tactics of physical obstruction and harassment as means of influencing policy. The sequence began with the bus boycott in Montgomery, Alabama. It spread next to the sit-in demonstrations at segregated lunch counters and restaurants. Later, there were instances of plain physical obstruction such as completely blocking the entrances to restaurants or crowding into libraries. Student activists gained first-hand experience with such tactics when they went into the south, and later into the northern urban ghettos, to work for racial equality. They could not fail to observe the effectiveness of the tactics, both in dramatizing a cause and in compelling concessions. Any moral or legal scruples were overwhelmed by the morality of the objective. There was virtually no condemnation of their action in segments of the community interested in reform.

Disruption, harassment, and physical obstruction then became common tactics in the peace movement, in which student leaders everywhere played dedicated roles. Again, although more doubts were expressed, there was no general outcry that the tactic was intolerable regardless of its goal.

Thus, the use of disruptive indoor demonstrations and sit-ins as methods of student protest against university policy—at least in relation to the black community or the war in Vietnam—resulted from the progressive extension of tactics encouraged by many moral and political leaders. Careful thought makes it plain that distinctions can, and probably should, be drawn. The Montgomery bus boycott involved neither physical obstruction nor disobedience to law. The sit-ins, at least where there was no physical interference with other patrons, involved the bona fide claim of a constitutional right to service in the lunch counter or restaurant. Both are a far cry from the seizure of buildings as a way of forcing action upon other issues, and from physical harassment or obstruction of others' activities as a means of compelling concessions. But the distinctions, vital as they are, were usually overlooked and the tactics lumped loosely under such heads as "civil disobedience," "non-violence," and "direct action." No one should be greatly surprised, therefore, that students, accustomed to the acceptability of one, should move gradually into the other. Nor is it altogether strange, in this milieu, that the crowded occupation of a college building by 250 protesting students was spontaneously converted into a sit-down, and then a seizure with barricaded doors.

DEMOCRACY AND THE CURRICULUM

by Carl Cohen*

Universities around the country are now engaged in heated controversy over two kinds of issue, often confused. The first is *substantive*—what requirements, if any, should be imposed for a B.A.;
should a program of black studies be initiated, and how; in what
form are examinations and grades to be used, if at all; and who
among the faculty are to be fired, promoted, given tenure and so on.
The second deals with *procedural* matters—how decisions on curricular and related matters are to be reached. Both kinds of issue
are important, but the latter is fundamental. Leaving the many
substantive questions (which vary from institution to institution)
for the present, I shall here propose some principles for the resolution of procedural conflicts. Within a university, what are the
appropriate decision-making processes for curricular affairs?

I begin with two assumptions that I think will be universally—
or almost universally—accepted. The first is that, where the conditions of its successful operation are met, democracy is the best form
of community government. I believe that very strongly, and I am
prepared to defend democracy with rational arguments against its
critics, both historical and contemporary. But, though we may differ
on what conditions its success does require, it is likely that most
members of most American universities will agree upon the ideal.

The second assumption is that all parties to the current controversy over curricular matters are acting honestly and in good faith. I
believe that to be true. Some students appear to think that faculty
judgments are masks for private interest; some faculty do think that
student arguments opposing them are duplicitous in the same way.
Perhaps there is some justice in both complaints; but by far the
greater number, among students, faculty and administrators, are
genuinely seeking the best interests of their university. I shall

* From *The Nation*, March 17, 1969.

assume that, and with such persons shall direct my attention to procedural questions of great consequence to the long-term well-being of our universities.

Democracy is a way of making decisions in a community. It gives to each member of the community the right to an equal voice in affairs that concern the whole. We are disposed by habit to think of democracy as a way of governing political communities, because that is where its results are most impressive, its absence most painful. But it can also apply to nonpolitical communities: a church congregation, the faculty of a college, a community chess club, a cooperative residence hall, many other kinds of community.

Among the host of issues which the practice of democracy presents in every context (most of which I cannot touch upon here) two points need to be emphasized:

(1) Democracy can operate only where there is a specifiable and self-conscious community of some kind. It must be clear who has the right to participate in deciding what affairs. That is one reason why citizenship is so important for a democratic polity or initiation for a fraternity, or membership for whatever community is in question.

(2) Democracy supposes that all members of the community in which it is operative are members *equally*. The equal voice of each member stems not merely from his serious concern in the outcome of a decision but from the equality of status within it. All citizens of a democratic nation are citizens equally, though some may be wiser than others; all members of a chess club are members equally, though some may play far more expertly than others. Wisdom in the polity and skill in the chess club may be grounds for respect; they do not justify greater decision-making powers for their possessors.

This far I think all can agree, but how does all this apply to the university? The university is not one community but many. There are the communities constituted by all undergraduate students, by all graduate students, and by all students. There are the communities constituted by the faculties of the several schools and colleges, by the several departments and institutes, and by the faculty as a whole. There are the communities constituted by groups—of both faculty and students—having special intellectual or aesthetic interests in common; dramatic societies for example, or philosophical discussion groups. There are the many residential communities of students, in the dormitories, cooperatives, etc., and some communities of combined residential-intellectual concern. There is also the greater community of the university at large. It would be hard to exhaust the list.

Probably everyone will agree that each of these communities ought to have the authority and power to decide the questions which are chiefly its business; and that within each community of equals those decisions ought to be arrived at democratically. The basic controversy in which our universities are now engaged (and are likely to be engaged for some time) arises in deciding which issues are the chief business of which communities.

This is not a simple matter, and anyone who supposes that simple answers can be given is being, literally, simple-minded. It is clear at the outset that the several communities in the university overlap, and that what is chiefly the business of one of them is also a matter of real concern to other, larger communities. Practically everyone in a university, and many outside it, are affected, more or less seriously, by the decisions of all or almost all of these internal communities. Whether, as an illustration, a colleague whom I respect and like is or is not given tenure in a department other than mine is a matter of deep concern to me. But my concern does not give me a right to participate in the decision. Tenure, in our healthy tradition, is bestowed by academic peers, persons qualified by long study and experience in that professional sphere. It is naive, in some circumstances dangerous to the well-being of the larger community, to insist that every person has a right to a decision-making voice in every affair that affects his life. That is a shallow view of democracy, and it is false.

More specifically, we are now deeply involved in questions regarding the curriculum of our colleges and universities. Whose chief business is it to make decisions in this sphere? I argue that it is the chief business of the community constituted by the faculty of the college in question. I believe that curricular decisions—say about requirements for degrees, standards and examinations—should be made democratically within the community responsible for the outcome of those decisions. I could defend this claim at great length. Briefly, I suggest two kinds of reasons why the responsibility lies there and not elsewhere.

First, the nature of the university as an institution places certain obligations upon the faculty which they can fulfill only if they control the curriculum. Faculty members are appointed to teach, to guide student study and research, and to do so in ways for which they are specially qualified. Further, the faculty has a certifying duty. Through boards of governors and deans the faculty ultimately must decide whether certain students are to receive the degree Bachelor of Arts, or other such certificates. If they are to make this decision, and if they are to mean what they intend to mean by doing so, *they* must decide what will qualify persons for the receipt of such degrees. They cannot delegate that power, or share it, any more than an attorney or a physician can delegate or share the power to make his professional decisions (except on occasion with other attorneys or physicians). Will we not agree that the decisions faced by the professor in the arts and sciences, the challenges faced by a professional educator, are as demanding, as intellectual, as professionally serious as those encountered in medicine or the law? Designing the curriculum, implementing it, evaluating the work of those students who pursue it, are all very important parts of the job of the faculty. It is quite understandable that students who are affected by such decisions would like to share in making them, but that desire does not give them a right to do so. Certainly they should not hope to get that right as a consequence of any reputable democratic theory. This factor of institutional responsibility I find compelling by itself.

Second, beyond the matter of responsibility, is the factor of competence. This is a delicate point, one upon which I know many good students are sensitive, and I want very much not to be misunderstood here. I believe it is possible to characterize groups—statistically, as it were—as having (or tending to have) certain talents or training, without making the ensuing distinctions invidiously. No doubt there are some matters on which students, as a body, are more competent than faculty; on other matters the faculty, as a body, is markedly more able and better prepared to act than are students. Among the latter are curricular affairs. I respect the integrity and intellect of my students. I am often proud of them; I know that a number of them will one day join the faculty of my own or like institutions. But false flattery is good for no one, and it is false flattery to refuse to make some discriminations that need to be made in this connection. To say that the faculty is the group most likely to reach wise curricular decisions is not meant offensively, or pejoratively, or condescendingly. It is plain honesty, the honesty we owe one another.

Curricular decisions are difficult. They have wide ramifications, for students (past, present and future), for the faculty itself (what they will teach, and how), for the secondary schools, for the graduate schools, for other universities, and for the society as a whole. It is hard to weigh all these factors fairly, and no person or body can be expected to do so perfectly. Corrections and adjustments will always be in order. But in a university there is no body more to be relied upon for the making of such decisions than the faculty itself. I emphasize again that this is not to express distrust or contempt for students, who are, in my view, for the most part serious, highly intelligent, and devoted to their university. The greater competence of the faculty in this sphere is largely a matter of education and experience. That does not mean the faculty is exempt from error. On the topics now hotly contested in some universities, they may well be in error. But our larger concern is how, over the long run, these decisions are likely to be best made. Careful reflection obliges me to conclude that entrusting those decisions to a body partly consisting of persons with a far smaller degree of experience and knowledge on the matters to be decided is simply foolish. It is not democracy but an unthinking Populism that supposes all persons, or all students, to be as competent to decide professional questions as persons who have devoted much of their lives to those very questions.

To this it is sometimes replied that students are lower in competence in this sphere simply because they are effectively kept from engaging in the very activities which develop this competence—so that the argument against student voting power is here viciously circular. I would respond first that a denial of the right to vote on these matters is not a denial of the right to participate vigorously in the deliberations upon them. But second, and more important, the criticism misses the force of my argument. The competence of which I have spoken is not simply a skill, to be developed with a few weeks or months of practice or experience. It is a competence flowing from long study, long association with liberally educated men, and long reflection upon the goals, methods and substance of university education. That competence is an essential element of the excellence of a faculty, in which the entire community takes pride. Is this character of the faculty something that serious students would really want to deny?

I find also the factor of competence by itself entirely persuasive in this argument. Unlike institutional responsibility, it does not speak to the question of the rights of respective bodies but to the widsom of entrusting certain tasks to certain bodies. Taken together, the two factors of competence and institutional responsibility are overwhelming in their force.

Still, the demand of some students for a role in curricular decision making does have some plausibility. Can we do justice to that demand, while adhering to the conclusions reached above? I think we can.

First, a clarification. Part of the plausibility of some student demands rests upon a confusion over the nature of the larger community in which the decisions are being made. There *is* a community consisting of both faculty and students, having the pursuit of learning as its central purpose; my students and I are bound together in an enterprise that marks us off from much of the rest of the world, and often brings us very close together. The university as a community of scholars *is* an honorable and appropriate ideal. But it is slipshod thinking to infer from the existence of this community that every decision having wide effect within it must be shared equally and universally by its members. Both students and faculty are members of the university community, to be sure, but they are not members of the same kind or status. In the nature of the case they cannot be members equal in every way. This is not paternalism; it is a fact, and one in which the serious student will take pride. His faculty has been carefully selected, screened, tested, in a host of ways, over a period of many years. The qualifications required of the faculty member for membership in the university, his authorization to participate, come from a wholly different source in a wholly different way from those of the student. To suppose that enrollment as a student, after completing high school, entitles one to a role on professional issues similar to that of the faculty is downright foolish.

On the other side, there are two respects in which the student quest for a voice in university affairs is entirely just. First, where the questions to be decided are not professional but concern every member of the community in the same way; or where they concern the rights of individuals to pursue their private business—questions, say, regarding the driving of automobiles on campus, or regarding the private lives of students or faculty—student voices are every bit the equal of faculty voices. In my view, our universities have been much too slow to recognize this, but in this area we are changing rapidly for the better. It is not the university's business how a student dresses, or whom he entertains in his room, or how; any more than it is the business of the high school how a student wears his hair. Students and faculty both are right in demanding control over what are chiefly their own affairs.

The second point is that students do have a major role in making curricular decisions. Their role is a key one because the curriculum is designed, not by them but for their use and benefit. Their voices must be heard, and their views should have a real effect upon the decisions made. The information students can provide, their judgments on how curricular matters have been and are being handled, can come from no other source. Their participation is vitally important.

But there is an important difference between having a role in the ongoing debate, and having part of the decision-making power. The students are the ones to whom the requirements and examinations and other such matters must apply. It is inevitable that in some cases these applications will result in disappointment or unhappiness. It is therefore inappropriate and unwise to make any student representative responsible for helping to determine these standards. He cannot avoid being utterly compromised when put in such a position.

When student decision-making power begins to operate in this sphere, the academic rigor of the institution is seriously threatened. A great deal of experience in this and other countries, attests to the accuracy of this warning. I have taught in several Latin American universities; I do not wish to denigrate them or their students, who evince more social responsibility than most other elements in their communities. But student power over purely curricular affairs has resulted there, as it may here, in a corruption of the appropriate intellectual relations of students and faculty. The focus of university affairs shifts from learning to intramural politics. Students play an increasingly larger role in the hiring and promotion of staff. Standards drop. I dread all that. I used to think that the analogy between these universities and ours was unrealistic; after reflecting upon recent events on my own and other American campuses, I am convinced that we are subject to what is essentially the same deterioration. The only way to avoid it is to develop rational principles for decision making in curricular (and similar) affairs, and stick to them. [See "The Yanqui University: Ships That Pass in the Night" by Ronald Hilton, *The Nation,* August 28, 1967.]

What then is the proper course? Specifically, I urge that students be given a full and genuine opportunity to present their views on curricular matters as forcefully and as rationally as possible. Along with this is the need for a rapid increase in the sensitivity and responsiveness of the entire university community to the needs and interests of students. How develop that responsiveness? We must work on two fronts. On the formal side, we must open up new channels for representative student participation in policy-making committees, both on college and departmental levels. Here it is important not only that faculty have an opportunity to hear student opinions and judgments but that such student spokesmen be genuinely representative of, and responsive to, their student constituencies. In this area it seems clear that good progress is being made. Perhaps even more important than these formal channels, however, are the informal patterns of student influence on academic matters. Here the problem is more severe, because the great size of our universities makes very difficult a comfortable, easy and effective communication between students and faculty. We must think hard about the redesign of our institutional structure into units with which students can identify themselves more closely—the Residential College at the University of Michigan is one good example—and in which their direct, informal participation can have appropriate influence.

But I also urge that the hard decisions on curricular design and requirements remain entirely in the hands of the faculty. This means, bluntly, that in resolving such matters student representatives ought not to have a vote, either in the faculty as a body, or in the curriculum committees which investigate for the faculty, deliberate as an arm of the faculty, and make recommendations to it.

One proposal that is frequently made must be rejected. It is that, to reduce the present tension, students be given two or three votes on certain key committees of the faculty or administration. This is only to throw the students a bone; it will irritate, frustrate, and do no good. In the first place, it is a mistake to vest such power in student members of committees with the thought that the faculty retains the right of review, because the faculty as a whole is not in a position to redo the work of its committees, and is obliged to rely upon them heavily. A committee of the faculty is its instrument and should represent it. Other interested parties must be heard, but neither justice nor wisdom requires their enfranchisement. In the second place, those who seek student control in this sphere will not be appeased. If they are right in principle, two or three votes are not enough; they ought then to have at least half the votes, probably two-thirds or three-fourths of them. After all, there are more of them and they are likely to be more directly affected by particular decisions than the faculty members who make them. We must reject on rational grounds the principle that simply being affected by a decision necessarily entitles one to a voice in making it. We must look to the proper business of our several overlapping communities.

If I am accused of undue conservatism, I would note that the long years of academic tradition in our universities, their respect for books and ideas, their intellectual standards, deserve very much to be conserved. Many things need to be changed in our universities and many more in our society. But it doesn't follow that everything needs to be thrown out.

A further dimension of the entire issue of decision making in the university has been too little appreciated on our campuses recently. A historical reminder is in order. American universities have long fought the battle against special-interest groups—the American Legion and others similarly well intentioned—that have sought to impose curricular requirements from without. Courses in American history, anti-communism and others, have been strongly urged as statutory requirements for university degrees. With some difficulty such pressures have, for the most part, been successfully resisted on the solid ground that degree requirements and like matters are professional affairs, the proper province of the faculty, not the general public, even though the public is affected by the decisions made.

If this principle be given up in the present disputes, universities —especially public universities—will be subject once again to a barrage of demands for curricular changes by nonprofessional groups which have strong convictions, some articulate support, and are genuinely affected by the outcome. The intellectual strength and independence of our universities will be threatened from without.

It is true, of course, that student demands for voting power are within the university, not outside it. But students are surely no more qualified than alumni in these affairs, or than graduates of other institutions who happen to hold political power. If the principle be now accepted that simply being affected by a decision gives one a right to help make it, the American university will suffer a series of major defeats. The result will not only be the wrongful subjection of the university to political pressure, and the weakening of its intellectual stance; it will tend, as well, to work directly against such wholesome progress as our student critics now seek.

In the interests of the universities as independent institutions, as well as the interests of its several members, it is important that faculty responsibilities be clearly recognized and firmly fulfilled.

Three final comments. First: Note that I have said nothing about the wisdom of specific curricular arrangements now in force, or of the changes in them that have been proposed. I am chiefly concerned here with how we ought to make the decisions on these matters. I hope that those who disagree with me will share my concern that we distinguish these questions, for the sake of intellectual clarity.

Second: My own view is that important decisions in a university, including those regarding curriculum, should be made, to the greatest extent feasible, democratically. Perhaps I am wrong in my understanding of democracy; but I earnestly hope that all those, students and faculty who share the democratic ideal, will do it the honor of reflecting carefully upon its proper application. Let us not be guilty of cheapening our own ideals with careless rhetoric, as so many of our political leaders have so frequently done to our distress and shame.

Third: Even if agreement on these matters is not reached, now or soon, I repeat my conviction that the vast majority of the participants in the ongoing debate are serious and honest. That seriousness and honesty can best be recognized and made effective in a context in which all of the arguments on all sides are carefully heard and weighed, composure and rationality maintained, threats avoided. That, as J. S. Mill remarked, is the real morality of public discussion. I urge that it be respected.

PART VI

Reform and Change

In a sense this entire volume is concerned with change and reformation in the schools. In this section it seems suitable to draw together only a few examples that show the directions that change, and ideas about change, have taken. They are suggestive and by no means exhaustive. Obviously the subject could easily absorb many volumes like this one, dealing as it does with all that is and could be in the schools.

The section includes a consideration of some barriers to change, an example of politically directed change in one urban system (Philadelphia), some suggestions about changing the attitudes of ghetto teachers, a discussion of how schools can be masculinized and better adapted to the needs of active boys (as well as girls), the concluding section of the influential English Plowden Report on primary schools, and finally an approach to manpower education and training outside the schools.

The three barriers to change described by Richard Carlson are the absence of a change agent in schools similar to the county extension agent, the lack of knowledge about what to change and how to do it, and the sheltered or "domesticated" nature of the school which makes it impossible for the child to reject the school or the school the child. He points to new research indicating, contrary to past findings, that the amount of money available to schools is not necessarily related to the rate of change.

The article by Wallace Roberts describes the political process by which change was begun in the Philadelphia schools. Among the more celebrated of the Philadelphia experiments has been the School without Walls. Students do not go to school in the usual sense. Instead, groups of about fifteen ungraded high school students and two teachers meet in any of a number of assigned public or private buildings. Usually the students spend several hours a day there learning math, language, and other subjects required by state law. Otherwise, they are free of the traditional classroom. They may choose from a wide range of specialized courses—zoology and anthropology at the Philadelphia Zoo, art appreciation at the Art Museum, biology at the Academy of Natural Sciences, physical education at the YMCA, journalism at the local newspapers. The "School" is integrated, mainly with disadvantaged children chosen from the city's eight public school districts, but suburban youths and Catholic parochial students also participate. The School was founded as an economy move and as an alternative to building a new 18-million-dollar high school. It has been widely regarded as one of the most successful innovations in curriculum and organization of our time. By 1972, 2,400 students will be enrolled in the program, the equivalent of a full four-year high school.

The Plowden Report on English schools endorses a style of education in the primary schools that permits small children to move about freely and work at individual and group tasks of interest to them. The Plowden Report, unlike the Coleman Report, deals not with massive quantities of data but with qualitative descriptions of schools that are succeeding while others fail.

Eli Ginsberg's article is included because it deals with a significant form of training and education that takes place largely outside the schools—manpower and vocational education. He notes the link between education and economic growth and the recognition by industry and government, stimulated by the world wars, of the need for on-the-job and institutional training of employees. The size and effectiveness of manpower programs, he observes, are shrouded in mystery; we know very little about how much business spends on training or how good the training is. He notes the enormous growth in funds spent on training by the federal government and its commitment to training as a means of reducing unemployment. He raises questions, in response to the views of Robert Maynard Hutchins, about the place of vocational education in our formal school system and suggests that education for jobs is a legitimate part of general education.

Educators and those who would reform our schools have much to learn from an examination of this vast complex of training programs which, in their totality, may closely rival the formal school system in size and usefulness.

BARRIERS TO CHANGE IN PUBLIC SHOOLS

by Richard O. Carlson*

A good many people, reflecting on our times, suggest that we are in the advanced stages of a revolution in education. Some of them are even prepared to argue the point, and there is considerable evidence to support their case. There are, for example, at least ten national projects in science, eleven in mathematics, one in English, two in foreign languages and four in social sciences that are currently preparing curriculum materials and testing them in the schools. The federal government has given considerable financial support to this so-called revolution in education. Over 12 million dollars has been disbursed by the Cooperative Research Branch of the U.S. Office of Education since 1956 for research on the improvement of education. This, of course, represents a very small amount in comparison to the support for the improvement of education

* From *Change Processes in the Public Schools,* Center for the Advanced Study of Educational Administration, U. of Oregon, Eugene, Oregon, 1965.

which has been provided by the National Science Foundation and Title III of the National Defense Education Act.

In spite of all of the current activity, it seems fair to say that there is quite widespread pessimism about the ability of public schools to make rapid and adequate adaptation to our fast changing times.

I am sure you have heard many times Paul Mort's fully publicized finding that it takes 50 years for the complete diffusion of an educational innovation which is destined to be fully accepted. I am sure, too, that you are well aware of the generalization that public educational institutions are painfully slow to change. You have, no doubt, marveled, as I have, at the tremendous change facility of other sections of our work world such as agriculture and medicine. Evidence of the ability of these enterprises to change is all around us and constantly forces its way to our attention.

Why is this the case? Why are educational systems reputed to be slow to change and medicine and agriculture quick to change? Could it be that there exists a greater need to change practices in medicine and farming than there is need to change educational practices? Is the practice of education so advanced and the practice of medicine and farming so primitive as to explain the diverse rates of adaptability? I think not.

THREE BARRIERS TO CHANGE

1. The Absence of a Change Agent

Part of the explanation of the slow rate of change in public schools, according to many students of organizational change, lies with the absence of an institutionalized change agent position in public education. A *change agent*, for the purposes of my remarks, can be defined as a person who attempts to influence the adoption decisions in a direction he feels is desirable. He is a professional who has as his major function the advocacy and introduction of innovations into practice.

The county extension agent is well recognized as a change agent as far as farming practices are concerned. But who is it that performs a similar role for educational practice? What office in public education as we know it has responsibility for the advocacy of change? Does such a function rest in the apparatus of state departments of education? Does it rest in the office of the county school superintendent? The answer to these questions seems clearly to be no. By and large, county and state levels of public education take as their major function one of regulation.

If the change agent role is not imbedded in county or state levels of public education, then perhaps it lies in the local school district unit. It would seem difficult to make a case that local school districts have developed positions wherein the superintendent takes as his major function the advocacy of change.

It seems easy to conclude that the change agent counterpart of the county extension agent has no office in our public school enterprise. And, as has been indicated, many attribute the slowness of change in educational practices to the absence of a change agent.

Let us assume, as seems reasonable to me, that by default of others, the change advocate role must be taken by the local school system through the office of the superintendent. This would seem to be not only a fair assumption, but, in the marked instances of rapidly adapting school districts, to be a fair description of reality.

Right away this makes obvious a difficulty: whereas the change agent prototype of the county extension agent operates outside of and free from the farm unit he is attempting to change, the school superintendent as a change agent is a central part of the unit he must take as his change objective. Being in and of the organization, the function of change advocacy for the school superintendent is difficult because he frequently must prescribe the change of his own practices.

In the area of providing public schools with a change advocate, the state of New York must be seen as a leader. During the last few years, through the Commission of Education in New York, a series of studies have been conducted aimed at the development of a plan for "improving the process of educational change in the elementary and secondary schools of the state." The plan for managing change that these studies have developed is worth your attention and can be found in a monograph titled "Organizing New York State for Educational Change," which is published by the New York State Department of Education. In essence, the plan suggests that in order to deal effectively with the problem of change in school practices, three distinct and separate units must be established under the control of the Commissioner of Education of New York. One unit is a design unit where ideas are generated. The second unit has the task of evaluating the ideas flowing from the design unit. The third separate unit has as its function the development and dissemination of the practices which emanate from the other two agencies. The extent to which this plan is successful in improving the process of educational change in the schools of New York is, of course, still to be seen. Nevertheless, it is very encouraging to see the human talent and effort that is involved in the undertaking. And it is clear that the problem of establishing a viable change advocacy function among the many levels in our system of education is one of extreme importance and one for which we should recruit our best minds.

2. A Weak Knowledge Base

In addition to the lack of a change agent, schools are also handicapped in change activities by the weakness of the knowledge base about new educational practices. This is apparent when one contrasts the knowledge base about innovations which is available to the school superintendent with that which is available to the county extension agent. As you know, the county extension agent is backed by very extensive and practiced research, experiment, and development operations. He is in a much more favored position than is the school superintendent to judge the merits of the innovations he attempts to have adopted, and to demonstrate these merits to the acceptors. It is rare indeed when an educational innovation is backed by solid research. It is even rarer to find an educational innovation which has been fully developed and subjected to careful trial and experimentation. Thus, the school superintendent as a change agent must ordinarily do not only the work of the county extension agent but also the work of the agricultural experimental station. This is a job of large dimensions. But, as you know from first hand experience, it is a job which is very exciting and satisfying.

The future may be brighter on this point: the school administrator may be relieved of some of the burdens of being both a county extension agent and an agricultural experimental station. The federal government has within the last year established four large educational research and development centers, (at the Universities of Oregon, Pittsburgh, and Wisconsin, and at Harvard) and more centers will be established in the future.

These centers are charged with research, development and dissemination responsibilities and in this sense can be seen as emulating the U.S. agricultural experimental stations. These centers have high potential and, given time to get into full operation, should have a large influence on public education. They should give school administrators a knowledge base about educational practices that is as firm as that from which the county extension agent operates.

3. "Domestication" of Public Schools

To the list of factors which hinder change activities in public schools, a list which so far in my remarks includes the lack of a change agent and a weak knowledge base about innovations, let me add a third factor. This third factor has to do with organizational characteristics of schools and specifically with the relationship between the school as an organization and its clients.

When we talk about service organizations, those organizations which provide a self-improvement or rehabilitation function to clients which the organizations must motivate, it is clear that some of these organizations have the power or exercise the right to select its clients. Other service organizations, of which the school is one, cannot select their clients.

It is also obvious that clients are free to accept or reject the services provided by some service organizations but with some service organizations, the clients are *not* free to accept or reject the service—the clients of these organizations must accept the service. The school is one organization in the latter category.

Thus, some service organizations operate in an environment where they can select their clients and the clients are free to take or leave the service according to their desire. One of many examples of this type of organization is the *private college*. And some service organizations operate in an environment where they *cannot* select the clients they are to serve and the clients *must* accept the service. One of several examples of this type of organization is the *public school*.

The significance of the relationship with clients is implied in the label of "domesticated organization" which is given to organizations like the school which cannot select clients and where the client must accept the service. The label of domesticated organization is used to indicate that this class of organization is protected and cared for in a fashion similar to that of a domesticated animal. They are not compelled to attend to all of the ordinary and usual needs of an organization. For example, they do not compete with other organizations for clients; in fact, a steady flow of clients is assured. There is no struggle for survival for this type of organization—existence is guaranteed. Though this type of organization does compete in a restricted area for funds, funds are not closely tied to quality of performance. These organizations are domesticated in the sense that they are protected by the society they serve. The society sees the protection of these domesticated organizations as necessary to the maintenance of the social system and creates laws over and above those applying to organized action in general to care for these organizations.

The consequence of domesticating organizations, as far as organizational change is concerned, is to restrict the need for, and interest in, change because the environment of the domesticated organization in many important respects is more stable than it is in other types of organizations. When important elements of the environment are stable, as you know, the necessity for change is reduced.

Therefore, it seems reasonable to suggest that the domestication of public schools is a hindrance to change along with the lack of a change agent and a weak knowledge base about educational innovation.

THE IMPACT OF RESEARCH FINDINGS ON INNOVATION ADOPTION

Now let us return to the problems of the school superintendent as a change agent and ask the question of what guide lines are suggested for his action by educational research. What does research about the adoption of educational innovations tell the school administrator?

Research on the spread of educational innovations has several characteristics which set it apart from many other streams of diffusion research. One distinctive feature is that a vast amount of work has been done. It seems fair to say that the diffusion literature is as sophisticated and as well developed as any other area of scientific study to which educators have given their attention. Further, the study of the spread of educational practices bears the mark of one man. The late Paul Mort and his students seemed almost to have cornered the market on studies of the diffusion of educational innovations. This last feature has, however, apparently permitted a third and very important characteristic of such studies: an implicit assumption that characteristics of chief school officials are unimportant in explaining rates of adoption of innovations.

Mort and his students have displayed considerable ingenuity in the isolation of variables—usually relating to the economic base of the school district, ranging from expenditure per pupil to teachers' salaries—and in fitting the variables into accounting schemes.

A conclusion based on over 100 studies done in what I choose to call the Mort tradition is this—"If but one question can be asked, on the basis of which a prediction of rate of adoption of educational innovations is to be made, the question is: 'How much is spent per child?' " Said another way, school systems that are first to adopt educational innovation spend the most money per child and those last to adopt educational innovations spend the least amount per child.

Assuming some causes and effect relationship to be at work here, what does this finding, which comes out of a vast amount of research effort, suggest to the school superintendent? I believe that it suggests a clear line of action. If a school administrator wants his district to be on the so called leading edge in the development of public schools, his efforts above all else should be directed toward securing for his district as much money as possible and as few students as possible. I am sure this is well understood for we can all cite examples showing that this is exactly what some school districts attempt to do.

I think it is indeed fortunate, however, that this finding of the relationship between money spent per child and rates of adoption of educational innovations is being challenged by data which are now emerging.

In a recent study of the adoption of such educational practices as team teaching, modern math, foreign language instruction in the elementary grades, programmed instruction, ungraded primary classes, and accelerated programs in high schools among school systems in a county in western Pennsylvania, it was found that amount of money spent per child had a negative, insignificant correlation. That is, amount of money spent per child had no predictive power in relation to the rate of adoption of these innovations.

This is not a single finding in one county. The general finding was replicated in two ways. First, another research project was undertaken in the state of West Virginia and again it was found that the rate of adoption of these innovations was not significantly related to expenditure per child. And second, even though the expenditure level per child is considerably lower in West Virginia than it is in western Pennsylvania, there was found to be no material differences in the rates of adoptions of these innovations between these two regions of the country.

To my way of thinking, these rather recent findings which indicate no significant relationship between rate of adoption of educational innovations and expenditure per child, are indeed happy ones. They should be popular with school administrators because, for one thing, they break away from a mechanistic explanation and show the school administrator as something other than a victim of his local budget.

These findings coupled with others, which I will not bother to recite, give very clear evidence of the important role of school superintendents in the process of adopting educational innovations, and in general of the centrality of human rather than monetary aspects in the adoption process.

CAN URBAN SCHOOLS BE REFORMED?

by Wallace Roberts*

Change comes infrequently in Philadelphia, but when it does, it is like the fundamental kind set in motion at Independence Hall in 1776, and it is led chiefly by merchant-revolutionaries, liberal businessmen from the upper or upper-middle class with a distinctly

* From *Saturday Review*, May 17, 1969, Vol. LII, No. 20. Copyright 1969 Saturday Review, Inc.

Anglo-Saxon heritage of patrician radicalism. Yet the world of Chestnut Hill, the Main Line, the Assembly dances, Rittenhouse Square, and the Pennsylvania Company for Insurance on Lives and Granting of Annuities connotes a class image of a cool reserve, an active disdain for the masses that goes beyond mere unconcern, and, finally, a rigid conservatism that is more than an injunction not to rock the boat.

It is hardly surprising, then, that change in the schools has taken 150 years. Philadelphia's public school system was set up in 1818 to serve the children of the poor. The city's upper class sent their own children to the many Quaker and Episcopal schools in the city and gave only passing notice to the public schools. In the early 1960s, however, a group of reformers led by a small band of gray-flannel radicals started a movement that has produced a series of decisive changes in the atmosphere surrounding the administration of the education of Philadelphia's 290,000 public school children.

Part of the change was a series of enabling laws that were jammed through the legislature to give the school system a measure of fiscal independence and administrative flexibility. The new laws, in turn, sparked the selection of a new school board to replace a group of men whose nineteenth-century outlook and frosty indifference to public criticism caused them to be called Philadelphia's House of Lords.

The new board brought in a dynamic and controversial superintendent, Mark R. Shedd, who is as unorthodox and as aloof as Eugene McCarthy; a doubled school budget in four years; more federal school aid per child than any other large city; an extensive and diverse collection of educational programs; and a $500-million building program that opens fifteen new schools a year. The changes have also produced tensions, fears, and distrust, as jobs have been eliminated, old power centers have been circumvented, and new powers or threats of power have been unleashed. The changes, however, have brought only barely perceptible gains in student achievement scores because they have been programed reforms aimed at providing the preconditions necessary for learning. The reforms have not gone far enough yet, but their future is already uncertain.

Some of the changes in the Philadelphia school system have been described as "revolutionary," but they are the fruit of a mixed heritage. The city's colonial tradition of genteel radicalism was conveniently forgotten once the nation was made. After the Republic's capitol moved to the mud flats of the Potomac in 1800, the merchant-revolutionaries of Penn's "greene Country Towne" turned their energies to making money, and, for the rest of the nineteenth century and up through the Second World War, the idea of reform movements led by the upper class was lost in the rush of a rapidly expanding economy.

The city's banks played the key role in the capitalization of basic industries, and its counting houses have dominated the city's life; their atmosphere of conservatism, frugality, orderliness, and a subtly imposed harmony pervaded the city up through the late 1940s. Because the city's white immigrant groups were roughly the same size, no one group emerged from the wide-open battles of ward politics to dominate the city, as did the Irish in Boston and the Germans and Scandinavians in Midwestern cities. James Tate, the current mayor, is the first Irish-American to hold the job; his predecessors all have WASP-sounding names, and most of them were office boys for the business elite.

Reform in Philadelphia began twenty years ago, when the mayor's office was captured by a reform movement under the leadership of a small group of liberal, upper- and upper-middle-class businessmen—the Old Philadelphians who discovered their legacy of dissent. Joseph S. Clark, a descendant of one of the city's foremost banking families, became the first Democratic mayor in the twentieth century when he took office in 1952. Under Clark and Richardson Dilworth, his successor, who is now president of the board of education, the reform movement in city hall cleaned out the light-fingered pols for a while, streamlined the administration of the municipal bureaucracy, and, most spectacularly, turned a dreary and decaying downtown area into a model of well-planned, if uninspired, renewal.

After reshaping the rest of the city, the reformers turned their attention to the city's school system, which, at the time, symbolized the disaster of urban education. Elementary and junior high schools' achievement scores were considerably lower than national norms in nearly every category tested; the high school scores, by contrast, were well above average, but this apparently reflected attrition not improvement, as Philadelphia had the highest dropout rate of the nation's ten largest cities. There were fewer professionals in relation to enrollment than in any other city except Pittsburgh, and even then one-sixth of the teachers were permanent substitutes. Philadelphia also had a higher proportion of its school-age children in private and parochial schools than any other major city, except, again, Pittsburgh. In 1959-60, it ranked seventh in school expenditures per student among the eleven largest systems in the nation.

In 1959, enrollment, which had been growing at the rate of 1,000 or 2,000 a year, jumped by 9,000. In 1965, nearly 60 per cent of the elementary schools, 83 per cent of the junior high schools, and 89 per cent of the high schools were overcrowded. Not only were the schools short of space, they were old. More than 70 per cent of the city's public schools were over thirty years old, and sixty-three elementary schools were built before 1907 and classified as fire hazards.

Dissatisfaction with public education was considered only slightly less than subversive in Philadelphia until the late 1950s when a few individuals, citizen groups, and civil rights organizations began carping about finances and the overcrowding, but the criticism was sporadic and without punch. What welded it into an effective tool was the Greater Philadelphia Movement (GPM), a nonpartisan group of about fifty businessmen, most of whom were corporation lawyers and bankers. GPM members had been active in liberal causes in the city even before its formation in 1948, and many of them were also members of the Philadelphia chapter of Americans for Democratic Action (ADA). GPM had actively supported Clark and Dilworth in their mayoral campaigns, yet GPM was composed of men who were primarily upper-class businessmen living in the city's fashionable suburbs along the Main Line. "GPM," says William H. Wilcox, its executive director, "made it respectable to criticize the public schools."

The 1965 Philadelphia Education Home Rule Charter, which established a new school board selection process and shifted control over school finances from the state to the city, was based on state enabling laws that were approved by the legislature in 1963 only because some GPM members and friends had political leverage in Harrisburg. Those state laws, in turn, were originally based on a 1962 study of the Philadelphia schools made by GPM.

Under the new school board selection process, the mayor picked the board members from a list drawn up by a nominating panel consisting of the chief officers of a number of civic, labor, business, and education groups. Previously the school board members had been named in a seemingly haphazard fashion by the judges of the city's Court of Common Pleas, who were themselves political appointees. The result was a succession of boards of education composed of respected businessmen who saw their job as a custodial one that required a minimum of public controversy and the operation of a school system at the lowest possible cost.

When the new school board took office in December 1965, its new president was Dilworth, a carpetbagger from Pittsburgh who looks like a Tory prime minister. Besides his two surnames, he is marked by another distinctly upper-class trait of speaking his mind bluntly (they say he was born with a silver foot in his mouth), so it might appear that the school reforms he has hammered through were the product of patrician impetuousness. But Dilworth, who is now an elegant and dynamic septuagenarian with a forty-three-year career as a lawyer in the city behind him, is acutely aware of the stagnancy that can strangle a system, a city, or an institution when its top leadership is an inbred coterie of powerful coupon-clippers that has no substantial contact with minds that think differently. He tells the story of how he could never understand why some of the city's banks and railroads were so badly run until he questioned a series of corporation presidents on the witness stand in court. "I'll never forget one man," Dilworth recounts. "He was a gentleman to his fingertips, don't you know, but stupid. My God, was he dumb."

Philadelphia's school bureaucracy was no different in this respect than the city government or business community had been. Dilworth and Clark had revamped city hall by bringing in outside experts, and the same tactic was quickly applied to the schools. Before Dilworth even took office, he set up three task forces composed almost entirely of the reformers and other people with no experience in education but with proven abilities in finance, planning, personnel relations, human relations, engineering, data processing, and purchasing. Many of these men and others like them are now working on the central headquarters staff under a clause in the GPM reform laws that permits the board to exempt 5 per cent of its professional employees from certification requirements.

Dilworth's task forces reviewed all the previous studies of the city's public schools, held public hearings, and then abstracted a long series of concrete demands and recommendations into a program for a goal-orientation set of policies that the board of education could institute without having to administer closely.

The board has since concentrated on two areas of the bureaucracy that are regarded as crucial to any changes in the system: financing and planning. The latter function was simply nonexistent, so it was not difficult for the board to establish a free wheeling planning office that doesn't just talk about bricks but tries to work out with the community and professionals involved just what should go on inside their school.

The same type of change has taken place in the office of administrative services. The schools' finances have come a long way from the days when two-page budgets were kept locked in the desk drawer of business manager Add Anderson, who, until 1961, had run the schools for twenty-five years like a Roman consul, extracting a tribute for the businessmen from each budget in the form of a low tax rate. Now the finances are on a "planning, programing, budgeting" system, a managerial technique under which the costs of general programs, such as elementary education, are tabulated in a way that facilitates the determination of priorities and gives the administration greater flexibility in allocating resources.

With new procedures being put into effect by new men at the second and third levels of authority, the board soon realized that it needed a new man at the top to match its own vision and style, and by mutual agreement, decided that C. Taylor Whittier, the superintendent whom the board had inherited, was not the man. In September 1967, he was succeeded by Dr. Shedd, the former superintendent of schools in Englewood, New Jersey, which had a school system with a total enrollment of less than that of some of Philadelphia's high schools.

Having Shedd as superintendent of the Philadelphia public school system is a bit like having a socialist as the president of General Motors; he is doing things that are so different they seem antithetical to the very idea of public education. It is not just that Shedd has chosen to build his constituency in the black community rather than among his professional staff and white middle-class parents, nor is it his use of confrontation and tension, nor even is it his abrasive style, aloof manner, or unconcern with tradition. Shedd is a gambler who has put his money where his convictions are. His conversations and speeches are marked by the explanation, "I don't know if it will work, but we've got to take the chance," and the reason the chance must be taken is that he believes leaders have an obligation to act, not soothe injured feelings. If one accepts the Kerner Report, the Coleman Report, and the facts that hit you in the face, Shedd feels, there is no choice for those charged with promoting the commonweal but to accept the high risks necessary for *any* gain.

Although Dilworth and the forty-two-year-old Shedd are separated in age by a generation, there is practically no gap in their thinking. If Dilworth is, as he has been tagged by his critics, "the pied piper of anarchy," then Shedd is his drum major. The public sees them as a father and son team (they even alternate fielding questions on a Sunday morning radio program), and if this situation has its benefits—such as those few instances during a board of education meeting when Dilworth has to pound the table and say, "We brought this man in and we've got to support him"—it also creates a sense of conspiracy among the school professionals and the public who feel they are being manipulated like serfs by a divine right king and his minister.

Shedd's own belief in the efficacy of bringing talent in from outside the system and his practice of surrounding himself with an "Ivy Mafia," have produced more than a "We–They" split among the staff. Apprehension is pervasive in Philadelphia, not just because 381 administrators one day found that their jobs had been eliminated on the pretext of belt-tightening and that they had a choice of either early retirement or lower-paying jobs, but also because Shedd has paid heed primarily to the grievances of the black community. It was not because the principals felt that Jimmy Hoffa was a great educator that this winter they tried to find some muscle of their own by threatening to join the Teamsters Union. Even before Shedd took office officially the signs were clear; he met almost continually with gang members, black militants, and parents and began championing their demands before he deigned to address the principals or central headquarters staff.

There are some very real and practical reasons for this tactic, however. Since 1930, Philadelphia's population has hovered at the 2,000,000 figure, but the proportion of Negroes has increased from 11 per cent to 34 per cent. Since 1960, the school enrollment ratio has shifted from 47 per cent to 60 per cent black. Negro children in the Philadelphia schools have significantly higher dropout rates and markedly lower achievement scores; they typically go to older and more overcrowded schools, are channeled into non-academic courses, and have less experienced teachers. If the Philadelphia public schools were not fulfilling their promises to white children in the early '60s, they weren't even making promises to the black students.

Shedd has made promises, perhaps too many, and is determined to see them fulfilled despite the inevitable tension such a course causes. In his speeches (he is probably the only superintendent in the country to have a speechwriter), he constantly urges parents, civic groups, and students to put pressure on the schools. On what has now come to be called Black Friday, November 17, 1967, 3,500 black high school students took him at his word, left school (sometimes with the blessings of their principals), and gathered at the board of education headquarters at 21st Street and Benjamin Franklin Parkway to demand better education generally, more black teachers and principals, permission to wear African clothes and form Afro-American societies in the schools, and black-oriented curricula.

While Shedd and the Reverend Henry Nichols, a Negro who is vice president of the school board, and several other administrators and board members met with a delegation of students, tension rose outside the building. The police eventually moved in swinging their clubs and twenty-two persons were seriously injured. The resulting controversy not only released latent racism, it opened the floodgates of criticism from everyone in the city who had listened to Shedd talk for almost a year about using the schools to make a "social revolution," and "breaking down the human walls of values and psychological distance." Color him black and he comes on like a pedagogical Martin Luther King, but to the principals, teachers, and working-class whites of Philadelphia, he sounds like Rap Brown.

The explosive issue had blown up several times since and threatens, along with the personnel policies, to be the pivot upon which the hopes of continued reform turn. Yet beneath all the public hauling and pushing, the process of change set in motion by the Dilworth board and accelerated by Shedd is continuing, albeit at sometimes uncertain pace. For instance, Shedd's conception of the central office as a supply depot rather than a military headquarters has resulted in attempts to decentralize its functions by setting up a "talent pool" of teachers from which principals can select their staffs instead of being forced to accept those chosen arbitrarily by the central office. Shedd has also taken similar steps with the budget and set up a fund from which principals can draw grants of up to $15,000 for special projects and another fund for teachers that makes grants up to $300. These kinds of changes are not complete and working smoothly yet, but the first steps have been taken.

More than the administrative devices, however, there is also a large variety of new educational programs—perhaps more than in any other school district in the nation. The system has developed Learning Center Projects, which are discovery-oriented classrooms aimed at finding new models for more effective classroom organization; there is also a growing network of "magnet" schools, each specializing in one academic area such as space science or social studies and drawing students from all over the city; long-term arrangements have been made with several colleges for intensive teacher training and urban studies; and Philadelphia has made the most extensive use of computer-assisted and individually prescribed instruction of any city in the nation—35,000 students used the facilities last year.

Most of these projects, which are directed at improving learning, are just getting off the ground or are still in the planning stages, so it will be several years before any judgment can be made about them. The results are in, however, or seem self-evident in two instances.

One is the Simon Gratz High School. In three years it has been completely transformed from a nightmare of noneducation with one of the city's highest dropout rates and lowest percentages of college-bound seniors into a school that feels itself to be alive and vital. The dropout rate has been halved and the number of students going to college has increased from 3 per cent to 22 per cent, but the school has something going for everyone, not just the scholars and the rejects. Work programs have been set up with medical laboratories, food markets, banks, the Philadelphia Navy Yard, the garment industry, and others, and now the school is investigating the ramifications of being adopted by Boeing-Vertol. There is probably no other school in the country with a foundation grant used solely to pay the bills incurred with a Diners Club card used for lunches with businessmen interested in working with the school.

The man responsible for all this is the principal, Marcus Foster, a veteran of twenty years in the Philadelphia school system, a man who grew up in a street gang in the South Philadelphia black community to become one of that rare breed of schoolmen who have never been beaten down by the bureaucracy, and, finally, a man who is able to impose his own humanity on an institution. But even if Marcus Foster walked out of Gratz tomorrow, it would be almost the same. Everyone in the school is turned on, even the war lords of the gangs with which Foster "collaborated" to put pressure on city hall to have fourteen neighboring homes occupied by white families condemned for an addition to the school that was built for 2,000 pupils and which serves 4,000 in split sessions, nearly all of whom are black.

What makes Gratz significant is that it could not have happened under the pre-reform regime. True, Foster had been in the system for a long time and had worked out his techniques while transforming first an elementary school and then a disciplinary school, but he was certified only as an elementary school principal; his appointment to Gratz by the Dilworth board under their 5 per cent exemption clause created a minor controversy, but the appointment stuck.

The opening up of the bureaucracy by Dilworth and Shedd has also resulted in the Pennsylvania Advancement School (PAS), a center for affective education that operates on two remodeled floors of a once-abandoned warehouse in the North Philadelphia slums. Shedd brought the Advancement School staff, started in North Carolina under Peter Buttenwieser, to Philadelphia in September 1967, and had it set up as a semi-autonomous, nonprofit corporation to "save" bright junior high school boys who were failing and potential dropouts.

The figures on the job being done by the PAS won't be in for a few years until the groups of students PAS has been working with for fourteen weeks each go through high school, but the Advancement School is concentrating not so much on becoming a service station for repairing the damage done by the city's regular schools as it is trying to become a development labooratory for new teaching techniques that will eliminate the reasons students become bored with or intimidated by schools.

In the school itself, walls are uncommon and movable, and the teachers are concentrating on breaking down the barriers that separate them from the students. They use games (poker spelling), drama improvisation, animal laboratories, sophisticated electronic equipment, urban studies, and a host of other carefully worked out curricula and techniques to reach the students.

The PAS is a radical change for Philadelphia (almost too

radical—in March it was closed down for a week on technical housing-code violations, apparently on orders from the office of the mayor who has criticized the school's orientation), but change has not yet pervaded the Philadelphia school system proper. Central High School, the city's highly selective boys' school, and its counterpart, Girls High, have hardly been touched by the tidal waves coming out of 21st and the Parkway. The principal of Central, the oldest public high school in the country outside of New England, is still called its president, and the school's most talked about innovation is the Advanced Placement Program which is fully eleven years old. There are more blacks now in Central, and the number of student radicals ("dirties," they're called) is growing. It's hard to argue with a 95 per cent rate of college-bound seniors, but the students, their parents, or their teachers may soon start to say that perhaps Central should be doing something else, too.

The story of the Philadelphia public schools is the story of change, but it is also the story of the implications of the process of change and the central administration's failure to decentralize control of the schools, despite repeated and varied attempts. Since the Dilworth board took office and began holding televised meetings in various sections of the city, the community's interest in the schools has become intense, and when Shedd arrived, he quickly converted a few vague ideas about community involvement and administrative decentralization into a program that sounded as if it were going to be implemented immediately. But not much has really changed in three years.

The failure of these efforts is explained easily by the fact that they were all essentially attempts at the redistribution of power, and any such attempt is bound to encounter large-scale resistance from those from whom the power would flow. It's not just a fear of the black community; schoolmen are really just as afraid of the upwardly mobile Italians and Irish in the Eastwick development or the upper-class WASPs in Chestnut Hill. But this explanation does nothing more than say that Southern Congressmen don't want to give up the seniority system because they enjoy controlling the most important committees.

More fundamentally, the failure of decentralization and community involvement in Philadelphia is tied to the limits of reform from the top. Nearly all the experiments were initiated in the central offices at 21st and the Parkway. Another attempt is now being made to work out some new approaches to decentralization and community involvement through a commission of sixty-eight widely varied members. The process still smacks of central initiative, especially the selection process used to determine the commission members. Nevertheless, it offers hope because it is symbolic of the kind of long and agonizing process that is necessary for dealing with problems as complicated as this one.

The black community, meanwhile, is under no illusion that its new relationship with the schools insures reform. As much as many Negroes respect Shedd and Dilworth, leaders such as the genial and politically astute Novella Williams of Citizens for Progress realize that the black community finally may be pushed into a position where for its own survival it must either take over the schools or establish its own independent, private system.

Survival has become the main concern of nearly everyone connected with the Philadelphia schools, and education has never really been able to emerge from the background. The reformers, for all their good intentions, have been primarily concerned with the same things that were important to the bankers and the House of Lords: orderliness, stability, and tranquility. They have not been able to follow up their attempts to go beyond the preconditions of learning by pushing for changes that would make Philadelphia's schools joyous, exciting, and liberating. The nation's urban schools have never been the vehicles for upward social mobility that we once thought they were and still think they should be, but it seems that there should be more to education than utilitarianism and administrative neatness.

All of this may seem irrelevant when the Philadelphia public schools are faced with a fiscal crisis of such proportions that it can be solved only by the federal government; with a state desegregation order for both schools and faculties; with a mayor who is openly antagonistic to Dilworth, and, hence, the schools; and with mounting pressure from all sides, even from the predominately white and once powerful Home and School Council, which, ignored by Dilworth and Shedd, has been demanding "parent power."

Yet the issues are part of the same problem. The liberal reformers have tried to make the schools into institutions that can cure the diseases of society, but the schools are a direct reflection of society and can't be changed until the society itself is ready to change.

A couple of weeks ago, a young teacher who had grown up in the city told Shedd of a recent visit to his old high school, Northeast. "They've integrated it since I was there," he said. "And as I left, I stopped at a traffic light and saw a Negro boy and a white girl talking and laughing at the corner. The white drivers in the two cars ahead of me saw them too and glared in disgust and rage. The city is *scared*, Dr. Shedd. You've alienated all the whites. You've got to do something!"

Shedd's face muscles tensed a little; he's been through this many times in the past few months. Finally, he slouched slightly in his chair and said, "There's only so much that one man can do. Eventually it's going to have to be people like you that are going to have to pull this city together."

There is also a limit to the amount of change that can be programed. Fear, tension, and racism cannot be qualified and fed into a computer with any expectation that a solution for achieving tranquility and an educational utopia will appear on the printout. With or without its gray-flannel reformers and their modern managerial techniques, Philadelphia will probably never be able to live up to the original meaning of its name, but it can try to find a way of life that does not make a mockery of it and that allows children to relish life, not rebel or run from it.

MASCULINIZING THE SCHOOL

by Patricia Cayo Sexton*

In public elementary schools, 85 percent of all teachers are women. In all public schools, women are 68 percent of the total. Men are now a bare majority in secondary schools. On the other hand, in higher education, women are a small minority of teaching facul-

---

* From *The Feminized Male*, by Patricia Cayo Sexton. Copyright © 1968 by Patricia Sexton. Reprinted by permission of Random House, Inc.

ties—and are heavily concentrated in the arts, education, nursing, social work, English, languages, and the social sciences.

Women multiply in the school when men are engaged elsewhere, during times of prosperity or war. During World War I, women were 86 percent of all public school teachers, and during World War II the figure was only slightly lower.

Though run at the top by men, schools are essentially feminine institutions, from nursery through graduate school. In the school, women set the standards for adult behavior, and many favor students, male and female, who most conform to their own behavior norms—polite, clean, obedient, neat and nice ones. While there is nothing wrong with this code, for those who like it, it does not give boys (or girls either) much room to flex their muscles—physical or intellectual.

Putting a man, any man, in place of women in school will not do. A man who is less than a man can be more damaging to boys than a domineering mother. The chances of getting feminized men in the school are fairly good because those eligible and willing, given present hiring codes and salaries, are usually those who made it through a feminine school system without conflict or failure.

One is inclined to say that the younger the student, the more feminine the tone of the school seems to be. But, then, some graduate programs seem far more oppressive to the male temperament than do kindergartens, even though there are more female teachers present in the latter. What does seem clear is that the system is spun round, like a cocoon, with threads woven by women and feminized males. The signs are found everywhere, in curriculum, standards, values, systems of reward, methods of instruction, personnel, remoteness from power and reality, and dispersal of authority.

To mention authority is not to suggest that the school is either too permissive or too authoritarian, too easy or too punishing, too chaotic or too disciplined. It is a difficult point, but the sketchy evidence we have about the way organizations operate indicates that they can be either very strict or very loose and still permit optimal masculine growth, depending on how authority is used, by whom, and to what ends. For example, the military is certainly not the least masculine of institutions, yet it is run with firm authority. The Wild West was an era of perhaps excessive masculinity, yet it ran almost without law and order. One would assume, based partly on speculation and some psychological evidence, that freedom and consent nourish the masculine temperament and are as essential to natural sex growth as protein is to body growth. But man does not live on protein and license alone. These must be taken along with other fuels.

The signs of femininity are even found in the sounds people make, quite apart from the words they speak. Many academicized people have a certain identifying sound—feminine and vaguely reptilian—which is made often by them, but rarely by others. The characterizing sound of the schoolmarm is *shhh* and among the university elites (faculty and students) the corresponding sound is *hisss*. Both are meant, like the serpent's rattler, to express hostile intent, and both often succeed in suppressing the expression of others. Made from behind closed lips, the sound does not always identify its source. Its expression is no act of brave personal dissent, but instead permits anonymity from antagonists. It is a cat sound—feline, sibilant, "female."

The schools mainly teach the words and number symbols of reading, writing, arithmetic. One hardly ever sees the *things* these symbols stand for. Deeds and actions are rarely the substance of school instruction, activity being viewed as disruptive of academic study. Schools set the standards—followed too religiously by others who judge people—by which people are measured. They are the academic measures of ability to deal with symbols on paper, rather than measures of performance or creativity.

School words tend to be the words of women. They have their own sound and smell, perfumed or antiseptic. Just as there are dialects of class, occupation, and region, so there are distinguishable dialects of gender. Women use different words, stress them differently, put them together in special ways, use them for different purposes, write them differently—and usually much more legibly. Boys, for example, usually prefer tough and colorful short words—while teachers and girls lean toward longer, more floral and opaque synonyms. School words are clean and refined—sugar and spice, and other things nice—idealized and as remote from physical things as the typical schoolmarm from the tough realities of ordinary life.

Active word usage, as in *speaking*, is usually discouraged in school; students are expected to speak only when addressed. Talking—a far more aggressive act than reading, listening, or even writing—is a favorite mode of male verbal activity. Even boys who refuse to read or write usually like to talk, but on their own terms. It is the school's most troublesome job to suppress most forms of spontaneous oral expression, and to keep boys quiet and in their seats.

The classroom cannot, of course, be an oral free-for-all. Nor can our primers become indistinguishable from locker-room talk. But some of the guts of male talk should be left intact. A boy would probably be run out of school for imitating Norman Mailer's prose, yet Mailer is one of our most gifted writers. Many well-meaning efforts to add the vernacular to our formal language look silly and seem artificially pasted on top of old packages. Still, the school primers need not fall so far behind the times. Much of the vernacular gets into formal language anyhow, enriching and simplifying it. More is needed, especially from the style, if not the vocabulary, of male talk. Some males are able to blend action words from the street with those that pass for proper English. Let them be the teachers of words and written language. And let there be more time in school for boys to talk and say what they want to each other.

Some science is taught in schools, but usually as words which are detached from things, from doing and discovering. Thus, the magic and adventure of science are missing. Physics, an academic subject with some natural appeal to average boys, is offered only to honor students, and often only in an unpalatable form, loaded with memorization and excessive detail, and drained of the spirit of scientific inquiry. So it is that many boys (and girls) with a natural interest in what lies at the heart of physical reality are by-passed. As for technology, aside from shop classes, which at least offer slow or troubled boys a chance to move around, there is a great glaring void, filled in by long hours of paper work.

Methods of school instruction require little more than passive receiving and repeating. The student listens to the teacher. He reads the book. He memorizes and repeats what the book and teacher have said. His "learning" is passive and feminine, not active. He sits, listens, reads, writes, repeats, and speaks when spoken to. Thus learning is reduced to a body of facts to be noted and stored, rather than a method of active and rigorous inquiry and a way to examine and master one's environment.

The feminized school simply bores many boys; but it pulls some in one of two opposite directions. If the boy absorbs school values, he may become feminized himself. If he resists, he is pushed toward school failure and rebellion. Increasingly, boys are drawn to female norms. The attraction is the rainbow that lies at the end of graduation with honor, the school diploma, the college degree. More than ever before in human history, a boy's fate will be determined by the number of diplomas he gets and where he gets them. As long as society and employers generally regard diplomas as *the* badge of merit, boys will be pulled ever deeper into a system that rewards conformity to feminine standards. While the rainbow lies ahead, voices at the rear (friends, or even parents, if they want a real boy) urge him to be himself and become an autonomous person. Following this course means trouble in school, but being your own man can, for many boys, be worth the sacrifice of gold stars in class.

Of course, school achievement is not identical with life achievement, though the two are very closely related. Many exceptional boys, of course, can break all school rules and still rise to the top in life. Nor are those who head the most powerful organizations usually the most feminized males. More often they are those who have managed, through fate or some ploy, to escape the feminizing influence of school and society. Many boys know better than female teachers that academic learning has little to do with what goes on in the real world, that it does not always produce top results in real life.

Elites in America, unlike the British (who tend to be born to privilege), have at least avoided the *extremes* of feminization. Our corporate and government elites have not come exclusively from school honor rolls—or from among those who went to the "right" schools and come from the "right" families. Though we may deplore the lack of vigor and humanity at the top, relative to elites in other societies we may be further ahead than we think.

Many top American political and corporate leaders have been poor or average scholars in college (Dwight Eisenhower, Franklin D. Roosevelt, Lyndon Johnson, Nelson Rockefeller, etc.), and we have not followed the Latin style of exalting academicians and artists to places of power. James Roche, president of General Motors, never went to college, nor did many other top executives. Walter Reuther, one of our greatest natural leaders, had trouble with written tests and was a college dropout, leaving the cloister to build a powerful union of industrial workers. Harry Truman was not a college man.

Carl Schurz wrote about Lincoln, "I grant that he lacks higher education and his manners are not in accord with European conceptions of the dignity of a chief magistrate. He is a well-developed child of nature and is not skilled in polite phrases and poses. But he is a man of profound feeling, correct and firm principles and incorruptible honesty. His motives are unquestionable and he possesses to a remarkable degree the characteristic, God-given trait of this people, sound common sense."

Such measures of men have carried more weight in the selection of elites (at least of those not born to privilege) than measures of academic aptitude. Performance and energy have counted more in selecting top leaders than ability to take written examinations. That elites are now taken increasingly from among honor students, may not invigorate our leadership.

Some American men of inherited, as well as earned, status (the Kennedys, Rockefellers, etc.) have been educated in all-male schools, and exposed to male societies when young. While sex segregation can be as bad as racism, boys can at least escape from other figures in the all-male school. Such schools may breed sexual inversion as British boarding schools apparently do; but some American prep schools clearly avoid the sadism, Spartan rigors, and snobbery that seem to stimulate inversion in British prep schools. Other males of the elite avoid feminization by pursuing a passionate interest in tough sports and a committed and disciplined style of life.

The present power elites, furthermore, are recruits from a different society—from a rural or small-town, rather than urban or suburban, way of life. On the farm, males can more easily be men. The farm boy does useful and manly work at the side of his father. He is free to wander, without fear of urban perils. He is close to nature and the ways of men. His father is home and his mother is busy with a large family—weaving, sewing, gardening, ironing, washing by hand, baking bread, milking cows, feeding chickens—without any idle time to lavish on the cultivation of her sons. Many men in current power elites grew up in rural settings, but those of the future will more often come from the city's or suburb's feminized hothouses.

REFORM OF ENGLISH SCHOOLS

(The Plowden Report)*

RECOMMENDATIONS AND CONCLUSIONS

Our terms of reference, "primary education in all its aspects and the transition to secondary education" were wide ranging. Our interpretation has been correspondingly wide. We conceived it as our duty to see the primary school not only in its strictly educational context but also as a part of society and of the economy.

The cost of the proposals we have made is large. This is in part the cost of bringing a system designed for "other people's children" up to the standard which "a good and wise parent" would accept for his own children. Neither in our staffing proposals, nor in our demand for buildings and equipment, have we been luxurious or extravagant. What we propose does not go beyond what is needed to provide a perfectly ordinary, well staffed school. Yet in the present difficult economic circumstances it is not a programme capable of being carried out in the next five years.

Since the war there has been a great increase in secondary education and in further and higher education. These developments were necessary if we were to hold our own with other advanced industrial countries. We are certainly not leading an advance party. This progress, however, has been in part at the expense of primary education. We think that a higher priority in the total educational budget ought now to be given to primary education. It is desirable in its own right: nobody ought to be satisfied with the conditions under which many of the four million primary school children are educated. It is also desirable in the interests of secondary and further education. A good deal of the money spent on older children will be wasted if more is not spent on them during their primary

* A Report of the Central Advisory Council for Education (England).

school years. Yet not everything costs money. Some of our recommendations call mainly for changes of attitude, understanding and knowledge in individual teachers.

In the introduction to our Report we posed certain questions. Now we attempt to answer them. We found that the Hadow reports understated rather than over estimated the differences between children. They are too great for children to be tidily assigned to streams or types of schools. Children are unequal in their endowment and in their rates of development. Their achievements are the result of the interaction of nature and of nurture. We conclude that the Hadow emphasis on the individual was right though we would wish to take it further. Whatever form of organisation is adopted, teachers will have to adapt their methods to individuals within a class or school. Only in this way can the needs of gifted and slow learning children and all those between the extremes be met.

The appraisal we have made of the curriculum, and of the methods which have proved to be the most fruitful, confirm many or most of the suggestions that our predecessors made. Their insights have been justified and refined by experience. "Finding out" has proved to be better for children than "being told". Children's capacity to create in words, pictorially and through many other forms of expression, is astonishing. The third of the three R'S is no longer mere mechanical arithmetic, French has made its way into the primary school, nature study is becoming science. There has been dramatic and continuing advance in standards of reading. The gloomy forebodings of the decline of knowledge which would follow progressive methods have been discredited. Our review is a report of progress and a spur to more.

This may sound complacent. We are not. The more dismal corners of primary education produce plenty of evidence of parochialism, lack of understanding of the needs of children and of the differing homes from which they come, lack of continued training of teachers and lack of opportunities for professional contact. Had we ignored these facts, we should have ignored what is well known to teachers and, increasingly, to parents. If all or most teachers are to approach the standards of the best, far more effort must be put into their in-service training.

There may be a good school without good buildings, though this is no excuse for the deplorable conditions in which many children are educated. There cannot be a good school without good teachers. Even one or two can leaven a whole staff. But there are staffs without leaven. We set these facts down here lest we should be accused of wilful ignorance because in the Report we have for the most part described English primary education at its best. That in our belief is very good indeed. Only rarely is it very bad. The average is good.

We hope we have described in the Report what good primary education is, and how robust, imaginative, sensitive and skilful the work of a good primary school pupil can be. Much of our thinking, however, has been given to considering those children to whose work none of these epithets could be applied. We know that in almost every primary school there are some such children. We know that in some districts almost every child is at a disadvantage that can only be removed by unusual excellence in the school. An outstanding trend in recent years has been the growing awareness of the importance for the individual of his family and social background. The last three reports by the Council and the Robbins report on higher education produced evidence that shows how closely associated are social circumstances and academic achievement. We have been able to set on foot research which has suggested that the most vital factor in a child's home is the attitude to school, and all that goes on there, of his mother and father. The interested parent has the interested child. In contrast we have been conscious of the unfairness that dogs many boys and girls through life. The loss to them, the loss to the community that arises because of the inequality of educational opportunity, is avoidable and in consequence intolerable. We have, therefore, deliberately given their needs the first priority among our recommendations even though this may delay for a while long overdue benefits for the greater number of children. Our proposal for the introduction of educational priority areas, a detailed plan for dealing with a situation to which the Council's last report also drew attention, is sufficiently urgent to be put forward for immediate action even in the present economic difficulties.

We think of primary education as something that ought to start gradually without a sudden transition from whole time home to whole time school, from the day with mother to the day with teacher. This lies behind our recommendation for half time education in nursery groups for nearly all four year olds and for a good many three year olds. That is why we have advocated a slightly later start than now to school, and why we have suggested that it may sometimes be right for a mother to be with her child in the classroom until he has settled down. Were this to happen, it would be a symbol of the partnership between schools and parents that we hope will persist in different forms through the whole length of education.

We have recommended a single term of intake to first schools and a complete three year course in them for all children. Perhaps the greatest benefit that time in the infant school gives is confidence in what has been learned. The child's own satisfaction in having really mastered something—whether it be riding a bicycle or telling the time—is important. If the beginnings of school work are only half learned and anxiety ridden, the effects may persist throughout school days. Confidence in the power to learn is vital.

The middle school will start and finish a year later than the junior school. Its staff will need to be drawn from secondary schools as well as primary. Both have a contribution to make. If the middle school is simply thought of as providing an "extra year" to the junior school, many children will be working well below their capacity and become bored. If the middle school is thought of as a junior secondary school to be organised and taught in the ways that secondary schools are run, there is an equal risk that we may lose too soon the enquiring spirit which drives a child to follow through an interest without respect to subject frontiers. We cannot give a description of a good middle school because such schools do not yet exist. They will have to work out their own pattern. We can only say that their work must be carried further than that of junior schools, their ways of learning be less stereotyped than those of secondary schools. In a world where secondary schools have increasingly to adapt their style to the needs of older adolescents and near adults, the middle school ought to provide the right environment for the last years of childhood as it passes over into adolescence.

No report on primary education today could be realistic if it did not attempt to deal with the revolutionary change that has come over the composition of the body of teachers. Before the war the schools could count on most teachers giving 40 years of service. A school staff was a body of experienced professionals in which a newcomer could easily learn to find his feet. Today the proportions are often reversed. A small body of experienced teachers is surrounded by a rapidly changing group of young women who expect to marry soon after they leave college and in many cases to leave within a few years, at least for the time being, in order to start their own families. Some return to teaching; more should. When they return they are the richer because they are themselves mothers, the poorer because they have often not had long enough to reach professional competence before they gave up teaching. Some can teach full-time; some part-time. The schools have to accustom themselves to being staffed in a novel way at the same time as they are developing new methods of individual and group work which demand greater competence and co-operation from teachers.

In these circumstances we make recommendations on the staffing of the schools on which we lay special emphasis. The first has only temporary application. It is that those who are planning now for the raising of the school leaving age should not reckon on any transfers from the primary schools to carry out the operation. The place for trained primary school teachers is in the primary schools. The second recommendation is that the work of teachers should be lightened by the provision of aides, who should be given one or two years training. The more individual the methods of teaching, the stronger the case for teachers' aides. The scheme will be expensive; we are sure the teachers deserve the relief it will provide.

The favourable judgment we have formed of English primary education as a whole, and the confidence with which we have made far reaching recommendations for its development, reflect the devoted and perceptive service of the vast majority of the 140,000 primary school teachers. Most of what is best in English schools has come straight from individual teachers. We could wish no child a happier fate than to encounter, as many do, a good teacher.

. . . Children are most severely handicapped by home conditions. The programme should be phased to make schools in the most deprived areas as good as the best of the country. For this it may be necessary that their greater claim on resources should be maintained.

A start should be made as soon as possible by giving priority to the most severely deprived pupils, starting with two per cent of the pupils and building up to ten per cent over five years. The purpose of the short term programme would be partly to discover which measures best compensate for educational deprivation. In the longer term, the programme may be expanded to cover a larger proportion of the population.

Every local education authority having schools in which children's educational handicaps are reinforced by social deprivation should be asked to adopt the measures suggested below and to report from time to time on the progress made. Local authorities should be encouraged to select schools within their areas for special attention even though they are not eligible for extra help from national resources.

A wide variety of criteria should be employed initially. Experience will show which of these criteria are most useful. . . .

Steps to be Taken: 1968 to 1972

(a) Measures should be taken to improve the ratio of teachers to children in educational priority areas to a point at which no class in these areas exceeds 30. Additions to salary amounting in total to £ 120 for every teacher in the priority areas should be paid. It should be open to authorities to award increases according to any plan approved by the Department of Education and Science as being likely to improve education in these areas.

(b) Teachers' aides should be provided in the priority schools at a ratio of one to every two infant and junior classes.

(c) In building programmes, priority should be given to these areas for the replacement or improvement of schools with old or out of date premises. . . .

(d) Extra books and equipment should be given for schools in priority areas.

(e) The expansion of nursery education should begin in the priority areas.

. . . Colleges of education should, wherever possible, establish a continuing link with priority schools. Students should do part of their teaching practice in these schools.

Teacher centres should be set up for in-service training. They might run longer courses with the co-operation of local colleges of education. Such courses might be recognised for salary purposes.

The development of social work in conjunction with schools should begin in priority areas and be more heavily concentrated there subsequently.

Community schools should be tried out first in priority areas.

Sustained efforts should be made to diversify the social composition of the districts where priority schools are so that teachers and others who make an essential contribution to the life and public services of the neighbourhood are not excluded from them. Coordinated action will be necessary on the part of authorities responsible for employment, industrial training, housing and town planning if educational deprivation is to be rapidly reduced.

Research should be started to discover which of the developments in educational priority areas have the most constructive effects, so as to assist in planning the longer term programme to follow.

Exchequer grants to local authorities with educational priority areas should be increased and the necessary changes in the grant making system made.

MANPOWER POLICY

by Eli Ginsberg*

There has been considerable excitement of late among academic economists in the United States and abroad who have suddenly rediscovered what Adam Smith knew a long time ago, that there is a close tie between the quantity and quality of a nation's educational services and its economic growth and welfare. As has been true in other instances, such as the tariff, the American public has acted on insights to which the economists either were not privy or in which they were little interested. There has always been a pronounced public concern in the United States with education, not without an awareness of its economic potential. One need only recall that Harvard College was established to train a local ministry; that West Point was authorized because of the need for engineers and surveyors to explore the West; and that the leaders of the new Republic discussed the advantages of founding a national university to

* From "Education and Moneymaking," by Eli Ginsberg, reprinted from *The World Year Book of Education* by permission of Evans Brothers Limited, London; © Eli Ginsberg.

harness the potentialities of science and technology to national goals.

Admittedly, there were also non-economic forces working to expand education: for the Puritans, religious requirements demanded literacy in order to read the Bible; for the immigrants who came from many different lands and spoke many different languages, the public school provided access to the melting pot. Nevertheless, the economic gains to be derived from educating the public were early recognized and, except for the special problems of the South with its large number of slaves, the value of an educated public was accepted.

In the midst of the Civil War, Congress passed the Morrill Act which committed the federal government to assist colleges so that they might contribute more effectively to the progress of agriculture and the technical arts. When one recalls that the principal type of entrepreneur in the middle of the nineteenth century was the independent farmer, the vocational implications of the Morrill Act cannot be overstressed. The linkage between education and the economic world of agriculture was made much more effective toward the end of the nineteenth century with the development of agricultural research stations at the land grant colleges and the establishment of a corps of agricultural extension agents. Federal funds made possible the rapid expansion of basic and applied research; the extension agents helped to diffuse the new knowledge; and, with assistance from farm machine companies, American commercial agriculture was on the way to becoming one of the most sophisticated of industries. Today we produce most of our food requirements, plus a considerable amount for export, with less than five million agricultural workers out of a total labour force of 80 million.

IMPORTATION OF SKILL

The situation with respect to industry followed a somewhat different track. The United States has long been a major importer of skill. The brain drain is not a recent phenomenon nor is it likely to disappear in the near future. We have long supplemented our local supplies of skill with young men trained abroad. The fact that we were able to attract immigrants, including skilled workers, with relative ease probably helps to explain the slow start and the limited success that the United States has shown in the elaboration of formal systems of skilled training.

The relative shortage of skill was unquestionably a major factor in spurring American industrialists to plan production so as to subdivide and standardize operations, making it easier to make use of the large numbers of unskilled manpower.

HIGHER EDUCATION AND TECHNICAL COMPETENCE

The foregoing remarks concern the training of craftsmen and the highly skilled workers, not of professional and technical personnel. With respect to the latter, we must take cognizance of the close interplay between the expansion of higher education and the preparation of a large number of technically educated persons. The single most important contribution of higher education to the technical competence of the American labour force has been through the large-scale education and training of engineers and, to a lesser extent, of chemists and other scientists.

Also important is the extent to which the general availability of higher education to women made it relatively easy to provide the large cadre of teachers required for the ever-expanding primary and secondary educational system. Many fathers were willing to send their daughters to college in the belief that the acquisition of a degree—easily convertible into a teaching license—would be insurance if they did not marry or if their marriages failed.

One of the explicit signs of the importance that business came to attach to the educational structure can be seen in the support that certain leading corporations provided a limited number of outstanding engineering and technical schools, such as the Massachusetts Institute of Technology. While broad support in the United States dates from after the world war and, therefore, lags considerably behind the German experience where industrialists had earlier become aware of the importance of science and technology to their own growth and development, it does represent one more evidence of the underlying importance of the vocational element in American education.

With the passage of time, particularly since the second world war, the ties between business and higher education became much closer. Large corporations have made it a practice to support colleges and universities through annual contributions, through grants to capital programmes, and through scholarships. They have also markedly stepped up their recruitment from among the graduates of institutions of higher education. While their interest remains centered on engineers and scientists, they also avidly seek mathematicians, economists, graduates in business management and many others. The fact that business is interested in the college and university graduate has not been lost on young people who are able to pursue higher education. The superior vocational opportunities that lie at the end of the educational road have been major spurs to entrance into the academic competition and to completion of higher studies.

One of the strengths of the American scene in which class background and family income, while important, never determined who went on to higher education to the same extent as in Western Europe, was the openness of the educational system. A student could proceed through college financed by his family; he could work his way through college; he could combine work and study in formal programmes; or he could start to study, drop out to earn money, and then return to complete his studies. The whole structure was highly flexible and remains so.

THE IMPACT OF WORLD WAR II

For education, as for many facets of American life, the second world war marks a watershed since the demands of the war led to a great many new developments. During the depressed 1930s American business had had little or no interest in training for skill. The market was able to provide all the trained persons that were needed, and more. But the vastly expanded levels of demand in wartime, particularly for military products, could be met only by a tremendous training programme, most of which was carried on within industry. The success of American industry in responding to the overriding demands of war through Training Within Industry (T.W.I.) reduced its interest, still further, after the war, in strengthening more formal skill training programmes, such as apprenticeships. Somehow or other, new workers had to 'pick up' the skills they needed.

But the war left an impact upon management training. Many American corporations came out of the war with their executive staffs seriously depleted after a decade of limited or no accessions. Moreover, rapid advances in technology and in management meant that many of the existing managerial group were poorly positioned to deal with the new opportunities that were developing. Taking a leaf from the military which devoted much time and effort to the advanced schooling of its officer corps, more and more companies decided to expand their educational and training efforts which, it should be emphasized again, were focused primarily on their executive personnel.

MANAGEMENT TRAINING

Once business decided to expand its efforts to educate and train its managerial personnel—a decision made easier by the excess profits tax, on the one hand, and the ability to write off training costs under government contracts, on the other—it faced a great many options about how to proceed.

Some companies decided to design a curriculum and to staff courses largely, if not exclusively, with their own resources. Others, seeing advantages in keeping reasonably close control over the effort but recognizing their limitations to cope with such a new and different task, invited outsiders—usually a neighbouring university—to design a programme and to furnish most of the instructional personnel.

Others moved to buy services from the outside. The 1950s saw a tremendous burgeoning of management training programmes under the auspices of universities, trade associations and other groups. Many companies directly associated themselves with one particular programme, while others sent men to different programmes in order to discover the one best suited to their purposes.

Some companies dealt with this matter on a more individualized basis. They arranged to pay the tuition, in whole or in part, for those of their managerial personnel who decided to pursue further education in their spare time. Some companies even went so far as to shorten working hours to enable some employees to attend approved programmes.

At the extreme, a few companies were willing to grant leaves of absence of a year or even of two years, sometimes with full or partial pay, so that staff members could study full-time to acquire higher degrees.

So far we have outlined various educational efforts on behalf of men who have been on the corporate payroll for varying lengths of time. Note must also be taken of the enthusiasm that American business began to show, after the second world war, for shorter or longer periods of training for new employees. There are major companies that provide up to three years of indoctrination. A man is sent from one division to another for periods of three to four months until he has been judged to have gained a good overall picture of the company. More typical are periods of initial training that run from six months to a year. On the other hand, many companies see no virtue in this approach. From the first day on the payroll the employee is assigned to an operational position.

COSTS AND RETURNS

Valiant attempts have been made to estimate the total sums expended by American business to educate and train its work force. Although there is no solid underpinning for such calculations as have been ventured, the total expenditure must be hundreds of millions of dollars, or possibly billions if every type of training is included. However, little serious effort, if any, has been made to determine the effectiveness of these expenditures. Even if no definitive information is available concerning the returns, a few general observations may prove illuminating.

Many companies use their educational and training opportunities as recruitment devices which, there is ground for believing, generate positive responses from many young men. Companies use various types of educational and training programmes as screening devices whereby they obtain evaluations, often from outsiders, of the abilities of men whom they may be considering for promotion. Then again, for many firms, especially those with overseas operations, training programmes serve as bridges for returning executives prior to reassignment. And there are other purposes to which these programmes are put that transcend the acquisition of knowledge or the acquisition of technique.

In an era in which cost-benefit analysis is gaining attention it would be highly desirable to assess more objectively than has yet been done what these several programmes do in fact contribute to management effectiveness and to company profits. But there is little likelihood that such studies can be designed and carried out. As is true of education, generally, the production and consumption effects are hopelessly intertwined.

One test of how important top management really believes these programmes to be will come if and when there is a marked decline in profits. If these training expenditures are not cut back, or are reduced only slightly, this will demonstrate top management's conviction of their worth. But the odds are that, under such conditions, these educational expenditures will be substantially reduced. If this happens we will still be in the dark as to their intrinsic value; all that we will have is a short run estimate of their worth by top management.

PLANT-COMMUNITY RELATIONS

One of the subtle and unsolved problems that has long plagued serious students of vocational education is the proper relationship between the needs of local business for trained workers and the extent to which the local school system should seek to be responsive to these needs. It is a fact that much of the credit for the few good vocational high schools that the United States has developed over the years goes to the active involvement of major local companies with educational authorities. But it is also true—and much more characteristic—that employers have sought to shift some of their training costs to the schools without making any corresponding contribution either by helping to strengthen the curriculum or by building sound bridges from school to the workshop. Only a very few employers have made significant contributions of machinery or materials, or even of ideas or guidance.

Perhaps the most successful pattern of industry-school relations has been developed in Southern California since the outbreak of the second world war. The aerospace industry would not have been able to make a smooth transition from two to four motor planes, from piston to jets, from aircraft to missiles, from missiles to spacecraft had it not been supported by the educational system which contributed both to the initial training and to the retraining of its work force. But California has a highly diversified and well-financed public educational system with a strong junior college system. It is not easy to find a second instance of such a successful interplay between industry and education.

Nevertheless, there are some important new trends worth noting. As late as the 1920s, in the shift of the textile industry from the high wage, high tax area of the North to the low wage, low tax area of the South, management had little concern with the quality of the schooling in the areas in which it was locating. Former farm hands could be quickly trained to operate the new machines. But since the end of the second world war, particularly in the rapidly expanding electronics and chemical industries, management has become much more concerned about the quality of the local educational system. Sophisticated industry needs a sophisticated labour force. Only good schools can produce competent technicians. Therefore, many leading corporations are willing to trade off higher taxes for better schools which can produce a more competent labour force.

There is a further dimension to this relationship between industry and education that must be noted. Top management is deeply concerned about the ready availabiltiy of university complexes with active research programmes and competent staffs. After the loss of its textile industry, the successful recovery of Massachusetts through the expansion of the electronics industry along Route 128 is directly related to the presence of Harvard and M.I.T. within commuting distance. And the same holds true for the growing electronics industry around Palo Alto, California on land owned by Stanford University. Another illustration is the location of the Manned Space Centre at Houston, Texas, which was determined in considerable measure by the presence of Rice Institute, the strongest technological institution in the South.

One safe forecast is that the future location of business enterprises dependent on high level competence will be conditioned more by proximity to educational complexes than by any other single factor.

TRAINING FOR FULL EMPLOYMENT

Although Congress passed the Employment Act in 1946 it did little if anything *directly* about establishing and maintaining a high level of employment in the following fifteen years. The federal government did of course make use of fiscal and monetary policy to keep the economy at a high level but with middling success. By 1961 unemployment was just below the 7 per cent level. At that point a spate of new programmes were enacted: Area Redevelopment (1961), Manpower Development and Training (1962), Vocational Education (1963), Economic Opportunity (1964), Economic Development (1965) and many others.

One theme predominated: Congress committed itself to training and retraining as a major instrument in reducing and eliminating unemployment. The logic of its position was as follows: the failure of large numbers of workers, old and young, to get and to hold jobs reflected either that their skills had become obsolescent because of automation or that they had never had the opportunity to acquire skill because of inadequate schooling and limited work experience.

With this diagnosis, remedial action lay in providing a host of new opportunities for workers to acquire skill. That Congress was not niggardly in its appropriations can be seen from the fact that in the four years since the passage of MDTA it has appropriated about $900 million. For the current year the MDTA budget is over $400 million annually. About 700,000 trainees have completed the programme or are presently enrolled.

Not only has Congress been liberal with funds, it also has been very responsive to the administration's repeated requests for additional flexibility as experience has been gained in handling the special problems of the hard-to-employ. Indicative thereof was the extension of the training period from one to two years with permission to use most of this time for instruction in basic education without which a man cannot profit from technical training.

In the context of the present essay on the relations of business to education and training it should be emphasized that for most of the first three years of the MDTA emphasis was primarily on institutional training with only slight attention to on-the-job training. Most large corporations had little or no interest in this new federal effort; they preferred to take care of their own manpower requirements.

But as the labour market tightened in 1965 and 1966; as the opposition of the trade unions to on-the-job training was reduced; and as the federal administrators recognized more clearly the advantages of on-the-job training over institutional training, a major shift occurred in the MDTA effort. Currently one-third of the MDTA budget is allocated to on-the-job training. In the past, such training had accounted for less than 9 per cent of the total funds although enrolling 25 per cent of those enrolled. Not only is the cost per person much less for on-the-job training but the slippage between training and employment is also greatly reduced. While 75 per cent of the graduates of institutional training are placed in jobs shortly after the completion of their course, the corresponding figure for on-the-job training is over 90 per cent.

Although the United States has gained much valuable experience about the role of training in an active labour market policy as a consequence of the new legislation of the last four years, there is a growing realization in the Congress and outside that the high hopes that had originally been placed on training as the open sesame to full employment were exaggerated. At the end of the summer of 1966 Congress took cognizance of this fact by passing new legislation for the first time aimed directly at the creation of job opportunities for the hard-to-employ.

VOCATIONAL EDUCATION

In 1963, on the basis of an exhaustive report of the deficiencies of vocational education, Congress passed new legislation which vastly increased the federal contribution; introduced flexibility in expenditures so that agriculture and home economics would no longer receive the bulk of the federal funds; and provided new monies for construction, particularly for the erection of area vocational schools. In 1963 the federal government contributed $55 million out of a total of $333 million; the states and the localities provided the remainder. In 1966, total expenditures are likely to total $863 million of which the federal government's share will be $241 million. These figures demonstrate that the last several years have seen a widespread perception at every level of government of the need to strengthen vocational education.

Business leaders have played a role in these efforts at reform and modernization but their role has not been of critical importance. Although they recognize the mounting dangers of the schools flooding the labour market with large numbers of young people without academic or technical competence and they welcome reforms that hold forth a promise of making better use of the public's money, most large companies still look to themselves to train their work force.

Today, there is rising public concern about such problems as the disadvantages of the Negroes; the way in which poverty cripples the young; the failure of most school systems to overcome the handicaps of the slum child; the dangers of an alienated youth; and the corrosive influences of unemployment, especially on youth. These conditions have aroused concern in the business community as well as among other sectors of the American public and have influenced some increase in the participation of businessmen in community planning and in reforms in education, including vocational education. But for every businessman who has become engaged, nine remain on the sidelines. The overwhelming problems of race, poverty, illiteracy, unemployment, alienation fall too far outside the conventional sphere and competence of the businessman to expect more than a minority to become heavily engaged in their solution. Even within the narrow confines of the reform of vocational education, it is questionable whether the business community has yet found a way to play a role commensurate with its knowledge and self-interest. Yet some progress has been made since 1963 and more can be anticipated.

PROBLEMS WITHOUT SIMPLE ANSWERS

While Robert Hutchins is convinced that vocational bias has been the principal source of weakness in American education past and present, most of his fellow citizens would not agree. They believe, and have long acted on the belief, that the educational system has a critically important role to play in preparing young people not only for citizenship but for work. Hutchins has always formulated his attack in extreme terms. Instead of addressing himself to the shifts that schools and colleges can sensibly make from narrow vocationalism to broader educational experiences, he has denied that occupational preparation is a relevant consideration at all and, in so doing, he has vitiated his criticism. However, he does have a point, especially in a world in which basic education is becoming more important. If business were able to recruit high school graduates with fundamental training in mathematics, language, and elementary science, it could train them rapidly on-the-job, but where educational foundations are weak or missing there is little, if anything, that business can do. The real challenge to vocational education is how to instruct the less academically-oriented in academic fundamentals. Few educators recognize this to be their challenge; and fewer still have any notion where the answers lie.

A second challenge relates to the tendency of business to hire specialists at the same time that top management continues to make speeches in favour of men with broad education. The trend to specialization is reinforced by large-scale government contracts for research and development which means that young men's doctoral studies can be supported only as long as they work on some very narrow problems of interest to the sponsoring agency. And there is still a further influence toward specialization caused by the sheer abundance of knowledge and by the organization of universities. The establishment and maintenance of a reasonable balance between general and specialized knowledge is a challenge to which there are no easy answers.

If it be true, as more and more students have come to believe, that the educational system can no longer educate a man for life but can only offer him the tools with which he can continue his education, the basic question arises as to what a man should learn initially in school—and the time he should spend learning it—and what he should learn after he has begun to work. The answers lie shrouded in darkness. We know that business has begun to make substantial investments to enable its managerial and technical staffs to keep abreast of changing knowledge and techniques but the presumptive evidence is that these investments must be substantially enlarged; something that it will not be easy for the profit-seeking enterprise to accomplish. Moreover, much has to be learned about the best ways of making these investments. There is no valid evidence that the experimentation which has been underway since the end of the second world war has really provided satisfactory answers.

Finally, it is necessary to recognize that a man's education is a single process carried on within a variety of institutions: home, school, job, society. The articulation among these several institutions still leaves much to be desired, and here, too, the solution will not come easily.

One concluding comment: the place of work in American life has always been pronounced, hence the counterpoint between education and money-making. Without for a moment subscribing to the doctrine that technology will put an end to want tomorrow, or the day after tomorrow, it is still important to consider whether the relations between education and money-making will alter as our society becomes more affluent, and to determine in what ways they should be altered.

PART VII

New Models and Radical Change

Considerable pessimism exists, especially among the more extreme critics, about the possibility of seriously improving schools by present methods and approaches. Many believe that the schools are incapable of real reform in goals and modes of operating and that not even more money can do the necessary job. They call for more radical forms of change. Usually this means diminished, rather than increased, attention to the existing school system.

Some ask that society, and especially employers, change their attitudes about schooling as a qualification for good jobs and other rewards in life. They argue that schooling does not necessarily prepare people to perform better at their work and that, indeed, many people are educationally "over-qualified" for the jobs at which they work. Not only do they have more formal schooling than their work requires, the education is often even a handicap to performance. As an example, it is said that during the depression of the thirties, dime stores for a time hired as sales girls only college graduates. They found that the girls became discontented with their work and acted snobbishly toward customers. They replaced the college girls with the more "qualified" high school dropouts.

Most employers have assumed that the more educated a person is—the more formal years of schooling he has—the better he will be as a worker and employee. Accumulating evidence suggests that this is far from the case and that schooling can in many cases actually detract from performance in a variety of jobs, from the least to the most highly skilled. The connection between schooling and performance is undoubtedly related to the quality and suitability of such schooling. Obviously, it does little good to teach a student in music to pilot a plane or survey a field. It may even be dysfunctional to insist that the music student study only classical exercises; indeed, it may incapacitate him for invention and creative effort. But suitable training, good education, can obviously contribute to his performance as a musician; in fact, he will not be able to perform at all without some form of instruction.

Unfortunately, much schooling is unproductive and often even fails to serve a useful purpose. We do not know the extent of either the waste or the harm because we have never really thought it necessary (*believing* as we do in the powers of school) to evaluate the effectiveness of schooling in relation to performance. We do not know to what extent law school (as contrasted with the old practice of "reading law," for example) equips the student to be a better lawyer, or how effective the colleges of education or medicine are in preparing students to be teachers and doctors.

In this section, S. M. Miller discusses "credentialism," the inclination of society to overvalue formal credentials and school diplomas. He argues that, if we are to insist on credentials, we should provide students with more ways of getting them than are now available. Specifically, he calls for the "second chance" university as a means of giving dropouts another chance to get the coveted diplomas.

Edgar Z. Friedenberg criticizes the reformers who would simply put a new or perhaps prettier face on an old and decrepit frame. Of the three books he reviews, he says Leonard's is "much more original in his constructions for the future. He is willing even to forego the school as a building and a set of routines altogether and to take the students and their teachers into the streets."

On the other hand, he says, the authors of the other two books "accept the basic social structure and its conventional liberal goals implicitly." They want only to incorporate the disadvantaged into this system. Yet Leonard, he says, "ignores the structure and distribution of power in American society and the ways in which its present schools support that structure, and gushes out in great springs of sentimentality."

None of them, he concludes, wants to change the "underlying social structure that supports the school." Schwebel's book, he says, "is mainly directed against the notion that the disadvantaged are really less capable of educational achievement than the more privileged," and is less concerned than the others, he feels, about the poor quality of educational goals.

Milton Schwebel's reply is really a response to the radical reformers, at least an influential group of them. It is not the idealist, he says, whom educators fear, but "those like many blacks (and their allies in the academic community) who are demanding a greater share of the nation's wealth for their education and for other benefits, and demanding it now." Dr. Friedenberg's alternative "to my opposition to homogeneous ability grouping and the use made of intelligence tests sounds very much like that taken by the opponents of integration." Southern whites have long said something like ". . . a common perspective . . . makes it possible for the people who share it to work together more effectively and enjoy one another less defensively."

The article by Kenneth B. Clark discusses the failings of the present educational system and suggests as alternate models, "possible, realistic, and practical competitors to the present form of urban public school systems": regional state schools, federal regional schools, college- and university-related open schools, industrial demonstration schools, labor union sponsored schools, army schools.

He suggests that such parallel systems of education might provide the competition that our school system needs—the kind of competition that brought abundance to our economic system. Only in this way, he feels, can we recover from the stagnation, discrimination, and segregation which characterize our schools.

BREAKING THE CREDENTIALS BARRIER

by S. M. Miller*

Education has in the past helped make our society more democratic by emphasizing qualifications rather than connections. In this way, it has freed us considerably from the rule of nepotism and arbitrariness. Paradoxically, however, this same insistence on education is now becoming a barrier to democracy—particularly to our national effort to remake the social class structure of this country by reducing the number of its poor and underprivileged.

We have built this barrier through our emphasis on credentials. Indeed, we have become a credential society, in which one's educational level is more important than what he can do. People cannot obtain jobs that they could well fill because they lack educational qualifications. Negroes who dropped out of the educational steeplechase before obtaining a high-school diploma cannot get jobs. Employers do not feel that they are discriminating against these dropouts; they merely regard them as "unqualified." And they persist in their beliefs despite a growing body of evidence, analyzed by Ivar Berg at Columbia University, that the higher-educated have a worse record than the poorly educated at every occupational level—more absenteeism, turnover, dissatisfaction, and probably lower productivity. Indeed, few companies even know the connections between the educational level of their employees and their performance. They have not bothered to probe their records to find out if their beliefs accord with the results of their practice.

I focus on the exclusion of the low-educated, but the processes that we are concerned about build Chinese walls of exclusion around an increasing number of occupations. We have a new guild system of credentials, licenses, certificates—largely built on the base of education—which keeps people out of many occupational chan-

* From *Breaking the Credentials Barrier*, New York University, 1969.

nels. There is increasingly, for many occupations, only one route in—that taken when young. Failing to take that route bars one from it forever.

It is assumed that these credentialing procedures assure a better product—that those who receive the credentials can do much better in the occupation than those who do not; that those who successfully go through the steps needed to gain the credentials are better fitted for the occupation than those who are not interested in doing so or fail in the prescribed climb.

I submit that we do not know if these two assumptions are true. To some extent they are undoubtedly untrue. And a broader assumption—that those who do not go through credentialing activities are unfit for the demands of the occupation—is clearly inaccurate. All of us know of individuals who cannot get jobs that they would be able to perform well because they lack the appropriate credentials—whether it is a high school diploma or a Ph.D.

THE REASONS FOR CREDENTIALISM

Schools today are not a humanizing or an educational force as much as a credentialing agency, sorting people out who do not fit into the regular channels of educational development. Schools function to certify that someone is not harmful rather than to develop the potential of all. Many of the poverty and job-training programs serve the same function.

Why is credentialism growing? One reason is that we like to assume that our world is rational and scientific. We invest confidence in the present structuring of occupations as optimal; then the question becomes how best to fit people into these wisely constructed occupations.

Then we presume that we know enough to sort out "potential" and "ability" from their opposites. Consequently, we repose an enormous misplaced confidence in testing and educational achievement, even when we have quivers of doubt about their "real meaning." Objective measures seem to remove irrationality and discrimination in favor of universally applied, objective rules. Where there has been oversupply of labor and talent, then processes of exclusion on some basis will occur. But when shortages occur as now in many professions, maintenance of exclusion as the core process is obviously peculiar. Such peculiarity is undoubtedly based on some fear—a fear of having to make choices and exercise judgment.

This fear is related to the third reason for the spreading tide of credentialism. Increasingly, the results and achievements are difficult to measure in a service-growing society. Norms of production output are difficult to use in the professions or in government service. Ambiguity of purpose further compounds the measurement problems. If 70 per cent of patients seeing a physician have no ascertainable medical reason for being there, how does one measure the achievement and productivity of the physician? Our uncertainty about what is the product and how to measure effectiveness throws us back to the input—that is, what is the training of the occupational incumbent?

A fourth reason for emphasizing exclusion is the "marshal's baton" syndrome. Napoleon asserted that his military prowess was based not only on his kitchens but on his promotion outlook—every soldier carried a marshal's baton in his knapsack, ready to jump into a command position. In many occupations and organizations, the notion, at least for men, is frequently to employ only "top-notchers" who can move to the peak of the pyramid. Yet the possibilities of moving to the top are slim indeed. In many organizations there is enormous turnover; only a very few stay long, and yet the notion is of "long-distance promotability." Furthermore, as Robert K. Merton has pointed out, there is no possible definition of "top-notchers" nor an adequate number of them, so that organizations and professions are doomed to feel that they are being shortchanged in their share of "top-notchers." The important thing in this context is that the "marshal's baton" syndrome serves to make it appear wise to exclude many, even when talent and ability are in short supply. And certainly it caters to the yearning for prestige to be able to say that the profession or organization has only top-qualified people.

A fifth reason for credentialism is the importance of social appearance. As organizations and professions not only become more uncertain about criteria or performance, but require more intricate "teamwork," getting along with others, appearing "mature," and more acceptable to the public to be serviced, the desirability of insisting on educational credentials grows. For the credentials certify not educational achievement, but personal serviceability—that one knows how to get by, conform, manage. The educational failures—at whatever level—are social failures, bad risks.

Does my attack on credentialism imply that there should be no standards of training, no qualifications for entrance into occupations? I do not think that these are the implications, but I do think my analysis implies the following paragraphs:

There should be a general downgrading of the importance of education as the major credential. Experience and performance should gain greater importance. Many people will not be seriously considered for a job because they lack educational credentials; prospective employers will not even pause to investigate whether the low-educated can perform well. The absence of certificates results in automatic exclusion. Individuals should be judged on what they can do rather than where and how long they have gone to school.

If we treated experience and performance seriously, civil service regulations would be changed so that low education was not an automatic bar to many positions. Testing would be downgraded in favor of trying people in jobs and then assessing their performance. Since much of the job training today is not relevant to work, there should be a strong movement toward "Jobs first, training later." The absence of this practice means that many minority group members are now serving lifetime sentences of low-income and unemployment for their educational delinquencies.

A LIFETIME "DROPOUT" LABEL

"Dropout" is a label assigned at age sixteen; it persists through a lifetime. The consequence is that individuals who may have outgrown the issues which propelled them out of schools or who now have demonstrated and developed considerable skill are still economically disenfranchised because of their youthful educational difficulties. Once a dropout, always a dropout. As in many other aspects of American life, we need a delabeling procedure which takes the curse off individuals who were labeled and cast aside—whether the label is "dropout," "delinquent," or "mental patient."

We need deepened awareness of the respect for the abilities of those who have educational difficulties. We should not believe that our educational hurdles infallibly pick those who should be successes and unerringly cast aside those who should be failures. As we increasingly face the manpower problems of scarce talent, the great hope will be in the cultivation of talents among those who are now disadvantaged.

I do not wish to imply that every poor individual deserves and can use a marshal's baton. But many can. The failure is in cultivating these talents. We have much to learn here that we shall not learn if we persist in the new fashion of denouncing poor families for their deficiencies as educational environments. We then excuse the schools for their failure to learn how to adapt to and develop different varieties of students.

The first step of liberation from the shibboleths of invincible ignorance is to recognize the educational and occupational potential of many who have difficulty with educational systems as presently conducted.

We need new channels of credentialing and new points at which credentials can be expanded. While I am eager to see reduced emphasis on educational credentials, I am realistic enough to know that this kind of change is slow. Consequently, we must make it easier for individuals to obtain educational credentials.

Today, if one does not get twelve or sixteen or eighteen or twenty years of education in the orthodox way of continuous immersion without a break in the apparatus of formal education, one has much reduced chances of gaining credentials.

We should more effectively develop school programs and procedures so that once out does not mean permanently lost. Education and training will be increasingly a discontinuous process for the highly-educated in American society, as they will need new kinds of education at various points in their careers. The same attitude should prevail towards those who have not successfully weathered the educational system to high school or college graduation or beyond. They should be in practice re-entering and benefitting from education and training at various points in their lives.

To some extent the poverty programs are new credentialing systems in our society. Experience in the Job Corps or in the Neighborhood Youth Corps or in Manpower Development and Training Act programs may not be primarily important in terms of providing skills. Rather, employers may be more willing to hire youth who have gone through one of these self-selection and molding systems.

Neighborhood Youth Corps experience may be a new way of getting a credential which employers will accredit and accept.

THE SECOND-CHANCE UNIVERSITY

By multiplying the number of credential channels, we make it easier for individuals to gain them. Those rejected by our educational system at age sixteen might be able to get needed credentials at age eighteen, twenty-two, or thirty. One should have second, third, fourth chances and ways of getting credentials. The more different ways of getting credentials, the fewer the people who would fail to get some brownie points needed for acceptance into the main economy.

What is needed is the idea of a Second-Chance University which permits "dropout" adults to get further and more useful opportunities to get credentials. Experience should be given educational credit; courses should be more relevant to activities—liberal-arts education need not be taught in traditional ways in order to reach traditional ends. While there is need for a formal structure to facilitate re-entry into the educational atmosphere, there is also need to recharge that educational atmosphere so that it is more hospitable and useful to those who have found the established educational practices less than useful or stimulating.

Every credential system should have an escape clause which permits the unusual person to be admitted to the realm of the elect. As professions tighten their qualifications, there is usually a "grandfather clause" which exempts oldtimers from meeting new qualifications. Similarly, at least 5 per cent of each year's entrants into a profession or other highly credentialed occupation should be individuals who have "qualified" in nonusual ways—by taking tests without the traditional educational prerequisites, or by getting credit for enriched experiences, for example. Some collective bargaining contracts have a similar provision: the company is allowed to hire back after a cutback up to 10 per cent of the labor force without paying attention to seniority; the other 90 per cent of the labor force must be rehired according to seniority. The company is permitted some margin of choice and selectivity to meet its production needs.

Without a minimum percentage, it is unlikely that a "creative minority" could in practice obtain unusual entrance into a field. Arbitrariness and favoritism could be avoided by a blue-ribbon panel of decision-makers.

The need here, as in so many other parts of our society, is for making pluralism possible in a complex society. We need a variety of social inventions to provide the structure and the reality of pluralism.

We should not assume that the present structuring of occupations is optimum. Many jobs, for example, call for too many different kinds of skills, and too many time-consuming tasks; they should be broken down into finer tasks for many hands. Many jobs, too, should be enlarged so that those holding them can accept greater responsibility.

The emerging position of the nonprofessional is interesting here. The tasks of a professional job—like those of a social worker or nurse or teacher—can often be broken down into smaller units and combined in ways that permit less trained people to perform them. Sometimes the recombination produces services which the professional was not able to provide. These new positions could reduce the great unmeetable demand for professional services. With the tightening up of educational qualifications, it will be increasingly difficult to turn out an adequate number of professionals. As a consequence, the role of professional should increasingly be that of making it possible for less trained people to do effective work.

But this rational role is moving very slowly. There are grave limitations on what nonprofessionals are allowed to do; there is the absence of a career structure that permits many nonprofessionals to move into the middle class and into the elite stratum of the professional activity.

Professionals are increasingly becoming the gatekeepers of the welfare state, deciding on "professional" grounds who receives what kinds of services and who is allowed to perform various services. The pivotal importance of professional and organizational services has led many of the New Left students to focus on the professionals as the "enemy." While the assault is overdone and frequently misguided, there is something to the view that professions are hardening into barriers rather than aids. The guild-like features of professional occupations frequently are more visible than their commitment to broad social concerns, though there does seem to be important growth here. The emphasis on "competence" and "quality" frequently means a lack of attention to the poor, and others.

The slowness with which the nonprofessional is catching on—in being permitted to do broad jobs, in having chances to move up the occupational ladder—is indicative of the failure of professionals to reassess their roles today.

But I do not want to criticize professionals alone. For business deserves criticism here as well. Private enterprise could probably get needed labor (and at high productivity levels) if it restructured jobs so that the less trained could perform at least parts of them.

In summary, we live in a pseudomeritocracy where individuals are presumed to be selected for talent and placed into appropriate squares. Education becomes the major route to social mobility as the historic alternative routes are shut off.

The general issue which the plight of the poor raises is that of a hardening and narrowing of society into fewer and fewer acceptable routes to economic improvement. We are slowly and rather hazily re-examining the core values and practices of our society. But we must press the search for equity and purpose rather than accept a patina of rationality through reliance on school processes in resolving our value choices.

SENTIMENTAL EDUCATION AND PHONEY REFORMS †

by Edgar Z. Friedenberg*

These books, taken together, are as depressing in their implications for American education as any set of documents could be. This is not because their authors are pessimistic. They are sturdily optimistic; Leonard is even joyful. What is unpleasant about them is not primarily their tone but their relationship to the reality they discuss.

† Comment on three volumes: *The Disadvantaged,* M. Fantini & G. Weinstein; *Education and Ecstacy,* G. Leonard; *Who Can Be Educated,* M. Schwebel.

* Reprinted with permission from *The New York Review of Books.* Copyright © 1968 The New York Review.

All are by influential people. Mario Fantini (Ed.D. Harvard University) is Program Officer of Public Education for the Ford Foundation, in which capacity he serves, in his own words, as a "Change Agent" and a "power source." George Leonard is Senior Editor and West Coast Editorial Manager for *Look*, which heralded *Education and Ecstasy* in a cover story. Milton Schwebel is Dean of the Graduate School of Education at Rutgers University. While it cannot be said that what these men urge will come to pass—for Leonard's vision of the future differs markedly from that of his fellow authors—it will certainly command attention.

The three books contrast sharply with the recent and by now familiar works of Herndon, Holt, Kohl, and Kozol in that their books were all based on the authors' own experiences as classroom teachers. While Schwebel and Weinstein have taught in public schools and Leonard, according to the dust jacket, "has received more national awards for education writing than anyone in the history of magazine journalism," none of these books is a concrete record of what public school teaching has meant—or done—to a particular individual. They are therefore less vivid than their precursors, though Leonard's has a sheen of its own.

They are no less critical of current school practice than Kozol and the others were; but the fact that their works all make specific recommendations for improvement of the schools commits tham to a fundamental acceptance of the American educational system. To compare Kozol and Fantini on schools is like comparing the views of Jonah and the managing director of Marineland on whales. Kozol knows he was lucky to get out again alive; Fantini makes his career by exhibiting an improved specimen each year. Leonard is much more original in his constructions for the future. He is willing even to forego the school as a building and a set of routines altogether and to take the students and their teachers into the streets. This is a very promising suggestion, as are most of Leonard's concrete proposals. But where Schwebel and Fantini and Weinstein accept the basic social structure and its conventional liberal goals implicitly, so that their programs for the disadvantaged stress more effective techniques for incorporating them within it on slightly more favorable terms than it now gives them, Leonard ignores the structure and distribution of power in American society and the ways in which its present schools support that structure, and gushes out in great springs of sentimentality. This glimpse of life in the Kennedy

School of Santa Fe, New Mexico on "Visiting Day, 2001 A.D." illustrates his tone:

"We couldn't go on," Johnny says softly, handing me a history-drama script, thin pages of opaque plastic bound by spiral wire. Thucydides' *The Peloponnesian Wars.*
Nodding, I say, "I know what you mean."
"We tried to become Athenians. We tried to stay in character. But look. . . ."
He hands me the script, pointing out a passage in "The Melian Dialogue." Tears start streaming down his face.
"Don't worry about it, Johnny," I say. "Anyone who can relive the Peloponnesian Wars—or any war without crying is somehow defective. Something's lacking."
"You know, Johnny, until recently education was mostly nothing more than the 'teaching' of facts and concepts. Even as late as the 1960s people could go completely through school and remain what might be called, in the words of those days, not only emotional imbeciles, but sensory ignoramuses and somatic dumbbells."

In calling Leonard's picture of future education sentimental, I am not of course putting down his conception that education is concerned as much with emotional as with intellectual development, or that the two are and should be inextricably linked. This, I agree, should be the heart of any reform in schooling, for the schools of today are as profoundly alienating as Leonard says they are. What is sentimental is his depiction of the necessary improvements as changes in the techniques and attitudes of educators rather than in the society that supports them and its goals. How will students as appropriately lachrymose as those in Leonard's dream manage to take their place in the military-industrial complex? It will certainly not tolerate schools which render the young unfit for its service; so that if the schools are to educate feeling people, the system itself must be changed—and not by T-groups and the Esalen Institute (to which Leonard, as Vice-President, devotes an admiring chapter) but by basic changes in the allocation of power and the functioning of the economy.

In its efforts to avoid confronting these not-very-mysterious determinants of American educational policy Leonard's book turns gimmicky, and wanders into neural physiology, genetics, and computer technology illustrated by snippet references to the thought of Harold Taylor, Marshall McLuhan, J. Bronowski, and a host of other less familiar names—even an old chemistry professor of mine at Stanford, now *emeritus,* who objects to air pollution. The irony of his dream reveals itself in the name he gives his school of the future. The Kennedy School, indeed! All America is a Kennedy School, to which has now been added the Onassis Institute for Advanced Study.

Still it is true, as Leonard observes, that "Education's new domain is not bound in by the conceptual, the factual, the symbolic, it includes every aspect of human existence that is relevant to the new age. . . . Experimenters all around the U.S. and in some other nations as well already have established beachheads in the new domain. . . . Powerful and respected institutions have begun to show strong interest in helping education break out of the old subject-matter entrapment. A Ford Foundation official has become an authority on what he calls 'affective education' (as opposed to 'cognitive education')." Whether Mr. Fantini is that official, Mr. Leonard does not say, though public education is Fantini's domain. His and Mr. Weinstein's study, *The Disadvantaged,* is surely the most important of the books reviewed here; and its limitations make it the most disturbing.

The Disadvantaged is, in many respects, the most sophisticated of the various recent books which are designed to induce the schools to improve instruction for disadvantaged children; and it takes an unusually broad view of who the disadvantaged are. The authors stress that middle-class children, too, are disadvantaged by their limited experience of life and lack of empathy for those less sheltered. While this is essentially the view that leads some English teachers to see Jane Austen and Virginia Woolf as more limited than Genet and Tom Wolfe, which is silly (I would certainly have liked to hear these ladies' appraisal of the Chicago convention, and wish *Esquire* could have sent them there), there is merit in the view when applied to the middle-class ethnocentricity of the schools.

There is a similar merit in the authors' emphasis on what they call, rather sententiously, "the hidden curriculum," by which they mean what the child learns about life from living it. What "the disadvantaged" learn in this way is certainly different from what the schools try, unsuccessfully, to teach them; and much of Fantini and Weinstein's book is devoted to devising ways of reducing this dissonance. But the value of the concept is largely vitiated by the fact that they are either unaware of or indifferent to the presence and function of "the hidden curriculum" in the school itself. The school is an excellent place to learn what life is like, especially for the disadvantaged, and especially if one does not listen to what it says—as they do not—but attend to what it does and what it is. The whole point of Fantini and Weinstein's book is that school should be something different and better for them; and they make concrete suggestions for bringing this about.

But here they find themselves in much the same bind as Leonard found himself in. They do not really want to change the underlying social structure that supports the school; they want to make the school a more effective device for incorporating, rather than excluding, "the disadvantaged." Their book is really about the dropout problem and how to solve it; and the methods proposed add up to a monument of bad faith. One reviewer has praised the book for its honesty—a better word would be brazenness. In consequence, though they have a chapter complaining of "The Phoney School," the reforms they propose would make the schools even phonier. In order to bring about change, they advocate introducing people called "change agents"—if possible funded by two or more outside "power sources"—into the school. "It is probably wise," they observe, "for the change agent to obscure his real role as reformer at the beginning, although gradual exposure of this role will inevitably occur during later stages of development. . . . His first reforms should be of the accepted and familiar variety, such as those which have received widespread publicity, and they should be chosen for their ability to relieve the needs which the school staff perceive to be greatest. . . . The wise agent realizes that, although such solutions are superficial and yield only limited benefits to learning, these concerns are vital to teachers, administrators, and parents [not pupils]; and, if he can satisfy these needs, he can later ask them to consider more radical and fundamental departures from the status quo. . . . As we have said, it is well for the change agent to conceal his true role from school personnel until he has their full confidence and support. By no means should this be construed as a cue for the change agent to alter his true role, but rather that he should disguise his position in such a way that his explicit role is immediately acceptable to school personnel. This leads the change agent to assume a kind of double identity, in which he can accomplish two or more objectives simultaneously. For example, an instructional change agent might be introduced officially as a Helping Teacher."

A bit further on, Fantini and Weinstein tell how they developed this program further so that by "teaming, the change agents were afforded maximum confrontation with the two main levels of the educational hierarchy. The administrative agent, to whom we shall refer as Agent A, and the instructional agent (Agent B) worked closely together and on parallel levels with respect to one another—toward common objectives." As they describe the games of Agent A and Agent B further, I saw that the Ford Foundation must think of itself as The Cat in the Hat, and that Agents A and B are really Things, turned loose in the school to make it more fun on a rainy day.

Dr. Seuss, however, is funny without being vulgar; this is not true of Fantini and Weinstein. Since they emphasize the need to alter the language of the school so that what they call "restricted-code" users will not feel put down or off by "elaborate-code" speakers, their conception of both elegant and gutter speech becomes a central issue in the book. Thus, they suggest:

Contrast the words of the restricted-code mother speaking of the past to her child—'Things were different then, not so messed up'—with those used by the school-teacher; an elaborate-code user—'During the colonial period the pilgrims had a tendency to engage in outdoor activities.' The child raised in an elaborated language may respond to the latter, while the child with a restricted language code may be unable to recognize the clues of 'during, colonial, period, engage, tendency, and activities.'

But whatever the consequences of being "raised in an elaborated language" may be—one, perhaps, is that it makes you write like Fantini and Weinstein—a child reared in a cultivated home would respond to the teacher's statement by recognizing it as the usual dreary nonsense—what specific pathology is meant by "a tendency to engage in outdoor activities"? Or, consider the following small but juicy triumph:

One of the first assignments given to a group of urban teaching trainees was a 'Pupils' Culture Survey.' As part of this assignment, each trainee was to list some of his pupils' most often-used slang expressions with illustrations of their usage. One trainee listed 'bustin' suds,' which, when translated, means 'washing dishes.' Such esoteric knowledge can often be utilized later, as illustrated by the following report from this trainee:
    The sixth-grade class had just returned from lunch, and the teacher expended a considerable amount of energy in getting the pupils settled

down. Then, one of her 'troublemakers' walked in late. 'Why are you late for class?' she asked. 'I was bustin' suds,' was the reply from the latecomer. The rest of the class became interested in the outcome of this exchange. 'Well,' the trainee said, 'I'm sorry you had to wash the dishes but still that's no excuse for coming to class late. Now sit down and start your work.'

The boy's expression changed from amusement to surprise. 'How did you know what "bustin' suds" meant?'

'Oh, I get around,' she replied smugly. 'Now take your seat.'

He did and the class continued its work.

It was a small victory for the trainee, but every new teacher will testify to the importance of such victories in developing control of a new class.

Fantini and Weinstein certainly do. Four bizarre pages of a chapter on "The Teacher: Strength with Sensitivity" are devoted to a precise, detailed, and approving account of a martinet named Miss Tyler in the process of intimidating her class into bewildered submission the first day. Not every young teacher will possess—or desire—all of Miss Tyler's skills, as the following brief excerpt shows:

Before the pupils reached the end of the hall, the teacher said, 'Stop.' Everyone seemed to freeze in place. The teacher again walked by and said, 'One person was not in order.' She did not indicate who this was, but expressed shock through her voice as she looked at each person. Again, mainly through her eyes, and after what seemed to be another very long pause, she said, 'Proceed.'

This sort of thing is probably easier with contact lenses.

I suspect that Fantini and Weinstein derive both their writing styles and their appalling examples from practicing what they preach; as Change Agents they are trying to win the confidence of school personnel by offering familiar-sounding approaches to problems of real concern to them, like keeping children quiet. Keeping children quiet does facilitate teaching, if not learning; and these authors are interested in improving that, too. But their book really shows how little capacity for improvement they attribute to the schools; and how determined they are, nevertheless, to get the disadvantaged into them and keep them there, until they become more like the rest of us. Knowing the grim realities better, they are less inclined than Leonard is to rhapsodize beneath the fantastic Basic Dome of the Kennedy School of the Future. But both authors are equally disinclined to ask what the function of the schools, and of the disadvantaged, in America really is. Leonard proposes that the schools teach people to be human, which would destroy the usefulness of the schools—and perhaps of the people—to American society. Fantini and Weinstein propose that the schools do a more effective job of helping the disadvantaged to realize their potential in society through the schools; they then demonstrate by every word they write how sad and banal a task that will prove to be, even if it can be accomplished. None of them proposes a basically different society in which different schools would be used differently by a society with quite different power-arrangements and purposes—as Paul Goodman, for example, has done. Leonard clearly believes that more humane education would lead to the development of people who would desire and build a better society; but in practice the process works the other way round, if it works at all.

It would be a pleasure to report that Dean Schwebel has contributed a deeper analysis of the failure of the schools with the disadvantaged, which is the social group that concerns him. But he has not. His book is more sharply focused than either of the others on a particular, and quite important issue: the bias that consistently leads school and society to underestimate the educability of the disadvantaged. He analyzes very thoroughly the various forms this bias takes. It is evident in the limitations and irrelevancies of intelligence testing and the homogeneous grouping that is based on the test results; in the sheer biological deprivation of the poor who are then said to be incapable of achievements they have not the energy to undertake; in the definition of achievement according to patterns of expression and social participation which are appropriate only to, and reinforced only by, the middle-class life-style. This last factor, of course, is also what Fantini and Weinstein emphasize, and, indeed, it is what is usually meant when middle-class bias is attributed to the schools.

But Schwebel's book is mainly directed against the notion that the disadvantaged are really less capable of educational achievement than the more privileged. He is less concerned than Fantini and Weinstein, and far less concerned than Leonard, about the poor quality of the goals themselves, even for those capable of achieving them. Sometimes this leads him into a ludicrous circularity:

How many years ago was it (post-Second World War) that educators were still declaring that only 15 or 20 percent of our youth could profit from higher education! How recent history has begun to belie them with increasing college enrollments! More than 53 percent of the 1965 high school graduates entered college, and they represented almost 40 percent of their age group. To those who assert that many of the new crop of college students are not benefiting, the answer is two-fold. How many, one must ask in response, even of the elite families of America 'profited' from their education twenty, thirty, and forty years ago? More affirmatively, one must point to the claims of that awakening giant, the educationally conscious college student body, that the college and university are failing the student, drowning him in irrelevancies, stultifying him with formalism and disciplines that remain immaculately removed from the harsh realities of a dying, addicted, sex-obsessed, hypocritical world bent on destroying its youth in war and its principles in continued deprivation of dignity and equality for millions of its citizens. . . . And if only 9.4 percent of the population twenty-five years and older (in 1964) has completed four or more years of college when it suffers from such shortcomings, imagine to what heights the figures might soar if education in the elementary and secondary schools as well as the colleges improved to meet the needs of contemporary life.

Imagine! Not only was the food terrible, as the old lady complained of her Catskill resort; but the portions were so small! Yet, in this passage, he raises—though he does not pursue—the issue that might have taken him to the heart of the matter that concerns him. How many people "profit" from their education under any circumstances; and what distinguishes them from people who do not? The answer to these questions determines whether bias can be eliminated from the educative process. It also helps in understanding what happens when we try to eliminate it.

Education, after all, is nothing but a set of institutionalized, planned experiences. As Fantini and Weinstein note, it does not teach people any better than the "hidden curriculum" does. In fact, it is much less effective, because people learn from experience by selecting from it what has meaning for them; while in school the personnel try to induce them to attend to symbols and events which may or may not have meaning for them or anybody else. Most curricula at any time or place have little effect on students; though college attendance today does confer one very real benefit—the 2S deferment, without which enrollments would probably fall very rapidly. Education, at any level, appears to be most effective and seems most satisfactory to students on precisely those occasions when its effects are least distinguishable from those of the "hidden curriculum." That is, parents and students are convinced that the schools are doing a good job, and teachers find them agreeable to work in, when curriculum and school routines are congruent with life at home and in the social class they are accustomed to. Under these conditions, students naturally seem to achieve more because what they are asked to achieve, though possibly of very little value in itself, is reinforced by all the students' experiences and serves as a basis for social cohesion between himself and his peers.

One can, of course, argue, as Schwebel does, that this means that intelligence tests are biased, and homogeneous grouping unfair, because they legitimate and rigidify social class differences that are unrelated to potential learning ability. Of course they are, but they are very much related to the present capacity to share experiences meaningfully; and this too is of basic importance to education. Instead of calling the tests biased, and the grouping undemocratic, one could just as truly declare that the tests identify and reward a common perspective which makes it possible for the people who share it to work together more effectively and enjoy one another less defensively. Even then, it is hard to prove that what they learn in school apart from the protracted experience of being there makes much difference—but the experience of being there makes all the difference, and is very different in quality if one is not forced to accommodate continually to routines which one finds bewildering or degrading, and people—teachers or students—who seem frightening, overbearing, or detestable.

To provide optimal educative experiences for children now judged "disadvantaged," what is needed may well be the very contrary of what Schwebel seeks; and much more nearly what the dissenting black communities of New York City demand—education that means something to them now and for the rest of their lives. The kinds of teaching that would help them most is surely not the seductive invasion of their language and life-style that Fantini and Weinstein seem to advocate, but the cool acceptance of that life-style and, with it, of the students' capacity to generate their own kind of order and meaning that James Herndon records so beautifully in *The Way It Spozed to Be*. His classwork, despite the initial handicap of a particularly asinine system of homogeneous grouping, is what I should call genuinely free of bias, and genuinely constructive in its approach to "the disadvantaged" in that it permitted them the opportunity to form as much of a community as their severe sense of degradation permitted; and to recover from that sense, albeit slowly, as Herndon continued to accept them and work with them for what they were.

The difficulty, as Herndon's readers will recall, is that his seemingly very practical approach proved as visionary as Leonard's most glittering proposals; his principal and colleagues could not accept an approach to the "disadvantaged" that respected them without regarding them as a challenge, a menace, or a problem to be solved. This, finally, is what any good teacher must do; and it is what the schools cannot tolerate—if they did, they would fail in their function of socializing the "disadvantaged." For socialization really means inducing them to abandon their old, developing selves as their price of admission to the opportunities afforded by the dominant social system the schools represent. It is this process which, it seems to me, the measures proposed by Schwebel and Fantini and Weinstein promise to facilitate. But acceptance of self is something else; and something that I do not think the schools of our society are likely to foster among those deemed "disadvantaged" within it, however ingenious they may become in dealing with such students.

A RESPONSE: THE STATUS QUO OF RADICAL REFORMERS

by Milton Schwebel*

Edgar Z. Friedenberg's review of my book, *Who Can Be Educated?* (November 21, 1968), missed the central theme and contained a grave error that is not uncommon among astute and liberal-minded writers, especially those who suffer from the ahistorical character of the behavioral sciences. His review is an example of how men of

* Reprinted with permission from *The New York Review of Books*. Copyright © 1969 The New York Review.

good will sometimes come up with solutions that are hardly different from those of their enemies. So strong are the subtle social influences to retain practices that favor the established order, that they must be unmasked in any analysis of human ability and education.

There are at least two ways of perpetuating the status quo in education in the guise of radical change, and Dr. Friedenberg employed both of them. One is to insist that goal-setting is an indispensable prelude to change in social institutions, when in fact institutions change as new groups enter them and gain power; and when in fact goals have meaning at all only as labels given to the direction in which social-historical forces are moving an institution. Goals based on wish and desire are ideals; they are the wonderful stuff of which dreams are made. What educator with body still warm would not identify with the goal of making all students "independent creative thinkers"? Who but the historically untutored is going to believe that our system in the foreseeable future at least could tolerate a population of such character? Revolutions in education we need; but anyone who knows the dynamics of change understands that the school system is not going to undergo such transformations except in the context of broad social upheavals. To make major goal change the central plank in the educational platform today is to divert attention from the demands of those who want not a change in goals but a fair share of education, 3 R's and all, the good and the bad—and who *in the process of entering it, help to change its very nature.*

No one in the educational establishment feels threatened by idealists who, in answer to the crying need for educational opportunity, demand that goals be changed, because leaders have no fear of modern-day Joshuas no matter how loud their horn. The establishment, in the form of one or another professional association, does in fact welcome the *enfants terribles* at national meetings to excite the membership and insure high attendance, and the impact on the beliefs and the behavior of the professional doesn't survive the hospitality hour that follows the lecture in the grand ballroom.

No, it's not the idealist who is feared but those like many blacks (and their allies in the academic community) who are demanding a greater share of the nation's wealth for their education and for other benefits, and demanding it now. They want the money and a voice on how it is to be spent. They want no pie in the sky; they want education now. They want their children to learn to read.

And learn to read they will. They value this ability and well they might for it is to their advantage and the benefit of the educational system that they enter it and compel it to assimilate them, a process which, as has been the case with the entry of other formerly alien groups, changes the system for the better.

To Friedenberg (and other idealists) the schools, being essentially socialization agents, demand of children in return for success the giving up of their "developing selves." How right he is (as I elaborated repeatedly) that our schools stifle curiosity and individuality, that they have many basic faults—but they also have the power to offer or deny the opportunity to learn those things that give individuals the power to read, to understand and change the system and even to recover a measure of what has been taken from them. And the black people today—like others before them—are insisting on that kind of opportunity for their children. No matter the shortcomings, they want it, and in their demanding and fighting for it, they are changing the schools, just as the struggles of the Berkeley and Howard students are inexorably, though all too slowly, altering the universities. Had Friedenberg taken note of the historical interpretation in the book, he would have understood what I meant when I said that much of the irrelevance and sterility in education was due to the need to exclude from the classroom those large realms of knowledge and human experience that explain the very inequalities in the schools and the larger society; and as black Americans change their status, they change—yes, too slowly— even the substance of education.

Those in America who have been oppressed—those now and in the past—haven't asked for isolation and alienation. And the black people didn't ask for it today. They were given no choice, and that is why they demanded their own schools. They wanted integrated schools and were denied them. Compelled now to have segregated schools, they want them to be their own. Very likely their own schools will soon take on some of the undesirable attributes of the others, if they don't already have them, but the people in the community will at least be able to see to it that the children have the chance to learn what others do and to become as others do, and it is no man's right in old paternalistic fashion to "protect" them from those evils. Segregated or integrated, all the people in the community have a right to more education even if this education is far from being as good as it could and ought to be, and even if it has harmful effects. That the schools participate in the alienating and dehumanizing processes of our society is a regrettable fact and good reason to attack the social-economic conditions that produce alienation. It most certainly is not good reason to decry, as Friedenberg did, this educator's prediction that higher education will be open to far more students "especially as the elementary and secondary schools as well as the colleges improve to meet the needs of contemporary life."

The second way of perpetuating the old system under the guise of advocating change is to equivocate about the only theoretical modification—that about educability—that could materially influence the behavior of all people involved in the education of children, including the parents and children themselves. I examined the long-functioning theory of mental ability that pervades our society and our schools, showed the historical role it has played, and gave evidence to the effect that an open-ended theory of ability is scientifically a more viable one and essential to achieve the objectives that all the oppressed people are or will be setting for us.

My reviewer is guilty of projection: he has ascribed to me his chief concern. I did not ask how many people "profit" from their education under any circumstances, nor was my book "mainly directed against the notion that the disadvantaged are really less capable of educational achievement than the more privileged." My aim was to help free the schools from the shackles of the prevailing closed theory which by definition precludes universal education.

Dr. Friedenberg's alternative to my opposition to homogeneous ability grouping and the use made of intelligence tests sounds very much like that taken by the opponents of integration. Southern whites have long said something like ". . . a common perspective . . . makes it possible for the people who share it to work together more effectively and enjoy one another less defensively." They said it before the Supreme Court. Of course, Dr. Friedenberg meant a common perspective as reflected in test scores but this, as many of us have pointed out, means social and racial separation.

The have-nots in education have a right to insist that teachers and educators be held accountable to see that their children get what others get. They have the right to demand it, and we the obligation to provide it. Our responsibility is to do everything possible to achieve that, and while the question of goals for education in general is a related issue, the first (new opportunity) is not dependent on the second (goal change) and, in fact, achievement of the first will lead to some positive changes in the second. However, the qualities in our educational system that are abominable are part of the fabric of our large system, and only the naive believe that one can establish ideological islands. That is why I wrote the following about big changes in a passage that Dr. Friedenberg seemed to have missed: "As to when this will come about, history's tentative answer is not a pleasant one. It will come after much travail and many wasted years, after more of what we have witnessed in the past few years in exacerbated form." In the meantime, those who strive to improve our schools will have to guard against the advice of our idealist friends, those stout defenders of individualism who like an overstuffed banker-type character in a Gropper cartoon of the Thirties luxuriously ensconced in his favorite chair at the club, brandy in one hand and thick cigar in the other, declaims about the need to protect the masses from the evils of overindulgence and idleness.

ALTERNATIVE PUBLIC SCHOOL SYSTEMS

by Kenneth B. Clark*

It is now clear that American public education is organized and functions along social and economic class lines. A bi-racial public school system wherein approximately 90 per cent of American children are required to attend segregated schools is one of the clearest manifestations of this basic fact. The difficulties encountered in attempting to desegregate public schools in the South as well as in the North point to the tenacity of the forces seeking to prevent any basic change in the system.

The class and social organization of American public schools is consistently associated with a lower level of educational efficiency in the less privileged schools. This lower efficiency is expressed in

* From Paper for U.S. Commission on Civil Rights, Nov. 16–18, 1967.

terms of the fact that the schools attended by Negro and poor children have less adequate educational facilities than those attended by more privileged children. Teachers tend to resist assignments in Negro and other underprivileged schools and generally function less adequately in these schools. Their morale is generally lower; they are not adequately supervised; they tend to see their students as less capable of learning. The parents of the children in these schools are usually unable to bring about any positive changes in the conditions of these schools.

The pervasive and persistent educational inefficiency which characterizes these schools results in:

(1) marked and cumulative academic retardation in a disproportionately high percentage of these children, beginning in the third or fourth grade and increasing through the eighth grade;

(2) a high percentage of dropouts in the junior and senior high schools of students unequipped academically and occupationally for a constructive role in society;

(3) a pattern of rejection and despair and hopelessness resulting in massive human wastage.

Given these conditions, American public schools have become significant instruments in the blocking of economic mobility and in the intensification of class distinctions rather than fulfilling their historic function of facilitating such mobility. In effect, the public schools have become captives of a middle class who have failed to use them to aid others to move into the middle class. It might even be possible to interpret the role of the controlling middle class as that of using the public schools to block further mobility.

What are the implications of this existing educational inefficiency? In the national interest, it is a serious question whether the United States Government can afford the continuation of the wastage of human resources at this period of world history. Although we cannot conclusively demonstrate a relation between educational inefficiency and other symptoms of personal and social pathology such as crime, delinquency, and pervasive urban decay, there is strong evidence that these are correlates.

Increasing industrialization and automation of our economy will demand larger numbers of skilled and educated and fewer uneducated workers. The manpower needs of contemporary America require business and industry to pay for the added burden of re-educating the mis-educated. This is a double taxation. The burdens of the present inefficient public education include this double taxation in addition to the high cost of crime and family stability and the artificial constriction of the labor and consumer market.

Beyond these material disadvantages are the human costs inherent in the failure to achieve equality of educational opportunity. This dehumanization contributes significantly to the cycle of pathology—poor education, menial jobs or unemployment, family instability, group and personal powerlessness. This passive pathology weakens the fabric of the entire society.

OBSTACLES TO THE ATTAINMENT OF EFFICIENT EDUCATION

The obstacles which interfere with the attainment of efficient public education fall into many categories. Among them are those obstacles which reflect historical premises and dogmas about education, administrative realities, and psychological assumptions and prejudices.

The historical premises and dogmas include such fetishes as the inviolability of the "neighborhood school" concept which might include the belief that schools should be economically and racially homogeneous. The administrative barriers involve such problems as those incurred in the transportation of children from residential neighborhoods to other areas of the city. Here again the issue is one of relative advantages of the *status quo* versus the imperatives for change.

The residual psychological prejudices take many forms and probably underlie the apparent inability of society to resolve the historical and administrative problems. Initially the academic retardation of Negro children was explained in terms of their inherent racial inferiority. The existence of segregated schools was supported either by law or explained in terms of the existence of segregated neighborhoods. More recently the racial inferiority or legal and custom interpretations have given way to more subtle explanations and support for continued inefficient education. Examples are theories of "cultural deprivation" and related beliefs that the culturally determined educational inferiority of Negro children will impair the ability of white children to learn if they are taught in the same classes. It is assumed that because of their background, Negro children and their parents are poorly motivated for academic achievement and will not only be unable to compete with white children but will also retard the white children. The implicit and at times explicit assumption of these cultural deprivation theories is that the environmental deficits which Negro children bring with them to school make it difficult, if not impossible, for them to be educated either in racially homogeneous or heterogeneous schools. This point of view, intentionally or not, tends to support the pervasive rejection of Negro children and obscures and intensifies the basic problem.

There are more flagrant sources of opposition to any effective desegregation of American public schools. White Citizens' Councils in the South, parents' and taxpayers' groups in the North, and the control of boards of education by whites who identify either overtly or covertly with the more vehement opposition to change are examples of effective resistance. School officials and professional educators have defaulted in their responsibility for providing educational leadership. They have tended, for the most part, to go along with the level of community readiness and the "political realities." They have been accessories to the development and use of various subterfuges and devices for giving the appearance of change without its substance and, in doing so, have failed to present the problem of the necessary school reorganization in educational terms. This seems equally true of teachers and teachers' organizations. In some cases, teachers, textbooks, and other teaching materials have either contributed to or failed to counteract racialism.

Within the past two years another formidable and insidious barrier in the way of the movement towards effective, desegregated public schools has emerged in the form of the black power movement and its demands for racial separatism. Some of the more vocal of the black power advocates who have addressed themselves to the problems of education have explicitly and implicitly argued for Negroes' control of "Negro Schools." Some have asserted that there should be separate school districts organized to control the schools in all-Negro residential areas; that there should be Negro Boards of Education, Negro superintendents of schools, Negro faculty, and Negro curricula and materials. These demands are clearly a rejection of the goals of integrated education and a return to the pursuit of the myth of an efficient "separate but equal"—or the pathetic wish for a separate and superior—racially-organized system of education. One may view this current trend whereby some Negroes themselves seem to be asking for a racially segregated system of education as a reflection of the frustration resulting from white resistance to genuine desegregation of the public schools since the *Brown* decision and as a reaction to the reality that the quality of education in the *de facto* segregated Negro schools in the North and the Negro schools in the South has steadily deteriorated under the present system of white control.

In spite of these explanations, the demands for segregated schools can be no more acceptable coming from Negroes than they are coming from white segregationists. There is no reason to believe and certainly there is no evidence to support the contention that all-Negro schools, controlled by Negroes, will be any more efficient in preparing American children to contribute constructively to the realities of the present and future world. The damage inherent in racially isolated schools was persuasively documented by the comprehensive study conducted by the United States Commission on Civil Rights.[1]

Furthermore, the more subtle and insidious educational deprivation for white children who are required to attend all-white schools is furthered by both the black and the white advocates of racially homogeneous schools.

ATTEMPTS AT REMEDIES

In spite of these obstacles in the path of genuine desegregation of American public schools and the attainment of effective, nonracially constrained education for all American children, there have been persistent attempts to compensate for the deficits of racial isolation in the American public schools. A tremendous amount of energy and money has been expended in the attempt to develop special programs designed to improve the academic achievement of Negro children, who are the most obvious victims of inferior, racially segregated public schools.

The United States Commission on Civil Rights report, *Racial*

[1] U.S. Commission on Civil Rights, *Racial Isolation in the Public Schools* (Washington: U.S. Government Printing Office, 1967).

Isolation in the Public Schools, has presented facts which raise questions concerning the long-range effectiveness of these programs. There is some evidence that these special programs do some good and help some children; but they clearly underline the inadequacy of the regular education these children receive. In addition to the fact that they obscure the overriding reality that underprivileged children are being systematically short-changed in their regular segregated and inferior schools, these programs may also be seen as a type of commitment to the continuation of segregated education.

If one accepts the premise which seems supported by all available evidence, and above all by the reasoning of the *Brown* decision, that racially segregated schools are inherently inferior, it would seem to follow that all attempts to improve the quality of education in all-Negro and all-white schools would have necessarily limited positive effects. All programs designed to raise the quality of education in racially homogeneous schools would therefore have to be seen as essentially evasive programs or as the first stage in an inferior approach to a serious plan for effective desegregation of public schools. Given the resistance to an immediate reorganization of the present system of racially organized schools so as to create a more effective system of racially heterogeneous schools, however, one may be required to attempt to increase the efficiency of education in all-Negro schools as a necessary battle in the larger struggle for racially desegregated schools.

The problem of the extent to which it is possible to provide excellent education in a predominantly Negro school should be re-examined thoroughly in spite of the basic premise of the *Brown* decision that racially segregated schools are inherently inferior. Some questions which we must now dare to ask and seek to answer as the basis for a new strategy in the assault against the inhumanity of the American system of racial segregation are:

(1) Is the present pattern of massive educational inferiority and inefficiency which is found in predominantly Negro schools inherent and inevitable in racially segregated schools?

(2) Is there anything which can be done within the Negro schools to raise them to a tolerable level of educational efficiency—or to raise them to a level of educational excellence?

If the answer to the first question is *yes* and to the second question is *no,* then the strategy of continued and intensified assault on the system of segregated schools is justified and should continue unabated since there is no hope of raising the quality of education for Negro children as long as they are condemned to segregated schools—there is no hope of salvaging them. If, on the other hand, the answers to the above questions are reversed, it would suggest that a shift in strategy and tactics, without giving up the ultimate goals of eliminating the dehumanizing force of racial segregation from American life, would be indicated. This shift would suggest that given the present strong and persistent resistance to any serious and effective desegregation of our public schools, that the bulk of the available organizational, human, and financial resources and specialized skills be mobilized and directed toward obtaining the highest quality of education for Negro students without regard to the racial composition of the schools which they attend. This attempt would demand a massive, system-wide educational enrichment program designed to obtain educational excellence in the schools attended by Negro children.

Recent experiences in New York City, Boston, Chicago, Philadelphia and other northern cities reveal that this temporary shift in the battleground will not in itself lead to any easier victory. School boards and public school officials seem as resistant to developing or implementing programs designed to improve the quality and efficiency of education provided for Negro children in segregated schools as they are deaf to all requests for effective desegregation plans and programs. The interests and desires of white middle-class parents, and the interests of the increasingly powerful teachers' federations and professional supervisory associations are invariably given priority over the desire of Negro parents for nonsegregated quality education for their children. The interests of the white parents, teachers, and supervisors are often perceived by them as inimical to the desires of the Negro parents. Furthermore, the capture and control of the public schools by the white middle-class parents and teachers provided the climate within which the system of racially segregated and inferior schools could be developed, expanded and reinforced and within which the public schools became instruments for blocking rather than facilitating the upward mobility of Negroes and other lower-status groups. One, therefore, could not expect these individuals and groups to be sympathetic and responsive to the pleas of Negro parents for higher quality education for their children. Negro parents and organizations must accept and plan their strategy in terms of the fact that adversaries in the battle for higher quality education for Negro children will be as numerous and as formidable as the adversaries in the battle for nonsegregated schools. Indeed they will be the same individuals, officials, and groups in different disguises and with different excuses for inaction but with the same powerful weapons of evasion, equivocation, inaction, or tokenism.

An effective strategy for the present and the future requires rigorous and honest appraisal of all of the realities, a tough-minded diagnosis of the strengths and weaknesses of the Negro and his allies. We cannot now permit ourselves to be deluded by wishful thinking, sentimental optimism, or rigid and oversimplified ideological postures. We must be tough-mindedly pragmatic and flexible as we seek to free our children from the cruel and dehumanizing, inferior and segregated education inflicted upon them by the insensitive, indifferent, affable, and at times callously rigid custodians of American public education.

In developing an appropriate strategy and the related flexible tactics, it must be clearly understood that the objective of improving the quality of education provided for Negro children is not a substitute for or a retreat from the fundamental goal of removing the anachronism of racially segregated schools from American life. The objective of excellent education for Negro and other lower-status children is inextricably linked with the continuing struggle to desegregate public education. All of the public school, college, and professional school civil-rights litigation instituted by the legal staff of the NAACP arose from recognition of the obvious fact that the segregated schools which Negroes were forced by law to attend were inferior and therefore damaging and violative of the equal protection clause in the 14th amendment of the United States Constitution.

The suggested shift in emphasis from desegregation to quality of education is not a retreat into the blind alley of accepting racial separation as advocated by the Negro nationalist groups, nor is it the acceptance of defeat in the battle for desegregation. It is rather a regrouping of forces, a shift in battle plans and an attempt to determine the most vulnerable flanks of the opposition as the basis for major attack. The resisting educational bureaucracies, their professional staffs, and the segment of the white public which has not yet been infected fatally by the American racist disease are most vulnerable to attack on the issue of the inferior quality of education found in Negro schools and the need to institute a plan immediately to raise the educational level of these schools. The economic, political, military, social-stability, international democratic, humane, and self-interest arguments in favor of an immediate massive program for educational excellence in predominantly Negro schools are so persuasive as to be irrefutable. The expected resistance should be overcome with intelligently planned and sustained efforts.

The first phase of an all-out attack on the inferior education now found in racially segregated schools should be coordinated with a strategy and program for massive and realistic desegregation of entire school systems. This more complicated phase of the over-all struggle will continue to meet the resistances of the past with increased intensity. It will be necessary, therefore, to break this task down into its significant components and determine the timing and phasing of the attack on each or combinations of the components. For example:

The evidence and arguments demonstrating the detrimental effects of segregated schools on the personality and effectiveness of white children should be gathered, evaluated, and widely disseminated in ways understandable to the masses of whites.

The need to reorganize large public school systems away from the presently inefficient and uneconomic neighborhood schools to more modern and viable systems of organization such as educational parks, campuses, or clusters must be sold to the general public in terms of hard dollars and cents and educational efficiency benefiting all children rather than in terms of public-school desegregation.

The need to consolidate small, uneconomic, and relatively ineffective school districts into larger educational and fiscal systems in order to obtain more efficient education for suburban and exurban children must also be sold in direct practical terms rather than in terms of desegregation of schools.

The need to involve large metropolitan regional planning in the mobilization, utilization, and distribution of limited educational resources on a more efficient level must also be explored and discussed publicly.

The movement toward decentralization of large urban school systems must be carefully monitored in order to see that decentralization does not reinforce or concretize urban public school segregation—and to assure that decentralization is consistent with the more economically determined trend toward consolidation and regional planning allocation of resources and cooperation.

A final indication that phase one, the struggle for excellent education for Negro children in ghetto schools, is not inconsistent with phase two, the struggle for nonsegregated education for all children, is to be seen in the fact that if it were possible to raise the quality of education provided for Negro children who attend the urban schools to a level of unquestioned excellence, the flight of middle-class whites to the suburbs might be stemmed and some who have left might be attracted back to the city. Hence, phase one activity would increase the chances of obtaining nonsegregated education in our cities. Similarly, some of the program suggestions of phase two such as educational parks and campuses and the possibilities of regional planning and educational cooperation across present municipal boundaries could lead to substantial improvements in the quality of education offered to inner-city children.

The goal of high quality education for Negro and lower-status children and the goal of public school desegregation are inextricable; the attainment of the one will lead to the attainment of the other. It is not likely that there could be effective desegregation of the schools without a marked increase in the academic achievement and personal and social effectiveness of Negro and white children. Neither is it possible to have a marked increase in the educational efficiency of Negro schools and the resulting dramatic increase in the academic performance of Negro children without directly and indirectly facilitating the process of public school desegregation.

PROBLEMS OF EDUCATIONAL MONOPOLY

It is possible that all attempts to improve the quality of education in our present racially segregated public schools and all attempts to desegregate these schools will have minimal positive results. The rigidity of present patterns of public school organization and the concomitant stagnation in quality of education and academic performance of children may not be amenable to any attempts at change working through and within the present system.

Until the influx of Negro and Puerto Rican youngsters into urban public schools, the American public school system was justifiably credited with being the chief instrument for making the American dream of upward social, economic, and political mobility a reality. The depressed immigrants from southern and eastern Europe could use American public schools as the ladder toward the goals of assimilation and success. The past successes of American public education seem undebatable. The fact that American public schools were effective mobility vehicles for white American immigrants makes even more stark and intolerable their present ineffectiveness for Negro and Puerto Rican children. Now it appears that the present system of organization and functioning of urban public schools is a chief blockage in the mobility of the masses of Negro and other lower-status minority group children. The inefficiency of their schools and the persistence and acceptance of the explanations for this generalized inefficiency are clear threats to the viability of our cities and national stability. The relationship between long-standing urban problems of poverty, crime and delinquency, broken homes—the total cycle of pathology, powerlessness, and personal and social destructiveness which haunts our urban ghettos—and the breakdown in the efficiency of our public schools is now unavoidably clear. It is not enough that those responsible for our public schools should assert passively that the schools merely reflect the pathologies and injustices of our society. Public schools and their administrators must assert boldly that education must dare to challenge and change society toward social justice as the basis for democratic stability.

There remains the disturbing question—a most relevant question probably too painful for educators themselves to ask—whether the selection process involved in training and promoting educators and administrators for our public schools emphasizes qualities of passivity, conformity, caution, smoothness, and superficial affability rather than boldness, creativity, substance, and the ability to demand and obtain those things which are essential for solid and effective public education for all children. If the former is true and if we are dependent upon the present educational establishment, then all hopes for the imperative reforms which must be made so that city public schools can return to a level of innovation and excellence are reduced to a minimum, if not totally eliminated.

The racial components of the present crisis in urban public education clearly make the possibilities of solution more difficult and may contribute to the passivity and pervading sense of hopelessness of school administrators. Aside from any latent or subtle racism which might infect school personnel themselves, they are hampered by the gnawing awareness that with the continuing flight of middle-class whites from urban public schools and with the increasing competitions which education must engage in for a fair share of the tax dollar, it is quite possible that Americans will decide deliberately or by default to sacrifice urban public schools on the altars of its historic and contemporary forms of racism. If this can be done without any real threat to the important segments of economic and political power in the society and with only Negro children as the victims, then there is no realistic basis for hope that our urban public schools will be saved.

The hope for a realistic approach to saving public education in American cities seems to this observer to be found in a formula whereby it can be demonstrated to the public at large that the present level of public school inefficiency has reached an intolerable stage of public calamity. It must be demonstrated that minority group children are not the only victims of the monopolistic inefficiency of the present pattern of organization and functioning of our public schools.

It must be demonstrated that white children—privileged white children whose parents understandably seek to protect them by moving to suburbs or by sending them to private and parochial schools—also suffer both potentially and immediately.

It must be demonstrated that business and industry suffer intolerable financial burdens of double and triple taxation in seeking to maintain a stable economy in the face of the public school inefficiency which produces human casualties rather than constructive human beings.

It must be demonstrated that the cost in correctional, welfare, and health services are intolerably high in seeking to cope with consequences of educational inefficiency—that it would be more economical, even for an affluent society, to pay the price and meet the demands of efficient public education.

It must be demonstrated that a nation which presents itself to the world as the guardian of democracy and the protector of human values throughout the world cannot itself make a mockery of these significant ethical principles by dooming one-tenth of its own population to a lifetime of inhumane futility because of remediable educational deficiencies in its public schools.

These must be understood and there must be the commitment to make the average American understand them if our public schools and our cities are to be effective. But it does not seem likely that the changes necessary for increased efficiency of our urban public schools will come about because they should. Our urban public school systems seem muscle-bound with tradition. They seem to represent the most rigid forms of bureaucracies which, paradoxically, are most resilient in their ability and use of devices to resist rational or irrational demands for change. What is most important in understanding the ability of the educational establishment to resist change is the fact that public school systems are protected public monopolies with only minimal competition from private and parochial schools. Few critics of the American urban public schools —even severe ones such as myself—dare to question the givens of the present organization of public education in terms of local control of public schools, in terms of existing municipal or political boundaries, or in terms of the rights and prerogatives of boards of education to establish policy and select professional staff—at least nominally or titularly if not actually. Nor dare the critics question the relevance of the criteria and standards for selecting superintendents, principals, and teachers, or the relevance of all of these to the objectives of public education—producing a literate and informed public to carry on the business of democracy—and to the goal of producing human beings with social sensitivity and dignity and creativity and a respect for the humanity of others.

A monopoly need not genuinely concern itself with these matters. As long as local school systems can be assured of state aid and increasing federal aid without the accountability which inevitably comes with aggressive competition, it would be sentimental, wishful thinking to expect any significant increase in the efficiency of our public schools. If there are no alternatives to the present system—short of present private and parochial schools which are approaching their limit of expansion—then the possibilities of improvement in public education are limited.

ALTERNATIVE FORMS OF PUBLIC EDUCATION

Alternatives—realistic, aggressive, and viable competitors—to the present public school systems must be found. The development of such competitive public school systems will be attacked by the defenders of the present system as attempts to weaken the present system and thereby weaken, if not destroy, public education. This type of expected self-serving argument can be briefly and accurately disposed of by asserting and demonstrating that truly effective competition strengthens rather than weakens that which deserves to survive. I would argue further that public education need not be identified with the present system of organization of public schools. Public education can be more broadly and pragmatically defined in terms of that form of organization and functioning of an educational system which is in the public interest. Given this definition, it becomes clear that an inefficient system of public systems is not in the public interest:

—a system of public schools which destroys rather than develops positive human potentialities is not in the public interest;
—a system which consumes funds without demonstrating effective returns is not in the public interest;
—a system which insists that its standards of performance should not or cannot be judged by those who must pay the cost is not in the public interest;
—a system which says that the public has no competence to assert that a patently defective product is a sign of the system's inefficiency and demands radical reforms is not in the public interest;
—a system which blames its human resources and its society while it quietly acquiesces in, and inadvertently perpetuates, the very injustices which it claims limit its efficiency is not in the public interest.

Given these assumptions, therefore, it follows that alternative forms of public education must be developed if the children of our cities are to be educated and made constructive members of our society. In the development of alternatives, all attempts must at the same time be made to strengthen our present urban public schools. Such attempts would involve re-examination, revision, and strengthening of curricula, methods, personnel selection, and evaluation; the development of more rigorous procedures of supervision, reward of superior performance, and the institution of a realistic and tough system of accountability, and the provision of meaningful ways of involving the parents and the community in the activities of the school.

The above measures, however, will not suffice. The following are suggested as possible, realistic, and practical competitors to the present form of urban public school systems:

Regional State Schools. These schools would be financed by the states and would cut across present urban-suburban boundaries.

Federal Regional Schools. These schools would be financed by the Federal Government out of present state aid funds or with additional federal funds. These schools would be able to cut through state boundaries and could make provisions for residential students.

College- and University-Related Open Schools. These schools would be financed by colleges and universities as part of their laboratories in education. They would be open to the public and not restricted to children of faculty and students. Obviously, students would be selected in terms of constitutional criteria and their percentage determined by realistic considerations.

Industrial Demonstration Schools. These schools would be financed by industrial, business, and commercial firms for their employees and selected members of the public. These would not be vocational schools—but elementary and comprehensive high schools of quality. They would be sponsored by combinations of business and industrial firms in much the same way as churches and denominations sponsor and support parochial or sectarian schools.

Labor Union Sponsored Schools. These schools would be financed and sponsored by labor unions largely, but not exclusively, for the children of their members.

Army Schools. The Defense Department has been quietly effective in educating some of the casualties of our present public schools. It is hereby suggested that they now go into the business of repairing hundreds of thousands of these human casualties with affirmation rather than apology. Schools for adolescent drop-outs or educational rejects could be set up by the Defense Department adjacent to camps—but not necessarily as an integral part of the military. If this is necessary, it should not block the attainment of the goal of rescuing as many of these young people as possible. They are not expendable on the altar of anti-militarism rhetoric.

With strong, efficient, and demonstrably excellent parallel systems of public schools, organized and operated on a quasi-private level, and with quality control and professional accountability maintained and determined by Federal and State educational standards and supervision, it would be possible to bring back into public education a vitality and dynamism which are now clearly missing. Even the public discussion of these possibilities might clear away some of the dank stagnation which seems to be suffocating urban education today. American industrial and material wealth was made possible through industrial competition. American educational health may be made possible through educational competition.

If we succeed, we will have returned to the dynamic, affirmative goal of education; namely, to free man of irrational fears, superstitions, and hatreds. Specifically, in America the goal of democratic education must be to free Americans of the blinding and atrophying shackles of racism. A fearful, passive, apologetic, and inefficient educational system cannot help in the attainment of these goals.

If we succeed in finding and developing these and better alternatives to the present educational inefficiency, we will not only save countless Negro children from lives of despair and hopelessness; and thousands and thousands of white children from cynicism, moral emptiness, and social ineptness—but we will also demonstrate the validity of our democratic promises. We also will have saved our civilization through saving our cities.

PART VIII

The Federal Presence

The federal government has undoubtedly played the leading role during the past decade in the formulation of new school policy. All branches of the federal government have been involved. Perhaps the U.S. Supreme Court has played the most central role, but Congress has also for the first time in American history entered into the formulation of policy for, and the financial support of, public elementary and secondary schools. The executive branch, too, has entered the educational scene, and its presence has been felt. President Johnson, for example, requested the report on civil disorder, a section of which is included here, and perhaps because he began his career as a teacher, he took a personal interest in educational affairs. The U.S. Office of Education—part of the executive branch—has sponsored many new programs and some pathfinding probes into the status of American education. Other executive departments have been similarly involved in educational change.

Considered in this section are two major topics: the fiscal problem and federal policy.

Until we find a way to buy better education with less money, we must concern ourselves with the fact that educational costs are increasing dramatically, while old sources of funding are drying up, and with the hotly debated proposition that more money buys better schools. School spending is rising faster than GNP or personal income. From 1957 to 1967, the average per-capita personal income increased 54 percent, while expenditures per pupil rose 86 percent.

Economist Leon Keyserling, in a selection from a monograph on the subject, tells us what we will need by 1977 to achieve a "nationwide minimum standard of equalized excellence." He then tells us that national outlays to schools should rise from $28.3 billion in 1967 to $70.1 billion in 1977 (in 1967 dollars) to achieve this goal. He proposes that the minimum standard be guaranteed by federal subsidies to schools.

The second article, "Nonproperty Taxes for Schools," describes some of the limits and inequities of the property tax on which schools have heavily depended for financing.

Localities and states obviously need financial assistance, particularly if they are to expand and equalize educational offerings. The following table (Figure 2) shows us something about (1) expenditure per pupil in each state and the state's rank among other states in expenditures, (2) the state and local school revenues as a percent of personal income in the state and the rank on this characteristic, and (3) the nonpublic school enrollment in each state as a percent of all public school enrollment. The latter is included to show how much of the school tax burden is lifted in some states by the presence there of large numbers of students who attend nonpublic schools. If these schools were closed, as many of them threaten to be, the tax burden in these states would correspondingly rise to pay for the new public school enrollments.

As we see from the table, the states spending most on schools are not necessarily those making the greatest "effort" in terms of income and ability to pay. New York State, for example, spends more per pupil than any other state, but it ranks 12 in effort. Since nonpublic school enrollments in that state are 21.7 percent of public school enrollments, much of the state's effort is being made by the nonpublic school system, with that share of the burden being lifted from taxpayers. In general, the Southern states are compelled to make extra efforts to finance their schools because of the relatively negligible nonpublic school enrollments there. Only eight states now

FIGURE 2. *Ability and Effort to Finance Public Education 1967–68*

STATE	LEVEL OF FINANCIAL SUPPORT		EFFORT		
	Estimated current expenditure per pupil in average daily attendance	Rank	Estimated state and local revenues for public schools as percent of personal income	Rank	Estimated non-public school enrollment percent of total elementary & secondary school enrollment
United States	$634		4.6		13.1
North Atlantic					
Connecticut	781	4	4.5	30	16.6
Delaware	726	5	4.9	16	15.0
Maine	517	36	4.6	27	14.3
Maryland	703	8	4.8	19	15.2
Massachusetts	625	21	3.9	43	20.7
New Hampshire	572	31	3.9	43	21.6
New Jersey	846	3	4.3	34	19.0
New York	1024	1	5.1	12	21.7
Pennsylvania	682	14	4.3	34	22.6
Rhode Island	680	15	3.2	50	25.7
Vermont	597	26	6.2	2	17.7
Great Lakes & Plains					
Illinois	683	13	3.9	43	20.8
Indiana	611	24	5.1	12	10.9
Iowa	640	20	4.7	23	14.3
Kansas	596	27	4.9	16	9.7
Michigan	617	22	5.1	12	15.1
Minnesota	649	18	5.3	9	17.3
Missouri	585	29	3.9	43	15.5
Nebraska	487	41	3.3	49	16.0
North Dakota	547	34	5.5	7	13.1
Ohio	584	30	4.2	38	15.4
South Dakota	541	35	4.6	27	13.3
Wisconsin	702	9	4.7	23	23.2
Southeast					
Alabama	376	49	3.9	43	3.8
Arkansas	448	48	4.3	34	2.8
Florida	563	32	4.5	30	6.9
Georgia	494	40	4.2	38	2.6
Kentucky	475	42	3.9	43	12.5
Louisiana	596	27	5.5	7	15.6
Mississippi	364	50	4.2	38	3.4
North Carolina	464	45	4.2	38	1.8
South Carolina	454	47	4.8	19	2.5
Tennessee	461	46	4.1	42	3.8
Virginia	552	33	4.5	30	5.6
West Virginia	500	39	4.6	27	4.4

FIGURE 2. (*Cont.*)

STATE	LEVEL OF FINANCIAL SUPPORT		EFFORT		
	Estimated current expenditure per pupil in average daily attendance	Rank	Estimated state and local revenues for public schools as percent of personal income	Rank	Estimated non-public school enrollment percent of total elementary & secondary school enrollment
West & Southwest					
Alaska	927	2	4.8	19	3.7
Arizona	687	10	6.5	1	8.1
California	686	11	4.7	23	8.8
Colorado	610	25	5.2	10	8.5
Hawaii	651	17	4.9	16	16.1
Idaho	516	37	4.8	19	5.4
Montana	684	12	5.9	5	11.7
Nevada	676	16	5.0	15	3.8
New Mexico	617	22	6.1	3	9.8
Oklahoma	474	44	4.4	33	3.6
Oregon	715	6	5.7	6	7.5
Texas	475	42	4.3	34	5.8
Utah	501	38	6.1	3	2.2
Washington	649	18	4.7	23	7.3
Wyoming	713	7	5.2	10	4.8

Sources:
    Personal income—U.S. Department of Commerce, Office of Business Economics. *Survey of Current Business,* Vol. 48. No. 8. Washington: Government Printing Office, August 1968.
    Other Data—National Education Association, Research Division: *Estimates of School Statistics, 1968–69.* Research Report 1968-R16; *Rankings of the States, 1969.* Research Report 1969-R1. Washington: The Association.
    U.S. Department of Health, Education & Welfare, Office of Education: *Digest of Educational Statistics 1967: Digest of Educational Statistics 1968.* Washingon: Government Printing Office.

NOTES:
    ...Personal income is on calendar year basis, and school data is on basis of school year beginning in the calendar year.
    ...When the figures for two or more states are identical, the states are given the same rank and the appropriate number is then picked up with the next state in rank.
    ...National figures include the District of Columbia; but, because the District is not comparable to state school systems, figures for it are not shown separately.
    ...Non-public school enrollment is included to correct possible distortion of "effort" column. While these children do not involve public tax effort, they do have to be paid for.
    ...Because of the relative purchasing power of the dollar in Alaska, dollar amounts for that state should be reduced by about one-fourth to make them roughly comparable.

spend less than 4 percent of personal income on public schools. Half of these states have more than 20 percent of total enrollments in nonpublic schools.

FEDERAL POLICY

While "federal aid to education" (that is, aid to elementary and secondary schools) is relatively new, the federal government has a long history of direct and massive intervention in education.

The federal government operates, tuition free, military academies at: West Point (Army), Annapolis (Navy), Norwalk (Coast Guard), King's Point (Maritime), and Boulder (Air Force). All are accredited four-year colleges, conferring thousands of bachelor degrees.

The Navy and the Army also sponsor schools at the graduate level, as does the Air Force and the Department of Agriculture. In the ROTC, thousands of undergraduates are trained in programs paid for, staffed, and administered by the federal government.

The Atomic Energy Commission and other government agencies offer extensive fellowship programs at the graduate level.

The Armed Forces Institute provides secondary education for enlisted men, as well as primary and secondary education for tens of thousands of servicemen's dependents overseas.

The Bureau of Indian Affairs provides education on reservations, and the Bureau of Prisons provides secondary education for inmates of federal prisons.

Much vocational education is federally subsidized. So also are the schools in areas where large numbers of federally employed workers are located—the so-called impacted areas. Federal aid is also given for school lunches in thousands of primary and high schools.

The federal government supports the National Science Foundation, one of the most influential policy-making groups in public education, and federal support is given to education in virtually every department in that government, perhaps most notably in the Departments of Labor, and Health, Education, and Welfare.

In general currency, the phrase "federal aid to education" describes the financial assistance voted by Congress to the states and through them to local school districts. Much federal assistance has been "categorical" in that it can be used only to support specific programs voted by the Congress. Such aid is granted only upon application by the affected school districts to the federal agency (generally the Office of Education) which administers the program. A typical example: the Head Start programs.

When categorical federal aid is voted, the federal government inevitably directly intervenes in the administration of local schools, since the agency dispensing the aid establishes rules and guidelines under which programs qualifying for assistance must operate. The agency can rescind or cut off financial support for programs that do not operate in conformity with its guidelines. Thus the federal government becomes to some extent the final arbiter of the shape, content, and administration of programs receiving categorical aid.

Quite understandably, local school administrators generally opposed categorical aid, because of the limitations placed on their powers. They strongly favor general federal aid which will enable them to use federal monies to support programs of their choice.

Civil rights organizations and others who are interested in reforming the schools, however, generally favor categorical aid. Minority groups, they claim, have little to say about the administration of local school districts and cannot easily affect their policies. They believe that their power to influence the Congress insures the poor, the blacks, and other excluded groups a degree of equity in the expenditure of school funds that they would not otherwise be able to win if all federal aid were voted to support education in general. It is around this issue of categorical, as against general, aid that much debate about the schools now revolves.

The selection on federal education policies and proposals is from a document on the subject issued by the House Committee on Education and Labor. It discusses the scope and potential of federal involvement in the system of education.

Another selection from a federally commissioned document, the Report of the National Advisory Commission on Civil Disorder, offers specific policy proposals to treat the sources of discontent and disorder in ghetto schools.

The brief selection on assessing schools describes the controversial but pathfinding National Assessment of schools. The public schools have never before been assessed systematically or nationally. Children are continually assessed by the schools, of course, but the schools themselves are never evaluated, marked, rewarded, or punished. We do not, in fact, know much at all about how our schools are performing throughout the nation. Few uniform records are kept, and many school administrators have consistently resisted any probing of school performance. National Assessment is certainly one of the major policy issues of our time.

The final article is drawn from a document that has received considerable attention nationally. *Toward a Social Report on Learning* is a first effort on the part of the federal government (and the U.S. Department of Health, Education, and Welfare) to provide an overview of our national situation. The report raises questions about social accounting and assessment in the areas of health and illness, social mobility, our physical environment, income and poverty, public order and safety, learning, science, and art, and participation and alienation. Though all these subjects relate to the condition of the schools, this volume includes, as the most germane, only the section on learning.

The Fiscal Problem

EQUALIZING EXCELLENCE BY 1977

by Leon H. Keyserling*

We need to start as soon as possible, under the galvanizing influence of new and adequate Federal legislation, but involving related efforts at all levels, a balanced 10-year program during 1968–1977 inclusive to achieve by 1977 an average level of public-school performance in every State at least equal to a nationwide minimum standard of equalized excellence. This does not mean a ceiling or straightjacket. Each State would receive enough Federal aid (contingent upon continued State and local efforts, based upon recent trends and capabilities) to reach these nationwide minimum standards of excellence by 1977. Yet the States and localities should and

---

* From *Achieving Nationwide Educational Excellence,* Conference on Economic Progress, 1969.

would be free to go as far beyond these nationwide standards as their own resources would permit.

The main goals for 1977 are:

(1) *Per-pupil outlays for all purposes related to public schools,* measured in 1967 dollars, should average $1,534 in 1977 in every region and State, compared with a nationwide average of $660 in 1967.

(2) *Enrollment in the public schools,* from kindergarten through four years of high school, should include every child aged 5–17 not served by private schools, i.e., a participation rate of 100 percent of the public-school population, by 1977. Today, the nonparticipation rate—the portion of the public-school population not enrolled—is as high as 9 percent in one region, and even higher in some States. To attain full participation of a group growing in number, nationwide enrollment needs to increase from 43.0 million in 1967 to 45.7 million in 1977, or 6.3 percent.

(3) *Classroom teachers* should increase greatly in number. By 1977, the ratio of fully accredited classroom teachers to enrollment should be 1 to 20 for the nation, and also in every region and State. The nationwide ratio in 1967 was 1 to 24. This calls for a nationwide increase in classroom teachers from 1,788,000 in 1967 to 2,286,000 in 1977, or 27.8 percent. Including replacements, more than 2,152,000 new teachers will be needed over the decade.

(4) *Teachers' salaries* in the public schools, measured in 1967 dollars, should rise from a nationwide average of $6,830 in 1967 to a nationwide average of at least $10,711 in 1977. This represents an average annual increase of 4.6 percent, exclusive of needed cost-of-living increases, with a more rapid rate of increase through 1970 to overcome the serious lag as of 1967. To attain the minimum standard of excellence in the treatment of both pupils and teachers, the average by 1977 should be at least $10,711 in every region and State.

(5) *Nonteacher instructional staff* throughout the nation should rise from 188,000 in 1967 to 1,523,000 in 1977. Some of this increase would be for principals, supervisors, librarians, and guidance and

psychological personnel. But more than 1,100,000 of the increase should represent individuals (not fully accredited teachers) assisting teachers in instructional functions. The average salaries of nonteacher instructional staff should rise at the same rates as those of teachers.

(6) *Noninstructional current outlays* need to be increased greatly for administration and operation and maintenance of plant, salaries of noninstructional personnel (including school aides), and programs for summer schools, adult education, and school lunches.

(7) *The available supply of classrooms* in the public schools should rise from 1,653,455 in 1967 to 2,285,000 in 1977, to take care of increased enrollment and reduced class size. Taking account also of elimination of unsatisfactory conditions and migration and abandonment, 1,232,000 classrooms should be constructed during 1968–1977 inclusive.

The Total Cost and How It Should Be Shared

Total nationwide outlays to meet public-school needs, up to the nation-wide minimum standard of excellence, should rise from $28.3 billion in 1967 to $70.1 billion in 1977, measured in 1967 dollars, or at an average annual rate of increase of 9.5 percent.

Drastic changes in the sharing of costs between the States and localities on the one hand, and the Federal Government on the other hand, are imperative to achieve the various goals. This is because of the very unequal distribution of economic and financial capabilities among regions and States; the fact that progress must be so much faster in some regions and States which, through no fault of their own, are now most below the 1977 goals for excellence; the fact that, during 1946–1966, State and local outlays for all purposes rose more than 3 times as fast as Federal outlays for all purposes, while State and local debts grew more than 10 times as fast as the national debt; and the preemptive advantage enjoyed by the Federal Government in raising revenues by methods consistent with equity and economic growth.

In 1967, the State and local share of the $28.3 billion of total outlays for our public schools was $26.0 billion or 91.9 percent, and the Federal share was $2.3 billion or 8.1 percent. By 1977, under the proposed program, the State and local share of the total $70.1 billion cost would be $42.8 billion or 61.1 percent, and the Federal share would be $27.3 billion or 38.9 percent, all measured in 1967 dollars.

The recommended formula toward this end is that the increases in outlays by each region and each State should continue approximately in accord with their respective recent rates of increase (adjusted somewhat upward in accord with goals for a somewhat more rapid average annual rate of income and economic growth throughout the nation), and that the Federal Government should make up the difference in each region and State, subject only to the modification that in no State in any year shall the Federal percentage share of total outlays be below what it was in 1967. This means, among the States, that there will be great variations in the relative rates of increase in total outlays and in respective State and local and Federal outlays, as well as in respective State and local and Federal shares. These variations are essential to equalize services in all regions and States, up to the minimum standard of excellence, despite vast differences among them in economic and financial capabilities and in the size of the job to be done.

We Can Well Afford the Cost of the Program

Under the proposed program, the increase in state and local outlays for our public schools would be approximately in accord with recent trends. The increase in Federal outlays, rising from $2.3 billion in 1967 to $27.3 billion in 1977, contemplates in 1977 total Federal outlays for education (public school and other) rising from $4.7 billion in the fiscal 1969 Federal Budget to $32.9 billion in calendar 1977.

In a fully-growing economy, the rise would be from an estimated 0.53 percent of total national production in fiscal 1969 to an estimated 2.36 percent in calendar 1977. By way of contrast, in fiscal 1969, proposed outlays of $89.5 billion in the Federal Budget category of national defense, space technology, and all international came to 10.11 percent of estimated total national production. Allowing for needed expansion in public programs and services across the board in response to all of our major national needs, and even assuming (without arguing for) substantial further increases in

Federal outlays for national defense, space technology, and all international, this would still be true: In a properly expanding national economy, total Federal outlays for all purposes, estimated at 21.02 percent of total national production in fiscal 1969, would be smaller in ratio to total national production in calendar 1977. The implication is that the proposed program would not require Federal tax increases.

Measured in fiscal 1969 dollars, our total national production was $829 billion in calendar 1967. With optimum economic growth, it should rise to $1,396 billion in calendar 1977, and, even at a considerably lower growth rate, to $1,170 billion. This means that our *average annual output* of goods and services during the 10 years 1968–1977 inclusive would be $303–178 billion higher than it was in calendar 1967. With an "economic growth dividend" within this range, we should be willing to use 7.2 percent of the higher "dividend," or 12.2 percent of the lower "dividend," or 21.8 billion dollars on the average 1968–1978, to increase our total investment in our public schools.

What About Inflation?

The problem of inflation is really irrelevant to the proposed public-school program. With optimum or even adequate economic growth, the program would place no excessive pressures upon our ability to turn out goods and services. But even if it should exert such pressures at some time, we should not sacrifice first what we need most, but instead should reorder our national priorities and values so as to put first things first by imposing some very small restraints upon the expendable or superfluous. Entirely hypothetically, if the proposed $70.1 billion level of total expenditure for our public schools in 1977 should require a cutback somewhere of even as much as $20 billion to curb inflation, that $20 billion would be only about 3.5 percent of our "economic growth dividend" in 1977 alone. It would be about 1.4 percent of our total national production in 1977 alone, under conditions of full resource use. We could certainly find better places to make cutbacks of this size than in our public schools.

The first essential step in the proposed 10-year program is Federal legislation, committing the nation and the people at large to action of incalculable benefit to the nation and people at large.

NONPROPERTY TAXES FOR SCHOOLS

by Albert L. Alford*

Taxation of property—real, personal, tangible, and intangible—is still the mainstay of school district local financing and plays a significant role in providing revenue for other local government services. In fiscal year 1960, over 87 percent of locally raised taxes came from the property tax.

The property tax began as a land tax in the colonial period. Additions of personal property—both tangible and intangible—to be taxed at the full rate resulted in the establishment of a general property tax by the time of the Civil War. Though constantly under attack because of inequities in administration, the general property tax remained the major tax source of revenue for both the State and local governments until the 1920's. By the end of that decade the general property tax had relinquished its dominant role in State finance to motor fuel and vehicle taxes as a result of the tremendous expansion in automobile production and ownership during the period.

The decade of the thirties brought the general sales tax and the income tax to such a significant number of States that the property tax was reduced in comparative yield to only a minor fraction of total revenue for State use. By 1942, the general property tax amounted to only 3.8 percent of all State revenues, as contrasted with 25.6 percent in 1922 and 42.7 percent in 1902.

This diminution in comparative yield resulted not only from the rapid growth of sales and income taxes, but also from a de-emphasis or abandonment of the property tax as a general revenue producer by State governments. This was a conscious effort on the part of most States to relieve the total property tax burden. The result was

* From Dept. of Health, Education, and Welfare, Office of Education (Washington, D.C., U.S. Government Printing Office, 1964).

a shifting of the use of the property tax almost entirely to the local level of government, including schools.

Instead of using 11.6 percent of all property taxes collected as was done in 1902, States on the average today use only 3.0 percent. There are wide ranges in this use between States ranging from 0 percent to 21.7 percent, but the trend has been steadily downward. Except for the depression years of the 1930's and the year 1953, the absolute amount of the property tax collected by the States has gradually increased, largely because property values have risen faster than State property tax rates have been cut or abandoned. While not significant percentagewise, the full release of State-imposed property taxes would add over $600 million to potential local sources, though some of the State-assessed property would pose administrative problems if local assessments were required.

EROSION OF THE PROPERTY TAX BASE

Although the local units of government have been given a virtually clear field in the use of the property tax, the potential base of this source has been gradually reduced to a point where it is only producing a fraction of what could be obtained if its full potential were realized. In absolute terms, of course, the dollar value of the base has increased. The gradual reduction of the potential property tax base has been brought about in two ways: (1) The extension of exemptions to the tax on grounds of equity, welfare, or administrative simplicity, and (2) the deterioration of the assessable base in relation to true value either through classification or maladministration.

CONTINUING ROLE FOR PROPERTY TAX

No local district is likely to consider abandoning the property tax altogether. The role of the property tax is too firmly implanted in the pattern of school finance, and this tax offers some advantages worthy of continuation. Stability of revenue and flexibility of rate are its two most highly claimed virtues. While it is easy to administer from the school district's point of view, since somebody else does it, the administration of the property tax is actually its major drawback. If the assessment practices could be sharply upgraded and provisions made for other than lump sum payment, the property tax would compare favorably with many others in use at the local level. . . .

The above "ifs" are so big, however, as to be almost insurmountable, in practice. The techniques and knowledge for sound practice are available, but the political pressures and lack of willingness to put them into effect limit severely the potential usefulness of the property tax. After generations of attempted reform, a substitute is more and more frequently being sought, rather than possible reform.

A danger to the schools in continued reliance on the property tax arises from the fact that school budgets may be starved more from a resistance to increases in the property tax than to increases in educational expenditures *per se*. In other words, education must bear a double burden: justification of its expenditure program and justification of the tax that supports it. Only the former should in reality fall upon the schools.

The property tax has had an understandable historic relationship with education as it has with virtually all local governmental functions. Other local governmental functions, however, have been able to draw to a greater extent from other local revenue sources, e.g., service charges, license fees, and nonproperty taxes, thereby lessening their dependence upon the property tax. So long as the property tax is not overburdened actually or psychologically this shifting of burden may benefit the schools, but once the limit of burden is passed, the schools more than any other function are left in the untenable position of having to defend the property tax as a tax. In spite of the many weaknesses and inequities of the property tax, however, no school district is likely to advocate a shift in tax base until this breaking point is reached.

Actually there is no reason, other than historical, why the school should be tied to the property tax. As a matter of fact, history would tend to support the proposition that the property tax, while appropriate in an agrarian economy, should give way to more adequate measures of wealth in our present-day industrial economy.

. . .

SCHOOL NEED FOR BROAD-BASED TAXES

One of the advantages of the property tax has been that it provides a broad base for the governmental functions it supports. There has traditionally been a relationship between income and property, and it is this relationship that has been modified in our modern economy. Since the benefits of public education are so broadly distributed, it is appropriate that public education should be broadly supported.

Broad tax support can be achieved theoretically in one of two ways: (1) Through a broad-based tax such as the income or sales tax, or (2) through a combination of lesser selective taxes which in total touch a very broad group. Of these two devices only the first, or use of broad-based taxes, is practical for school districts. . . .

Designated Taxes for Schools

Even though in most cases school districts do not actually collect the taxes they use, the taxes which go to schools are usually earmarked or labeled and are, therefore, closely related to education in the public mind. Proposed new taxes at the State level have often been justified by educational needs. Sometimes these taxes are in fact earmarked for schools, but occasionally the revenue from such taxes is later diverted to other uses.

Selective sales taxes.—A number of selective sales taxes and even general sales taxes have been earmarked in whole or part for schools even though levied by a municipality or county. The selective sales taxes have frequently been the so-called "sin" taxes on tobacco products and alcoholic beverages. These taxes are often easiest to levy particularly if the revenues produced are going for a good cause. There is some question, however, as to whether education should be tied to a selective sales tax which draws revenue from only a portion of the population. No school district is likely to turn down the revenue from any particular tax because it is tainted, a questionable concept at best, but having public education directly supported by a small variety of special or "nuisance" taxes may have the same limiting effect ultimately as the property tax.

Income and general sales taxes.—The schools would best seek to utilize the general sales tax or a form of income tax and leave the area of selective sales taxes to general government which supports a variety of activities from its general fund. The income tax may have special justification because of the documented relationship between level of education and expected life earnings.[1] Some of this

[1] See Herman P. Miller, "Annual and Lifetime Income in Relation to Education: 1939–1959," p. 962–986; and "Income and Education: Does Education Pay Off?" p. 129–146.

additional income might be tapped to support the educational system which allows its production with possible multiplier effects even though there may not be a direct or perfect relationship between the locality where the education is provided and the place where the income is earned.

Other broad-based taxes.—There may be exceptions to this general rule in the case of some taxes which are also broad-based. The poll or per capita tax properly applied is as broad-based as any tax and has some advantage in that it elicits a modicum of direct support from each adult citizen. It, of course, violates any progressive or proportional tenets of taxation and, because of its tie to voting in several States, it becomes less than desirable in the eyes of many.

Public utility taxation is certainly as broad-based as the property tax. It can produce sizable sums from a captive consumer group, though there is no reason other than availability which should dictate support of public education by utility users.

Finally the real estate transfer tax, if justified on a capital investment basis, might qualify for support of education though there are other capital costs of government which would equally qualify. The possible irregularity of yield might also indicate a desirability for the revenues from this source going to a general fund rather than a school fund.

RELATION OF TAX PROGRAM TO ECONOMY OF AREA

In order to be productive and equitable, a tax program must be related to the economic structure of the community. The economic structure will in turn be closely related to the geography and population of the area.

Wealth Necessary for Taxes

It becomes a truism that no tax program can produce adequate revenue if economic wealth is not present. Some school districts may have so little economic wealth in relation to the population that no local tax program, property or nonproperty, can provide relief. In these cases either the districts must be geographically modified to bring in additional economic wealth or aid from another level of government must be obtained. These are problems which have been long recognized, and various solutions of reorganization and State aid have been applied or recommended. . . .

CONCLUSIONS

Local nonproperty taxation for schools has not been widely adopted even though it has been widely discussed. There are several explanations for this limited use. The property tax has until fairly recently provided adequate local revenue in most cases where there was sufficient wealth to meet local needs. Where this wealth did not exist, it was necessary to look to other levels of government which could draw on a broader tax base. In the case of schools this has been predominately at the State level.

The States have withdrawn from the property tax field and this withdrawal has provided more leeway at the local level, at least until governmental service demands increased sharply. It is generally assumed that the larger units of government can best administer nonproperty taxes and the States have moved extensively into the fields of income, general sales, and selective sales taxation. The Federal Government has long dominated the income tax field and is also heavily involved in selective sales and excise taxation.

At the local level the major adoptions of nonproperty taxes have been made by the municipalities with the net result that the school districts are left in the residual position of being the major users of the property tax and, in turn, dependent almost entirely upon the property tax for their local sources of revenue.

So long as abandonments by other units of government have provided additional potential revenue from this source, or so long as the States have provided additional sums of money from State sources, the fiscal needs of the schools could be met. In more and more cases today, however, the property tax has reached its limit, either constitutional, legal, practical, or emotional. Additional State appropriations have not been forthcoming, and the local district is faced with the direct problem of seeking additional sources of revenue.

. . . Many nonproperty taxes are administratively feasible for use by local school districts, though they may not always be suitable for other reasons. The property tax is no better suited to efficient local administration than are most of the nonproperty taxes and not as well suited as several. The main advantage that the property tax holds is that it is in existence and being administered at the local level in spite of many inefficiencies. Resistance to change and fear of the unknown are always strong factors.

While an attempt has been made to dispel some of the misconceptions and fears of nonproperty tax use at the local school district level, this study does not necessarily recommend the use of nonproperty taxes, as such. From the point of view of adequate educational financing, there may be several alternatives which are more desirable. There are certain economies in the administration of taxes by a larger unit of government as well as the tapping of a broader base of wealth. Increased State aid, therefore, is held out by many as a most desirable alternative. Some support Federal aid on similar grounds.

Improvement of property tax administration is offered by others as a way to obtain larger revenues on a fairer basis at the local level. This is a hope, however, which has been held out for generations, and does not appear much closer to fruition today than 50 years ago.

Reorganization of school districts into larger and more efficient units has had strong support in recent years with substantial results.

All of these methods are useful and desirable. When, however, these alternatives are not being utilized and when the school district is being handicapped in its function of providing adequate education for its children, those responsible for the district's operation have a right and duty to examine other possibilities. If resistance to the property tax has reached the point where school budgets are endangered and if for political reasons the school district must rely on its own resources, then it may well turn to one or more of the nonproperty sources discussed herein.

The broadest based taxes should be used where possible, specifically the income and general sales tax, but conditions may not always allow this. . . . Nonproperty taxation for school districts cannot solve the major problems of educational finance, but it may alleviate the particular problems faced by many school districts in the never ending struggle for adequate revenue.

Federal Policy and
Research and Development

FEDERAL EDUCATION POLICIES
AND PROPOSALS

U.S. House Committee on Education and Labor*

Should an American statesman of the 19th century step down from his portrait in the Capitol and thumb through this survey, his first reaction would probably be one of astonishment over the great number of Federal educational programs existing in the fiscal year 1967—some 750, or, 250 more than when the last such survey was made, only 8 years before. The statesman's second reaction would probably be one of incredulity, upon his noting that the Federal Government spent more than $12 billion to carry out its educational programs in fiscal 1967.

This oldtimer would not be likely to be either shocked or overly impressed by the mere fact of Federal involvement in education, because the Federal Government has been thus involved since 1785. However, upon taking a closer look, he certainly would find significant differences between 1867 and 1967—the centennial of the U.S. Office of Education—not only in the extent and purposes of the Federal role but also in the whole structure of educational leadership. These differences some persons today are lamenting as "departures from tradition," and others are hailing as triumphant breakthroughs toward better educational opportunities for all and a better, stronger America.

Almost every Federal "aid" program is authorized by Congress for a specific purpose: to improve instruction in mathematics and science in the elementary and secondary schools; to improve instruction in modern foreign languages; to help "disadvantaged" children; to train and retrain both youth and adults for better job opportunities; to provide for educational television, and so forth.

* From *Federal Educational Policies, Programs and Proposals,* House document No. 398. 90th Cong., 2d sess., 1968 (Washington, D.C.: Government Printing Office, 1968).

However, a careful study reveals a definite pattern of Federal support of education in the interest of (1) national defense, (2) international good will, and (3) the general welfare.

Under the heading "National Defense" fall not only all the education and training programs of the Department of Defense, the Atomic Energy Commission, the National Aeronautics and Space Administration and the National Science Foundation, but also all the programs of the National Defense Education Act (NDEA), passed in 1958 in response to Russia's challenge to our scientific knowledge and know-how, expressed by the launching of her first sputnik. These NDEA programs include: loans to students in institutions of higher education; financial assistance for strengthening science, mathematics and modern foreign language instruction; national defense fellowships; financial assistance for guidance, counseling and testing and identification and encouragement of able students; grants for counseling and guidance training centers; language development centers and institutes; research and experimentation in more effective utilization of television, radio, motion pictures and related media for educational purposes; area vocational education programs; and a science information service.

Under the heading "General Welfare" falls almost everything else, covering a multitude of purposes. Here we find the "war-on-poverty" programs, including not only the OEO's Job Corps, community action programs, "Headstart," "Upward Bound," and so forth, but also the Elementary and Secondary Education Act's title I programs which provide Federal funds to equalize the educational opportunities of "disadvantaged" children; the "war on prejudice" programs to provide new educational tools, education, and training to further integration in the schools; education programs for the physically handicapped and for the retarded; vocational education and training programs for better job opportunities; vocational rehabilitation programs for juvenile delinquents and for prison inmates; adult educational programs; teacher training programs; student aid programs; higher education programs; and in-service training programs of great variety.

Also under "General Welfare" fall the Elementary and Secondary Education Act, title III programs for innovation and experimentation in education and most of the U.S. Office of Education cooperative research grants to or contracts with State or local education agencies, universities, private nonprofit organizations, and individuals for a wide variety of research projects, surveys, and demonstration, including educational laboratories, new curriculum development and information dissemination. Also here included are USOE contracts with profitmaking private corporations for research and development in the field of educational technology, such as the manufacture and programing of teacher computers.

THE BALANCE OF EDUCATIONAL POWER

As a result of the great number and variety of Federal categorical educational aid programs, this survey suggests, educational decision-making has largely moved from the grassroots to Washington. Our statesman from the past would find, no doubt to his surprise, that no State or local government, or community action group, or university, or individual may receive aid for education under certain major laws passed in the last two decades, without first submitting a plan for study, research or training following criteria spelled out in the legislation and/or regulations compiled by the administering Federal department or agency, and then having such plan federally approved.

The question arises as to whether this Federal categorical aid policy changes the Federal-State-local balance of educational power.

There are those who think that it does, and are backing the drive for "general aid" or "bloc aid" as opposed to categorical aid.

On the other hand there are those who think that the Federal designation of programs and the Federal money flowing to the grassroots for specific educational purposes have strengthened the foundations of the whole structure of American education.

The old structure was built on the concept of the neighborhood school; the local school board; State, local and individual responsibilities for the individual's welfare, including his education; and a strong belief in Federal responsibility in education limited to West Point, the Naval Academy, schools for the Indians, and land or money grants to the States for education "with no strings attached."

The new structure is built on what President Johnson and former Secretary of Health, Education, and Welfare John W. Gardner, have called partnerships among Federal, State, and local governments, the universities, the community action groups, and private corporations. Examples of such intended partnerships may be found in this survey in the administration of educational television grants, the Office of Economic Opportunity grants to community action groups and Elementary Secondary Education Act, title III, programs.

That the new balance of educational powers, the new educational structure, is both heatedly attacked and stoutly defended is revealed in the following few quotations:

Malcolm Bauer, in an article in the Christian Science Monitor, entitled "School Boards Favor U.S. Aid Without Strings," declared on May 1, 1967:

> The nation's school boards welcome federal aid to education, but they want no strings attached.
>
> This theme was strong in speeches and resolutions applauded by more than 8,000 delegates here for the annual convention of the National School Boards Association.
>
> A key resolution read: "Federal funds for public-education purposes should include funds in the form of general aid, administered without federal control . . . in accordance with state policy."
>
> State and local resentment over real or fancied federal intrusion in local school affairs was apparent in many discussion groups during the convention.

At this meeting Dr. Leon Minear, Oregon Superintendent of Public Instruction, said:

> State educational authorities have been bypassed by community-action programs, Head Start, Upward Bound, Job Corps, Housing and Urban Development neighborhood-innovation programs, church-related school programs, and Title II of the Elementary and Secondary Education Act.

Mr. Bauer's article concluded:

> Senator Wayne Morse (D) of Oregon, chairman of the Senate education subcommittee, assured delegates in their final session that the federal government would not control local schools so long as Congress was elected by the people "who believe, as I do, that educational decisions should be made at the local level."

On July 9, 1967, the New York Times education editor, Fred M. Hechinger, said in an article entitled "The Problem Is To Separate Aid From Control":

Three years ago, the Educational Policies Commission, the ideological voice of the National Education Association and the American Association of School Administrators, dropped a bombshell when it urged educators to throw their support behind "categorical" Federal aid to education. These powerful organizations had always demanded general aid— money which the states and local school districts could spend as they wished—and had rejected Federal subsidies with "categorical" strings attached, such as the requirement that funds be used to aid the disadvantaged or to improve science instruction.

Last week, during the annual convention of the N.E.A. in Minneapolis, the commission returned to its pre-1964 stand. It denounced categorical aid as a form of Federal control and urged that Washington henceforth strengthen the public schools with dollars to be used as the states see fit.

The commission charged that "special-purpose Federal aid . . . is in itself a form of Federal control of education." It cited the N.D.E.A. as "an indirect but nevertheless powerful influence . . . upon what is taught; how it is taught; and the priority of resources, time, and money allocated to it."

Those who reject this view say that the professional educational leadership, over a considerable period of time, failed to establish priorities attuned to the needs of the nation. For example, those who hold this view recall that educators virtually struck foreign language study from the list of essential academic subjects and permitted a majority of students, including highly gifted ones, to leave school without instruction in physics.

Former HEW Secretary Gardner in an address before the American Statistical Association in Washington, D.C., on December 27, 1967, said:[1]

Any effort to plan and rationalize the allocation of resources tends to reduce pluralism, and to introduce new kinds of institutional controls. If we have less than enough to spend in constructing hospitals, then we must be sure that those constructed are properly located and designed to accomplish the greatest good.

In doing so, we move toward a measure of social control. The Federal Government has avoided infringement of local autonomy by asking the States to perform the necessary planning functions.

But whether the controls are at the Federal, regional or State level, rational use of resources tends toward the creation of large-scale interconnected systems, and to comprehensive planning of those systems.

Traditionally we have had no appetite for such systematic planning. And our non-governmental institutions, whether universities or hospitals

[1] Processed copy of the address, obtained from the Department of Health, Education, and Welfare, pp. 5–6.

or scientific laboratories, are not accustomed to think of themselves as parts of large-scale interconnected systems.

I believe it is possible to accomplish a large measure of rational social planning and still retain the most important features of local and institutional autonomy. But it will require a conscious effort and a knowing grasp of the problems involved.

U.S. Commissioner of Education Harold Howe 2d, also has seen planning and congressional decisionmaking as being necessary and desirable. Said Commissioner Howe on January 12, 1968:[2]

Except for a few perennial holdouts, virtually nobody contends any more that Federal aid to education is essentially evil.

The major argument about Federal aid today is not whether it ought to go to the schools but how. And this argument, in turn, revolves around two methods of channeling Federal aid to the schools.

The first is categorical aid, a term referring to Federal programs aimed at buttressing some particular aspect of the educational enterprise, such as the teaching of handicapped children or instruction in the sciences or providing library books.

The second term is general aid, funds given to educators for any purpose they choose.

As of now, general aid largely remains a discussion piece, since most of the 80-odd programs administered by the United States Office of Education are of the categorical variety, each designed by Congress to focus on a specific educational problem common to every region of the country.

A high-handed stand?

This business of having the Congress decide which educational tasks most need doing is taken by many state and local educational officials (though by no means all) as being high-handed, the assumption being that it is based on a we-know-what's-good-for-you Federal philosophy.

If this assumption were true, I would share the hometown resentment. But Federal domination is neither the fact nor the spirit of the categorical approach.

Rather, this approach has emerged as the most effective mechanism for the development of national programs for education that address themselves to national problems, problems that would in all likelihood be given inadequate attention unless special Federal funds were provided to focus on them. From such categorical aid we get the biggest bang for our national educational buck without undermining our traditions.

The Legislative Conference of National Organizations, representing the American Association of School Administrators, the

[2] New York Times, Jan. 12, 1968, p. 53.

Council of Chief State School Officers, the National Association of State Boards of Education, the National Congress of Parents and Teachers, the National Education Association, and the National School Boards Association, unanimously passed the following resolution on January 10, 1968:[3]

General Federal support of public education

We recommend that federal participation in the financing of public education be primarily through substantial general support based on an equitable equalization formula and with minimum limitations on the use of federal funds.

We support categorical aid programs when such programs are necessary for the national welfare and are needed to meet urgent and unique national educational problems.

All funds should be channeled through state departments of education.

The Hon. Edith Green, chairman of the Special Subcommittee on Education of the House Committee on Education and Labor, remarked early in 1968:[4]

Congress has started a reversal—small but real—in the tendency to centralize the power and the authority of Federal education programs in Washington.

Some parts of the 1967 Elementary and Secondary Education Act and the "war on poverty" legislation, as well as the Teacher Corps legislation, were amended to give State and local authorities more responsibility in planning programs, establishing priorities, selecting personnel and controlling funds.

This major change in direction rests on the assumption that all initiative and wisdom does not somehow automatically flow to, and collect upon, the banks of the Potomac.

RELATED ISSUES

While the question of Federal control remains the pervasive issue in education today, closely related thereto are such other issues as:

[3] "Proposals on Education Legislation Recommended for Consideration by the President and the Congress in 1968 by a Legislative Conference of National Organizations." Processed copy obtained from the Council of Chief State School Officers, Washington, D.C.

[4] Green, Edith, "Who Should Run It?" The New York Times, Jan. 12, 1968, p. 53.

(1) the manner of bringing about integration in the schools—whether by busing, the establishment of educational parks, the development of "magnet" schools, each specializing in a different subject area, or extra Federal assistance for school districts which become models of desegregation; (2) Federal aid for private schools and colleges and parochial school children, continuing the church-state constitutional question; (3) the proposal to coordinate most Federal educational programs in one new department—the Department of Education; (4) the proposal to create a National Foundation for the Social Sciences, and (5) copyright revision.

CURRENT ASPECTS OF THE
INTEGRATION QUESTION

U.S. Commissioner of Education Harold Howe II, promulgator of the famous "segregation guidelines" of 1966, explained at the time:[5]

Title VI of that Act (the Civil Rights Act) as you know, prohibits Federal aid to any program of activity that discriminates among its recipients on the basis of race, color, or national origin.

Thus the Civil Rights Act makes of every Federal program, whether it be for education, urban development, or water pollution control, a powerful financial tool in the drive against racial inequity. The rationale behind this Act is simple: no desegregation, no Federal money.

But though the rationale may be simple, its operation is both frustrating and complex. The Nation sees that frustration in the Office of Education's attempts to secure compliance with our school desegregation guidelines in the South. We in the Office see this frustration in an even more acute form in our attempts to define what constitutes racial discrimination in the cities of the North and West, where segregation depends less on stated community policy than upon patterns of residence.

To say this is by no means to say that the Office of Education is caving in on *de facto* segregation—on segregation Northern-style. It is to say that the issues are complicated and subtle, that establishing a clear-cut legal basis on which to take action—and be confident of withstanding any challenge—has required far more investigation and study than we would have preferred.

[5] "The Heat in Our Kitchen," an address by Harold Howe II, U.S. Commissioner of Education, HEW, before the School Administrators' Conference sponsored by the National Urban League and Teachers College of Columbia University, June 18, 1966.

M. A. Farber reported in the New York Times on February 19, 1968:[6]

A resolution prepared for adoption at the American Association of School Administrators 100th annual meeting here held that "integration is simply one of the methods of approaching the real aim—excellent education for all children."

It recommended that integration "be sought wherever it can reasonably be implemented." But quality education, it added, is universally imperative and should be attained by "whatever means are suitable to the particular situation. . . ."

According to the association's president, William H. Curtis, it does not signal a softening of the group's opposition to racial imbalances in classrooms.

However, he explained that many big-city superintendents, faced with the "practical" difficulties of achieving integration, were being encouraged to place "more and more emphasis" on upgraded schooling, whatever the degree of segregation.

Educational parks, busing and other means of attaining "racial balance" are still being urged. At the same time, "Black Power's" demand for "separate but equal" schools, despite the Supreme Court's ruling that "separate educational facilities are inherently unequal,"[7] will have to be reckoned with in the years ahead.

THE CHURCH, THE STATE, AND EDUCATION

It was the hope of some and the fear of others that the Elementary and Secondary Education Act formula which granted Federal textbook and other aid, not to private church-connected schools but to private, church-connected school children, would not come afoul of the First Amendment to the Constitution.

The U.S. Supreme Court, in *Board of Education* v. *Allen*, held, June 10, 1968, that a law of the State of New York requiring local public school authorities to lend textbooks free of charge to all students (including students attending parochial schools) in grades 7 through 12, is not in violation of the Constitution.

On the same day, the Supreme Court in *Flast* v. *Cohen* expressed no view on the merit of the appellants' claims in the case.

---

[6] P. 29.
[7] *Brown* v. *Board of Education*, 847 U.S. 483 (1954).

(Florence Flast et al. had filed in the United States District Court for the Southern District of New York to enjoin the allegedly unconstitutional expenditure of Federal funds under Titles I and II of the Elementary and Secondary Education Act of 1965; and the lower court ruled that merely as taxpayers they did not have the right to sue.) The Supreme Court decided that "their complaint contains sufficient allegations under the criteria we have outlined to give them standing to invoke a Federal court's jurisdiction for an adjudication on the merits."

It is apparent that, although in *Board of Education* v. *Allen,* the Supreme Court gave its blessing to State textbooks for church-connected schoolchildren, in *Flast* v. *Cohen,* it opened the way for the bringing up of many cases. It opened the courthouse door to suits under some nine Federal aid acts. Although the opponents of judicial review seem to believe that *Board of Education* v. *Allen* has made *Flast* v. *Cohen* largely immaterial, Senator Irvin and other proponents of judicial review intend to press for legislation to provide guidelines for challengers under the first amendment, whom they feel may have legitimate complaints in spite of *Board of Education* v. *Allen.* In any event, the church-state issue is bound to complicate the Federal-aid-to-education picture for some time to come.

SUMMARY OF THE SURVEY

It is conceivable that an observation of the extensiveness of Federal educational activities set forth in this report might lead some readers, particularly foreigners, to the erroneous conclusion that education in the United States is principally supported and administered by the Federal Government. Education is principally supported and administered by the central government in many other countries.

It is observable even from this limited study, however, that the United States has no national system of education. Under provisions of the Federal Constitution, in the United States the local and State governments have assumed through the years the major responsibility for formal education, which they principally control. Nevertheless, in this country education at all levels is supported from local, State, and Federal Government funds, and from many private sources. The Federal Government principally controls the programs it directly administers. There is widespread disagreement concerning the nature and extent of any controls or influences which it exerts over education otherwise.

The regular, formal elementary and secondary schools and institutions of higher education are supported principally from State and local sources. According to data compiled by the Office of Education, U.S. Department of Health, Education, and Welfare, during the school year 1966–67 the total estimated expenditures for the regular, formal schools, colleges and universities, public and private, amounted to $49,100 million. Of that amount 32 percent was derived from local, 29.9 percent from State, 12.6 percent from Federal, and 25.5 percent from all other sources.[8]

Federal activities in the field of education have multiplied in recent years. In his annual message to Congress on Education, on February 5, 1968, President Johnson said that within "the past 4 years":

The Federal Government has raised its investment in education to nearly $12 billion annually, almost triple the level 4 years ago.[9]

Practically all of the departments and other agencies of the Federal Government are carrying out one or more educational programs. Federal educational activities cover all levels of education from elementary schooling to graduate training at the Nation's leading colleges and universities. The instruction includes virtually all subject fields known to man. Federal educational activities directly affect a large percentage of the population and indirectly affect the remainder of the population of the United States and its possessions.

[8] U.S. Department of Health, Education, and Welfare. Digest of Educational Statistics, 1968 edition.
[9] Weekly Compilation of Presidential Documents, vol. 4, No. 6, Feb. 12, 1968, p. 215.

PREVENTING CIVIL DISORDER
THROUGH EDUCATION

(The Kerner Commission Report)*

Education in a democratic society must equip the children of the nation to realize their potential and to participate fully in American life. For the community at large, the schools have discharged this responsibility well. But for many minorities, and particularly for the children of the racial ghetto, the schools have failed to provide the educational experience which could help overcome the effects of discrimination and deprivation.

This failure is one of the persistent sources of grievance and resentment within the Negro community. The hostility of Negro parents and students toward the school system is generating increasing conflict and causing disruption within many city school districts.

But the most dramatic evidence of the relationship between educational practices and civil disorder lies in the high incidence of riot participation by ghetto youth who had not completed high school. Our survey of riot cities found that the typical riot participant was a high school dropout. As Superintendent Briggs of Cleveland testified before the Commission:

"Many of those whose recent acts threaten the domestic safety and tear at the roots of the American democracy are the products of yesterday's inadequate and neglected inner-city schools. The greatest unused and underdeveloped human resources in America are to be found in the deteriorating cores of America's urban centers."

* From *Report of the National Advisory Commission on Civil Disorder,* Bantam Books, 1968.

BASIC STRATEGIES

To meet the urgent need to provide full equality of educational opportunity for disadvantaged youth, we recommend pursuit of the following strategies:

INCREASING EFFORTS TO ELIMINATE DE FACTO SEGREGATION

We have cited the extent of racial isolation in our urban schools. It is great and it is growing. It will not easily be overcome. Nonetheless, we believe school integration to be vital to the well-being of this country.

We base this conclusion not on the effect of racial and economic segregation on achievement of Negro students, although there is evidence of such a relationship; nor on the effect of racial isolation on the even more segregated white students, although lack of opportunity to associate with persons of different ethnic and socio-economic backgrounds surely limits their learning experience.

We support integration as the priority education strategy because it is essential to the future of American society. We have seen in this last summer's disorders the consequences of racial isolation, at all levels, and of attitudes toward race, on both sides, produced by three centuries of myth, ignorance and bias. It is indispensable that opportunities for interaction between the races be expanded. "The problems of this society will not be solved unless and until our children are brought into a common encounter and encouraged to forge a new and more viable design of life."[1]

We recognize that the growing dominance of pupils from disadvantaged minorities in city populations will not soon be reversed. No matter how great the effort toward desegregation, many children of the ghetto will not, within their school careers, attend integrated schools.

If existing disadvantages are not to be perpetuated, we must drastically improve the quality of ghetto education. Equality of results with all-white schools must be the goal.

[1] Testimony of Dr. Dodson.

We see no conflict between the integration and quality education strategies we espouse. Commitment to the goal of integrated education can neither diminish the reality of today's segregated and unequal ghetto schools nor sanction the tragic waste of human resources which they entail.

Far from being in conflict, the strategies are complementary. The aim of quality education is to compensate for and overcome the environmental handicaps of disadvantaged children. The evidence indicates that integration, in itself, does not wholly achieve this purpose. Assessing his report in light of interpretation by others of its findings, Dr. Coleman concludes that:

"it is also true that even in socially or racially integrated schools a child's family background shows a very high relation to his performance. The findings of the [Coleman] Report are quite unambiguous on this score. Even if the school is integrated, the heterogeneity of backgrounds with which children enter school is largely preserved in the heterogeneity of their performance when they finish. As the Report indicates, integration provides benefits to the underprivileged. But it takes only a small step toward equality of educational opportunity."[2]

Moreover, most large integrated schools retain a form of ability grouping, normally resulting in resegregation along racial lines. The Civil Rights Commission found that "many Negro students who attend majority-white schools in fact are in majority-Negro classrooms."[3]

In short, compensatory education is essential not only to improve the quality of education provided in segregated ghetto schools, but to make possible both meaningful integration and maximum achievement in integrated schools.

Attainment of this goal will require adoption of a comprehensive approach designed to reconstruct the ghetto child's social and intellectual environment, compensate for disadvantages already suffered and provide necessary tools for development of essential literary skills. This approach will entail adoption of new and costly educational policies and practices to provide intensive educational efforts beginning with early childhood and continuing through elementary and secondary schools. It will require extraordinary efforts

[2] "Towards Open Schools," James S. Coleman, *The Public Interest*, Fall 1967, p. 23.
[3] "Racial Isolation in the Public Schools," p. 162.

to reconnect parents with the schools. It will also require unique experimentation with new methods to bring back into the educational process street-oriented teenagers and sub-teenagers who have lost all connection with existing school institutions.

IMPROVING COMMUNITY-SCHOOL RELATIONS

In an atmosphere of hostility between the community and the schools, education cannot flourish. A basic problem stems from the isolation of the schools from the other social forces influencing youth. Changes in society—mass media, family structure, religion—have radically altered the role of the school. New links must be built between the schools and the communities they serve. The schools must be related to the broader system which influences and educates ghetto youth.

Expansion of opportunities for community and parental participation in the school system is essential to the successful functioning of the inner-city schools.

EXPANDED OPPORTUNITIES FOR HIGHER AND VOCATIONAL OPPORTUNITIES

To increase the relevance of education to the needs and aspirations of disadvantaged youth and to prepare them for full participation in American society, we recommend expanding opportunities both for higher education and for vocational training.

SUGGESTED PROGRAMS

Increasing Efforts to Eliminate De Facto Segregation

Increased aid to school systems seeking to eliminate de facto segregation either within the system or in cooperation with neighboring school systems. Local school boards have experimented with a variety of techniques designed to accomplish desegregation. Among those commonly employed are school pairing, busing, open enrollment, boundary changes, strategic use of site selection, en-

largement of attendance areas, and consolidation of schools to overcome racial imbalance. The results have not been uniform. Much
appears to depend on the size and racial composition of the city and
the attitudes of its suburbs.

Some of the smaller cities have achieved considerable success.
In many of our larger cities, however, the population shift earlier
described has proceeded so far that integration is not feasible without the active cooperation of suburban communities. In others,
distances between the white and Negro populations living within
city boundaries make these methods of accomplishing integration
unfeasible. While the desegregation technique best suited for it
should be determined by each community we believe substantial
federal assistance should be provided.

Title IV. Under Title IV of the Civil Rights Act of 1964, the U.S.
Commissioner of Education is authorized to provide "technical
assistance to . . . [state and local education agencies] in the preparation, adoption, and implementation of plans for the desegregation of public schools." However, such aid is not available in
support of locally-designed programs to overcome racial imbalance
in the schools. Moreover, this program has never been adequately
funded, even to accomplish its limited objectives. Applications for
Title IV funds have consistently exceeded the amounts requested by
the Administration and the far lower sums appropriated by the
Congress.

We believe that the Title IV program should be reoriented and
expanded into a major federal effort to provide comprehensive aid
to support state and local desegregation projects.

To accomplish this purpose, Title IV should become the vehicle
for a comprehensive federal construction, technical assistance and
operating grant program. Successful implementation of such a program will require repeal of the present statutory prohibition against
provision of assistance to support and encourage desegregation
through "assignment of students to public schools in order to overcome racial imbalance." To stimulate needed planning, formulation
of long-term integration plans by applicant state and local agencies
should be required as a condition to receiving assistance. Title IV
aid would be available only for projects which promote integrated
education in accordance with such plans.

Bonus Support. As an additional incentive to integration, the Title IV program might well be modified to provide substantially increased support upon attainment of specified levels of racial integration. Such bonus assistance should be large enough to enable each recipient school to attain a clearly superior quality of education in comparison with non-integrated schools.

Exemplary Schools. The Title IV program should stimulate development of exemplary city or metropolitan schools offering special courses and programs designed to attract, on a voluntary basis, students of varying racial and socio-economic backgrounds on a full or part-time basis.[4] These model programs should make extensive and imaginative use of resources uniquely available to city schools —the city itself, its museums, galleries, governmental institutions, and other public and private facilities.

To the extent that the quality of city schools influences migration to the suburbs, development of exemplary schools could operate to retain middle-class white families in the city and induce others to return, so increasing opportunities for integration. Through educational planning on a metropolitan basis, fostered by direct federal grants to cooperative planning bodies encompassing city and suburban school districts, opportunities for engaging central-city and suburban students in common educational experiences can be provided.

Specific methods of providing integrated educational experiences under this program could include the following:

Establishment of major educational magnet schools: depending upon the size and racial character of the city and its suburbs, these schools could serve all the students of a small city, students living in different sections of a large city or subdivisions of a metropolitan area. Special curricula could include intensive instruction or specialized educational programs (for example, science or commerce).

Establishment of supplemental education centers: these centers would offer specialized facilities and instruction to students from different schools in the city or its suburbs for a portion of the school day. It is most important that courses be developed and scheduled to provide

---

[4] Limited funds have been provided for this purpose under Title III of the Elementary and Secondary Education Act (ESEA). This aspect of the Title III program could be used to supplement the Title IV program here proposed or could be discontinued, releasing limited ESEA funds for other purposes.

racially integrated educational experiences for both white and Negro students.

Educational Parks. Such a reoriented Title IV program could provide substantial support, including construction funds, for communities choosing to develop the promising but costly educational parks now under consideration in several cities.

As contrasted with the magnet schools and supplementary centers described above, educational parks would consolidate or cluster existing schools, thereby broadening attendance areas to bring within the school zone a racially and economically heterogeneous population. These parks could be developed in conjunction with metropolitan plans to serve students from the suburbs, as well as the city. Their location should be selected to accomplish this objective.

Because of the economies of size made possible through consolidation, the quality of education offered all of the students attending educational parks could be improved. Problems raised by the size of such institutions could be overcome through inclusion of smaller sub-unit schools and individualized instruction made feasible by educational technology (computers, television) and savings resulting from the school consolidation program.

Eliminating Discrimination in Northern Schools. While racial isolation in the urban public schools results largely from residential segregation, there is evidence that racial discrimination also plays a part in reducing opportunities for integration.

For example, the Civil Rights Commission found that, when crowding in certain Cleveland and Milwaukee Negro schools became acute, school authorities began busing students to nearby underutilized white schools, where they were segregated in separate classrooms and luncheon facilities. When Negro residents objected, school officials in Milwaukee canceled busing altogether as "educationally undesirable," even though white students had been bused and integrated into receiving-school classrooms for years. In Cincinnati, to relieve overcrowding in a Negro school, students were bused past several nearby white schools with available space to a 98 percent Negro school, 5.5 miles away.

The Civil Rights Commission also reported that in many cities school attendance boundaries and location of new schools have been designed to perpetuate racial segregation.

Title VI. Under Title VI of the Civil Rights Act of 1964, the Congress prohibited federal financial aid to any program or activity which practices racial discrimination.

Federal law requires that Title VI be applied uniformly in all states. Implementing this provision, the Department of Health, Education and Welfare has recently instituted a survey to examine compliance with Title VI in school districts of all 50 states. The Department has made clear that its investigation is not directed at *de facto* segregation arising from reasonable application of neighborhood attendance policies.

We support this survey and urge that it be followed by vigorous action to assure full compliance with federal law in all sections of the country. Sufficient staff and resources should be provided HEW, so that this program can be effectively carried out without reducing the level of activity in the South.

Provision of Quality Education in Ghetto Schools

Improving the Quality of Teaching in Ghetto Schools. The teaching of disadvantaged children requires special skills and capabilities. Teachers possessing these qualifications are in short supply. We need a national effort to attract to the teaching profession well-qualified and highly motivated young people, and to equip them to work effectively with disadvantaged students.

The Teacher Corps program is a sound instrument for such an effort. Established by the Higher Education Act of 1965, it provides training in local colleges or universities for teacher interns—college graduates interested in teaching in poverty areas. Corpsmen are assigned to poverty area schools at the request of local school systems and with approval of state education agencies. They are employed by the school system and work in teams headed by an experienced teacher.

The National Advisory Council on the Education of Disadvantaged Children and the National Education Association found the Teacher Corps to have succeeded in attracting dedicated young people to the teaching profession, training them to work effectively in poverty areas, and making substantial contributions to the education of students.

The impact of this highly promising program has been severely restricted by limited and late funding. There are now only 1,506 interns and 337 team leaders in the entire nation.

The Teacher Corps should be expanded into a major national program.

The Education Professions Development Act ("EDPA") provides grants and fellowships to attract qualified persons to the field of education, and improve the ability of present teachers through advanced training and retraining. The Act also provides funds for institutes and workshops for other educational personnel, including guidance counselors, social workers, teacher aides and administrators. Finally, EDPA offers grants to local educational agencies experiencing critical shortages of teachers and teacher aides.

We recommend that the EDPA program focus on the special need for expanding the supply and improving the quality of teachers working in schools serving disadvantaged students and that it be substantially funded.

Concomitantly teacher training institutions should place major emphasis on preparing teachers for work in schools serving disadvantaged children. Courses should familiarize teacher candidates with the psychology, history, culture and learning problems of minority group pupils.

Class work alone, however, cannot be expected adequately to equip future teachers of disadvantaged children. Intensive in-service training programs designed to bring teacher candidates into frequent and sustained contact with inner-city schools are required. Other professionals and non-professionals working in ghetto-related activities—social workers, street workers—could be included as instructors in teacher training programs.

Year-Round Education for Disadvantaged Students. The present, anachronistic practice of releasing hundreds of thousands of children from a relatively full school schedule to idleness in the summer months is both a substantial factor in producing disorders and a tragic waste of time and facilities. Financing should be provided, through ESEA, for large-scale year-round programs in the disadvantaged areas of our cities. The testimony before this Commission, including that of Cabinet members and public educators, was unanimous in its support of this proposal.

What is needed is not 12 months of the same routine, but innovative programs tailored to total educational needs, and providing a wide range of educational activities (verbal skills, culture and arts, recreation, job training, work experience and camps).

Planning on a 12-month basis will be required. To meet this need, ESEA assistance should be provided through a single grant program (rather than separate 10-month and summer grants) and conditioned on development of year-round educational plans. Technical assistance should be provided for such planning.

As a step toward year-round education, federal funds should be made available for school and camp programs this summer.

The National Advisory Council on Education of Disadvantaged Children studied summer programs set up with ESEA funds and found that they offer special opportunities for new approaches to teaching disadvantaged children.

Summer camp programs for disadvantaged children offer significant educational and recreational opportunities, and should be encouraged. Educational components, particularly verbal skills, should be incorporated. It is essential that federal aid for such projects be committed well before the end of this school year, so that adequate time is available to design effective programs.

Early Childhood Education. Early childhood education is the very heart of the effort to reconstruct the environment which incapacitates disadvantaged children educationally, even before they enter the school system. Comprehensive preschool programs are essential to overcome the early language deprivation and conceptual disabilities of these children. Yet in most urban areas, no more than a maximum of 40 percent of the eligible school population in disadvantaged communities is receiving even one year (age 4) of preschool training.

We believe that the time has come to build on the proven success of the Head Start and other preschool programs in order to bring the benefits of comprehensive early childhood education to all children from disadvantaged homes, and to extend the reach to younger children. For this purpose, the Office of Economic Opportunity should receive substantially increased funds.

Effective implementation of this expanded program will be vital to its success. We recommend the following guidelines:

Early childhood education programs should provide comprehensive educational support tailored to the needs of the child, and should not be simply custodial care. Both day care and Head Start components are part of comprehensive early childhood education; each should be designed to overcome the debilitating effect on learning ability of a disadvantaged environment.

Parents and the home environment have a critical impact on a child's early development. Early childhood programs should involve parents and the home, as well as the child. This can be accomplished through community education classes, and use of community aides and mothers' assistants. To reduce the incidence of congenital abnormalities, these community-based programs should be tied in with prenatal training.

Since adequate facilities are scarce in many disadvantaged communities, where schools are overcrowded, and buildings deteriorated, the program should provide funds for special early childhood education facilities.

There is a need for maximum experimentation and variety. Funding should continue to support early childhood programs operated by community groups and organizations, as well as by the school system.

Early childhood education programs should include provisions for medical care and food, so that the educational experience can have its intended impact.

Improving Educational Practices—Elementary Schools. Without major changes in educational practices, greater expenditures on existing elementary schools serving disadvantaged neighborhoods will not significantly improve the quality of education. Moreover, current assessments of preschool programs indicate that their gains are lost in the elementary grades, unless the schools themselves are improved.

We suggest adoption of the following educational practices to improve school performance:

Extra incentives for highly qualified teachers working in ghetto and economically and culturally deprived rural area schools. The most effective means to attract such teachers is to make these schools exciting and attractive places to work. The practices set forth below contribute toward this end. In addition, we suggest that opportunities for creative and imaginative teaching be expanded by allowing the teacher greater discretion selection and presentation of materials. Such an approach is likely to produce benefits in terms of attraction and retention of excellent teachers and improved student performance. Rewards related to attainment of career objectives should be provided for teachers working in schools serving disadvantaged children. For example, all school systems should consider requiring service in such schools as a condition to advancement to administrative positions, where the experience gained would be of great value.

Reduction in maximum class size: It is clear that disadvantaged students require more attention and exert greater demands on teacher time than middle-class students. While reduction of class size may not in itself improve pupil achievement, it will free teachers to devote more time to educating disadvantaged students. It is of vital importance, therefore, that efforts to reduce the maximum class size in schools serving disadvantaged students be coupled with programs designed to improve the skills and capacities of teachers of disadvantaged children.

Recognition of the history, culture and contribution of minority groups to American civilization in the textbooks and curricula of all schools: In addition, school curricula should be adapted to take advantage of student experiences and interests in order to stimulate motivation.

Provision of supplementary services in the schools for severely disadvantaged or disturbed students. Such services should be made available within the schools, rather than at centralized facilities, and should include medical and psychiatric care.

Individualized instruction through extensive use of nonprofessional personnel: There is impressive evidence that these workers can make a meaningful educational contribution by providing individualized tutoring and incentive lacking in segregated schools.

In the *Homework Helper* program in New York City, pupils in the fourth through sixth grades were tutored after school by senior high school students. Tutoring was provided four afternoons a week under the supervision of a master teacher; the tutors received training on the fifth day. Initiated with a grant from the Ford Foundation primarily to provide employment for high school students, the program had significant educational impact on both the pupils and the tutors. The pupils who received 4 hours of tutoring showed a gain of 6 months on reading tests, compared to 3.5 months by the control group. An even more dramatic finding was that: "In the six months of the research, the mean score of the tutors improved 3.4 grade levels while the mean score of the control group improved 1.7 grade levels."

The Neighborhood Youth Corps and the College Work-Study program provide the tools for reproducing this program in every major city in the country. In some cities, NYC students are already working in these schools. But in many, NYC job assignments are far less stimulating. Colleges and universities should be encouraged to assign more students participating in the College Work-Study program to tutorial projects.

Both programs, NYC and College Work-Study should be expanded and reoriented for this purpose.

Intensive concentration on basic verbal skills: A basic problem in schools in large cities is the low achievement in the fundamental subjects of students from disadvantaged areas. This has been documented in the Haryou Studies in New York, the study prepared for the McCone Commission following the Watts riot of 1965 and nationally in the Coleman Report. The lack of reading and writing skills affects detrimentally every other aspect of the later school program. Intensive assistance in fundamental literacy skills, including remedial assistance, should be provided in all schools serving disadvantaged children.

We recognize that the enrichment programs we recommend will be very costly. ESEA provides financial assistance for such programs, but the amounts available do not match the need. To make a significant improvement in the quality of education provided in schools serving disadvantaged students, ESEA funding should be substantially increased from its current level.

In addition, Title I should be modified to provide for greater concentration of aid for school districts having the greatest proportion of disadvantaged students. This can be accomplished by altering the formula governing eligibility to exclude affluent school districts with less than specified minimum levels of poor students.

Improving Educational Practices—Secondary Schools. Many of the educational practices recommended with respect to the elementary schools are applicable at the secondary level. In addition, secondary school students require extensive guidance, counseling and advice in planning their education program and future careers. Such assistance, routinely provided by middle-class families, is lacking for the ghetto student. To promote its acceptance, indigenous personnel—college students, returning Vietnam veterans—should be utilized.

The new Stay in School program, for which the President recently requested an appropriation of $30 million, could provide funds for this and other projects designed to motivate disadvantaged high school students to pursue their education. We recommend that this program be fully funded.

Intensive National Program to Increase Verbal Skills of Ghetto Residents. For the products of the ghetto schools, many of them unemployed and functionally illiterate, these efforts will come too late. To compensate for educational disadvantages already increased we recommend a substantial appropriation to support an intensive year-round program beginning in the summer of 1968 to improve the verbal skills of people in low-income areas, with primary emphasis on the language problems of minority groups.

The present effort simply does not match the need. Current estimates indicate that there are approximately 16,300,000 educationally disadvantaged Americans (those who have less than an 8th grade education). While exact figures are not available, it is likely that a disproportionate number of the educationally disadvantaged are Negroes. Census data establishes that 36.9 percent of Negroes over 25 years of age, but only 14.8 percent of whites, are functionally illiterate.

The principal federal literacy program—Adult Basic Education —is meeting only a small fraction of this need; as of June 1966, it had provided assistance to some 373,000 people.

The Adult Basic Education program is a sound instrument for implementing an intensive literacy program. By affording both the public schools and community-based organizations the opportunity to conduct literacy projects, this program provides desired flexibility. It should be strengthened and expanded to make a major impact on illiteracy.

To concentrate its effect where the need is greatest and the potential payoff high, we suggest that priority be given to the unemployed and underemployed, and to welfare mothers. Increasing literacy levels would eliminate a major barrier to productive employment, and improved support for education in the home.

The high school dropouts should be brought into the program by lowering the age limit from 18 to 16, as proposed by the President. Course offerings should be expanded to include matters of interest and concern to residents of low-income areas.

Expanded Experimentation, Evaluation, and Research. Much remains to be learned about the most effective methods of teaching disadvantaged children in schools segregated by race and class. Research efforts should be oriented in this direction.

In addition to research, federal support should be provided for promising, but as yet unvalidated, experimental programs designed to involve the talents and resources of the entire community in support of education of disadvantaged children, and develop new and better educational techniques particularly adapted to the interests and needs of these students.

Among the educational approaches which we believe should be considered and evaluated are the current efforts to develop new patterns of education (such as storefront schools and street academies) for students who do not fit the traditional pattern, possible forms of competitive education (such as the use of businesses, universities and neighborhood corporations as subcontractors for the operation of certain education programs), concentration of assistance to a few schools serving ghetto children in order to test the effects of a maximum compensatory education effort, development of model experimental subsystems (high school and several feeder schools to provide specialized instruction) and teaching English as a second language to ghetto students whose dialect often constitutes a first language.

Finally, there is great need to evaluate not only these experimental programs but the entire enrichment effort. The Elementary and Secondary Education Act should be amended to require recipient school systems to undertake a thorough evaluation of their compensatory education effort, as a condition to receiving ESEA funds.

Improving Community-School Relations

Administrative Obstacles to Community Participation in the Educational Process Should be Eliminated. The school systems of our largest cities have become highly centralized, with decision-making responsibility for a large and disparate population concentrated in a central board of education. While this process has produced substantial benefits—city-wide tax base and nonpolitical administration—it has sometimes entailed serious sacrifices in terms of accountability and community participation. What is necessary is to preserve the worthwhile features present in the existing system while eliminating the liabilities thus far encountered. The objective must be to make public education more relevant and responsive to the community, and to increase support for it in the home.

This can be accomplished through maintaining centralized control over educational standards and the raising of revenue, while decentralizing control over other aspects of educational policy. The precise mix must be determined locally. However, specific mechanisms for seeking the advice and consultation of students and parents such as Parents Advisory Councils or other similar bodies should be adopted.

Ghetto Schools Should Serve the Educational and Other Needs of the Total Community. School facilities should be available during and after normal school hours for a variety of community service functions, delivery of social services by local agencies (including health and welfare), adult and community training and education programs, community meetings, recreational and cultural activities.

Decentralization and the establishment of Parents Advisory Councils will afford the community a means through which to communicate needs for such services and to play an active role in shaping activities. In addition to making better use of the major capital investment in school plants, this approach will encourage ghetto residents to regard their schools not as alien institutions but as vital community centers.

Use of Local Residents as Teacher Aides and Tutors. We have noted the educational gains accomplished through use of local, subprofessional personnel in the schools. These workers can contribute to improving community-school relations by providing a close link between the school system and the parents.

Results of Achievement and Other Tests Should be Made Public on a Regular Basis. To increase the accountability of the public schools, the results of their performance should be made available to the public. Such information is available in some, but not all, cities. We see no reason for withholding useful and highly relevant indices of school (but not individual student) performance and recommend that all school systems adopt a policy of full public disclosure.

EXPANDING OPPORTUNITIES FOR HIGHER AND VOCATIONAL EDUCATION

Higher Education

By enactment of the Higher Education Act of 1965, the Congress committed this nation to the goal of equal opportunity for higher education for all Americans, regardless of race or economic circumstance. While progress has been made, this goal, the key to virtually all managerial and professional jobs, remains for the disadvantaged student an unfulfilled promise.

Mr. Harvey Oostdyck, Educational Director of the New York Urban League, testified that less than one percent of the youth in Harlem go to college. In the nation, approximately eight percent of disadvantaged high school graduates, many of whom are Negro, attend college; the comparable figure for all high school graduates is more than 50 percent.

The fundamental reasons for this disparity lie in the cost of higher education and the poor quality of the elementary and secondary education available to minorities. In the preceding sections, we have recommended programs which we believe will ultimately eliminate these differences. But the full effect of these changes will not be felt for some years. In the interim, if we are to provide equality of opportunity for that segment of disadvantaged youth with college potential, special programs are needed.

Expansion of Upward Bound and Establishment of Special One-Year Postgraduate College Preparatory Schools. The Upward Bound program of the Office of Economic Opportunity, a program under which students from poverty backgrounds attend intensive six to eight week summer sessions on college campuses and receive special assistance throughout the school year, is designed specifically to meet the problem of motivating and preparing disadvantaged youth for college. The program has been effective. Of the 23,000 students covered in 1967 (52 percent of whom were Negro), 83 percent went on to college. However, the size of the program is far short of the need. Estimates indicate that some 600,000 poverty-area students could usefully be helped.

We believe that the Upward Bound concept is sound and recommend that it be substantially expanded.

Even an expanded Upward Bound program will not overcome the poor level of secondary school education attained by ghetto youth. We recommend that federal funds be made available for special one-year educational programs with the sole function of providing college preparatory training for disadvantaged youth. These programs could be operated by community colleges or local boards of education.

Removing Financial Barriers to Higher Education. The effort to assist qualified but needy young people to obtain a higher education should be strengthened and expanded.

Through the Educational Talent Search program, the Federal Government provides financial assistance to public and nonprofit agencies to identify and encourage disadvantaged young people with college potential to enter or re-enter educational programs.

The President's proposed Educational Opportunity Act of 1968 would provide combined grant, work and loan aid to poor college-bound students in need of financial assistance. Such assistance should be sufficiently flexible and substantial to accommodate the differing needs of individual students.

These programs can make an important contribution to realization of the goal set by the President in his 1968 Education Message to the Congress "that every qualified young person . . . have all the education he wants and can absorb." If this promise is to become a reality, these programs must be funded at a level commensurate with need.

The benefit gained by increasing opportunities for disadvantaged students to seek and obtain higher education can be amplified by providing incentives for college-trained public service personnel (particularly, teachers and health workers) needed to work in poverty areas. This might be accomplished by including a forgiveness feature in programs providing financial assistance in the form of loans to college and graduate students. This feature, like that now included under the National Defense Education Act loan program, would provide for the cancellation of loans at a reasonable annual rate, if the recipient works in a low-income area.

Vocational Education

Despite substantially increased efforts made possible by the Vocational Education Act of 1963, quality vocational education is still not available to all who need it. The recent report of the Advisory Council on Vocational Education, established to evaluate the Act, concluded that, although five out of six youths never achieve a college education, only a quarter of the total high school population in the country received vocational education. Similarly, a 1964 Labor Department survey found that less than one-half of the non-college-trained labor force had any formal training for the jobs they held.

Existing vocational training programs are not effectively linked to job opportunities. The Advisory Council found "little evidence of much effort to develop programs in the area where critical manpower shortages exist"—the health occupations and technical fields.[5]

[5] "Vocational Education: The Bridge Between Man and His Work," Report of the Advisory Council on Vocational Education, 1968, p. 29.

The special need of the dropout is still being neglected. With an unemployment rate for Negro youth more than twice that for white youth, this need is particularly acute.

To improve the quality and expand the availability of vocational education, provision of additional funds as recommended by the Advisory Council may well be required. The federal vocational education program should be strengthened by enactment of the proposed Partnership for Learning and Earning Act of 1968.

Significant improvement of vocational education, however, will depend on the use made locally of federal and other funds. We suggest the following guidelines:

Inclusion of intensive literacy training: literacy skills are obviously indispensable to productive employment. All vocational education programs should provide literacy training, either directly or in conjunction with Adult Basic Education or other programs.

Greater emphasis on part-time cooperative education and work-study programs through use of release time: the Advisory Council found that these programs, which provide students with jobs upon completion of the course, are the best available in the vocational education field. They consistently yield high placement records, high employment stability and high job satisfaction. The most important factor in improving vocational education is that training be linked to available jobs with upward mobility potential. To accomplish this goal, the active cooperation of the business community in defining job needs and effective training practices should be engaged. Consideration should be given to releasing students to attend pretraining Opportunities Industrialization Centers.

Full implementation of vocational training programs for high school dropouts: the Advisory Council found that assistance available under the Vocational Education Act for the training of this group is not being adequately utilized. The need for doing so is critical.

Elimination of barriers to full participation of ghetto youth in vocational education programs: some vocational schools attempt to improve the quality of their student body and enhance their prestige by raising entrance requirements. This policy eliminates those in greatest need. This practice should be discontinued and support for these students expanded.

Follow-up support and assistance to ghetto youth receiving vocational training: the Advisory Council reported that "the most successful vocational programs are those which assume responsibility for placing their graduates and thus get feedback on their strengths and weaknesses." Vocational educators should continue to provide counselling and guidance for their students until they have been successfully placed in training related jobs.

Increased training to meet the critical need for more workers in professional, semi-professional and technical fields: demand for public service workers alone exceeds supply by five to one. Preparation of disadvantaged students for these desirable positions should be greatly intensified.

IMPLEMENTATION OF THESE PROGRAMS

The Federal Role—The principal burden for funding the programs we have proposed will fall upon the Federal Government. Caught between an inadequate and shrinking tax base and accelerating demands for public expenditures, the cities are not able to generate sufficient financing. Although there is much more that state governments can and should do, the taxing resources available at this level are far from adequate.

The Federal Government has recognized and responded to this need. Federal expenditures for education, training and related services have increased from $4.7 billion in fiscal 1964 to $12.3 billion in fiscal 1969. These figures include aid for preschool, elementary, secondary and higher education, vocational education, work-training and activities not related to the education of disadvantaged students. This network of federal educational programs provides a sound and comprehensive basis for meeting the interrelated educational needs of disadvantaged students. We need now to strengthen that base, as we have proposed, and to build upon it by providing greatly increased federal funds for the education of the disadvantaged.

The State Role—Many states provide more support for suburban and rural schools than for city education systems. Designed at a time when the suburban school systems were poorer than those in the cities, state aid formulas now operate to extend existing inequities.

We urge that every state reexamine its present method of allocating funds to local school districts, not merely to provide equal funds for all political subdivisions on a per-pupil basis, but to assure more per-student aid to districts having a high proportion of disadvantaged students. Only if equalization formulas reflect the need to spend larger amounts per pupil in schools predominantly populated by disadvantaged students in order to achieve equality of educational results with other schools will state aid be allocated on an equitable basis.

To assist the states in devising equalization formulas which would accomplish this objective, we recommend that the Office of Education develop prototype formulas. Federal programs aiding states should require that funds be allocated within each state in accordance with formulas which conform with the criteria set forth above.

We recognize that virtually all school districts need more money than they now receive. Provision of expanded state aid to education may well be justified. Whatever the amounts may be, we believe that allocation should be made in accordance with the standards described above.

Finally, the states and, in particular, the state education agencies, have a key role to play in accomplishing school integration. The states are in a unique position to bring about urban-suburban cooperation and metropolitan planning. We urge that the efforts of state educational agencies in this area be given clear direction through adoption of state-wide, long-term integration plans and intensified through active promotion of such plans.

The Local Role—We have emphasized that more money alone will not suffice. Accomplishment of the goal of meaningful educational opportunity for all will require exercise of enlightened and courageous leadership by local government. The programs which we have proposed can succeed only if imaginative and effective use is made locally of funds provided by Federal and State governments. Mayors, city councils, school boards and administrators must lead the community toward acceptance of policies which promote integration while improving the quality of education in existing, racially segregated schools. The cooperation of their suburban counterparts is no less essential.

This responsibility is not limited to public officials. It is shared by the private community—business leaders, professionals, clergymen, civic organizations. Attainment of the goal of equal and integrated educational opportunity will require the leadership, support, talents and energies of the entire community.

THE NATIONAL ASSESSMENT

by Eleanor L. Norris*

Basically, the National Assessment's purpose is twofold: To gather and make available to educators and the general public the first censuslike data on the educational attainments of young Americans; and to measure what growth—or decline—takes place in selected aspects of those attainments over a period of time.

The recognition of the need to gather information about the effectiveness of education is certainly not new. When the U.S. Office of Education was first established in 1867, one of the duties given the Commissioner of Education was to determine the progress of education. Through the years a great deal of information about what goes into the educational system has been compiled—the number of school buildings and their average age, the average educational level of our teachers, what percent of our schools have hot lunch programs, and so on. Information about what comes out of the system exists also: how many youngsters graduate from high school and college, test scores that allow schools or districts to compare their students with those in other schools, and the like.

The kind of information that is not available, however, is a description nationally of what Americans know or can do and indices showing actual progress in education—or lack of it. Results of a standardized test tell us that Johnny, an eighth grader, scores at the 90th percentile on a reading test. But this score does not tell us what kind of material Johnny can actually read, or what percentage of 13-year-olds can read and answer questions on a major article in the *New York Times*. Such test scores do not tell us what percentage of students can determine whether the larger size of a product is more economical than the smaller size. And they don't

* From *American Education,* October, 1969, U.S. Office of Education (Washington, D.C.: U.S. Government Printing Office).

tell us whether more or fewer people can do this now, compared to, say, five years ago. This is the kind of descriptive information the National Assessment is looking for. Over a period of years, when the assessment has been repeated two or three times, it will also have data to show whether educational attainment has improved or not.

This ambitious undertaking really began during the summer of 1963 when Francis Keppel, then U.S. Commissioner of Education, and Ralph Tyler, then director of the Center for Advanced Study in the Behavioral Sciences at Stanford, Calif., broached the feasibility of conducting such an assessment. They concluded that it was feasible. The Carnegie Corporation then held two meetings on the feasibility and desirability of an assessment, and John Corson of the Woodrow Wilson School of Public and International Affairs at Princeton did a further study. Corson also supported the idea, but recommended that an exploratory committee be established to look into how such an assessment could be done, and to develop the instruments to conduct it. With Carnegie support, later supplemented by the Fund for the Advancement of Education, a committee was appointed, with Dr. Tyler as its chairman and Stephen Withey of the University of Michigan as its staff director.

The Exploratory Committee on Assessing the Progress of Education (ECAPE) worked with hundreds of teachers, subject matter experts, other educators, and interested laymen to set out the boundaries of what and who would be assessed, and how. Ten subject areas were chosen with the recognition that other areas probably would and should be added later. They were science, writing (composition), citizenship, mathematics, music, literature, social studies, art, reading, and career and occupational development.

The committee also decided that four age groups would be included in the assessment: nine-year-olds, most of whom would have completed the primary grades; 13-year-olds, most of whom would be nearing the end of intermediate grades; 17-year-olds, who would be finishing secondary grades; and a group of adults of ages 26–35, most of whom had completed all their formal education.

Rather than attempt to gather information about individual schools, school districts, or even States, the committee divided the United States into four geographical areas for the purpose of sampling and reporting results—Northeast, Southeast, Central, and West. They decided that information about other sub-groups should be investigated also: people living in different types of communities —large city, urban fringe, smaller city, and rural-small town; boys and girls and men and women; people from varying socioeducational backgrounds; and people of different races.

Another important decision of the committee was to administer the assessment as an on-going, cyclical process. Consequently, three of the 10 areas are being assessed this year; three will be assessed in the second year, and four in the third year. Then the cycle will begin all over again. This plan allows for hiring a permanent, full-time field staff to contact schools and administer questions to those in the sample.

The committee's decision to gather descriptive data about knowledge and skills, rather than to get scores for individuals, meant that questions totally different from those in the usual classroom test had to be prepared. Before these questions (called exercises in the National Assessment idiom) could be written, it was necessary to determine the objectives that the American educational system is trying to achieve. Four private research organizations— Educational Testing Service, the American Institutes for Research, Science Research Associates, and the Psychological Corporation— were awarded contracts with ECAPE to develop objectives that 1) schools currently are seeking to attain, 2) scholars in the field consider authentic to their discipline, and 3) thoughtful laymen consider important for American youth to learn.

When the objectives for all 10 subject areas were developed, they represented a reorganization, restatement, and something of a summarization of the objectives that frequently have appeared in print in the last quarter century. This general agreement, however, does not mean that the objectives developed are the only ones possible or the ones on which all educators and lay people agree. To keep objectives current and to make them reflect the best thinking in the field is part of the National Assessment plan. Objectives for the 10 subject areas will be reviewed regularly as the assessment proceeds.

Each objective and the rationale behind it was clearly spelled out. One of the objectives for citizenship reads as follows: "*Support rationality in communication, thought, and action on social problems.*" The habit of approaching problems rationally should have begun to form by age nine. This approach includes being informed and openminded, communicating with others, and thinking independently. In 13-year-olds, rational thought is rapidly developing toward its full capacity. Although their own personal lives are still their main concern, children of this age should be gaining information, communicating, and thinking independently about broader matters of social interest. Seventeen-year-olds or adults realize that if informed rationality is the most promising approach to problem-solving, then in a democracy it is essential that informed rationality be widespread among the citizenry, for in the long run the burden of solving society's problems is theirs. Universal education and free open communication help a society to solve its problems rationally, first, by stimulating the spread of wisdom as widely and quickly as possible, and consequently by the more enlightened judgments which the citizenry conveys to its leaders.

This major objective is then broken down into sub-objectives, and model exercises are prepared. One of the sub-objectives for this citizenship objective, for example, is that the students *try to inform themselves on socially important matters and to understand alternative viewpoints.*

This sub-objective can then be assessed in a number of ways. One possible exercise, prepared as an example of the kind of question presented to 17-year-olds, would be: Some people want strict gun control laws passed. They would like laws requiring, for example, that a person have a permit from the police to own a gun. Other people do not want such strict laws.

A. Give two reasons why some people want strict gun control laws.

B. Give two reasons why some people do not want strict gun control laws.

Clearly, this is not the kind of question one finds on the usual standardized test. It presents difficult problems of scoring and analysis, but the information the assessment is seeking is worth the effort.

In the summer of 1968, ECAPE completed its task of designing plans and instruments for assessment. At that point, the "Exploratory" was dropped from its name, and it became the Committee for Assessing the Progress of Education (CAPE). In the early days of the project, certain educational organizations were less than enthusiastic about such an assessment if not completely opposed to it. These groups did indicate, however, that they would support the project if it were directed by a non-Federal educational organization responsible to the public. Thus, last July, the Education Commission of the States (ECS) officially became the agency responsible for National Assessment. The policymaking board now consists of representatives from the former CAPE and from ECS.

In the spring of 1969, the exercises developed for the year's subject areas—science, writing, and citizenship—were administered to 17-year-olds enrolled in school. The schools to be assessed had previously been chosen by random sampling procedures and notified by mail. Then in March, 27 district supervisors—young college graduates who are in charge of administering the exercises—visited more than 550 schools throughout the country to explain the project to school personnel and get their cooperation.

These district supervisors are actually employees of either Research Triangle Institute (RTI) in North Carolina or Measurement Research Center (MRC) of Iowa City, Iowa, contractor and subcontractor respectively for administering the exercises. The district supervisors also hire and train assistant exercise administrators, of whom some 500 to 600 will be needed in the course of the assessment.

On his second visit to a school, which sometimes was several weeks after his initial contact, a district supervisor took with him exercise booklets, pencils, training manuals for the exercise administrators, instructions concerning how to choose the sample of students, two assistants whom he must train to administer exercises, and a tape recorder. The exercises, along with pertinent instructions such as where to write the answers, were tape recorded, and the students listened to the tape as they worked through their booklets. National Assessment is perhaps the first measurement project of its size to use taped instructions and exercises to standardize administration procedures, and to facilitate reading for slow readers and for children who might have trouble with the English language if not given assistance. In addition, many students were given assessment exercises in individual interviews with the supervisor or administrator.

One of the supervisor's first jobs was to draw the sample of students to participate. In most schools, no more than 75 students, and usually fewer, were chosen. In a school with a very large enrollment, however, as many as 150 students might be chosen.

Exercises were administered to groups of no more than 12 students by the supervisor, or one of his administrators, who gave a brief introduction to the project before passing out the packages of exercises. The tape recorder took over the groups for the rest of their administration time. Youngsters seemed to respond well to the tape, although some fast readers found it too slow for them. One supervisor remarked on the students' apparent acceptance of the machine: "They might not pay much attention while a person was talking, but once the tape recorder was turned on, they were all business."

When the booklets were completed, they were collected, checked to be sure they had been marked clearly, and set aside to be mailed in, with all other exercise packages from that school, at the end of the week. No student's name appeared on the packages or left the school with National Assessment personnel, ensuring complete anonymity.

Assessment procedures took about a week. In most locations more than one school in a district fell within the sample, so that once the supervisor had set up his procedures for one school and had seen his exercise administrators begin their work, he left for the other school or schools to perform the same tasks there.

At the end of a hectic week, the supervisor completed the necessary report forms, boxed up the exercise packages, and mailed them to MRC, where they would be scored and prepared for analysis.

The same procedures are being followed to assess the 13-year-old sample in science, writing, and citizenship. They will be followed with the nine-year-olds, and in all future assessments of the in-school sample. A maximum sample size of 32,000 youngsters at each age level is being sought.

By and large the exercise administration went well. The response of schools to the assessment was excellent—87 percent of the 770 schools asked to participate agreed to do so. A questionnaire sent by the National Assessment staff to principals and superintendents brought comments such as: "I think a wonderful job was done. We were happy to participate. Your representative was most impressive and a pleasure to work with." "We are willing to cooperate at any time with any assessment that you are doing on the progress of education. Thank you for including us in this study."

There were problems, of course. Scheduling the administration of the exercises ran into difficulties such as temporary school closings because of student demonstrations, power failures, bomb scares, and holidays. Finding a place in which to give the exercises was sometimes a problem. One supervisor found himself using a boiler room reached by climbing up and down a ladder; others met in the teachers' lounge, a boys' locker room, closets, and, in one extreme case, a girls' restroom. Although the project was generally well received by students, one supervisor got a rude welcome. He took some blows from a few boys who objected to his presence in the school.

The procedures for assessment in the summer of 1969 were quite different, because adults between ages 26 and 35, and 17-year-olds who had not enrolled in school the previous spring were being assessed. Supervisors first had to locate these people. This meant going to randomly chosen houses in geographical areas selected by the sampling experts at RTI, finding someone at home, determining whether anyone lived in the home who fell within the desired age limits, and if so, making an appointment to have the individual take the package of exercises. The sample design was planned so that 20,000 young adults and from 1,500 to 1,800 out-of-school 17-year-olds would be located and assessed. Complete information about the sample size actually obtained is not yet available.

Preparations for the assessment of the seven other subject areas in the second and third years of the project, and for starting the cycle over again in the fourth year, are under way. The objectives and exercises in citizenship, science, and writing are being refined in anticipation of a second round of testing. New exercises will need to be written to replace the 40 percent of the exercises that will be reported to the public. Once exercises are made public, they cannot be used in the assessment without opening the way to criticism that schools will "teach to" the exercises.

What of future plans? The first-year administration now under way will of course continue, as will preparation for the assessment of mathematics, music, and literature next year, and of social studies, art, career and occupational development, and reading in the year following. Other subject areas will be added to the assessment in the future as funds for development became available.

The major new work to be done is in data analyses and reporting of results. Detailed plans for analyses are still being worked over by the National Assessment staff aided by an advisory committee of experts in statistical analyses. Generally the plan is to prepare the data in such a way that the percent of responses to exercises may be reported both for the Nation as a whole and according to such breakdowns as the four regions, type of community, sex, socioeducational status, and race.

The approximately 60 percent of the exercises in each area that will not be publicly reported will, of course, be used again. Consequently, results of the first and second assessments may, to a large extent, be compared to see whether any change has occurred.

Results for all four age groups will be ready for publication during the summer of 1970. They will be made public through technical reports prepared by the National Assessment staff, and through news releases to educational and general interest publications, radio, and television.

Many school administrators were at first fearful that the assessment would lead to harmful comparisons between school districts and between States. These fears proved groundless, because the sample of people participating in the project is too small to make it possible to generalize about any school district or State. These administrators now ask, "Why don't you have results for my schools that I can use?" Influential educational organizations that once opposed the project now support it.

The complexities of the assessment, and the needs of educators and the general public will undoubtedly lead to further changes in the assessment itself, and in the public's attitudes and expectations about it. It's this flexibility, this openness to progressive change that makes the project so promising for American education.

TOWARD A SOCIAL REPORT ON LEARNING

U.S. Department of Health, Education, and Welfare*

Knowledge, intellectual skills and the creative capacity of scientists and artists are an important part of the Nation's wealth. Health, national defense, and the quality of the environment in future years depend on the success of research and education now. So does the future performance of the economy. Some studies have suggested

* From *Toward a Social Report*, U.S. Department of Health, Education, and Welfare (Washington, D.C.: U.S. Government Printing Office, 1969).

that as much as one-fourth of our growth in per capita income can be traced to increased schooling and as much as one-third to inventions and "advances in knowledge." The decisive productive potential of the supply of knowledge is illustrated by the surprisingly rapid recovery of the German and Japanese economies after the devastation of World War II. However much physical capital had been destroyed, the stock of useful knowledge remained.

This chapter will first attempt to bring together available information on how much Americans are learning. It will then turn to the sources of the knowledge that there is to teach: to the stock of systematic knowledge which we call science, and to the unstructured collection of human wisdom and creativity which we call art.

LEARNING

Exposure to Learning

The average American has spent far more time in school than his parents did. Today, three-fourths of the Americans just old enough to have done so have finished high school—roughly the same proportion that finished the eighth grade in 1929. Today, about 15 percent of Americans in their late twenties have graduated from college—about the same proportion that had graduated from high school at the time of World War I.

In addition there has been an increase in the proportion of each year that the student spends in school. Since 1900, 34 days have been added to the average academic year. Pupils are also absent much less often, so the actual number of days of school attendance per year by the average pupil has increased by more than half.

The difference in years of schooling received by different groups of Americans has at the same time decreased. Among Americans born in 1901 or shortly before, those in the 90th percentile had 13.5 years of schooling, and those in the 10th percentile 2.6 years of schooling, for a difference of almost 11 years. Among those born between 1932 and 1936, those in the 90th percentile had 16.4 years of schooling, and those in the 10th percentile, 8.4 years, for a difference of 8 years. This difference is projected to decline to about 5.5 years for those born between 1956 and 1960. The gap in median years of schooling between whites and Negroes has fallen from an average of 3.4 years for those born in 1901 or before to one-half year for those born between 1942 and 1946, and appears to be narrowing still further.

The amount of resources used to educate each pupil is also increasing. In 1956, there were 27 pupils for each teacher; now there are 24. Teachers have also had more formal training; 93 percent of the teachers now have college degrees, as compared with 78 percent only 13 years ago. The one-room school, commonplace in rural areas as late as World War II, has largely disappeared. Total expenditures per pupil in elementary and secondary public schools increased from $2.25 to $3.43 per day (in constant dollars) between 1954 and 1964. There have also been improvements in curricula, especially in science and mathematics.

It is generally assumed that these increases in the length of schooling and expenditures on education have brought about an increase in the amount children have learned. There is, however, almost no direct evidence on this point—unless it be the evidence that parents often have difficulty with their children's homework. The *Digest of Educational Statistics,* for example, contains over a hundred pages of educational statistics in each annual issue, yet has virtually no information on how much children have learned. The Department of Health, Education, and Welfare has recently encouraged an attempt at a "national assessment" of educational achievement in the United States. This assessment would involve administering tests measuring standard academic skills to a representative sample of Americans of various ages. Such an assessment, if repeated periodically, would yield for the first time a series of estimates of the change taking place in the intellectual skills and knowledge of the population.

Are We Learning More?

In 1870, 20 percent of the white and 80 percent of the Negro population were illiterate. Now only 2.4 percent are deemed illiterate. They are mostly older people and Negroes, and are concentrated mainly in the South. The rate of illiteracy among Americans from 14 to 24 years of age is only about one-half of 1 percent. These facts mark our progress in bringing most Americans up to the rudimentary but critical point of being able to read and write.

What about higher levels of skill and knowledge? Although there is no national assessment of what students are learning, testing is widespread and some clues to changes in test performance of school-age children are available.

The Educational Testing Service recently assembled 186 instances in which comparable tests have been given to large and roughly representative national samples of students at two different times over the past two decades.

In all but 10 of the 186 paired comparisons, the later group performed better than the earlier group. On the average an additional eight percent of the students in the more recent group scored higher than the median student in the old group.[1]

The results that have been described cannot be accepted uncritically; neither can they be casually dismissed. Until better evidence is presented, the tentative judgment must be that American children in the sixties are learning more than their older brothers and sisters learned in the fifties.

This collection of achievement test data also suggests that high school students, and perhaps students in the higher grades generally, have not improved as much as students in the lower grades. Typically, the test comparisons for high schools showed a smaller gain in performance than was usual in the elementary grades. In addition, the Preliminary Scholastic Aptitude Test and the American College Test program, which are given to juniors and seniors in high school, showed no improvement on balance.[2]

One possible reason for this disparity is that the increase in the proportion of teenagers attending high school may have reduced the average level of intellectual ability and cultural background in high schools. The increase in preschool education may also have had a particularly beneficial influence on the lower grades. Television may have at the same time significantly raised the intellectual level of

---

[1] This amounts to an improvement of one-fifth, assuming a normal distribution of scores. These test results must be interpreted with extreme caution. There is the possibility students are becoming increasingly "test wise" as time goes on, and this might account for the improvement in test scores. Moreover, test results do not measure all types of intellectual achievement. There could have been retrogression along those dimensions of intellectual development that the tests did not measure.

[2] Average scores on the Medical College Admission Test and the Law School Admission Test have been increasing. But this does not show that college students are necessarily learning more, since the sort of students who apply for medical and law school admission may change over time.

younger children, but seldom stretched the minds of high school students.

How Much More Could We Be Learning?

One way to answer this question is by comparing the performance of American students with those in other countries to see if we are doing as well.

One of the few sources on how well American students do as compared with foreign students is the International Study of Achievement in Mathematics. It deals with only one subject, but this is probably the one in which performance can best be compared among nations with different languages and cultures. The study considered only developed nations, and found that American students had one of the poorest levels of performance of the nations which were studied.

The fact that the United States did badly in this comparison is probably due in part to the fact that a larger proportion of young people go through the secondary education system in the United States than in most other countries. Still, American 13 year olds also did comparatively poorly, and this is an age at which none of the countries concerned have excluded many children from the educational system. Thus, if we contend that American youth have on the average as much aptitude for mathematics as children of other nations, we must conclude that we can do much better than we are doing.

In estimating the potential for improvement in American education, international comparisons are probably less relevant than measured differences in learning among different groups in the United States.

For estimating differences in learning among groups, the two best sources of information are the Armed Forces Qualification Test (with its forbear, the Army General Classification Test), and the tests done for the *Survey of Educational Opportunity* (also called the "Coleman Report") carried out under the Civil Rights Act of 1964.

These tests, like others, inevitably incorporate cultural bias. Verbal performance, for example, tends to be measured in terms of the student's command of literary English or the standard conversation of the majority, not in terms of the special dialects of minorities. Mathematics tests include fractions and compound interest, but rarely deal with the probability of "making a six" in craps. Nonetheless, the tests measure skills which are needed in order to do well in contemporary American society.

The Armed Forces Qualification Test is used to evaluate the trainability of prospective servicemen for military service. Because the proportion of young men who are drafted changes from time to time, place to place, and group to group, the test does not provide entirely satisfactory information. Nonetheless, it shows clearly that Negroes and Southern whites score, on the average, lower than whites from other regions, and Southern Negroes score less well than Northern Negroes. These groups receive, on average, different amounts of schooling, but this difference accounts for only part of the differences in performance.

A 1964 study by the President's Task Force on Manpower Conservation revealed that a majority of young men failing the Armed Forces Qualification Test, white and black alike, were brought up in poverty. Forty percent had never gone beyond eighth grade, four out of five failed to complete high school, and half came from families with five or more children.

The *Survey of Educational Opportunity* was based on a nationwide sample of 564,000 students in grades 1, 3, 6, 9, and 12. The tests covered verbal ability, nonverbal intelligence, reading comprehension, mathematics, and general information in the practical arts, natural sciences, social studies and humanities. With the exception of Oriental American children, the average minority group pupil (Negro, Mexican-American, American Indian, Puerto Rican) scored distinctly lower on these tests than the average white pupil. Students in the South, both white and Negro, scored below students of their own race in the North.

The schooling which the disadvantaged groups had received had apparently done nothing to lessen the gap between them and more fortunate pupils. Their disadvantage was evident from the start of their school experience through grade 12. The relative position of the different groups was about the same for all the grades tested (except in the South, where Negroes fell to a lower relative position in the later grades). This means that in terms of absolute grade level the disadvantaged fell further behind. Negro pupils in the metropolitan Northeast, for example, were 1.6 years below the norm in grade 6 and 3.3 years below the norm in grade 12.

The Armed Forces Qualification Test and the *Survey of Edu-*

cational Opportunity thus show that persons from both poorer groups and poorer areas performed less well on achievement tests, and that the existing pattern of schooling does not compensate for the initial handicap entailed in being brought up in a disadvantaged group or area.

If talented individuals do not get a full education, the Nation is obviously not developing its capacities as much as it could. And as the chapter on "Social Mobility" showed, only half of those who are in the top ability quintile, but from families in the lowest socio-economic quartile, go to college, whereas 95 percent of the equally able students from the top socioeconomic quartile go to college. Socioeconomic status also has a major effect on college attendance at other ability levels.

If high school graduates from all socioeconomic levels went to college in the same proportion as high school graduates of the same ability level in the top socioeconomic quartile, more than half a million additional students would enter college each year. This would increase the number who attended college from each high school graduating class by about one-half.

If the environmental and social handicaps of poor children could be overcome, and the elementary and secondary education they receive improved, an even larger number of high school graduates could profit from a college education.

We have seen that American students did less well in mathematics than students in a number of other countries, and that the pattern of results in the Armed Forces Qualification Test and the *Survey of Educational Opportunity* implied that there is an un-tapped reservoir of intellectual capacity in the Nation's disadvantaged groups and areas. It is also clear that those young people from poor families who do nonetheless score well on achievement tests are much less likely to enter college than those who come from a higher socioeconomic level. Thus there is no doubt that the Nation has failed to take full advantage of its children's capacity to learn.

The Policy Challenge

The greatest challenge to American education today is to find effective ways of helping low income children learn the basic intellectual skills so that they can be more successful in school and compete more successfully for jobs and rewarding positions in the community when they become adults.

How much a child learns depends upon his mother's diet before he was born, his own nutrition and health, his access to books, and the psychological and intellectual influences in the home. Most psychologists seem to agree that the preschool years are a period of particularly rapid development, and that attitudes acquired in these years can have enduring effects. Even after he reaches school age, a child typically spends only one-third of his working hours in school. Television programs and conversations with parents and playmates take up much of a child's time. The motivation to learn is obviously important, and there is every reason to believe it is decisively influenced by the home environment.

Some of the findings in the *Survey of Educational Opportunity* suggest the importance of the educational impact of factors outside of school. The *Survey* found that the socioeconomic status of a child's parents, and of his classmates, were major determinants of a student's academic performance. Once the impact of the socioeconomic status of parents and peers had been accounted for, such differences in quality of schooling as were observed and measured explained very little of the remaining variation in student performance.[3] The only observed school characteristic that had a significant effect was the verbal ability of its teachers, and this effect was much smaller than that of socioeconomic status of parents and classmates.

Despite the limitations of the *Survey* the conclusion that a child's socioeconomic environment is an important determinant of how much he learns is almost certainly right. This conclusion, in turn, suggests that we cannot take full advantage of the potential for learning simply by spending more on schools. Higher incomes and better jobs for parents may have more influence on their chil-

[3] The *Survey* did not measure the quality of schools well and its conclusions are subject to varying interpretations. The conclusion that the socioeconomic status of the families of a student's classmates is an important determinant of a student's performance could be interpreted as evidence that differences in the quality of schooling are important, because high status parents usually want and can afford to live in neighborhoods with good schools. Since variations in the quality of schooling were measured only partially and crudely in the *Survey*, it is possible that the average socioeconomic status of the families of the students in a school measures the quality of that school better than the explicit measures of school quality used in the *Survey*.

dren's learning than any "compensation" which can be given to the
children themselves. Better television programing and help for
parents in how to talk with and stimulate their own children may
also be important. Improved housing arrangements which give
children from poor families the opportunity to attend schools and
live in neighborhoods with children of different social and economic
status may also be of crucial importance.

Nevertheless, it is clear that schools could do far more to
stimulate and foster the curiosity and creativity of children—not
just poor children, but all children. We must somehow find a way to
do two things. First, we need to channel more resources into education especially in areas where the needs are very high in relation
to the tax base and present spending. It takes money to attract
sensitive, intelligent, and highly trained people into teaching and
education administration, and to replace rat-infested old schools,
especially in the center cities, with attractive convenient structures.

But resources alone will not solve the problems of American
education. A new spirit of acceptance of change and desire for
improvement is needed. Progressive industries often spend 5 to 10
percent of their funds on research and development. But expenditures on education research and development are now miniscule,
perhaps a half of 1 percent of the total education budget.

Furthermore, much "research and development" in education
consists of small projects having little impact on actual learning in
the schools. There is a need for major departures, for developing
whole new curricula and approaches to education, for trying the
new approaches with real children and real schools. This kind of
effort is expensive, by the present standards of education research,
although not by the standards of military and industrial research
and development.

But even a major effort to find more effective methods in education through research and development will not be sufficient
unless the schools as a whole adopt a new attitude toward change.
School systems must learn to see themselves as continuous laboratories trying new things, evaluating results, and making changes.